OWEN TUDOR

OWEN TUDOR

FOUNDING FATHER OF THE
TUDOR DYNASTY

TERRY BREVERTON

AMBERLEY

First published 2017

Amberley Publishing
The Hill, Stroud
Gloucestershire, GL5 4EP

www.amberley-books.com

British Library Cataloguing in Publication Data.
A catalogue record for this book is available from the British Library.

ISBN 978 1 4456 5418 8 (hardback)
ISBN 978 1 4456 5419 5 (ebook)

Family tree design by User Design Illustration and Typesetting.
Typeset in 10pt on 12pt Sabon.
Typesetting and Origination by Amberley Publishing.
Printed in the UK.

Contents

Acknowledgements

Professor Ralph Griffiths and Dr Roger Thomas have carried out groundbreaking research into Wales and the Hundred Years War. Without their work, my books on Richard III, Jasper Tudor, Henry Tudor and Owen Tudor would have been almost impossible to research and write.

Due to an old rugby injury, I was on crutches for the final ten weeks of writing this book, and thus was unable to take photographs of associated places. Fellow researchers Paul Remfry, Jeffrey Thomas, Lise Hull and Susan Booth came to my rescue.

The historian Paul Remfry assisted with medieval French and Latin translations (all translations unless otherwise stated are his work), and Dr Gideon Brough has recently added greatly to our understanding of the Tudor family's part in initiating revolt before the Glyndŵr War. I also sincerely thank Dr Heledd Haf Williams and Professor Ann Parry Owen at the universities of Bangor and Aberystwyth for their research and Welsh translations.

Introduction

In 1485, young Henry Tudor, whose claim to the throne was so weak as to be almost laughable, crossed the English Channel from France at the head of a ragtag little army and took the crown from the [French] family that had ruled England for almost four hundred years.

G. J. Meyer,
The Tudors: The Complete Story of England's Most Notorious Dynasty

Calling the Tudors 'notorious' possibly demonstrates a lack of awareness about their Plantagenet predecessors, or a lack of knowledge of the Normans who preceded them. Regarding the 'weak' and 'laughable' qualities of Henry Tudor's claim, the history of English royal succession had long been a matter of much discussion on the Continent – 'the English kill their kings', as we shall find. There has been much nonsense written about the rights of royal inheritance in recent years from a modern, politically correct perspective. Henry's claim to the throne was as strong as that of anyone else who took it. That was how things worked centuries ago. Indeed, the most 'laughable' claim to the throne belongs to the present Hanover dynasty, whose first king, George I, was actually 58th in line but the first Protestant. Of course, in today's terms, Henry Tudor 'usurped' the throne from Richard III. However, Richard III's elder brother Edward IV had killed Henry VI and himself 'usurped' the crown. Richard III, in his time, had 'usurped' his nephews Edward V and Prince Richard, by calling them illegitimate and disposing of them. Henry IV had 'usurped' and killed Richard II. Any claim to the throne of England through the Danes and Germanic Saxons, to the Franco-Danish Normans, to the French Angevins and Plantagenets was nearly always disputed. There never was any solid lineal right of succession, and in contrast to the Hanoverian line,

Henry VII had the first 'British' blood of any king of England since the pagan Saxon invasions.

The English tendency to constantly fight for the kingship was noted by our nearest neighbours, as Samuel Lewis explains:

> The regicidal proclivities of the English had a considerable fascination for fifteenth-century Frenchmen. '*Ilz ont une manière en Angleterre,*' wrote Jean Juvenal des Ursins in 1444, '*quilz ne tiennent comte de changer leur roi quant bon leur semble, voir de les tuer et faire mourir mauvaisement.*' ['They have a way in England which takes account of changing their king at their convenience: they kill them and kill them evilly.']

The Chancellor of France alleged in 1484 that the English had been through twenty-six changes of dynasty since the foundation of their monarchy. One political treatise on the English claim to the throne of France, written soon after Henry V's occupation of Normandy, posted that the English

> ... *ne pourroient bien faire a autrui quant ilz traisent et destruissent leurs roys et souverains seigneurs, comme on puet savoir par le roy Richart et par plusieurs autres de leurs roys jusques au nombre de xxij quilz ont desappointez et faulsement traiz et fait morir ou temps passe par leurs falses et mauvaises traisons...* [They do not do well when dealing with others and they destroy their kings and sovereign lords, as we know concerning King Richard [II] and many other of their kings up to the number of twenty-two (including Saxon monarchs), in which they were disappointed and treated falsely, and put them to death as time passed through their false and evil treasons...]

The theme was later taken up by Noel de Fribois in 1459: '*La seconde chose que les Anglois ont fait dogmatiser et semer est que ils sont a recommander sur toutes autres nations en vraie subjection & ferme obeisance envers les roys & princes et seigneurs temporelz dicelle nation d'Angleterre...*' ['The second thing is that the English are dogmatic, and always they advocate that all other nations should be in true subjection and firm obedience towards the kings, princes and lords temporal of that nation of England.' *Angleterre* is, of course, the land of the Germanic Angles.]

Lewis noted an illustration in de Fribois' second recension of 1461, and an identical miniature elsewhere:

Prominent in the foreground is a pile of six dead kings of England and a sainted bishop (St Thomas of Canterbury). At the head of a military group behind it a soldier sheaths his sword and an ecclesiastic looks down regretfully at the holocaust. In the left foreground six substantial figures – perhaps doctors? – are engaged in lively discussion of the scene. Their agitation is expressive of the disquiet with which the literary in fifteenth-century France claimed they observed the homicidal tendencies of their neighbours. For the English *did* kill their kings...

This has not been an easy book to research. Much of Owen Tudor's life has been obscured, and there does not seem to have been any detailed research on the life of his wife, the French Princess Catherine of Valois, widow of Henry V. The elder sister of Catherine of Valois, Isabelle, had married Richard II, who was killed by Henry of Bolingbroke, who became the first Lancastrian king, Henry IV. With France torn apart by civil war, an English presence and Henry V's invasions, Catherine was virtually forced by her parents to marry Henry V to bring peace. They disinherited her brother, the Dauphin, and Henry was to succeed as King of France. She witnessed sieges against her countrymen before returning to England. Henry hardly bothered with her, but in their few months together, Catherine conceived before the king returned to France. He died there, never seeing his son, who became King Henry VI at the age of nine months.

The great nobles of England did not want the dowager-queen to remarry, and a statute was passed prohibiting her to do so. However, she secretly married Owen Tudor. Their children were also born in secrecy, and although their eldest sons, Edmund and Jasper, were eventually raised to be the premier earls in England, they were taken from Owen upon Catherine's early death. Owen, for his temerity in marrying the dowager-queen, was hunted down and imprisoned three times, but a few years later, in a previously little-known episode in his life, he was captaining a garrison in Normandy as the French and Bretons overran that English possession in the Hundred Years War. As his life was finally settling down, the Wars of the Roses erupted between the Lancastrians and the Yorkists, and Owen lost his eldest son, Edmund, Earl of Richmond, in the conflict. Edmund's wife, Margaret Beaufort, then gave birth to his posthumous son, Henry Tudor, Earl of Richmond, future king of England. Like Henry VI, Henry VII would never meet his father.

With Edmund's death, Owen allied with his son Jasper, Earl of Pembroke, to fight for his stepson Henry VI on the Lancastrian side, but was executed in 1461 after fighting alongside Jasper at Mortimer's Cross. After the Battle of Tewkesbury in 1471, Jasper's nephew Henry was the only adult Lancastrian claimant remaining and was therefore in incredible danger. Jasper took Henry into exile in Brittany, then France. The Plantagenets had almost wiped the Lancastrians out, and the Yorkist kings Edward IV and Richard III made great efforts to capture Jasper and Henry Tudor. Henry knew that his only choice if he wished to live was to take England. Supported by many of Edward IV's followers, he led a Welsh-Scottish-French-Breton invasion into England in 1484 (this, not 1066, was the last successful foreign invasion), to defeat the deeply unpopular Richard III. Thus, the grandson of a clandestine marriage between a disenfranchised Welsh noble and the French widow of England's 'warrior-king' was to become England's greatest king.

I have included a chapter on Owen Tudor in literature, as various works seem to indicate that Owen knew Catherine of Valois in France, which assumes that he served Henry V as well as Henry VI overseas. One play makes him a friend of Henry V, having saved Catherine of Valois from drowning, and also having saved a French count from being killed. There may be more information to be found on his years up to 1420, when he appears in France as one of Hungerford's men. Fortunately, in recent years, Owen's captaincy in France from 1445 to 1449 has emerged from obscurity, but there are still gaps in his career. His may well be the strangest marriage in English royal history, to a French princess and dowager-queen who seems to have been one of the most neglected queens of England. For any omissions I apologise, but this was a time of multiple wars, alliances, mistakes and betrayals set in several countries, spanning the six decades of Owen's life.

The Ancestors and Birth of Owain ap Maredudd ap Tudur (Owen Tudor)

G. A. Williams writes:

'An unknown like Henry Tudor', 'the unknown Welshman', 'an obscure and penniless exile in Brittany', 'a moderately obscure magnate of Welsh descent', 'the forgotten exile'. These are among a selection of descriptions used by historians when referring to the early career of Henry Tudor before his triumph at Bosworth and coronation as Henry VII. Valid though these may be as indicators of England's perception of the future king as pointers to his contemporary fame and reputation in Wales, they are very wide of the mark. Hailed since infancy by the bards in their prophetic verse as the long-awaited *mab darogan* or son of prophecy, the national liberator who would win the crown of London and restore British, that is, Welsh, hegemony within the island, Henry was far from 'unknown' or 'forgotten' in the land of his fathers. It is this Welsh bardic perception of the founder of the Tudor dynasty that paved the way for his enthusiastic reception in Wales in 1485, thus contributing in no small measure to his success at Bosworth and seizure of the crown.

This grandson of Owain ap Maredudd ap Tudur (Owen Tudor) only gained the crown because of the British belief, held for a millennium, that England would be regained from its Germanic, then Danish, then French, conquerors. The Welsh were described as the British until late Elizabethan times. Indeed, the word 'Welsh' comes from Germanic languages and means 'foreigner' – the Germanic invaders, after the Roman departure, called the Britons 'foreigners' in their own land before pressing them back to the West Country, Cymru

(Wales), Cumbria and Ystrad Clud (Strathclyde). Crucial to the deeply held liberation ideal was the genealogy of the deliverer, the 'chosen one' who would reconquer British land and expel the enemy from British shores. The British had been fighting foreign invaders for 800 years when the conquest of 1283 took place, and even then the struggle had never stopped, with the Tudors being crucial to the beginning of the Glyndŵr War of 1400–1421.

Most Welsh literature from this period has been destroyed in incessant wars, especially the earliest illuminated manuscripts, as cathedrals and abbeys were sacked. The only such manuscript to survive, *The Book of Teilo*, was somehow taken to Lichfield Cathedral and cleverly renamed *The Book of Saint Chad*, and the earliest dateable Welsh poem of vaticination (prophecy) is the early tenth-century *Armes Prydein Fawr* (*The Prophecy of Great Britain*, from the *Book of Taliesin*), which foretells the retaking of Britain by a Celtic alliance under the resurrected Welsh princes Cynan and Cadwaladr and with the spiritual patronage of Saint David. In it, the Saxons are described as intruders and usurpers, to be massacred as they had done to the British in England, and it was followed by over 300 surviving vaticinal poems during the Middle Ages. There is a legendary prophetic figure in medieval Welsh literature called Myrddin; the Latin version of Myrddin would have been Merdinus, with faecal connotations (as in the French *merde*), so the twelfth-century chronicler Geoffrey of Monmouth instead named him Merlin. His true name is remembered in Caerfyrddin ('fort of Myrddin'), the Welsh name for the Roman camp of Carmarthen. In the *Armes Prydein Fawr*, Myrddin foretells that:

> The Brython will be outcasts, when they shall have done,
> Far will be foretold the time they shall be.
> Kings and nobles will subdue them ...
> ... And a banner will come, rough it will descend.
> And like the budded blossoms the Saxons will fall.
> The Cymry gathering strength with union of actions ...
> The armies of Cadwaladr, mighty they come,
> The Cymry were exalted, a battle they made.
> A slaughter without measure they assailed ...
> Saxons against the Brython, woe they will sing.
> Cadwaladr a pillar with his princes...
> The Allmyn [Germans] will not go from the places they stand on,
> Until they shall have paid seven times the value of what they did.
> And death shall scatter to the value of their wrong ...
> When the carcases stand according to their race,
> Even to Aber Santwic it will be noised,

That the Allmyn are about to emigrate abroad,
One after another, breaking afresh upon their race.
The Saxons at anchor on the sea always.
The Cymry venerable until doomsday shall be supreme
They will not seek books nor be covetous of poets.
The presage of this isle will be no other than this.
We will praise the King that created heaven and earth.
May David be a leader to the combatants ...

G. A. Williams writes:

Welsh vaticination also must have circulated in writing: a number of poets
refer to books of *brud* or prophecy. In the main, however, like other forms
of contemporary Welsh poetry, it must have depended for its dissemination
on oral performance; indeed, there are textual features in many poems
that unmistakeably indicate that they enjoyed an oral currency. The extant
vaticination of the period is the work of higher-grade bards, and would normally,
one supposes, have been declaimed to relatively sophisticated audiences in the
halls of the gentry. Such audiences, though not large, were, of course, crucial
politically. Some of the poetry, however, may occasionally have reached a wider,
more popular audience. A manuscript dated *circa* 1600 emanating from the
Council of the Marches mentions outdoor gatherings of 'the multitude of all
sortes of men woomen and childeme of everie parishe where theire harpers
and crowthers singe them songs of the doeings of theire auncestors, namelie, of
theire warrs againste the kings of this realme and the English nation.'

(A crowther was a *crwth* player, and a *crwth* was one of the Welsh traditional
stringed instruments along with the harp and timpan.)

Without the writings of the bards, much of early British history would
remain unknown. The bards were given lists of duties in the laws of Hywel
Dda (*c.* 880–950) as one of the twenty-four officers of the royal court, and
each noble house followed the same system. J. Hugh Edwards writes:

In addition to his social prestige, the bard had certain defined functions. He
had the charge of the historical documents of the tribe and its chief, and
was his recognised laureate. Most of the bards were accustomed to tour
through Wales every three years, the chief bards being entertained at the
houses of the nobles, and the lower class order finding free access to the
homes of the common people.

In his biography of Lloyd George, Edwards notes their importance in history: 'It would be difficult to overestimate the influence and service of these poets in behalf of the literature of Wales. They deepened the channel of the Welsh language and widened its course ... Let it never be forgotten that these bards were, for their age, learned men. Whatever was known, they knew; their theology was in advance of that of the Church, and they were as far advanced in knowledge as any contemporaneous class of persons.' The result was, as Meic Stephens has so aptly observed, that

> ... at a time when all the languages now spoken in Europe were beginning to be formed, the people of Wales had not only a copious language fully developed, but also a class of men enriching its literature with poetical compositions ... Before Gower sang, or Chaucer wrote, or England had a literature of its own, there were poets in Wales who left behind them, in the course of two hundred years, upwards of four hundred poems, many of which are more than three hundred and fifty lines in length.

These remaining works are a wonderful reference for historical research, with Welsh bards contemporaneously writing of Richard III's habits and murders, for instance. Jacques Nicolas Augustin Thierry, in his 1841 French history of the Norman Conquest, calls the Welsh the most intellectual and civilised people of the age, saying that they lost their territory but enriched their literature. Even on the murder of Prince Llywelyn in 1282, when the Welsh mourned like 'the sullen wash of the waves upon the grey beach', they 'laid fresh foundations for their nationality on which subsequent generations of their countrymen might build'. The bards never stopped proclaiming that Wales would drive the 'Saxon' out of their nation. This belief was to lead to a Welsh army under Owen Tudor's grandson defeating the last of the Yorkist Plantagenets in 1485.

Around AD 550 the Glamorgan cleric Gildas ap Caw, sainted in the British Church, wrote *De Excidio et Conquestu Britanniae* (*On the Ruin and Conquest of Britain*), condemning the acts of his contemporaries after the departure of the Romans and describing the resulting pillage of Christian Britain by the invading pagan Germanic tribes. It is the most significant book of its era. We can see Gildas' great admiration for Emrys Wledig, Ambrosius Aurelianus, who pushed back the ravaging Saxons for a time, in his writing:

> They first landed on the eastern side of the island, by the invitation of the unlucky king, and there fixed their sharp talons, apparently to fight in favour of the island, but alas! more truly against it. Their mother-land, finding her first brood thus successful, sends forth a larger company of her

wolfish offspring, which sailing over, join themselves to their bastard-born comrades. From that time the germ of iniquity and the root of contention planted their poison amongst us, as we deserved, and shot forth into leaves and branches ... For the fire of vengeance, justly kindled by former crimes, spread from sea to sea, fed by the hands of our foes in the east, and did not cease, until, destroying the neighbouring towns and lands, it reached the other side of the island, and dipped its red and savage tongue in the western ocean ...

So that all the columns were levelled with the ground by the frequent strokes of the battering ram, all the husbandmen routed, together with their bishops, priests and people, while the sword gleamed, and the flames crackled around them on every side. Lamentable to behold, in the midst of the streets lay the tops of lofty towers, tumbled to the ground, stones of high walls, holy altars, fragments of human bodies, covered with livid clots of coagulated blood, looking as if they had been squeezed together in a press; and with no chance of being buried, save in the ruins of the houses, or in the ravening bellies of wild beasts and birds; with reverence be it spoken for their blessed souls, if, indeed, there were so many found who were carried, at that time, into the high heaven by the holy angels. So entirely had the vintage, once so fine, degenerated and become bitter, that, in the words of the prophet, there was hardly a grape or ear of corn to be seen where the husbandman had turned his back ...

Some, therefore, of the miserable remnant, being taken in the mountains, were murdered in great numbers; others, constrained by famine, came and yielded themselves to be slaves for ever to their foes, running the risk of being instantly slain, which truly was the greatest favour which could be offered them; some others passed beyond the seas with loud lamentations instead of the voice of exhortation. 'Thou hast given us as sheep to be slaughtered, and among the Gentiles hast thou dispersed us.' Others, committing the safeguard of their lives, which were in continual jeopardy, to the mountains, precipices, thickly wooded forests, and to the rocks of the seas (albeit with trembling hearts), remained still in the country.

But in the meanwhile, an opportunity happening, when these most cruel robbers were returned home, the poor remnants of our nation (to whom flocked from divers places round about our miserable countrymen as fast as bees to their hives, for fear of an ensuing storm), being strengthened by God, calling upon him with all their hearts, as the poet says, 'With their unnumbered vows they burden Heaven,' that they might not be brought to utter destruction, took arms under the conduct of Ambrosius Aurelianus, a modest man, who of all the Roman nation was then alone in the confusion of this troubled period left alive. His parents, who for their merit were adorned with the purple, had been slain in these same broils, and now his progeny in these our days, although shamefully degenerated from the worthiness of our ancestors, provoke to battle their cruel conquerors, and by the goodness of our Lord obtain the victory.

Memories of the invasion and the genocide and displacement of the Britons by incoming pagan Angles and Saxons ran through the works of the bards for a thousand years. The surviving British in Wales were not just bitter; they were not allowed to forget the barbarian treatment of the native Christians. It is hardly surprising from this contemporary writing of Gildas that the Celtic Church refused to evangelise the Saxons in later years, incurring the wrath of Bede, who indeed praised a pagan Saxon victory over the Christian Welsh.

Nennius, a Welsh monk, copied much of Gildas and wrote about the legendary King Arthur and his famous twelve battles in his *Historia Brittonum* around 830. Arthur is also referred to in *The Gododdin*, written around the end of the sixth century, as well as in early Welsh poetry, some saints' lives, and in the sixth-century *Welsh Triads of the Islands of Britain*. All of these predate the romances by Geoffrey of Monmouth and Chrétien de Troyes that made King Arthur famous. Many of the characters in Arthurian legend were already present in pre-medieval Welsh legend and literature, with Arthur becoming the potent symbol of the rebirth of the British nation. In British and Breton legend (Brittany was settled by Christian Britons fleeing from the Welsh borders and West Country because of Germanic pressure), Arthur never died and would come back to lead his people.

The cleric Geoffrey of Monmouth (Gruffudd ap Arthur) wrote the influential *Historia Regum Britanniae* around 1130, and used Nennius as its source. In it he describes the descent of the Britons from Brutus of Troy, and writes of the heroic Arthur fighting the Anglo-Saxon invaders, recalling an angel's prophecy to Cadwaladr, the last British king of Britain, that the red dragon of Cadwaldr would defeat the white dragon of the barbarians. Knowing his heritage, Henry VII was to call his eldest son Arthur 'in honour of the *British* race', as he had been seen in Wales as the deliverer of that old prophecy.

Geoffrey's work became an important source for prophetic poetry by the fifteenth century. Also, his *Prophetia Merlini*, the seventh book of the *Historia*, which was allegedly translated from a Welsh original, set a trend in writing for employing animals as a stylistic device. As G. A. Williams writes: 'Thus, whilst the son of prophecy is often given the name of a hero such as Cadwaladr or Owain, he appears just as frequently in a perplexity of animal and bird guises, as a lion, a stag, a bull, a wolf, an eagle, and so on.' This use of animals would have been understood by the audience, but would also have acted as a shield against prosecution for bards as they could defend their work by saying that they were simply writing about animals, not issuing subversive calls to action.

Of course, the bards were the only real source of information at this time in Wales. Each important local lord would have his own 'house bard', and there were others who travelled the land, staying at important houses. They were incredibly important in preparing Henry Tudor's path through Wales and his acceptance in 1485 when he won the English crown. The power of the bards had been acknowledged before, after the treacherous entrapment and murder of Llywelyn ap Gruffudd, Prince of Wales, by the Mortimers in 1282, which had led to the massacre of his surrendered army, the brutal disembowelling of his brother Dafydd and the domination of Wales, with its royal line systematically wiped out and enormous occupying castles built with unrepaid foreign loans. With Wales having lost its independence, the victorious Edward I ordered the suppression of the bards.

William of Malmesbury (*c*. 1095–1143) wrote two versions of *Gesta Regum Anglorum* (*Deeds of the English Kings*), in 1125 and 1127, and continued the chronicles with *Historia Novella* of 1128–1142. William had noted that Arthur was still to return to lead the Britons, so Henry II arranged the 'discovery' of the bodies of Arthur and Guinevere (her original name being Gwenhwyfar) at Glastonbury in 1170 to 'prove' that Arthur was not returning to lead the British race once more. This was designed to demolish British hopes – the 'finding and translating [of his body] is an objection to the fantasticall sayinge of the Welshe men that afferme his commynge again to reygne, as he before dyd' (Fabyan's *Chronicle*, *c*. 1509).

Higden's fourteenth-century *Polychronicon* relates of the British: 'They extol the blood of Troy of whom they took beginning ... the prophecy of Merlin and often his witchcraft was wont to beguile them and to move them into battle.' Recent research has indeed placed the original British as being of Anatolian origin, part of the Celtic dispersal from that region that brought agriculture, language, metalworking, navigation and the like into western Europe. A contemporary of Edward II wrote the *Vita Edwardi Secundi* around 1326, claiming in it that Merlin's foretelling of the British taking back England caused them to frequently rebel, the entry for 1315 recording that

the Welsh habit of revolt against the English is an old-standing madness ... and this is the reason: the Welsh, formally called Britons, were once noble crowned over the whole realm of England, but they were expelled by the on-coming Saxons and lost both the name and the kingdom. The fertile plains went to the Saxons, but the sterile and mountainous districts remained to the Welsh. However, from the sayings of the prophet Merlin they still hope to recover their land [England]. Hence, it is that the Welsh frequently rebel, hoping to give effect to the prophecy; but because they do not know the appointed time, they are often deceived and their labour is in vain.

The account of Llywelyn ap Gruffudd's last campaign in the thirteenth-century *Flores Historiarum* (*Flowers of History*) reminds us of the prophecy of Merlin that Llywelyn was destined 'to be crowned with the diadem of Brutus', that is to say he was the one chosen to retake Britain for the British. In the late fourteenth century, Owain Lawgoch (*Yvain de Galles* in Froissart and other French chronicles), the exiled grand-nephew of Llywelyn and the last survivor of the princes of Gwynedd, was acclaimed as the *mab darogan*, or son of prophecy. The Tudor family was involved helping Lawgoch before he was assassinated in 1378 on the orders of John of Ghent, the father of Henry IV. Roger Mortimer, Earl of March, was a descendant of Gwladus Ddu, daughter of the Prince of Gwynedd Llywelyn ap Iorwerth ('the Great'), and allegedly the designated heir of Richard II. Because of his Welsh connection, Mortimer was another fêted as the new deliverer. He had been followed by Owain Glyndŵr, Owen Tudor, Edmund Tudor, Jasper Tudor and Lord William Herbert of Raglan in the line of false hopes before Henry Tudor succeeded as Henry VII.

Owen Tudor's father Maredudd, with his brothers Rhys and Gwilym, were first cousins to Owain Glyndŵr, and instrumental in his 1400–1421 war of independence. One source relates that Maredudd died in 1411 (G. A. Williams), and others that he died in 1406, the means being unknown. What Williams calls 'the nationalist pedigree of the family' would have been known by the bards, 'the most consistently nationalistic section of Welsh society', especially the connection with Glyndŵr. Williams writes:

There are instances in vaticinal poetry where the later Tudors Owen, Jasper and Henry are portrayed as the successors of Glyn Dwr: 'Do not sheathe the sword of Owain Glyn' urged Ieuan ap Rhydderch in a poem addressed to Jasper. Henry Tudor no doubt perceived the advantage of cultivating this image: his display of the red dragon standard at Bosworth, a standard formerly used by Glyn Dwr, may well be a case in point. Relevant also in any consideration of bardic enthusiasm for Henry is his family's past role as patrons of poetry. There is evidence which suggests that it was they who replaced the vanished princes as the foremost patrons of the bards during the fourteenth century. Eurys Rowlands, a leading scholar of Welsh poetry, has pointed out that over half the eulogies to patrons in the *Red Book of Hergest*, our main repository of fourteenth century Welsh verse, are addressed to members of the Penmynydd clan, despite the manuscript being of South Walian provenance. It is very likely, as Mr. Rowlands has asserted, that Owen Tudor and his descendants inherited the understanding that had developed between the bards and the Penmynydd family. When the Tudors, as a result of Owen Tudor's liaison with Katherine de Valois, obtained a toehold in the powerful world of English dynastic politics, the bards, mindful of the family's illustrious Welsh past, were roused to attention, and in due course Henry Tudor, his potential enhanced by the trace of English royal blood inherited through the Beauforts, became the focus of old and unfulfilled bardic yearnings and expectations.

G. A. Williams also informs us:

Just as crucial to Henry's role as *mab darogan* was his ancient princely descent was his more recent ancestry, his descent from the Tudors of Penmynydd in Anglesey'. According to Paul Murray Kendall 'So far as anyone knew [Henry] came of an Anglesey family of no great pretensions'. In fact, the bards very definitely knew of his descent from the Tudors whom they regarded as a family of quite considerable pretensions. Descendants of forebears who over three generations, beginning with Ednyfed Fychan, seneschal to Llywelyn the Great, had served the princes of Gwynedd in high ministerial office, after the conquest they had retained a leading position in native Welsh society.

In the 1804 edition of *The New Baronetage of England*, the biography of Sir Robert Williams of Penrhyn, born in 1764, reads:

This family [the Tudors] is lineally descended from Marchudd, ap Cynan, Lord of Abergeleu, in Denbighshire, one of the fifteen tribes of North-Wales, who lived in the time of Rodri Mawr (Roderick the Great), King of the Britons, about the year 849. Of him was descended Ednyfed Fychan, who being one of the princes host (*Llewelyn ap Jerworth*), was sent to the marches, to defend the frontiers from the advance of the English army, which was ready to invade them, under the command of Ranulph, Earl of Chester, and killed three of their chief captains and commanders, and a great many of the common soldiers. The rest he put to flight, and triumphantly returned to his prince; who, in recompence for his good services, gave him among other honours, a new coat of arms; for the coat, what he and his ancestors had always used before, was the coat of Marchudd, viz. *Gules, a Saracen's head erased, proper, wreathed, or.* — The new coat was thus displayed, *Gules, between three Englishmen's heads couped, a cheveron, ermine.* From the death of the last Llewelyn, Ednyfed's posterity were the greatest men of any in Wales, and from him was descended the royal line of Tudor. The pedigree of Marchudd is deduced from Brutus, the first King of the Britons.

The elements of ancestry, Arthur, the *mab darogan* and verbal transmission by the bards were incredibly important to the remaining British people. They had been largely pushed out of England by aggressive Germanic barbarians, with the consequence that Brittany acquired the British language and was Christianised by British missionaries. The remaining British had seen their populations in Strathclyde, Cumbria and the West Country being taken over or exterminated, although the Cornish language lasted for a millennium after the invasions. The people of Wales had held what is virtually the existing border against the Saxons, and fought off the Danes when that nation took over England. When the Normans landed in 1066 they overcame the Saxons of England in under two years, but did not manage to conquer the whole of Wales until 1283. The people of Wales had fought off invasions by the Irish, Vikings, Romans, Danes, Anglo-Saxons, Normans and French kings of England until this time. They had seen over a thousand years of almost constant war.

Throughout it all there was a belief that they were the chosen people – the people with the longest unbroken Christian heritage in the world, who Christianised pagan Ireland via Patrick and other British saints. The religion had died everywhere for periods after the fall of Rome – except for where the remaining British lived in defiance. The sense of retaining their religion, identity and language throughout a millennium of invasion had given the British in Wales a belief in survival, and with success came renaissance. The ancient Tudor family was at the heart of this nation, lords under the last Welsh princes, descended from nobility. The Tudor clan had been fighting for their lands since Roman times, intermarrying with other leading families across Wales all along.

The Tudor properties included Aberlleiniog and Trecastell on Anglesey, then part of the kingdom of Gwynedd. The important Aberlleiniog Castle is the only visible evidence of a Norman foothold on Anglesey in the eleventh century. It is a large motte-and-bailey castle, erected by Earl Hugh of Chester in the 1080s and held by Robert of Rhuddlan, the earl's military commander in North Wales. Around it grew Trecastell (town of the castle), an important township granted to the heirs of Ednyfed Fychan in the thirteenth century. It has some of the largest historical fish traps on the Menai Strait shoreline. In 1093, Hugh of Chester diverted the revenues of two Anglesey manors and the profits of fishing rights in the Menai Strait to build St Werburgh's Abbey in Chester.

Gruffydd ap Cynan took power in Gwynedd for the second time in 1081, and agreed to a meeting with Red Hugh, Earl of Shrewsbury and Hugh the Fat, Earl of Chester, at Rug, near Corwen. Hugh the Fat had bribed one Meirion Goch to bring Gruffydd to supposedly discuss peace between the Welsh and Normans. Upon arrival Gruffydd was seized and imprisoned in Chester Castle, while Hugh the Fat and Robert of Rhuddlan invaded to take possession of Gwynedd, building castles at Bangor, Caernarfon and Aberlleiniog. Hugh the Fat held Gruffydd as a prisoner in chains at Chester for twelve years, but in 1093 ordered that Gruffydd be displayed at its marketplace so that the people (Chester and its environs were then mainly Welsh-speaking) could see the fall of this great Prince of Gwynedd. In the busy market, one Cynwrig Hir rescued Gruffydd, and was said to have carried away the weakened prisoner on his shoulders. A blacksmith had knocked off Gruffydd's chains and the small rescue party managed to escape to Aberdaron, afterwards sailing to safety in Ireland.

Returning to Wales, Gruffydd besieged and burnt Aberlleiniog Castle, regaining most of Gwynedd. In 1098 a Norman force led by Hugh the Fat and Red Hugh again invaded Anglesey. However, a Norwegian fleet under King Magnus 'Barelegs' intervened off Trecastell, and Hugh the Fat was killed. Gruffydd ap Cynan was the father of the great Owain Gwynedd, and the great-grandfather of Llywelyn the Great, whose leading advisor, steward, general and principal administrator was Ednyfed Fychan of Trecastell and Aberlleiniog, ancestor of Owen Tudor.

The existing remains of the old Tudor manor house of Trecastell consist simply of one angle of the building. Edward Lhwyd (1660–1709) noted: 'This ancient castellated mansion, after having long been the abode of the descendants of Marchudd, Lord of Uwch Dulas, in Denbighshire, was at length conveyed into the family of Mostyn by the marriage of Evan ab Adam ab Iorwerth Ddu of that house with Angharad, heiress of Ednyfed ab Tudor of Trecastell.'

The Ancestors of Owen Tudor

Eldest Son	Married
Marchudd ap Cynan ab Elfyw ap Mor, 'Lord of Brynffenigl' (Abergele), Lord of Rhos fl.950	
Edryd ap Marchudd, Lord of Brynffenigl	
Idnerth ab Edryd, Lord of Brynffenigl (*c.* 1035–*c.* 1100)	
Gwgan ab Idnerth, Lord of Brynffenigl	
Iorwerth ap Gwgan, Lord of Brynffenigl	Gwenllian ferch Ririd ap Pasgen (descended from Brochwel Ysgithrog, Prince of Powys.)
Cynwrig (Kendrig) ap Iorwerth, Lord of Brynffenigl and Llansadwrn (Anglesey)	Angharad ferch Hwfa ap Cynwrig, descended from Prince Owen Gwynedd
Ednyfed (Fychan) ap Cynwrig (1170–1246), 'Baron of Brynffenigl', Llansadwrn and Cricieth in Eifionydd	(firstly) Tangwystl Goch ferch Llywarch of Menai, by whom he had (Sir) Tudur ap Ednyfed (*c.* 1200–1281), giving one line of the family
[this second marriage gives us the 'Tudors of Penmynydd' line of Owen Tudor, via the eldest son Goronwy]	(secondly) Gwenllian ferch Rhys ap Gruffydd, 'Yr Arglwydd Rhys', King of Deheubarth
Goronwy ab Ednyfed Fychan (1195–1268) Lord of Trecastell	Morfydd ferch Meuric ap Ithel, Lord of Gwent
Tudur (Hen) ap Goronwy (1235–1311), Lord of Penmynydd	Angharad ferch Ithel Fychan, of Englefield, Flintshire
Goronwy ap Tudur (1265–1331), Lord of Penmynydd	Gwerfyl ferch Madoc ap David, Baron of Hendwr, Merioneth, derived from Owain Brogyntyn, Lord of Edeirnion, Dimnael, and Abertanat
(Sir) Tudur 'Fychan' ap Goronwy (1310–1367) Lord of Penmynydd	(firstly) Gwladys ferch Hywel, by whom he had Goronwy (d.1382), Ednyfed Fychan (d.1382), Gwilym (pardoned 1411) and Rhys ap Tudur (exec. 1412)
	(secondly) Marged ferch Tomos ap Llywelyn, Lord of South Wales, the last male representative of the royal house of Deheubarth

Maredudd ap Tudur (*c.* 1465–c. 1406)	Marged ferch Dafydd Fychan ap Dafydd Llwyd of Anglesey, a descendant of Hwfa ap Cynddelw, Founder of the First Noble Tribe of North Wales
OWAIN AP MAREDUDD AP TUDUR (*c.* 1400–1461)	Catherine of Valois (1401–1437), the widow of Henry V and mother of Henry VI
Edmund Tudor, Earl of Richmond (*c.* 1430–1456) [brother of Jasper, Earl of Pembroke, *c.* 1431–1495]	Lady Margaret Beaufort (1443–1509), daughter of John Beaufort, Duke of Somerset and Margaret, daughter of Baron Beaumont
Henry VII, King of England (1457–1509)	Elizabeth of York (1466–1503)

In the years before the birth of Ednyfed Fychan in 1170, relations between the Welsh and English had worsened considerably under Henry II's reign. After the disorder of the years of Stephen and Matilda, Henry decided that the power of the Marcher Barons needed to be curbed. As they were the guardians of the buffer zone between Wales and England they had great military power, and to disarm them Henry first had to crush and conquer Wales. He fostered dissent between the Welsh princes as part of this process, and then invaded with three armies in 1157. Henry's army was defeated at the Battle of Ewloe (Coleshill) in July by Owain Gwynedd, but he secured Rhuddlan Castle before agreeing peace and returning to England, taking hostages including two of Owain's sons. William of Newbugh reported that Henry was nearly killed, that two of England's noblest barons died and that Henry of Essex, the king's hereditary standard-bearer, had thrown down the royal banner and fled. He was sentenced to death, but the king commuted this to his becoming a monk at Reading 'and enriched himself with his ample fortune'. Another army passed along the coast of Glamorgan and penetrated past Carmarthen to Pencader before retreating, and a third force ravaged Powys around Oswestry; however, according to Giraldus Cambrensis all three 1157 expeditions were unsuccessful.

Henry's second expedition, of 1163, marched through Glamorgan to Carmarthen, wreaking destruction. Making peace at Pencader, Rhys ap Gruffydd gave Henry hostages, including two of his sons, and the king returned to England, accompanied by Rhys. By 1164 Henry had 'fulfilled nothing of what he promised' according to *Brut y Tywysogion* (*Chronicle of the Princes*). Rhys's nephew had been 'treacherously killed', and Rhys took over Ceredigion, burning Aberystwyth Castle. The following year, Dafydd ab Owain Gwynedd ravaged the Vale of Clwyd and Englefield, and Henry II took a force to Rhuddlan Castle to prepare for his third invasion. He returned to England to raise an army of Englishmen and mercenaries from Normandy, Flanders, Anjou and Gascony, gathering at Oswestry. In 1165 the massive army marched to Corwen, but they were met there by the greatest Welsh force ever assembled. On a hill above the town were gathered Owain Gwynedd and Cadwaladr, the sons of Gruffydd ap Cynan and the army of Gwynedd. Alongside their force was the 'Lord Rhys', Rhys ap Gruffydd, with his sons and the army of South Wales. Cadwallon and Einion Clud, the sons of Madog ab Idnerth, had brought the men of Rhwng Gwy a Hafren, the lands between the Wye and Severn. Owain Cyfeiliog and Iorwerth Goch ap Maredudd led an army from Powys.

Henry could not attack their position so retreated to the woods of Cyfeiliog, cutting down trees as he went and suffering constant attacks in dreadful weather. One skirmish was called the Battle of Crogen. The *Brut* records that:

> … when provisions failed him, he removed his army to the open plains of England; and, full of extreme rage, he ordered that the hostages who had previously been long imprisoned by him, to be blinded, to wit, the two sons of Owain Gwynedd, Cadwallon and Cynwrig, and Howel, and Maredudd, sons of the Lord Rhys, and many others.

Twelve young men from the leading families all had their eyes plucked out before the English king, and other hostages were dismembered. The king burned churches on his way back to England and never invaded again, instead appointing Rhys ap Gruffydd as Justice of South Wales in 1172. Against this background of invasion we can examine Owen Tudor's North Welsh ancestors, who will have followed Gruffydd ap Cynan, Owain Gwynedd and other princes of North Wales into battle.

The leading Welsh families of the fourteenth and fifteenth centuries could trace their descent to the 'five royal tribes of Wales' or the 'fifteen noble tribes of Gwynedd'; genealogical lists were compiled by Welsh bards around the middle of the fifteenth century. Marchudd ap Cynan, Lord of Brynffenigl, was the founder of the eighth 'noble tribe' of Gwynedd, which was North Wales and Powys at that time. Ednyfed Fychan was the direct descendant of Marchudd by the male line, which carried on to Owen Tudor. The Tudors were the most important non-royal family in Wales for around two centuries, and in the *Dictionary of Welsh Biography* Professor Glyn Roberts writes:

Ednyfed [Fychan] ap Cynwrig (d. 1246), claiming descent from Marchudd, was a member of one of a group of kindred long settled in Rhos and Rhufoniog. As seneschal (in Welsh, *distain*) of Gwynedd *c.* 1215–1246, his political and military services to Llywelyn the Great [Llywelyn ap Iorwerth, Prince of Wales] were rewarded, not only by the grant to Ednyfed himself of bond vills in Anglesey, Nantconwy, Arllechwedd Uchaf, and Creuddyn, but also by the concession, made to all the descendants of Ednyfed's grandfather (Iorwerth ap Gwrgan) that they should for the future hold their lands throughout Wales free from all dues and services other than military service in time of war. This special tenure, known as that of 'ŵyrion Eden,' is prominent in the 14th century in the lordship of Denbigh [then much larger, including Conwy etc.] amongst the collateral branches of the family. Ednyfed's own descendants in the same period are found in the townships of Trecastell, Penmynydd, Erddreiniog, Clorach, Gwredog, Trysglwyn, and Tregarnedd in Anglesey, and in Crewyrion, Creuddyn, Gloddaeth, Dinorwig, and Cwmllannerch in Caerns. They are also found in Llansadwrn in Carms. and at Llechwedd-llwyfan, Cellan, and Rhydonnen in Cards. Even before the conquest of 1282, therefore, Ednyfed's immediate descendants formed a 'ministerial aristocracy' of considerable wealth, and their widespread possessions, combined with the favourable terms on which they were held, made them the forerunners of that class of Welsh squires whose emergence is characteristic of the post-conquest period.

Ednyfed (Fychan) ap Cynwrig, Lord of Brynffenigl ('Baron of Bryn Ffanigl', Abergele), Lord of Lansadwrn and Lord of Cricieth in Eifionydd (*c.* 1170–1246)

Ednyfed was the chief counsellor, chief justice and general of Prince Llywelyn ap Iorwerth (Llywelyn Fawr, 'the Great'). He may have been involved in the negotiations when Gwenwynwyn ab Owain, Prince of southern Powys, swore allegiance to Llywelyn the Great in 1202, and in the subsequent fighting when Gwenwynyn made incursions into Gwynedd. Partly because Llywelyn married King John's daughter in 1205, Gwenwynwyn was arrested by John in 1208 and had his lands annexed by Llywelyn, with John's agreement. In 1209 Llywelyn accompanied his father-in-law John on campaign against William I of Scotland, and Ednyfed Fychan was almost certainly in his army. However, in keeping with John's reputation as an untrustworthy king, Gwenwynwyn was released by John around 1210 to recover Powys and accompanied the English on an expedition into Wales against Llywelyn.

In 1211, John summoned the Welsh nobles to meet him at Chester and demanded their loyalty, to which most acceded. Robert of Shrewsbury, the English Bishop of Bangor who had been placed there instead of being elected (Giraldus Cambrensis wanted the post), refused to attend, giving John's excommunication as an excuse. John's army drove Llywelyn and Ednyfed back into Gwynedd in May, but lengthy supply lines forced his withdrawal. In July and August an expanded English army returned, and John sent Brabant mercenaries to burn Bangor while the bishop sheltered in the cathedral. Troops entered Bangor Cathedral and dragged Bishop Robert away from the high altar, where he had claimed sanctuary. He had to pay a tremendous fine of 200 hawks to regain his freedom, John not being allowed to confiscate money from the Church. John was supported by Welsh nobles jealous of Llywelyn's power, and penetrated deep into Gwynedd, but it seems that Gwenwynwyn had changed allegiance again and switched to Llywelyn's side. On 8 July 1211, John's earls and barons marched from Whitchurch to Snowdon, 'destroying all the places he came to; he received twenty-eight hostages for their submission for the future' (*Brut y Tywysogion*).

In 1212 Pope Innocent III released Llywelyn and the other Welsh princes and nobles from their oaths of allegiance to John, and Llywelyn reconquered most of Gwynedd with Ednyfed at the head of his army. Ranulph de Blondeville, Earl of Chester, along with Peter des Roches, Bishop of Winchester, then led another king's army into Gwynedd. Llywelyn partly destroyed his own castle at Deganwy to hinder their progress, and the English eventually retreated. The *Brut* records that John's lieutenant in Powys, Robert Vieuxpont (Vipont), 'hanged at Shrewsbury Rhys, son of Maelgwyn, who was a hostage to the king, not being yet seven years old … that year, three illustrious men of the nation and chief princes of Wales were hanged in England, that is to say, Hywel, son of Cadwaldr, and Madog, son of Maelgwn, and Meurig Barach.' Ednyfed is said to have first come to notice in battle at this time, fighting against the army of Ranulph de Blondeville. De Blondeville had attacked Llywelyn at the request of King John. Ednyfed killed three Franco-English lords in battle and carried their heads, still bloody, to Llywelyn. Llywelyn commanded Ednyfed to change his family coat of arms to display three heads in memory of his valour, and the arms were carried by his descendants.

John was angered, and Roger of Wendover (d. 1236) writes:

About this time the Welsh burst forth fiercely from their hiding places, and took some of the English king's castles, decapitating all they found in them, knights and soldiers alike; they also burnt several towns, and at length, after collecting great quantities of booty, they again betook themselves to their retreats without any loss to themselves. When these events became known to the English king, he was very indignant, and collected a numerous army of horse and foot soldiers, determined to ravage the Welsh territories, and to *exterminate* [author's italics] the inhabitants. On his arriving with his army at Nottingham, before he either ate or drank, he ordered twenty-eight youths, whom had had received the year before as hostages from the Welsh, to be hanged on a gibbet, in revenge for the above mentioned transgressions of their countrymen.

Whilst he was, after this, sitting at the table eating and drinking, there came a messenger from the King of Scotland, who delivered letters, warning him of premeditated treachery against him; soon after which there came another messenger from the daughter of the same king, the wife of Llywelyn, King of Wales; this second messenger brought letters, like the former ones, and told the king that the contents were secret. After his meal the king took him aside and asked him to explain the content of the letters; these, although they came from different countries, were to one and the same effect, which was that, if the king persisted in the war which he had begun, he would either be slain by his own nobles or delivered to his enemies for destruction. The king was greatly alarmed on hearing this, and as he knew that the English nobles were absolved of their allegiance to him, he put more faith in the truth of the letters; therefore, wisely changing his intention, he ordered his army to return home.

Deganwy and Rhuddlan castles were captured by Llywelyn and Ednyfed in 1213, and in 1214 the earls and northern barons entered into a treaty with Llywelyn against John. The next year the earls took London, and on 4 December 1215 Shrewsbury surrendered to the Welsh.

Ednyfed was seneschal to Llywelyn from about 1215 to 1240 (and then to Dafydd ap Llywelyn from Llywelyn's death until Dafydd's death in February 1246). Ednyfed probably represented Llywelyn the Great at Runnymede when the barons forced John to sign *Magna Carta* on 15 June 1215, ensuring that Llywelyn's conditions were met. A clause compelled the release of Gruffydd ap Llywelyn Fawr and other Welsh nobles being held by John as hostages. (Gruffydd was Llywelyn's son by his first wife Tangwystl, who probably died giving birth to him). The successive relevant clauses applying to Wales are:

(56) If we have deprived or dispossessed any Welshmen of land, liberties, or anything else in England or in Wales, without the lawful judgment of their equals, these are at once to be returned to them. A dispute on this point shall be determined in the Marches by the judgment of equals. English law shall apply to holdings of land in England, Welsh law to those in Wales, and the law of the Marches to those in the Marches. The Welsh shall treat us and ours in the same way.

(57) In cases where a Welshman was deprived or dispossessed of anything, without the lawful judgment of his equals, by our father King Henry or our brother King Richard, and it remains in our hands or is held by others under our warranty, we shall have respite for the period commonly allowed to Crusaders, unless a lawsuit had been begun, or an enquiry had been made at our order, before we took the Cross as a Crusader. But on our return from the Crusade, or if we abandon it, we will at once do full justice according to the laws of Wales and the said regions.

(58) We will at once return [Gruffydd] the son of Llywelyn, all Welsh hostages, and the charters delivered to us as security for the peace.

Originally known as the Charter of Liberties, it was not translated into English for another three centuries. Its terms were upheld for just three months before John violated them.

By August 1215 Pope Innocent III had annulled *Magna Carta*, declaring it null and void having been sealed under duress. John died of dysentery aged fifty in October that year. In 1225, a new version was issued by Henry III and became the definitive version. Shakespeare did not mention it in his *Life and Death of King John*, and its importance was not noted until centuries later. It had little to do with the ordinary people of England, basically enshrining the rights, privileges and liberties of the clergy and the nobles while limiting despotic behaviour by the monarch. Most of its sixty-three clauses deal with the specifics of feudal rights and customs and the administration of justice. It was a temporary yet practical solution to a political crisis and 'primarily served the interests of the highest ranks of feudal society by reasserting the power of custom'.

Only three of the original clauses in *Magna Carta* are law today. The first defends the freedom and rights of the English Church. The second confirms the liberties and customs of London and other towns, and the third states that no man can be arrested, imprisoned or have their possessions taken away except by 'the lawful judgment of his equals or by the law of the land'. This last eventually paved the way for trial by jury. It certainly was not some torch for democracy, but a method for the upper classes to control the king's power – the idea that the monarch was not above the law was possibly its main element.

With John's powers curtailed, by December 1215 Llywelyn and Ednyfed had rampaged through the princedom of Deheubarth, south-west Wales, taking the castles of Cardigan, Cydweli (Kidwelly), Cilgerran, Carmarthen and Llansteffan (Llanstephan). The *Brut y Tywysogion* relates that Llywelyn gathered the other Welsh princes in a vast army at Carmarthen and after five days took the royal castle there and razed it to the ground, then demolished the castles of Llanstephan, Talacharn (Laugharne) and St Clears. They moved north and took Newcastle Emlyn and Newport castles, then Aberystwyth and Cilgerran. John died in 1216, and the accession of the nine-year-old Henry III temporarily relieved tension between England and Wales. In 1217 Llywelyn's son-in-law Reginald de Braose turned to fight for England and was attacked by Llywelyn, who took Swansea Castle and district. Ednyfed was Llywelyn's chief negotiator in the discussions leading to the Peace of Worcester in 1218, a peace treaty with Henry III. Trying to stabilize the eleven-year-old king's reign, the regency government under William Marshal, Earl of Pembroke, came to an agreement with Llywelyn. He effectively became Henry's justiciar across Wales, underlining the weakness of the king at this time. Henry's great barons were jockeying for power, with the trusted Marshal nearing the end of his days.

Ednyfed was also involved in the 1218 recognition by Henry III of Dafydd ap Llywelyn as Llywelyn's heir, an agreement on which Henry was to renege upon Llywelyn's death. In 1220 Ednyfed and Llywelyn invaded Pembrokeshire with other Welsh princes because the Flemings of Rhos and Pembroke had broken a peace treaty, and the men of Gwynedd took Narberth and Wiston castles before burning Haverfordwest, when the Flemings accepted peace. Both Giraldus Cambrensis and *Brut y Tywysogion* record that 'Flemings' were settled in south Pembrokeshire, part of the princedom of Deheubarth, soon after the arrival of the Normans in the early twelfth century.

There had been Norse settlements before this time, and in the sixteenth century Camden called the area *Anglia Transwalliana*; it has been known since as 'Little England beyond Wales'. In Welsh the area is known as Sir Benfro Saesneg, and in English it is Pembrokeshire. There is still a cultural and linguistic difference between north (Welsh-speaking) and south (English-speaking) Pembrokeshire, to this day delineated by the 'Landsker Line' of castles and earthworks from Amroth on the south coast to Newgale on the west coast. A study of place-names is instructive in this respect, with the southern part being full of names such as Rosemarket, Walwyn's Castle, Johnston, and Maiden Wells.

In 1222 Ednyfed was witness to the peace agreement with the Earl of Chester, but in 1223 Marshal took an army and recovered Pembroke, and then Cardigan and Carmarthen, expanding his Marcher lordship into Llywelyn's lands. In 1225 Llywelyn had asked for his wife Joan, Lady of Wales, the illegitimate daughter of King John, to be legitimised, and Pope Honorius III agreed in 1226. Marshal was ordered by the king's new regents to surrender Cardigan and Carmarthen back to Llywelyn, but in 1228 Gloucester led an army capturing an ally of Llywelyn, Morgan ap Caradog, Lord of Neath. Also in that year, Henry III was defeated at Ceri and William de Braose was captured. To set him free, Llywelyn was to be given Builth Castle, its district and a huge ransom. In 1229 Henry accepted the homage of Prince Dafydd for the lands he would inherit from his father Llywelyn.

The year 1230 witnessed an interesting incident. William de Braose was found in the bedchamber of the Lady Joan. *The Chronicle of Ystrad Fflur* states, 'In this year William de Breos the Younger, lord of Brycheiniog, was hanged by the Lord Llywelyn in Gwynedd, after he had been caught in Llywelyn's chamber with the king of England's daughter, Llywelyn's wife.' William Marshal died without issue in 1231, succeeded as earl and Lord Marshal of England by his brother Richard.

Ednyfed represented Llywelyn in a meeting with Henry III in 1232. In letters patent of Henry III dated at Shewsbury to 17 December 1232, Ednyfed is styled '*Idnevet Seneschallo ipsius Lewelini*'. There was more fighting in 1233, with Walter de Clifford defending Bronllys Castle against his father-in-law Llywelyn. Llywelyn and Owain ap Gruffudd allied with Richard Marshal, the new Earl of Pembroke, as he led a baronial revolt against the crown having been declared a traitor. They burned Monmouth, killing the castle garrison, before taking Abergavenny, Cardiff, Pengelli and Blaenllynfi, razing all except Cardiff. Routed by Marshal at Grosmont in 1233, Henry returned to Gloucester. In January 1234 Llywelyn and Marshal burned Shrewsbury, and Marshal agreed a truce with Henry. Unfortunately for Llywelyn, the Earl of Pembroke died in April 1234. Realising he had won all that he could, Llywelyn decided that peace was a good option. His country was in ruins.

At last, on 21 June 1234, Ednyfed attended the Peace of Middle, ending over two decades of Llywelyn's wars against the English. The agreed two-year truce was extended year by year for the remainder of Llywelyn's reign. Ednyfed's name appears as one of the arbitrators in a convention between

Henry III and Dafydd ap Llywelyn at Gloucester in 1240. Until his death in 1246, his name appears frequently as ministering to Dafydd's son Llywelyn.

Llywelyn the Great died in 1240, being buried in Aberconwy after first becoming a monk there, probably after suffering a stroke. The *Annales Cambriae* record: 'The died that mighty man, the second Achilles, namely Lord Llywelyn, son of Iorwerth, son of Owain Gwynedd, then Prince of Wales ... his deeds I am unworthy to narrate.'

In April 1240, his son Dafydd ap Llywelyn succeeded as Prince of Gwynedd and Wales, with Ednyfed as his seneschal. In March 1241, Ednyfed was at the peace treaty of Gloucester, signed by Dafydd and Henry, confirming Dafydd's princeship, but in August Henry invaded Gwynedd. Dafydd was forced to sign the Treaty of Gwerneigron with Henry in August 1241, having to give up most of modern Flintshire and being forced to give up his half-brother Gruffydd ap Llywelyn for imprisonment in the Tower. Gruffudd ap Llywelyn died in an escape attempt in 1244, and Dafydd, prompted by his people's discontent, began a war in the Marches, recovering most of Flintshire and taking Mold Castle in 1245. Henry III invaded Gwynedd, but was defeated and withdrew to England. Following representations from Henry, the Vatican reversed its decision to recognise Dafydd as rightful ruler of Wales. Ednyfed lost a son in the fight against the English in 1245. Dafydd was possibly poisoned at his court at Abergwyngregyn, dying in 1246.

Ednyfed remained in the employ of the princes of Gwynedd until his own death in 1246, bringing to an end a lifetime of loyal service. He was buried in Llandrillo-yn-Rhos Church on the north coast of Wales, which was his own chapel, only a few hundred yards from his mansion at Llys Euryn. His descendants were called 'Bryn Euryn's trophied race'. Llys, or Bryn Euryn, near Conwy, was one of the thirteen residences of Ednyfed Fychan, said to have been his favourite, 'royally adorned with turrets and garrets'. It is a testament to his political standing that Ednyfed's death was recorded in the *Annales Cestriensis* (the *Chronicles of St Werburgh*) at Chester as being an event of great importance in the region, a rare obituary for a Welshman in an English chronicle.

He had first married Tangwystl 'Goch' ferch Llywarch ap Brân of Llanedwen, Lord of Menon. By Tangwystl Ednyfed had a son, Tudor ap Ednyfed, who is mentioned in King Henry III's Patent Roll for 1248. Tudur ab Ednyfed Fychan owned Penrhyn and in 1450 a bard wrote of a descendant '*Un llin a'i Frenin fu'r ach*' – his descent is the same as that of his king.

Ednyfed's second wife was Gwenllian, daughter of Rhys ap Gruffydd, Prince of Deheubarth, known as 'Prince of the Welsh'. From this union came the Tudors. (In 2000 *The Sunday Times* ran an article on 'the Richest of the Rich' of the preceding millennium. Rhys ap Gruffydd, who made his fortune from 'land and war', was rated 95th richest, with a fortune estimated in 2000 values at £4.3 billion.) Ednyfed Fychan himself had great riches, and endowed his son Goronwy by his second marriage with the manors of Trecastell, Penmynydd and Erddreiniog in Anglesey, and many fine houses 'royally adorned with turrets and garrets', of which few traces remain. His sons and descendants also acted as seneschals.

Bezant Lowe records that according to folk tradition, Ednyfed is said to have composed a 'farewell song' to Gwenllian before leaving to take part in the Crusades. He was away for several years, and his family thought him dead. Ednyfed disappears from history for some time around 1234, and Harrison writes: 'Ednyfed Fychan embarked on his journey to the Holy Land in 1235, a journey that he would take with his retinue and, while lodging in London before he left, King Henry ordered his treasurer, Hugh Pateshull, to find out where he was lodging and to take him the gift of a silver cup… on his breastplate was a Saracen's head, a sign he or his ancestor had taken part in Crusades.' Pateshull, Bishop of Coventry and Lichfield, was Lord High Treasurer from 1234 to 1240.

Due to his prolonged absence Gwenllian accepted another offer of marriage, and on the wedding night a 'pitiable beggar' arrived at the house, asking permission to borrow a harp with which to entertain the party with a song. According to this legend the beggar sang 'Ednyfed's Farewell song', and as he reached the last verse he removed his hat, revealing himself to be Ednyfed. He sang, 'A wanderer I, and aweary of strife, / Get ye gone, if ye so desire; But if I may not have my own wife / I'll have my own bed, my own house, my own fire!' Ednyfed then announced to the wedding guests, 'This was the tune "Farewell" to my dear Gwenllian. Hence let her go with her new husband. My faithful harp, come to my arms.'

Over the following century, several townships in Llywelyn's possession were granted to the heirs of Ednyfed Fychan. Trecastell was one of these grants, whereby the land was held on exceptionally free terms in recognition of past service and in expectation of the same in future. The only requirements were attendance at court and the promise that a member of the Trecastell family would follow the prince of Gwynedd and his heirs in war, at the clan's own cost within the Marches of Wales and at the lord's cost outside it. Trecastell was also granted the privilege of holding its own court, which the tenants were required to attend, every three weeks.

Apart from Aberlleiniog Castle, which adjoined his mansion of Trecastell, another favoured stronghold of Ednyfed was at Tregarnedd, near Llangefni. In 1887, John Bartholomew's *Gazetteer of the British Isles* described

Tregarnedd as an 'old mansion, now a farm-house, in par. and 1 mile SE. of Llangefni, Anglesey; was built in time of Henry VII., and succeeded an older mansion of 13th. The south and western branches of Tre-Garnedd moat are the only remains of a medieval mansion on the edge of Malltraeth Marsh.' Tregarnedd was later the seat of Gruffydd ap Rhys ap Gruffydd ab Ednyfed Fychan (Gruffydd Llwyd, d. 1335), knighted before 1301, when he did homage to Edward of Caernarvon as the new Prince of Wales, becoming a member of the prince's household. He was the leading Welshman of North Wales through the early fourteenth century. There were visible traces of the house in the early twentieth century. The barns and farm have recently been converted into ten very modern holiday cottages and apartments, unsympathetic to the medieval moated site. Llwyd is described in Welsh pedigrees as lord of Tregarnedd in Anglesey and Dinorwig in Caernarfon. He also held lands in Denbighshire, Carmarthen and Ceredigion. Tregarnedd and the Denbigh lands were inherited from his father Rhys ap Gruffydd, who died in 1284. Llanrhystud in Ceredigion came to him from his uncle Sir Hywel ap Gruffydd, who died in a battle with the English army invading North Wales from Anglesey at 'the bridge of Anglesey' in November 1282. Llwyd's father and his uncle Hywel were active supporters of Edward I in the Welsh wars. Llwyd joined Queen Eleanor's household, and in 1283 was admitted as a yeoman of the king's own household.

Goronwy ab Ednyfed Fychan, Lord of Tref-Gastell (1195–1268)

Goronwy, or Gronw, was Ednyfed's son by Gwenllian ap Rhys ap Gruffydd of Deheubarth. He served Prince Dafydd ap Llywelyn ap Iorwerth until that prince's death, possibly by poison. Goronwy was also seneschal to Llywelyn ap Gruffudd from 1458, fighting to retain Welsh independence. He was the founder of the line of the Tudors of Penmynydd. Robert Williams, following an article on the Tudor tomb at St Gredifael's Church, Penmynydd, wrote that Ednyfed Fychan 'had two sons, Gruffydd and Grono. To the second, Grono, he bequeathed the three manors of Penmynydd, Tre Castell, and Arddreiniog, with other extensive estates. Grono ab Ednyved, an illustrious and powerful man, resided at Tre Castell, near Llanvaes.' Goronwy ab Ednyfed married Morfudd ferch Meurig ap Ithel, Lord of Gwent.

Goronwy's step-brother [Sir] Tudur ab Ednyfed Ffychan, of Nant and Llangynhafal married Adlais (Adles) ferch Rhisiart ap Cadwaladr, a descendant of Gruffydd ap Cynan, Prince of Gwynedd. He was born at Tregarnedd, Langefni, died at Y Nant Llangynhafal. He one of the commissioners for the conclusion of peace between Edward I and Llywelyn ap Iorwerth, Prince of Gwynedd. Tudur ab Ednyfed was captured during Henry III's inconclusive campaign against Prince Dafydd ap Llywelyn in September 1245, being released in May 1247 upon swearing fealty to Henry. Henry's army retreated in 1246, Dafydd died, thought to have been poisoned, in 1246 at his palace at Tŵr Celyn, and Tudur received royal favour in the following years, but became one of Prince Llywelyn ap Gruffudd's leading advisers after 1256, succeeding his brother Goronwy as seneschal until his death in 1278. Tudur's son Heilyn was a hostage in the king's hands between 1246 and 1263, submitting finally to Edward I in 1282. Other sons of Ednyfed Fychan in the following of the later princes of Gwynedd were Hywel (Bishop of St Asaph, 1240–7), Cynwrig and Rhys.

Tudur (Hen) ap Goronwy ab Ednyfed, Lord of Penmynydd (*c.* 1235/45–1311)

According to Thomas Pennant, Tudur Hen, son of Goronwy ab Ednyfed, founded the House of the White Friars, the Carmelites, in Bangor, about 1276, enriched it in 1299 and was buried there in 1311. The foundation supposedly exists in the Friars Grammar School, but the traces left by the Carmelites are 'exceedingly meagre'. Like his father, Tudur Hen was Seneschal of Gwynedd for Llywelyn ap Gruffudd.

At this time there was almost constant fighting against the English across Wales, brought on by cruelty, enslavement and excessive taxation. Petitions to John Peckham, Archbishop of Canterbury, for the actions of the king's officers in Wales included these against Roger Cifford and Roger Schrochill, his deputy:

... to the men of Strath Alyn, where Mold lies:
Item – the said Roger took the lands of the men of the country as forfeit, and for one foot of a stag found in a dog's mouth, three men were spoiled of all they had...
Item – Ithel ab Gwysty was condemned to a great sum, for the fact of his father, done forty years before...
Item – We were given to Maister Maurice de Cruny, and were sold to Roger Clifford, which was never known in our parents' time.

Mathew Paris notes that in 1247 'Wales was in a most straitened condition, and, owing to the cessation of agriculture, commerce and the tending of flocks, the inhabitants began to waste away through want; unwillingly, too, did they bend to the yoke of the English laws'. In 1252 the *Brut y Tywysogion* noted the lack of crops, fish in the rivers and fruit on the trees due to a massive drought that was followed by floods, leading to destruction of bridges, roads and buildings. To compound difficulties, Llywelyn ap Gruffudd was faced with civil war, winning at Bryn Derwyn in 1255 before the events of 1256, as recorded by Paris:

> ... the Welsh, who had been oppressed in manifold ways, and often sold to the highest bidder, were at last so outrageously and tyrannically oppressed by the king's agent, Geoffrey Langley, knight, that they roused themselves for the defence of their country and the observance of their laws. Entering into a confederacy, they invaded the provinces of England adjoining Wales, and attacked the subjects of Edward, their lord, which however they did not acknowledge as such; and they succeeded so well in their warlike expedition, that it was believed they had the goodwill of the neighbouring people.

Henry III's son Edward now invaded, causing widespread damage, and Welsh nobles told Llywelyn that they would rather die in war than be 'trodden down in bondage by strangers'. In the ensuing war Llywelyn was successful, taking lands back from English nobles across the nation. Henry III led another expedition in 1257 but had to withdraw.

Matthew Paris wrote of Llywelyn's successful war of 1256–57, where Tudur and Goronwy would have fought alongside him, that the Welsh 'had sworn upon the gospels boldly and faithfully to fight to the death for the liberty of their country and the laws of their ancestors, declaring that they would rather die with honour than drag on an unhappy life in disgrace. This manly and brave determination might justly shame the English, who lazily bent their necks to foreigners, and to every one that trampled on them, like vile and timid rabble, the scum of the human race.' Matthew Paris was an English Benedictine monk at St Albans Abbey from 1217. He took over from Roger of Wendover as the abbey's recorder in 1237, and was strongly nationalistic and critical of Rome. He was on friendly terms with Henry III, who wanted his history to be as exact as possible. In 1257, during a week's visit to St Albans, Henry kept the monk beside him, with Paris recording that the king 'guided my pen with much goodwill and diligence'. However, his *Chronica Majora* is not overly complimentary to the king.

Tudur Hen led a successful raid against the Marcher Lords in support of his mother's family in Gwent in 1263, and Llywelyn reasserted the authority of Gwynedd and extended its supremacy over much of the rest of Wales. In 1267 his position as overlord was recognised by Henry III in the Treaty of Montgomery when the king accepted Llywelyn's homage as Prince of Wales. Ten years after his recognition as the Prince of Wales, Llywelyn was to suffer a humiliating defeat at the hands of the new king, Edward I. He had refused to offer the homage and payments owed to the king under the terms of the Treaty of Montgomery. He had also arranged to marry Eleanor, daughter of rebel baron Simon de Montfort. Llywelyn strengthened his grandfather's castles at Cricieth, Ewloe and Dolwyddelan, and in 1273 he started to build a new fortress at Dolforwyn, above the Severn, creating a direct challenge to the nearby royal castle of Montgomery. Llywelyn refused to abandon the project, and Edward arrived at Chester in July 1277; by August he had mustered 15,600 troops via moneylenders and foreign banks. Llywelyn had no choice but to sue for peace. The ensuing Treaty of Aberconwy was a humiliation. He was stripped of his overlordship of Wales, and Gwynedd was again reduced to its traditional heartland west of the River Conwy. On 21 March 1282, Llywelyn's brother, Dafydd, attacked Hawarden Castle and sparked off the war of 1282–83. Llywelyn was to side with his brother and led the Welsh resistance to the inevitable invasion by Edward I.

During Tudur Hen's lifetime there occurred the final conquest of Wales by Edward I, after Llywelyn ap Gruffudd was lured into a trap and killed, and his supporting army surrendered and was slaughtered. (Tudur Hen was probably with the rest of Llywelyn's army with Prince Dafydd in Gwynedd at this time.) Anian, the Bishop of Bangor, was suspected in the treachery leading to Llywelyn's death, and it became politically correct for the remaining Welsh nobles to henceforth endow the clergy of Bangor.

The wonderful elegy for Llywelyn by Gruffydd ab yr Ynad Coch describes the heartbreak felt across the nation. It is noted as one of the greatest poems of medieval literature. Below is an excerpt assisted with translations from Greg Hill:

> For us now the blackness,
> The hatred of Saxons [English] –
> A time of lamenting
> In the life left to us
> ... Horror chills my heart.
> Do you not hear the storms of wind and rain?
> Do you not see the oaks together hurled?
> Do you not see how ocean scours the land?
> Do you not see the sun bend from his course?

Do you not see the stars rush from their spheres?
Does not the end of all things now draw near?
To Thee, O God, I cry; why does not now
Earth sink engulfed, our agony to end?
… His head has fallen, and with it our pride
Fear and surrender are all we have left.
His head has fallen – a dragon's head,
Noble it was, fierce to our foes.
His head is stuck with an iron pole,
The searing pain of it runs through my soul
The land is empty, our spirit cut down.
His head had honour in nine hundred lands.
Proud king, swift hawk, fierce wolf,
True Lord of Aberffraw [his Anglesey court]
His only refuge
The kingdom of Heaven.

The penalty for treason was hanging until dead, with the head being spiked somewhere, usually London, while the quarters of the body were despatched for display in other parts of the kingdom. Edward I personally refined this into one of the worst tortures known to mankind, in 1283 dragging Llywelyn's brother Prince Dafydd, the last Prince of Wales, through Shrewsbury on a hurdle. He was then hanged slowly and cut down to be castrated, with his genitals placed before him and burnt. Then he was slowly disembowelled, the skill of the executioner being to prolong the process for the delight of the king. Only then was Dafydd's head taken to be spiked alongside that of his brother in London, and his quarters sent for display. Now Edward I ordered a valuation to be made of Anglesey showing what he might expect to derive from 'the granary of Wales' in revenues. The commissioners met at Llanfaes, but the valuation 'did not include those places of local and self-contained importance, from which the crown, having seized only the rights of the Welsh prince, and not those of his subjects, could demand nothing'. It did not include Penmynydd, Erddreiniog or Trecastell, the manors Ednyfed Fychan left to his second family.

Tudur Hen had not only acted as seneschal for Prince Llywelyn, but over a decade later took part in the great Madog ap Llywelyn uprising of 1294, acting as his seneschal as well. Madog was said to have been taken to the Tower after his capture, never to be heard of again. Tudur was probably known as *Hen*, or old, because of his longevity in public office and to distinguish him from others of the same name. (*Bychan*, mutated to *Fychan*, means small, and can either refer to size, or to distinguish from a senior family member.)

Tudur married Angharad ferch Ithel Fychan of Tegeingl (Englefield, Flintshire), and divided his lands at his decease among his three sons, Goronwy (Grono), Howel (Hywel) and Madog. He was buried in Llanfaes Friary at Bangor, which he had completed, in a tomb made for him in the south wall of the chapel. The House of the Grey Friars in Llanfaes, near the more recent Beaumaris, was said to have been founded in 1237 by Llywelyn the Great. After Tudur's death, his sons enjoyed the whole inheritance of their father. Edward Lhwyd notes: 'Sir Tudor was one of the great proprietors who, holding their estates in capite did homage to Edward Prince of Wales at Chester, in the twenty-ninth of Edward I.' However, this must have been at Lincoln in 1301 where the future Edward II became the first English prince to be invested with the title Prince of Wales, where the king also granted him the earldom of Chester and lands across North Wales. 'His three sons were in their time styled the three temporal lords of Anglesey, viz., Ednyfed of Tre'r Castell; Gronwy of Penmynydd, and Rhys of Arddreiniog; the three spiritual being the Archdeacon of Anglesey, the President of Holyhead, and the Prior of Penmon.' According to Williams, 'Howel [ap Tudur Hen] died without issue; Madog [ap Tudur Hen], having received holy orders, became the first Archdeacon of Anglesey, and afterwards a most renowned Abbot of Conwy, left his lands to his own monastery of Conwy.'

Goronwy ap Tudur Hen ap Goronwy ab Ednyfed, Lord of Penymynydd (*c.* 1285–1331/32)

Goronwy was captain of twenty archers serving in Aquitaine and was later Forester of Snowdon. He married Gwerfyl ferch Madoc ap David, Baron of Hendwr, Merioneth, a descendant of Owain Brogyntyn, Lord of Edeirnion, Dimnael and Abertanat. The eldest son of Sir Tudor obtained Penmynydd for his share, where he lived and died. He left an only daughter, Morfudd, who was married to William ab Gruffydd ab Gwilym (ap Gruffydd ap Heilyn ap Sir Tudor ap Ednyfed Fychan) of Penrhyn, Caernarvonshire. Robert Williams states:

> It is clear that Grono inherited Penmynydd and Dinsylwy Res, together with most of the honours of the family. Grono – commonly called Grono Vychan ap Tudor, was in favour with Edward the Black Prince, and very probably accompanied him abroad. When, therefore, the entire government of Wales was placed by Edward III in the hands of his gallant son, the latter

appointed Grono ap Tudor for life to the responsible office of Forester of Snowdon, – a district which comprehended the greater portion, if not the whole, of Carnarvon, Merioneth, and Anglesey. His salary was 3d. per diem – £10 13s. per annum. This office he held until the day of his death. Although the Black Prince never succeeded to the throne, his son did, and, as Richard II, not only continued the prince's appointments, but promoted his father's friend, Grono ap Tudor. The Patent Roll for 1331 contains a grant to him of the office of Constable of Beaumaris Castle, with a yearly fee of forty marks, – he to provide a chaplain, sub-constable, and warder; but it would seem that he did not live to enter into possession of the post. The Chamberlain's accounts, which record the payment of salaries to all high officers of state, do not in any year include the name of Grono ap Tudor as Constable of Beaumaris. David Cradock, or Caradoc, whom he was to have succeeded, remained for many years in charge of the castle, and Grono, or his representatives, drew his salary as Forester of Snowdon only, up to the day of his death, March 23rd, 1332 ...

We have the following excellent evidence of this date. The lands of Penmynydd were taken possession of by King Richard's escheator, the heir being a minor, and the escheator recorded them thus:

The Lands which were Grono's ap Tudor. – Of certain proceeds or profits of lands or tenements which were Grono's ap Tudor, in the townships of Penmynyth and Dynsilwy Res, who died on the Sabbath day next before the feast of the Annunciation of Blessed Virgin Mary, in the fifth year of the now king; and which the same Grono held of the king in capite by service of going with the said king in his war within the marches of Wales at his own cost, and beyond at the cost of the said king and suit, at the County Court of Anglesey: remaining in the hands of the lord the king by the death of the said Grono, on account of the minority of age of Tudor, the son and heir of the said Grono; and which are extended by the year at twelve pounds beyond, etc. He answereth not, because respited by the justiciary and others of the council of the lord the king until it should be discussed whether they ought to belong to the lord the king, or whether they should be de-livered to Mevanwy [sic], who was the wife of the said Grono, for surety in answering the lord king, etc.

Goronwy had been one of the leaders of Welsh troops who assembled in Newcastle-upon-Tyne in 1314 to invade Scotland, and fought in the two-day battle at Bannockburn. Peter Reese writes that 'only one sizeable group of men – all footsoldiers – made good their escape to England.' This force of Welsh spearmen, commanded by Maurice de Berkeley, probably included Goronwy, and they managed to escape to Carlisle. Reese states, 'It seems doubtful if even a third of the footsoldiers returned to England', and of 16,000 infantrymen, possibly 11,000 were killed fighting for Edward II against Robert de Brus. Goronwy was appointed a King's Yeoman and appointed Forester of Snowdon in 1318–19. By the time of his death, the Tudurs were no longer tainted with rebellion, but firmly in the favour of the new king, Edward III. One report tells us that 'Grono, the eldest son, having acquired the property of his brother Howel, made his son Tudor his heir, and was buried with his father at Bangor'.

(Sir) Tudur 'Fychan' ap Goronwy ap Tudur Hen ap Goronwy ab Ednyfed, Lord of Penymynydd (1310–1367)

Goronwy ab Ednyfed Fychan held Trecastell, Penmynydd and Erddreiniog, in the commote of Dindaethwy, in the thirteenth century. His grandson, Goronwy ap Tudur, also held the townships, along with the township of Tregaian. The townships then passed on Tudur Fychan ap Goronwy, who probably maintained Trecastell as his principal residence. Tudur Fychan and his brother Hywel were in 'possession of Trecastell, Erddreiniog, and half of Penmynydd in Anglesey and 'Gavell Gron ap Eden' (which included the nucleus of the later Penrhyn estate) and half of 'Gavell Kennyn in Crewyrion in Caernarfonshire', as well as some Cardiganshire possessions. Tudur Fychan was Rhaglaw (prefect) of Dindaethwy, Trecastell and Penrhyn.

J. Williams (*Penmynydd and the Tudors*) informs us that:

Edward III bestowed Wales upon his gallant son, the Black Prince, and then a more complete extent [valuation] was made to show the value of the gift. It bears date in 1352, and has since been printed in the Record of Carnarvon ... Military tenure, of course, obtained in Wales as elsewhere, and, subject to such tenures, the crown claimed all the land. Most occupiers owed, in addition to this service, others of a more menial nature: repairs of the king's house, food for his troops, beef for his household, work in his fields, and many more remarkable feudal exactions. *The manors, however, of Trecastell, Penmynydd, and Erddreiniog were held free from all such claims as these* [author's italics] – the first by Howell ap Grono and his brother Tudor; the second half by them, and half by the Abbot of Conway, to whom King Edward and Bishop Anian of Bangor had granted the tithes when the Abbey of Conway was removed to Maenan. The third manor was held by Howell ap Grono, his brother Tudor, and Res ap David. Their tenure is thus described in the extent:– Trefcastell. This township is a free one. The tenants are Hoell ap Grono and his brother Tudor, and they pay no rent or duty to the Prince, except suit at his court. And one man of the stock of that township, that is, of the stock of the grandchildren of Ednyfed, shall go to the king's wars for all the blood of the said Ednyfed, at his own cost within the marches of Wales; but beyond them, at the cost of the king. And they and their bondmen make suit at both of the great sheriff's tours in the year.

Penmynydd was held on similar terms. These two brothers, with Rhys ap David, represented the Tudor family in 1352. Hywel ap Goronwy took a career in the Church, becoming a canon at Bangor Cathedral and later Archdeacon of Anglesey, dying in 1366/67, being buried in Bangor's friary.

Tudur was a wealthy royal officer for Anglesey, living at Trecastell, and first married Gwladys ferch Hywel, by whom he had several children, the most important for us being the sons Goronwy, Ednyfed, Gwilym and Rhys, the uncles of Owen Tudor. After this Tudur married Marged ferch Tomos ap Llywelyn ab Owain, Lord of Iscoed, South Wales, and they had Maredudd, the father of Owen Tudor. Tomos ap Llywelyn was married to Eleanor ferch Philip. Marged's paternal grandparents were Llywelyn ab Owain, Lord of Gwynnionith, and Eleanor, daughter of Henry III, Count of Bar (c. 1262–1302), and Eleanor of England (1269–1298). Eleanor of England was the eldest surviving daughter of Edward I of England and Eleanor of Castile. Marged's maternal grandparents were Philip ap Ifor, Lord of Iscoed, and Catherine ferch Llywelyn, the reported daughter of Llywelyn the Last and Eleanor de Montfort. Tomos ap Llywelyn was the last male representative of the royal house of Deheubarth, which would later strengthen Owain Glyndŵr's claim to be Prince of Wales. Marged was the sister of Elen ferch Tomos, the mother of Glyndŵr, which made Tomos' son Maredudd a blood cousin of Glyndŵr.

Tudur served under Edward III in France in 1337 and assumed the rank of knight, although he may have done so without the king's permission. In 1345, Tudur and his brother Hywel were the main suspects in the death of the hated attorney William de Shaldford, who was killed near Hywel's home. De Shaldford was in the employ of Edward the Black Prince across North Wales. The brothers were arrested and placed in custody, but later released without charge. Local English burgesses complained that 'no Welsh man dare indict them' because of their influence. The Anglesey poet Gruffudd ap Maredudd ap Dafydd (*fl.* 1352–1382) was the household bard of the Tudors of Penmynydd, and wrote eulogies for both Hywel and his brother Tudur Fychan. He suggested that they were as 'strong as oak trees' and 'protected all those under their branches'. On Tudur's death in 1367, his body was placed with those of his ancestors in the south wall of the chancel of Llanfaes Friary, near Beaumaris. The possessions of Tudur and his unmarried brother Hywel in Anglesey and Caernarvonshire passed to Tudur's sons. Tudur divided the estate among his five sons Goronwy, Ednyfed, Gwilym, Rhys and Maredudd. With the exception of Ednyfed, they all seem to have held positions of administrative responsibility in the royal government of North Wales at the end of the fourteenth century, and Rhys and Gwilym had a personal relationship with Richard II, being appointed that king's squires.

Iolo ab Ithel Goch ap Cynwrig ab Iorwerth ap Cynwrig Ddewis Herod ap Cowryd (*c.* 1325–1400) was known as Iolo Goch ('the red-haired', like his father Ithel), and only thirty-nine of his poems are known to have survived. Born at Lleweni in the Vale of Clwyd, he described Glyndŵr's splendid mansion at Sycharth before it was burnt by Prince Henry. Some of his poems are of relevance to our subject. He wrote a wonderful seventy-two-line *Marwnad Tudur Fychan o Benmynydd* (*Elegy for Tudur Fychan of Penmynydd*), translated by Professor Dafydd Johnston. Tudur is called '*carw Tre'rcastell*', the stag of Tre'rcastell, and praised as 'he was more used to wearing finely / in a joust, strong gentle lord, / a helmet always richly crested. / And a habergeon, swift straight hawk, / and a closely linked mailcoat / heavy and loose to enable him to fight, / a shield which was a heavy weight to him, / a squire's crow-feeding arm-burdening spear'. Brynffanugl was one of the courts of Ednyfed Fychan, near Abergele.

… Gwedy marw y rhygarw rhugl,
Ffyniant hil naf Brynffanugl,
Ffeleaig, ysgithddraig uthrddrud,
A phen Môn rhag ffo na mud;
Aesawr gwlad fawr, golud fu,
Yswain brwydr sy'n ei brydu;
Dillyn Môn, frehyrion fro,
Dalltai bwyll dellt ebillio; …

After the death of the great swift stag,
Flourishing of the line of Brynffanugl's lord,
Chieftain, ferocious tusked dragon,
And Môn's head against retreat or flight;
Great land's shield, he was wealth,
A swain of battle is singing his praise;
Darling of Mon, land of nobles,
He understood the art of piercing a shattered shield; …

The Sons of Tudur Fychan, the grandfather of Owen Tudor

Iolo Goch also wrote the poems *Praise of Tudur Fychan's Sons* and *Elegy for Tudur Fychan's Sons*. The four sons mentioned in these poems were all the children of Tudur's first wife (probably Maredudd was too young to be included), so unlike Maredudd they were not blood relatives of Glyndŵr.

In the elegy, Rhys and Gwilym are dressed as black-robed monks because of the deaths of Goronwy and Edynfed. Goronwy was Constable of Beaumaris Castle, and was drowned with Ednyfed on 22 March 1382, being buried at Llanfaes Friary. At the time of Goronwy's death, as the eldest brother he lived at Penmynydd, with Ednyfed at Trecastell, Rhys at Erddreiniog and Gwilym at Clorach. (Iolo Goch gives us these homes for the brothers.) Goronwy was succeeded as Forester of Snowdon by Rhys. The Tudurs had controlled Anglesey and much of north-west Wales in the fourteenth century, and the family seemed destined to pass out of history until the fifth Tudur brother, Maredudd, established a new destiny for the family.

Iolo Goch's eighty-eight-line *Praise of Tudur Fychan's Sons*, translated by Johnston, calls them 'chief jousters of Mon, / Gronwy, Rhys, lords of the island, / Ednyfed, Gwilym, keen spear; / Rhys, Ednyfed, gift-bestowing lord, / grim and keen his spear, Gwilym, Gronwy, / Ednyfed, Gronwy, Rhun's pride / ... cubs of fierce Tudur Llwyd...' Iolo writes of his visits to the 'fortress of Pen Môn, stag of Penmynydd', where 'Gronwy of the shining spear' has a 'pleasant court'. He writes of Rhys' home of 'Erddreiniog, it ennobled the island', and how 'Tre'rcastell is not far off, chamber of gifts, / heavenly land, Ednyfed's dwelling'. Iolo travels between their houses to Clorach: 'Gwilym's court, a mansion full of herbs, / golden leopard, place of ready talent / dragon's nature, there will I dwell, / in heaven, and I will do right, / Clorach's dwelling, brilliant building.' According to Johnston, Pen Môn is not the Penmon Priory situated in the south-east of Anglesey, but a fort on the northern tip of Anglesey. However, Ednyfed's court at Tre'r Castell, now Tre-Castell Farm, is less than 2 miles from Penmon Priory, near the 60-foot-square, four-towered Castell Lleiniog, which is surely the '*Caer Pen Fon*' of Tudur Fychan. Erddreiniog is near Tregaian, and Clorach is between Llanerch-y-Medd and Llanfihangel Tre'r Beirdd.

Goronwy ap Tudur Fychan (*c.* 1340–1382)

Goronwy and his brothers Rhys and Gwilym were in the personal following of Richard II, noted as the king's esquires. Eighteen years after the deaths of Goronwy and Ednyfed, the three surviving brothers, Rhys, Gwilym and Maredudd, and their near kinsmen were prominent supporters of Owain Glyndŵr, with Rhys being hanged, drawn and quartered at Chester in 1412. Their lands were forfeited to the crown and came into the possession of the Griffiths of Penrhyn, also descended from Ednyfed Fychan through Tudur ab Ednyfed. However, a remnant of the Tudur estate at Penmynydd remained in the possession of the descendants of Goronwy ap Tudur through his daughter Morfydd and her husband Gwilym ap Gruffydd of Penrhyn. Goronwy had married Myfanwy, daughter of Iorwerth ap Ednyfed Gam of Pengwern.

Goronwy had campaigned in France, probably under the Black Prince in Aquitaine, and was rewarded for his services. Goronwy ap Tudur, Forester of Snowdon like his namesake, also held the stewardship of the Bishop of Bangor's Anglesey manors. A favourite of the Black Prince, on 18 March 1382 he was appointed Constable of Beaumaris Castle with a salary of forty marks, an office only held once by a Welshman before his time. He died, as the escheator of Anglesey reported, on 22 March 1382. His possessions in Penmynydd and Dinsylwy Rees, to the net value of £12 a year, were held 'by service of going with the lord King in his wars, within the march of Wales at his own proper costs and without the marches at the cost of the lord King and by suit of the county court of Anglesey'. These were also the terms on which his father and uncle had held their lands in 1352. Grace Lloyd-Williams states that his youngest brother Maredudd 'succeeded Gronow as steward of the Bishop of Bangor's lordship in Anglesey', which may have been around 1382.

Bards state that Goronwy and his brother Ednyfed died by drowning during disembarkation in Kent in 1382. In Iolo Goch's elegy, he writes that he would not have been surprised at this as Goronwy probably frequently crossed both in the service of Richard II. Gruffydd ap Maredudd and Llywelyn Goch both confirm the cause of death by drowning. Gruffydd and Iolo tell us that Goronwy's body was brought from London and buried at Llanfaes, where his tomb represents the most costly and elaborate type of monument of the period, demonstrating his prestige and wealth. Llanfaes was the burial place in 1282 of Eleanor de Montfort, Princess of Wales, who died giving birth to Prince Llywelyn ap Gruffudd's only child, Princess Gwenllian. The child was incarcerated in a nunnery in England for life in an attempt to wipe out the last remnants of the House of Gwynedd.

Llanfaes was founded by Llywelyn the Great, and his wife Princess Joan, the daughter of King John, was also buried there. It was thus the favoured burial site of local Anglesey nobility. Goronwy's splendid tomb was moved to St Gredifael's at Penmynydd, possibly during the Dissolution. Gruffudd ap Meredydd ap Dafydd wrote an elegy to Goronwy and Ednyfed, and J. Williams gives a partial translation:

> Of excess of mead it happened –
> His arms that prevailed in battle
> Prove an utter evil to the leader of the host.
> There was deep grief around
> For the bright-helmed, wine-loving leader;
> For the drowning of a leader of wolves –
> A wild boar in battle – the eagle of the host
> … Many of the people will be astounded
> In England, that the sleep of his eyes
> Has come upon the leader of bright thousands.
> Dire offence, double lament, heavy
> Senseless loss the black pool caused
> By covering the dread lion
> …The grief of Menai was placed in a marble tomb.
> Sad indeed was it to put in oak and earth
> A pillar of the coast; the ardent pursuer of France;
> The powerful friend; chief of the court of Penmynydd:
> The choir of the Barefooted Friars [Llanfaes] covered him.

The bard Hywel ap Einion Llygliw wrote a song to the beautiful Myfanwy Fychan before she married Goronwy. It is said that he would hide his poems in a tree on the hillside beneath Castell Dinas Brân for Myfanwy to find. Myfanwy is reported as having come from Castell Dinas Brân or Llys Pengwern. The castle overlooks Llangollen, and there is an area in the modern town called Pengwern. It is believed that Myfanwy's grandfather, Ednyfed Gam, is buried locally at Valle Crucis Abbey. A translation of Hywel ab Einion's contemporary poem begins:

I am without spirit, O thou that hast enchanted me, as Creirwy enchanted Garwy. In whatever part of the world I am, I lament my absence from the marble castle of Myfanwy. Love is the heaviest burden, O thou that shinest like the heavens, and a greater punishment cannot be inflicted than thy displeasure, O beautiful Myfanwy. I who am plunged deeper and deeper in love, can expect no other ease, O gentle fair Myfanwy with the jet eyebrows, than to lose my life upon thy account. I sung in golden verse thy praises, O Myfanwy; this is the happiness of thy lover, but the happiness is a misfortune...

The fourteenth-century love story of Myfanwy and Hywel was the subject of the poem *Myfanwy Fychan* (1858) by John Ceiriog Hughes (1832–87). In 1875 the tale was set to a tune by Joseph Parry with Welsh lyrics by Richard Davies, and it remains a favourite of Welsh choirs. When Myfanwy's tomb was opened in the 1850s restoration, it reportedly contained a body with 'thick yellow hair'.

Ednyfed ap Tudur Fychan (1345?–1382)

Less is known of Ednyfed than Goronwy, but he died about the same time as his brother Goronwy, apparently of the same cause. Iolo Goch's elegy is to both brothers and implies the death of both, with Ednyfed predeceasing his brother. Ednyfed held Trecastell with his brother Gwilym. The Tudur branch of Mostyn in Flintshire believe he was married to Gwenllian ferch Dafydd ap Bleddyn Fychan of Tegeingl. Ednyfed's daughter Angharad, heiress of Trecastell, married Ieuan ap Adda ap Iorwerth Du of Pengwern in the late fourteenth century and their son Ieuan Fychan married another Angharad, the daughter of Hywel ap Tudur.

Maredudd ap Tudur is not mentioned, being the youngest son, by Tudur Fychan's second wife, and also is not noted in Iolo Goch's ninety-eight-line elegy for Tudur Fychan's four sons by Mallt, his first wife, *Marwnad Meibion Tudur Fychan*. Iolo Goch notes the 'deserted court' of Penmynydd, with Rhys and Gwilym in black mourning robes, and indeed, 'there is hardly a single nobleman in Môn, / who is not in black clothes'. Much work has been done upon translating medieval Welsh poetry into modern Welsh, but unfortunately very few have been translated into English, which makes Professor Johnston's work so important. He translates the circumstances of Goronwy's death and burial:

... Ni ryfeddwn, gwn ganwaith,	I would not wonder, I know of 100 occasions
Pe boddai ar Fenai faith,	Had he died on broad Menai,
Neu ar Fôr Udd, arfer oedd,	Or on the North Sea, it was customary
Penadur byd pan ydoedd;	When he was a ruler of the world;

Braw eisoes oedd i'r bresent	But it was a shock to the people of the world
Suddo ei gruff yn Swydd Gent;	That his body sank in Kent;
Mewn pwll trydwll troëdig,	In a pitted whirlpool
Y bu ar Sadwrn, dwrn dig;	It happened on a Saturday, grievous accident;
A'i arwain ar elorwydd	And he was carried on a bier
O Loegr i Fôn, chwŵl garw fydd,	From England to Môn, it will be a grim turn of events
O Gaer Lludd, hen drefudd draw,	From London, old dwelling yonder,
I gwr Môn, garar Manaw.	To the edge of Môn, the border of the Isle of Man.
Ni ddoeth at Frawd llednoeth Llwyd	There never came to the half-naked Grey Friar
I'w briddo – wb o'r breuddwyd! –	To be buried – oh the nightmare! –
I lawr Llan-faes elorllwyth	To the coffin-burdened ground of Llan-faes
Cyfryw gorff, bu cyfa'r gŵyth	Such a body, the grief was entire.
Aed I nef at Ednyfed	May he go to Heaven to Ednyfed
Ei frawd un giwdawd un ged;	His brother of the same family and the same generosity;
Erbynied Duw, ar bwynt dwys,	May God receive, in a severe plight,
Y brodyr I Paradwys	The brothers into Paradise.

Rhys ap Tudur Fychan (*c.* 1350–1412)

In 1383–84, Rhys ap Tudur and Richard Pykeme had shared the escheatorship of Anglesey. The escheator was the officer appointed in every county to look after property that, lacking inheritors, reverted to the crown or the local feudal lord. Although it is generally true that escheators were somewhat less wealthy and important than sheriffs, their ranks included some knights and a number of future and former sheriffs. Although burdensome, the office was potentially lucrative. The standard fee seems to have been 40*s* by the fifteenth century, and escheators might also receive payments or other inducements for carrying out an inquisition promptly.

Between 1385 and 1397, Rhys was *rhaglaw* of the commote of Dindaethwy. In 1386, according to Adam Chapman, Rhys and his brother Gwilym ap Tudur raised 120 archers from Caernarfonshire in response to a threat from France. In 1394–95, Rhys ap Tudur and two companions, whom Chapman says are Rhys' brothers Gwilym and Maredudd, led eighty foot archers and twelve mounted archers and two beadles. Both Rhys and Gwilym were probably with Richard II in Ireland in 1399. In that year, the year in which Richard II was murdered, Rhys was granted £10 per annum for life 'to serve the king personally'. They resented the usurpation of Henry of Bolingbroke, and were possibly unaware that Richard II had been murdered when they rebelled against Henry IV.

Gwilym ap Tudur Fychan (*c.* 1355–1413)

Gwilym was in the personal service of Richard II, and both he and Rhys ap Tudur Fychan were captains of archers in the king's service. This appears by the issues of pay made to them out of the Exchequer. In 1399 Richard II granted 'Will'o ap Tydore de Wallia armigero quern penes se retenuit', £10 per annum for life, similar to the payment made to Rhys. Like Rhys, Gwilym was *rhaglaw* of the commote of Dindaethwy at one point, and lived at Clorach. The brothers appear to be the king's squires, partially explaining why they rose in revolt after the king's death in 1400.

Maredudd ap Tudur Fychan (*c.* 1365–1406)

'Historians' wishing to blacken the name of the house of Tudor have called Maredudd an alehouse-keeper, probably not realising that alehouses were generally run by the women who brewed their ale. Rapin repeats the tale that Maredudd was a brewer living at Bangor. In fact Maredudd, father of Owen Tudor and great-grandfather of Henry VII, was *rhaglaw* of the Anglesey commote of Malltraeth from 1387 to 1391 and again from 1394 to 1396. Maredudd was also *rhaglaw*, like his brothers Gwilym and Rhys, of the commote of Dindaethwy. He was escheator of Anglesey from 1388 to 1392, although the office of escheator was normally given to Englishmen. His family was much in favour with Richard II. He and Hywel ab Adda farmed the lucrative receipts of Newborough in 1395–96. Lloyd-Williams states that Maredudd succeeded 'Gronow as steward of the Bishop of Bangor's lordship in Anglesey', which would have been in 1382, probably because his older brothers were serving the king. Maredudd lost all appointments in 1399 owing to rebellion, and then with his surviving brothers joined the Glyndŵr War in 1400. Unlike his brothers, he was pardoned in 1401; however, he did not regain any offices, instead finding employment with a sympathiser in the Church.

By 1405 Maredudd was described as an 'esquire' of the bishop of Bangor, possibly to protect him after his involvement in the Glyndŵr War. Pennant styles him a *scutifer*, a similar designation as a man-at-arms, and others say he was butler or steward serving the bishop. In 1405, Llywelyn Byford became Bishop of Bangor. Byford was a supporter of Glyndŵr, as was John Trevor, Bishop of St Asaph, a brother-in-law of Glyndŵr, and Henry

IV wished to get rid of them. In 1405 Maredudd was said to be leading rebellions in Snowdonia, and in 1406 all freeholders in Anglesey were fined on account of his activities. Maredudd then vanishes from history. On 1 May 1408, Pope Gregory XII was persuaded at Lucca to relieve Bishop Byford from his obligation to his see – even though Byford had not been heard – and gave Benedict Nichols the diocese. Clearly, Maredudd had been protected by a Glyndŵr supporter.

Maredudd had married Margaret (Marged) ferch Dafydd Fychan ap Dafydd Llwyd of Trefeilir. She was descended from Hwfa ap Cynddelw, Lord of Llyslifon, Anglesey, founder of the first of the fifteen Noble Tribes of North Wales and Powys. During his absence from home, around 1400, Marged bore Maredudd a son, Owain ap Maredudd ap Tudur (Owen Tudor). They may have had a daughter, 'Annes ferch Maredudd', who is said to have married Sir William Norris of Cheshire, but this seems unrecorded. Thomas Nicolas, in his *Annals and Antiquities of the Counties and County Families of Wales*, gives us the maternal ancestry of Owen Tudor:

> ... from Cynddelw, a founder of one of the fifteen noble tribes of North Wales. Dafydd Fychan ap Dafydd Llwyd ap Cynwrig ap Goronwy ap Iorwerth ap Hwfa ap Cynddelw. By a second marriage, Dafydd Fychan had a daughter and co-heiress, Marged, who married Maredudd ap Tudur ap Gronw (Goronwy). [On his paternal side] Maredudd was a descendant of another of the fifteen noble houses, that of 'Marchydd ap Cynan'.

The deposition of Richard II by Bolingbroke and his usurpation as Henry IV in 1399 was to destroy the comfortable livings of Rhys, Gwilym and Maredudd, who are only now being recognised for their leading roles in the great war of independence of 1400–1415. Under Richard II, the Anglesey descendants of Ednyfed Fychan, in the words of Griffiths and Thomas,

> reached heights of influence and responsibility in North Wales that were almost comparable with those reached by Ednyfed Fychan himself 150 years before. All five of Tudur's sons, Goronwy, Ednyfed, Rhys, Gwilym and Maredudd, were well integrated in the society and government of a North Wales that was part of the king's principality of Wales.

Rhys and Gwilym, as mentioned, were personal retainers of Richard II. However, in 1399, the deposition of their king and the usurpation of Henry of Bolingbroke was to transform the Tudurs of Penmynydd, with their cousin Glyndŵr, back into rebels and destroy the family influence and inheritance.

2

The Ancestry and Birth of Catherine of Valois

Catherine's great-great-grandfather on the paternal side was Philippe VI, the first Valois king of France. Philippe *le Fortuné* (the Fortunate, 1293–1350) reigned from 1328 until his death in 1350. His predecessor Charles IV *le Bel* (the Fair), the last Capetian king, had died without a male heir, the nearest male relative being Edward III of England. Edward III inherited his claim through his mother Isabeau, sister of the dead king, but French assemblies decided that Edward was ineligible to inherit the French throne through the female line under a convention known as Salic law. Philippe's father Charles of Valois had been the third son of Philippe III, and as the cousin of Charles IV and therefore the nearest male relative in the male line, Philippe of Valois took the French crown. Edward III continued to press his claim to the throne of France, resulting in the beginning of the Hundred Years War in 1337. After the French navy, which intended to take troops to invade England, was destroyed at the Battle of Sluys in 1340, the war continued on the Continent. By 1345, increasing numbers of Norman lords were paying homage to Edward III, constituting a major threat to the legitimacy of the Valois dynasty. The loss of Calais and the disastrous defeat at Crécy in 1346 further weakened French support, and the Black Death crippled both countries, though it hurt France more than it hurt England.

On his death in 1350, Philippe VI was succeeded by his son, Catherine's great-grandfather Jean II *le Bon* (the Good, 1319–64). He was faced with a plague that perhaps killed almost half the French population, accompanied by widespread uprisings, known as *Jacqueries*, against local nobility. Charles the Bad, King of Navarre, a claimant to the crown, was also a constant enemy, plotting with the English and leading French nobles against the Valois family. Also 'free companies', or *routiers*, roamed and looted the country, unrestrained as society was breaking down. English successes included that at Poitiers in 1356, where King Jean II and his youngest son, the fourteen-year-old Philippe (later Philippe 'the Bold', Duke of Burgundy) were captured. Charles the Dauphin (later Charles V), with his brother Prince Louis of Anjou, commanded a battalion at Poitiers but hardly fought; they fled in the middle of the battle. The flight allowed them to avoid capture, but their reputations suffered badly. King Jean and Philippe were kept in comfortable surroundings in the Tower of London, and his son Charles became Regent of France but faced several rebellions.

To free the king, Charles agreed the Treaty of Bretigny in 1360, giving many territories to the English and agreeing a huge ransom of 3,000,000 crowns. Giving forty high-born hostages, including his son Louis of Anjou, as guarantee for payment, Jean was released to return to France and raise his ransom. The hostages sailed to England in October 1360, but conditions in France meant that it was difficult to pay the ransom and repayments were delayed. Prince Louis was expecting to be held at Calais for only six months and, because of the delay, approached Edward III to negotiate terms but Edward refused, and Louis escaped in July 1363. Jean disapproved of his son's behaviour, considering himself personally dishonoured and, because of the ransom arrears, returned to English captivity to try to redeem his honour. He died, aged forty-five, of unknown causes in England in April 1364, being succeeded by his son Charles V, Catherine's grandfather. His brother Philippe, known as the Bold, for his fighting at Poitiers, had been made Duke of Burgundy in 1364, and was to become a leading character in the Hundred Years' War.

Charles *le Sage* (the Wise, 1338–1380), was the king that France needed to rebuild a shattered nation. Using a coterie of trusted and efficient advisers, he restored royal finances and the image of the House of Valois. Charles V established the first permanent army paid with regular wages, and began to exterminate the companies of *routiers* that were plundering the country. Under Bertrand du Guesclin, France began to recover lands lost to the English, and eventually reconquered almost all the territories ceded in the 1360 Treaty of Bretigny. However, he was succeeded by Catherine's father, Charles VI (1368–1422), appropriately called *le Fou* (the Mad), under whom the English began again to take territories across France.

Charles VI was only eleven in 1380 when he succeeded to the throne in the midst of the Hundred Years War. Mental illness had been passed down for several generations on the side of his mother, Joanna of Bourbon. Her father, Peter I of Bourbon, Grand Chamberlain of France, had a series of mental breakdowns, as did Joanna and her only surviving brother, Louis II of Bourbon. As he was only eleven, the government of France was placed in the hands of the four uncles of Charles VI: Philip the Bold, Duke of Burgundy; Jean the Magnificent, Duke of Berry; Louis I, Duke of Anjou; and Louis II, Duke of Bourbon. Although Charles VI could have assumed regal authority aged fourteen, his uncles, led by Philip, maintained their power until the king was twenty-one. The royal uncles wasted the resources built up by Charles V, having to raise taxes, leading to revolts. Charles VI married Isabeau of Bavaria in 1385, when he was seventeen and she was fourteen. They had twelve children, most of whom died young, including the first two. Her third child, Isabella, was born in 1389, and was married, aged six, to the twenty-nine year-old Richard II, king of England, who was likely murdered in 1400/1401 by Henry IV. Henry IV wished Isabella to then marry his son, the fourteen-year-old who was to become Henry V, but Isabella refused and eventually was allowed to return to France.

In 1388, Charles VI dismissed his uncles and returned his father's former advisers to power to rebuild the nation's finances and restore law and order. However, in July 1392, en route to Brittany with his army Charles had his first bout of insanity, killing a knight, wounding others and almost killing his brother Louis of Orléans. Charles continued to suffer from periods of mental instability throughout his life. In one attack in 1393 he could not remember his name and did not know he was king. When Isabeau came to visit, he asked his servants who she was and ordered them to see to what she wanted and send her away. He claimed he was St George, and although he recognised all the officers of his household, he did not know his wife or children. Sometimes he ran to exhaustion through the corridors of his palace, the Hôtel Saint-Pol, and entrances were walled up to keep him inside.

In September 1394, Charles suddenly published an ordinance in which he expelled the Jews from France. With the king often mentally incapacitated, from 1393 Isabeau presided over a regency council consisting of the great magnates. Philip the Bold had acted as regent during the king's minority, from 1380 to 1388, and was a great influence on the queen. However, influence progressively shifted to the less capable Louis I, Duke of Orléans, who was the king's brother. Antagonism built between the Orléans party (who would become the Armagnacs) and the Burgundy party, leading to outright civil war. Against this tumultuous background – French civil war while fighting against England – Catherine of Valois was to be born in 1401.

Ancestors of Catherine of Valois

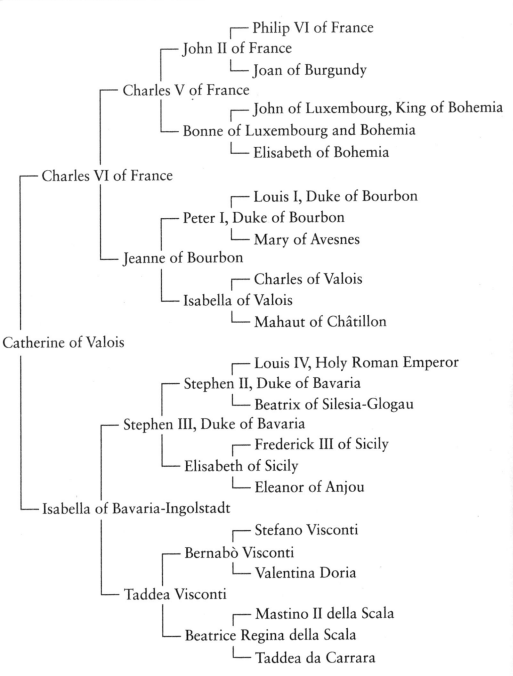

Philip VI of France
John II of France
Joan of Burgundy
Charles V of France
John of Luxembourg, King of Bohemia
Bonne of Luxembourg and Bohemia
Elisabeth of Bohemia
Charles VI of France
Louis I, Duke of Bourbon
Peter I, Duke of Bourbon
Mary of Avesnes
Jeanne of Bourbon
Charles of Valois
Isabella of Valois
Mahaut of Châtillon
Catherine of Valois
Louis IV, Holy Roman Emperor
Stephen II, Duke of Bavaria
Beatrix of Silesia-Glogau
Stephen III, Duke of Bavaria
Frederick III of Sicily
Elisabeth of Sicily
Eleanor of Anjou
Isabella of Bavaria-Ingolstadt
Stefano Visconti
Bernabò Visconti
Valentina Doria
Taddea Visconti
Mastino II della Scala
Beatrice Regina della Scala
Taddea da Carrara

3

The Early Life of Owain ap Maredudd ap Tudur Fychan c. 1400–1427

Agnes Strickland in her book on the queens of England says:

Deep obscurity hangs over the birth and origin of Katherine's second husband, Owen Tudor. Some historians declare that the father of Owen was a 'brewer at Beaumaris'. Nevertheless, he drew his line from a prince of North Wales, called Theodore; which, pronounced according to the Saxon tongue, was corrupted into Tudor, and even to the meaner sound of Tidder. There is an ancient house in the county of Anglesey, called Glengauny, still pointed out as the residence of Owen Tudor, and the Welsh say that he possessed there property to the amount of three thousand pounds per annum. But this wealthy heritage is by no means consistent with the assertion of his accurate country-man, Pennant, who has proved that Meredith, the father of Owen, was the fourth son of a younger son of the line of Tudor, and that he filled no higher office than that of scutifer, or shield-bearer, to a bishop of Bangor. When in this office, Meredith, either by design or accident, killed a man; and being outlawed, fled with his wife to the fastnesses of Snowdon, where Owen Glendower upheld the banner of defiance against the house of Lancaster. If young Owen were not born in this stronghold of freedom, he was probably baptized there, for a tradition declares that he was godson to the great chief Glendower. He was thus brought up from his cradle as a hardy, predatory soldier. The next fact regarding Owen is, that he certainly belonged to the brave Welsh band with whom Henry V. most prudently entered into amicable terms, on the death of the warlike Glendower. These hardy warriors, it is well known, under the command of Davy 'the One-eyed,' did good service at Agincourt. Tradition says that young Owen Tudor aided his countrymen in repelling the fiery charge of Alencon, and that Henry V made him, for his bravery, one of the squires of his body; hence his title of armiger. There is great reason to suppose that the brave and handsome Owen fought only as a common soldier in the Welsh band; but when once he had received the preferment of squire of the body to Henry V, he certainly continued the same office about the person of the infant king, and hence his acquaintance with the queen-mother; in this station he is next found keeping guard on the royal child and his mother at Windsor castle.

The marriage of Owain's father Maredudd ap Tudur Fychan and Margaret ferch Dafydd of Taefeilir, Lord of Anglesey, has been dated to 1399. Maredudd ap Tudur is said to have been born around 1365, dying in 1406 at Llancloudy, Herefordshire, where he is buried.

I can find no other link between Maredudd and Llancloudy, but other sources also state that he died in 1406. The only fighting was in Anglesey in 1406, and this may have been the time he died, as he was noted as leading rebels in that year, for which Anglesey freeholders were fined. There certainly seems no reference to him after that date, and it seems likely that Owain grew up fatherless. Llancloudy is 2 miles west of Llangarron, between Monmouth and Ross-on-Wye, but there is no remaining church of St Lowdy. If the dating of Maredudd's death is correct, one could speculate that he may have fought for Glyndŵr at the battles of Grosmont (near Abergavenny) and Pwll Melyn (near Usk) in spring 1405, being injured there and hiding locally. The battles were disastrous for the Welsh, faced with superior forces led by Henry of Monmouth (later Henry V). Owain Glyndŵr's eldest son Gruffydd was captured, dying in the Tower of London. Glyndŵr's brother Tudur and brother-in-law John Hanmer were killed, along with his war captain Rhys Gethin and John ap Hywel, Abbot of Llantarnam, slain as he tended the wounded. Adam of Usk (who was in Glyndŵr's company for some time) wrote that 300 Welsh prisoners were beheaded outside the walls of Usk Castle.

Owain ap Maredudd (hereafter referred to as Owen) was born around 1400, and the absence of his name from official records before and during the Glyndŵr War of 1400–1415 seems to give some proof of this date. Records from that time in Wales are sparse, many having been destroyed. Lloyd-Williams tells us that his kinsman Owain Glyndŵr stood godfather, which could well be the case, but this is not found in other sources. If not killed in the war, members of Owen's family, such as his father, were stripped of estates and offices, which were given to incomers and loyalists. Owen was probably too young to fight, unlike his father and uncles Rhys and Gwilym, who were involved in rebellion in favour of Richard II even before Glyndŵr's war began. According to old editions of *Burke's Peerage*, Owen had a sister named Anne (also called Annes), also born around 1400, who married Sir William Norreys and had a son called Robert Norreys. George Ormerod, in 1851, records:

> Sir William Norres, a Cheshire Knight, whom Sir Samuel Meyrick refers, conjecturally, to the Speke line, [was the] husband of Anne Tudor of Penmenydd [sic], in Anglesea, sister of Owain Tudor. His descendants adopted the patronymic of Robinson, (as stated, in Dwnn's *Visitation of Wales*, by Bishop Robinson, whose elevation to Bangor might be helped by this relationship to Elizabeth,) and they were of Gwersylt in Denbighshire, in the seventeenth century, as shewn by the monument of the Royalist, Colonel Robinson, at Gresford.

I can find no evidence for Owen's sister, but she may have wished to disguise her involvement with her family, which lost virtually everything as a result of the wars. It was also at this time both unwise and illegal to marry a Welsh person.

The eighteenth-century Anglesey antiquarian Henry Rowlands declared that Owen's father Maredudd was in exile when Owen was born because he had committed a murder. This was at a time of societal breakdown across Wales after the capture of Richard II.

Angharad Llwyd tells us that the murdered man was William de Sutton, Justiciar of North Wales, a theme repeated by Thomas Pennant, but there is no evidence whatsoever for this, and Henry Percy ('Hotspur') was justiciar from around 1399 to 1403. Lloyd-Williams believes that Maredudd took the law into his own hands and lynched the 'unjust' justiciar for 'reviving an ancient overcharge on the poverty-stricken inhabitants of Penrhos in Mona, a grievance sufficiently genuine to be immediately redressed by the next Justiciar'. There is a later reference to 'Kenrig ap Madoc' (Cynwrig ap Madog), who held bond land in Dindaethwy, Anglesey, being hanged for de Sutton's murder, possibly as an accomplice of Maredudd. It has been said that Maredudd fled to Snowdon with his wife, and that there Owen Tudor was born, but it seems far more likely that Maredudd fled alone, if indeed the murder occurred. Certainly he was involved with his elder surviving brothers Rhys and Gwilym in resistance shortly after Richard II was deposed in 1399.

Lloyd-Williams states that before 1392 Maredudd ap Tudur Fychan was 'also escheator of Anglesey, though he did not live there, but at Glan Conwy, on the road to Pentrevoelas [Perntrfoelas], a house which now belongs to Lord Penrhyn. There was no road then. It was up the River Conway that travellers must sail if they were desirous of making their journey a safe or a short one.' Llansanffraid Glan Conwy, shortened to Glan Conwy, formerly had a marine-based economy, and faces Conwy Castle and walled town across the estuary of the River Conwy. The parish was created by Maelgwn Gwynedd in the sixth century and five royal manors were given to the church to create the parish. The site of Glan Conwy Manor is immediately to the south-west of Plas Isa Farmhouse. There are some Tudor-period remains, although the medieval hall had disappeared around 1800, replaced by a low bakehouse and/or brewhouse. (It was probably the birthplace of John Williams (1582-1660), Archbishop of York and Lord Keeper under Charles I, although local tradition also ascribes nearby Garlleg to be his birthplace.) Thus it may well be that Owen was born at Glan Conwy, rather than the traditionally held Penmynydd.

Dr Gideon Brough has recently altered our perceptions of the Glyndŵr War of 1400–1415, placing it in the context of previous uprisings across the nation, and particularly placing the three Tudur brothers Rhys, Gwilym and Maredudd as a locus of discontent. In the summer of 1399, there had already been a rising in Carmarthenshire. Brough:

Neither the initial outbreak of violence, nor the episodes which immediately followed, were instigated by or connected to Owain Glyn Dŵr. The earliest incident of revolt was consequent to Henry Bolingbroke's uprising against Richard II. Henry's aims were, apparently, to win enough support to oblige Richard to reinstate his inheritance, seized after the death of his father, John of Gaunt, in February 1399. He returned from exile in France in June 1399, landing in Yorkshire where he began to gather an army. Richard received news of Bolingbroke's revolt while on expedition in Ireland, from where he set sail with his advisors and his army as soon as weather permitted. Richard returned from Ireland in late July 1399, landing in west Wales by the 24th of that month. Contemporary evidence is clear that significant disorder broke out between the Welsh and the English following Richard's landing in Wales.

The Dieulacres Chronicle described how Richard's army landed in west Wales and dispersed as he travelled to Carmarthen. As it did so, violence erupted; 'thus they (the Englishmen in the army) were all scattered, and the Welsh despoiled them to a man, so it was only with difficulty that they got back to their homes'.

Thomas Walsingham, who recorded in his chronicle corroborated this: 'While the king's followers – magnates, lords or lesser men, regardless of their status – were harassed by Welshmen … Of those who had been with or followed the king, scarcely one escaped unless he was prepared to hand over not only his arms but whatever was in his purse as well.'

Two of those robbed when they left Milford were the Earl of Rutland and Sir Thomas Percy. By the time Richard reached Flint in north east Wales, they had joined Bolingbroke … Therefore, the Welsh had attacked the king's troops – clearly an act of rebellion – as well as those of Bolingbroke, the pretender who became king shortly after. These independent, contemporary sources plainly show that considerable numbers of Welshmen, similarly to many in England, had risen in revolt by August 1399 at the latest.

Brough's research is detailed in his 2016 book (his second on Glyndŵr), and tells us how Jehan Creton wrote that he witnessed much fighting between the Welsh and the English, often involving large numbers of combatants: 'The Welsh, who saw their treason for what it was (Englishmen deserting Richard en masse), attacked them in strength, in groups of one or two thousand … Thus were the English despoiled by the Welsh.' Another contemporary source mentioned Welsh-English violence just over the border in England: 'As soon as the Duke (Henry) and his people set out from Chester, the Welsh did him great damage; for, whenever they could entrap the English, they killed and stripped them without mercy.' My own biography of Glyndŵr followed the accepted reasoning of Lloyd and Davies that the initiation of the war was because of Glyndŵr's treatment by the new English usurper, Henry IV, Parliament and the Marcher Lords, especially Lord Grey of Ruthin, but this 1399 rebellion had nothing to do with Glyndŵr. Indeed, the unfolding of the war shows the incredible importance of the Tudor brothers in its instigation and initial successes. Also, in legal proceedings against a Denbighshire man, Dafydd ap Cadwaladr Ddu, we note that his rebellious activities, in league with others, were retrospectively dated to 17 August 1400, again prior to Glyndŵr's actions.

Before Glyndŵr was in rebellion, the Tudor brothers Rhys and Gwilym, personal squires in attendance on Richard II, attacked royal forces in Anglesey, probably because of the imprisonment and murder of their king. Davies also relates a rising in north-west Wales in 1400, which is probably the Tudor rising, before Glyndŵr's September attack on Ruthin. Maredudd will have been active with his brothers, soon being proscribed as a traitor. On 18 September 1400, Glyndŵr's small force rode into Lord Grey's base of Ruthin, looted the fair and fired the town. No one was killed, but fourteen rebels were captured and hanged. Glyndŵr's warband quickly learned about fast-moving guerrilla warfare. Lord Grey of Ruthin reported the disorder 'across North Wales' to Henry, Prince of Wales, requesting immediate action. By 24 September, the Welsh had fired and looted Denbigh, Flint, Hawarden and Rhuddlan, and were moving on to Welshpool. However, the Sheriff of Shrewsbury had raised men from the Borders and the Midlands, and defeated Glyndŵr's small force on the banks of the Vyrnwy River, driving them back.

On 19 September 1400, the day after the first Glyndŵr attack, Henry IV issued two orders from Northampton. This could not have been in response to Glyndŵr's actions 120 miles away at Ruthin the day before, and must have been to punish other activities in Wales, probably centred on the Tudor brothers and/or Dafydd ap Cadwaladr Ddu, Lord of Bachelldref near Montgomery (the subject of praise by at least four bards). One order called for troops from several counties to suppress an unspecified rebellion in Wales, and one demanded the mobilisation of troops for the defence of castles in Cheshire against the Welsh.

With a 13,000-strong army marching from Scotland, the king's first invasion of Wales picked up some of Lord Grey's forces from Ruthin, and passed through Shrewsbury and Bangor to Caernarfon, which was (with nearby Conwy) the centre of Tudor possessions outside Anglesey. On 26 September Henry arrived in Shrewsbury with his army, and on 28 September dismembered Goronwy ap Tudur of Anglesey, a first cousin of the Tudur brothers, sending his limbs along the Welsh borders to Chester, Hereford, Ludlow and Bristol as an example to those thinking of supporting Glyndŵr. Goronwy had been captured with eight others at Ruthin, and they were all hanged, drawn and quartered without trial. After witnessing the disembowellings, Henry IV left Shrewsbury on 28 September, reaching Bangor to threaten the Tudurs by early October.

Owain Glyndŵr's mansions and estates at Glyndyfrdwy and Sycharth were untouched, and Glyndŵr was not involved. There were executions and fines along the army's progress. It is telling that the campaign terminus was in Tudur lands rather than Owain's. Near Beaumaris, at Rhos Fawr, a small army under Rhys Tudur was defeated but managed to melt away before it was destroyed.

There is an alternative version of the events of 1400, given by Griffiths and Thomas:

Gwilym and Rhys ap Tudur put themselves at the head of a rising in Anglesey in September 1400. When Henry IV arrived with an army, Rhys and his men set an ambush for them on Rhos Fawr ('the Great Moor'), one of the highest spots on the eastern part of the island. The harrying of Anglesey and its population by the angry king was severe: Llanfaes Priory was set alight, some of the friars were killed, and the countryside roundabout was devastated. But when he encountered Rhys and his men on Rhos Fawr, Henry was forced to turn tail and retired to the safety of Beaumaris. It is hardly surprising that when the king tried to pacify North Wales by issuing a general pardon in March 1401, he excluded Rhys and Gwilym, as well as Owain Glyndŵr, from its terms.

To try to prevent fresh support for Glyndŵr and other rebels, Prince Henry and Henry Hotspur had taken control of the North Wales campaign, and they convinced the king to issue a general pardon for North Wales. The English army marched to the coast at Mawddwy and returned to Shrewsbury.

Glyndŵr and the rebels had been condemned as traitors at Bangor on 7 October 1400. On 18 October Henry's force passed back into England, and orders were issued 'to David Gamme and John Havard to arrest Rees Kiffyn, esquire, and bring him before the king in person'. There were no orders to arrest Glyndŵr, which seems to implicate 'Rees Kiffyn' (Rhys Gethin) as the most important rebel among several at this time. Henry now declared the lands of the brothers Rhys, Gwilym and Maredudd forfeit, along with those of Glyndŵr. There was a general pardon for the Welsh rebels on 30 November, only valid until the next parliament.

That parliament, of 20 January to 10 March 1401, reaffirmed the pardon covering the year from 14 January 1400 to 6 January 1401. (In January 1400 serious civil disorder had also broken out in Chester, after the public execution of an officer of Richard II.) On 10 March 1401 a pardon was granted to various rebels at Prince Henry's request, 'to all the King's lieges for all treasons and insurrections, except Owyn Glendowrdy, Rees ap Tudour, William ap Tudour and those who have been captured, detained in custody or persisted in rebellion'. On 10 May this pardon was extended to 'the men of Oswestry hundred in Wales' and the following week to 'the men of the lordship late of John Lord Lestrange of Knockyn decd of the Hundred of Ellesmere in Wales'. Interestingly, both Oswestry and Ellesmere are firmly placed in Wales. Maredudd ap Tudur was pardoned, possibly on account of his having less property than his brothers. Henry also offered a pardon to Glyndŵr's brother Tudur, which he accepted.

Owain Glyndŵr's lands, and those of the Tudurs, were given to the Earl of Somerset, John Beaufort. Brough points out: 'It might not be a coincidence that three of the wealthiest native Welsh landowners were not pardoned by a new regent in need of gifts with which to reward his supporters.' It looked as if Glyndŵr's days were numbered at the end of the year 1400. The Marcher

Lords were now allowed to take any Welsh land that they could by force of arms or subterfuge. On top of this, in 1401, the English parliament passed laws that no Welsh person could hold official office, nor marry any English person. The Welsh could not live in England, and had to pay for the damage caused by the 1400 rebellions. This racial purity enforcement enraged the Welsh of all classes. Rees Davies wrote that this was 'simply putting into statutory law a century and more of customary practices and discriminatory ordinances employed by the English toward the Welsh; a process that had begun with Edward I's ordinances of 1295 in the wake of the last great Welsh revolt [of Madog] before that of Owain [Glyndŵr]'. In fact, Henry IV only codified anti-Welsh legislation from existing practices and prohibitions. Stephens elaborated:

> Nearly all the Henrician measures either built on those Edwardian ordinances no Welshman could reside in a town, bear arms in them or conduct trade outside them or the several types of restraints placed upon Welshmen by the burgesses of some town in Wales at some point or other; restraints also incorporated into borough charters in some places. One such restraint and further injustice that most burgesses made sure of was that they could only be tried by fellow Englishmen in Wales, though the same right would not be afforded the Welsh. For example, according to the Charter of Laugharne of 1386, 'A burgess cannot be convicted or adjudged by any Welshman, but only by English burgesses and true Englishmen.'

One cannot underestimate the resentment felt by the Welsh, and constantly fuelled by the bards, against their treatment by non-British incomers. These tensions were inflamed by a singular action of the Tudur brothers. According to Williams-Jones, 'in the annals of insurrection in these islands there is hardly a single exploit to compare with it in sheer audacity and cunning'. This was the Tudur brothers' seizure of Conwy Castle, which sparked real rebellion across Wales, with men now flocking to join Glyndŵr. *The Chronicle of Adam of Usk* informs us that in 1401,

> William ap Tudor and Rhys ap Tudor, brothers, natives of the isle of Anglesey, or Mona, because they could not have the king's pardon for Owen's rebellion, on the same Good Friday (1 April) seized the castle of Conway, which was well stored with arms and victuals, the two warders being slain by the craftiness of a certain carpenter who feigned to come to his accustomed work; and, entering therein with forty other men, they held it for a stronghold. The Welsh held out against siege engines, but,

straightaway being besieged by the prince and the country, on the twenty-eight day of May next following they surrendered the same castle...

With a company of just forty men, the Tudurs had tricked their way into the walled town of Conwy, part of the 'Iron Ring' of fortresses built by Edward I in the late thirteenth century to subdue the Welsh. Some say they were disguised as workmen, or just mixed with the country people entering the town to trade at the weekly market. On Good Friday, they knew that most of the the small garrison of fifteen men-at-arms and sixty archers would be at prayer in the parish church of St Mary's.

Once in control they demonstrated that with just a few dozen men this magnificent castle could be easily defended against massive forces. The castle's constable, Massy, and his men raced back from the church, as the town had been set ablaze and the smoke alerted his men. Safe inside the castle, the Welsh burned all the records of the town's exchequer. The town gate had also been destroyed, and the king's justiciar's quarters were burnt along with the chamberlain's lodgings. The Tudurs held out against assaults by 500 men under Hotspur for weeks, until the English decided to try to starve them out instead of fighting. Importantly, the Welsh now knew that the 'impregnable' Iron Ring of castles could be taken. Hotspur, justiciar of Chester and North Wales, was helpless. Lloyd tells us that this amazing capture was to secure a pardon for themselves, and that their actions were unconnected to those of Glyndŵr, which seems to be the case from their negotiations.

The Tudurs refused to surrender until they were granted the pardon previously refused them. Hotspur, leading the besiegers, did not want the great royal castle damaged too badly. On 13 April, twelve days after it was taken, negotiations were authorised, conducted by Hotspur himself. Gwilym ap Tudur then managed to publicise the brothers' demands. They wanted a comprehensive pardon, as given to other rebels; a safe-conduct to return home; no hounding by the authorities for at least six months; the recovery of lands and possessions confiscated from Welshmen; no charges for robbing the burgesses of Conwy and the houses of royal officials; and no charges for burning the town of Conwy, leading to £5,000 worth of damage (around £3.25 million today) and the loss of official records. The siege negotiations with Henry Percy never mention Glyndŵr, his rising or his assumed title of prince. 'William ap Tudur and Rees ap Tudur his brother' won pardons for themselves 'and their accomplices', presumably including Maredudd, but on 20 April the agreement was disowned by Henry IV and the Tudurs stayed in the castle. Gwilym sent a second, more conciliatory set of demands to

Henry, and a settlement was reached on 24 June, and confirmed on 8 July 1401. From 1 April to 8 July, around fourteen weeks, the castle was held. All the Welsh were pardoned, disproving Adam of Usk's accusation that the Tudurs handed over some of their own men for execution when leaving Conwy. (Adam was the only chronicler to state this, and few men would have followed them for years after if it had been true.)

There was another insurrection not involving Glyndŵr, beginning at Abergavenny in April 1401 and continuing for some months. 'On the feast of the Lord's ascension [12 May 1401] this year, the tenants of Abergavenny rose up against their lord, Lord William Beauchamp, freeing three men from the gallows and killing with their arrows Sir William Lucy, knight, who had been given the task of executing them; these three had been condemned to death for theft, and were, by order of that second Jezebel, the lady of the lordship, going to be hanged that very day, heedless of the festival being celebrated at the time.' It was against Christian faith that any men should be executed at a holy time, and Abergavenny Castle was sieged. In Gloucestershire troops were raised and sent to the area, and in May 1401 the noted Sir John Greyndour of Abenhall, Gloucestershire (c. 1356–1404) was one of those commissioned to relieve Abergavenny.

At the time Prince Henry noted other rebellion across South Wales, with crown tenants refusing to pay dues, which had no connection with Glyndŵr. Other incidents tell us the situation across Wales had deteriorated widely. Brough tells us: 'The contemporary accounts do not give Owain's actions the same pre-eminence, but instead place him as one among a number of men such as Gwilym and Rhys ap Tudor, Rhys Gethin, Llywelyn ap Gruffydd Fychan, John Filz Pieres and Maurice ap Meweryk.' The first act, which began in Carmarthenshire in July 1399 and spread across Wales, saw Welshmen attack supporters of Richard and Henry. Unable to resolve the crisis, Henry IV had reluctantly granted pardons to the Tudurs and their troops in 1401, but issued warrants to arrest John Filz Pieres and Maurice ap Meweryk, who were leaders in the Abergavenny rebellion. The king took an army to Carmarthen, where the rising does not seem to be related to Glyndŵr. There is a list in the Peniarth MS of 'men of noate… out with Glendower', at the beginning of the 1400–1415 war, which includes 'Meredith ap Tudor' and his brothers Rhys and Gwilym. Although pardoned, their estates had not been returned to them and they became leading figures as revolt across most of Wales flourished under the leadership of Glyndŵr.

Royal letters of 28 May 1401 summoned troops from twenty-eight counties and cities to oppose 'Owen Glendourdy and other rebels', claiming that the Welsh were poised to overrun Carmarthen, even before their victory at Hyddgen in June. Heading south-west, a new army under Henry IV executed without trial a number of men deemed rebels, such as Llywelyn ap Gruffydd Fychan at Llandovery. He was hanged, drawn and quartered in Llandovery market place, with the king watching. A marvellous stainless steel statue outside the castle commemorates his actions in not revealing the whereabouts of Glyndŵr, in whose army Llywelyn's sons were captains. Glyndŵr appears to have achieved little since the retreat from Ruthin in September 1400, but the Conwy Castle capture had sparked revolt across Wales. He still only led a small force, camped in the barren hills of Mynydd Pumlumon, and in June 1401 a band of Flemings, long settled Pembrokeshire, rode north to find him. Bradley writes:

> The Flemings (so called, though doubtless by this time largely infused with immigrant English blood) of South Pembrokeshire and the Carmarthen littoral, now marched against Owen fifteen hundred hundred strong, and engaged him on a spur of Plynlimmon. Outnumbered and surrounded, the Welsh leader only escaped by cutting his way through his enemies, leaving 200 of them dead on the mountain. Pembrokeshire, well able to protect itself, seems to have been little further concerned with the rebellion till much later. Owen's personal prowess on Plynlimmon seems to have been noised through South Wales, for he accumulated sufficient forces there to ravage the country ruthlessly. The lands of the Lord Marches and of the Welsh who would not join him were swept bare, homesteads burned and even such castles as were caught unawares or under-manned.

At last men started joining his force in numbers, even students from the universities at Oxford and Cambridge.

Chronicle evidence describes fighting before Midsummer 1401 at Welshpool in north-east Wales and Henry IV's desecration of Strata Florida in the west. In the summer of that year, Gwent, Gwynedd, Merionethshire and Carmarthenshire were all in revolt. In November 1401, Glyndŵr wrote asking for support from the lords of Ireland, stating that 'we (the Welsh) have manfully waged (war) for nearly two years past', which predates his Ruthin involvement by over a year, if we date insurrection from the Carmarthenshire rising of July 1399. He next attacked and took Radnor Castle near the border in August, but at the same time Harlech was besieged for several months by another band of Welshmen, with no record of Glyndŵr's involvement. Bradley states: 'This winter [1401] Owen made a dash for his old enemy Grey, defeated his force, captured the Earl himself and shut him up in the remote castle of Dolbadarn, between the two Llanberis lakes, for a year, when a high ransom was paid for him. His Ruthin property being destroyed, he returned to England for life under bonds not to serve again in Wales.'

Four more royal armies were to invade Wales between 1402 and 1405, following a great raid by the Welsh into Maelienydd (modern Radnor), part of the Mortimer heartlands, in 1402. The army rested near Pilleth, knowing that a hastily levied English force was going to follow it. On 22 June 1402 the waiting Welsh defeated an English army at Bryn Glas, upon which sits Pilleth Church, when Edmund Mortimer was captured and some English knights killed, along with hundreds of men-at-arms and other soldiers. Welsh archers on Mortimer's side defected to Owain en masse and Rhys Gethin is credited with the surprise tactic of hiding the bulk of his force behind the crest of the hill, charging the English as they were struggling up towards what they thought was an easy victory. Shakespeare gives us a tale of Welsh women mutilating the corpses of the English dead, which is nonsense. There are burial mounds near the church. Female camp followers and local people would have stripped the dead of any useful armour, weapons and clothing. Any bodies or body parts left of the field would have attracted hundreds upon hundreds of corvids, buzzards, badgers, foxes, rats and the like within hours of the battle. The Welsh army would not have waited in the Marcher area, but quickly moved back into Wales carrying whatever useful items had been stripped from the dead. They had no foreign loans or taxes to pay for their campaigning, and so had to take what they could.

Lloyd-Williams records a long raid, probably by this force: 'Abergavenny, Usk, Caerleon, Newport and Cardiff were attacked by a great host and the Welshmen of Glamorgan rose in sympathy.' There were raids into Gloucester, Hereford, Shropshire and Cheshire, trying to raise the Welsh in the Marches to the cause. By the end of 1403, most of Wales had fallen back to the Welsh. Another march towards the *bastide* of Brecon was feared by its inhabitants, and Glyndŵr's presence at Dryslwyn Castle (in the Tywi Valley between Llandeilo and Carmarthen) is attested on 4 July 1403. Carmarthen Castle had already been taken, and Dryslwyn's constable, Rhys ap Gruffydd, simply surrendered to Owain's massive force and joined his army. At this time a contingent of Glyndŵr's army had marched from Llandeilo to nearby Carreg Cennen Castle, one of the most impressive of all Welsh castles, instead of joining the main army on its route to Carmarthen and Dryslwyn. Its keeper, Sir John Scudamore, visited Glyndŵr to seek a safe-conduct for his wife and mother-in-law out of the castle, and was refused. The women had been trapped within the castle by Glyndŵr's swift advance. John Scudamore had previously replaced his brother Philip as constable of Dryslwyn, as Philip

Scudamore had joined Glyndŵr's forces. We mention Scudamore in a little detail here and later, as he may well have come across the three Tudur brothers, and Owen Tudor may have been taken into his care shortly after, Owen's father being Glyndŵr's cousin.

Bradley tells us that Glyndŵr's wife 'was the daughter of Sir David Hanmer of Hanmer in Flint, one of Richard II's Justices of the King's Bench, a family which it is hardly necessary to state in these pages still survives on the Welsh Border. We hear a good deal of two sons, at this time mere boys, and vaguely of three more still younger ones. His daughters must have been older, as four seemed to have been married when the troubles began, one to a Welshman, Adda ap Iorwerth; a second to Sir John Scudamore of Holme Lacy and Kentchurch; a third to a Crofts of Croft Castle and the youngest to Roger Monnington of Monnington, all in Herefordshire. The fifth, Jane [Catrin], made a notable match with her father's captive, Sir Edmund Mortimer, during the war. It is she, of course, whom Shakespeare in *Henry IV* puts upon the stage to sing Welsh songs to Hotspur and others.'

One story is that around this time, Sir John Scudamore's wife died, possibly owing to the siege, but within a year he had secretly married Alys ferch Owain Glyndŵr. Another version is that they were married before the war, and another that they were to marry in 1423. They definitely married, however, although it was illegal for an Englishman to marry a Welsh woman, and from the time of the Carreg Cennen siege, if not before, Sir John Scudamore seems to have been ambivalent in his support of Henry IV. Perhaps he had been an ally of Glyndŵr's even before this. Other family members were leading supporters of Glyndŵr, so Scudamore may have been 'loyal' to the king in order to retain the family estates if Glyndŵr lost the war. Equally, if Glyndŵr won, the Kentchurch and Monnington estates would be secured.

Carreg Cennen is one of Wales' most evocative castles, perched over a 300-foot drop. Sir John Scudamore wrote of it:

I may not spare any man from this place away from me, to certify neither my king nor the lord my prince, in the mischief of the countryside about, nor no man pass by anyway, hence I pray you and require you that you certify them how all Carmarthenshire, Kidwelly, Carnwaltham [Carnwallon] and Yskenyd [the hundred of Iscennen] were sworn to Owain yesterday. And he lay tonight in the castle of Drosselan [Dryslwyn] with Rhys ap Griffith and there I was on truce and prayed for a safe conduct under his seal to send home my wife and her mother and her train, but he would not grant me. This day he is about Carmarthen and thinks to abide there until he may have town and castle; and his purpose then is to go into Pembrokeshire for he holds all the castles and towns in Kidwelly... Gowersland and Glamorgan for the same countries have undertaken the siege of them until they be won... Excite the king's advisors that they should excite the king here in all haste to avenge himself on some of his false traitors he has cherished overmuch, and to rescue the towns and castles in these countries for I dread full sore there be few to maintain them...

The siege of Carreg Cennen lasted around eight months and it was not taken.

There is an indenture from Henry IV to 'John Skydmore, Steward of the King's lordships of Kidwelly, Carn Waltham and Iskenny... the grantee is to receive 12d. a day for two homes d'armes and 6d. a day for 10 archers for the safe keeping of the castle of Kidwelly'. (The large hundred of Iscennen includes Llandybie, Llanarthne, Llanddarog etc., and the hundred of Carnwallon includes Llanedi, Llanelli, Llangennech and Llannon.)

In his letter above, Scudamore indicates that Glamorgan and Gower were already under attack, the war having spread across south Wales. The last sentence seems to indicate that he knows he will fall under suspicion, not only because of his kinsmen but because news of his secret marriage to Glyndŵr's daughter might be discovered. We have little idea of how Scudamore met Alys, but Owain's other daughters married into prominent Marcher families, which Scudamore knew. His estates at Ewyas and Kentchurch in Herefordshire were bordered by the lands of Roger Monnington of Monnington Court, on the Wye, who married another daughter, Marged ferch Owain; Jonet married John Croft(s) of Croft Castle in Hereford; and the ill-fated Catrin married Lord Edmund Mortimer. There is a legend that another daughter, Jane, married Glyndŵr's great enemy Lord Grey of Ruthin, when he was in captivity. There is a strong possibility that the Scudamores knew Maredudd ab Tudur, and at least one source states that his son (Owen Tudor) was taken in by the family when Maredudd died.

Hotspur was disenchanted by being chastised by the king for allowing Conwy to be taken, by being demoted in favour of Prince Henry in Wales and by the king refusing to pay the debts he had incurred in his service, so he entered talks with Glyndŵr. He had won the Battle of Homildon Hill in 1402 with his father Northumberland, and was discontented by the king taking his valuable hostage, the Earl of Douglas, from him. Hotspur was also angry at the king's refusal to ransom his brother-in-law, Edmund Mortimer. Rhys Tudur was known to have been involved in the negotiations, and had also negotiated with Hotspur at the siege of Conwy Castle.

Returning from Scotland, Hotspur issued proclamations in Cheshire accusing Henry of 'tyrannical government'. His uncle Thomas Percy, Earl of Worcester, joined him and they marched to Shrewsbury, where he intended to meet the armies of his father, Northumberland, and Glyndŵr. However, Northumberland was slow to move south and missed the battle. Owing to a breakdown in communications – perhaps messengers were intercepted – at the time Glyndŵr was besieging Carmarthen and Dynefwr, some 100 miles away. Some men from North Wales joined Hotspur, perhaps including the Tudurs, and on 21 July 1403 they encountered the king and Prince Henry with a large army at Shrewsbury. Here we see the first occasion where massed troops armed with the longbow faced each other on English soil, in tactical formations that would be later used so effectively against the French. Hotspur was killed, apparently shot in the face when he opened his visor. Henry, Prince of Wales, was also badly wounded with an arrow in the face. There were heavy casualties on both sides, but when Hotspur was struck down and killed, his troops fled. Hotspur was quartered and put on display in various corners of the country, his head being impaled on York's north gate. If Glyndŵr and Northumberland had attended the battle, there would have been a Mortimer dynasty.

In 1404, Welsh troops took the great Edwardian fortresses of Aberystwyth and Harlech, and Glyndŵr was negotiating alliances with France and Scotland. Across Wales, Glyndŵr was hailed by the people and bards as the *mab darogan*, the son of prophecy, and Rees Davies notes that it was a 'people's war': 'As to the native population of the countryside, native annalists and hysterical English correspondents were at one in observing how they defected en masse "all the nation, except a few".' Hundreds of men-at-arms defected from English forces. From 1404, Harlech became Glyndŵr's family residence, court and military headquarters for four years, suppliable by sea through its Watergate Tower.

Holding court at Harlech, Glyndŵr appointed Gruffydd Yonge as his Chancellor, and soon afterwards called his first parliament or *Cynulliad* (gathering) of all Wales at Machynlleth. He held his second parliament in Harlech in August 1405, and probably a third in August 1406. The three Tudur brothers, the Scudamores, the Hanmers, Rhys Ddu, Rhys Gethin, Cadwgan of Abergorci, Robert ab Ieuan of Ystymcegid, Bishop Trefor and Lewis Byford all assembled here. Glyndŵr and his wife Marged had their quarters in the Constable's home in the massive gatehouse. Edmund Mortimer, Catrin and their children resided in what is now known as Mortimer's Tower. Glyndŵr was fully occupied governing his fledgling state, conducting diplomatic relations with France and Scotland and dealing with ecclesiastical matters.

Returning to Scudamore, perhaps with Owen Tudor in his protection around this time, in August 1405 John Oke accused Scudamore of having been a secret supporter of Glyndŵr as early as 1400. He claimed that Scudamore had received £6,870 (£4.8 million today) in gold and silver from twenty-seven disaffected persons for the support of the Welsh uprising. He said that support against the king was strong, especially in East Anglia, and stated that high-ranking clergymen were also involved. Oke said he had been an agent of Glyndŵr, collecting funds from English religious houses for the war. Another prisoner, John Veyse, supported the claims. The criminals turned informer to escape the death penalty, but named abbots and priors across the country as conspirators. Luckily for Scudamore, Oke and Voysey were hanged, but Henry IV ordered six separate inquiries into their testimonies. These strongly implicated Sir John Scudamore, who had defended Carreg Cennen in 1403, and had illegally married Alys ferch Owain Glyndŵr. Clerics were arrested but released, and Scudamore escaped punishment but fell from royal favour. However, his lands were not forfeited.

Waurin's Chronicle tells us that in 1405 a French army of between 4,000 and 5,000 men, in 140 ships, landed at Milford Haven, having many of their horses at sea. This French army, under the Marshal of France and the Master of Archers, marched on Haverfordwest and burnt the town before meeting the Welsh army at Tenby, which was also burnt. Having met the Welsh lords, they marched to Carmarthen and thence to Worcester, where they met Henry IV. The king

...went forward till he came to the place that he had chosen, within three leagues of Worcester. His enemies, warned of his coming, were ranged in battle order upon a mountain [Woodbury Hill, nine miles north-west of Worcester]. The king, having surveyed their numbers and their position, saw that he could not, without great los of his own men, fight them there. Wherefore, with all his battalions, he drew up to another mountain right opposite that on which his enemies were. There, with a deep valley between, each party waited for the other to begin the attack – and waited in vain. Thus the armies faced each other for six days [actually eight] doing nothing save that every morning they put themselves in battle array, which they kept till evening. But know for a truth that many skirmishes and fine deeds of arms were done daily in the valley, in the course of which about two hundred men were slain and many wounded...

Meanwhile, the French and the Welsh were much tormented by famine. Only with great difficulty could they get any food for themselves or their horses, because the English king, who was valiant and prudent in the business of war, had placed men in the passes so that provisions could not come to his enemies. Finally, on the eighth day... King Henry, seeing that his enemies would not attack him, retired in the evening to Worcester. The French and the Welsh pursued, destroying eighteen carts laden with provisions and other royal baggage. Then, with their spoil, they retired into Wales to rest themselves a little.

While these things were going on the French fleet was cruising at sea. Upon the appointed day it returned to Wales, whereupon the Admiral of France, the Master of the Archers, and their advisers (seeing that their army could do nothing useful because the King of England was too powerful in the field, and because every day came to him fresh men and supplies, while to them came neither) put to sea again ... and returned to France.

Rhys, Gwilym and Maredudd will have been captains in the Welsh army, and it may have been that Maredudd stayed in the area if there is any truth in the rumour that he died at Llancloudy in 1406. Glyndŵr's army, short of supplies, had been forced to return to Wales. It was to be the high point of the wars from the Welsh perspective. This left Henry free to ride to Hereford and assemble a larger force. Henry's 1405 campaign eventually set out from Hereford on 10 September. His purpose was, as always, to be seen by the people at the head of an army. This time he also had the specific war aim of relieving Coity Castle in Glamorgan, which was then being besieged by the Welsh. The garrison was supplied with victuals and reinforced, but Henry lost men and part of his baggage train in flash floods. Forty or fifty carts had to be abandoned to the swollen rivers and the impassable roads. By the end of the month, when Henry's bedraggled army staggered back into Hereford, his frustration must have been immense. Having had such grand plans of crushing the Welsh, all he had managed four months later was to relieve one castle. Disappointed, he returned to Kenilworth.

However, Welsh forces lost at the battles of Pwll Melyn and Grosmont in 1405, where Rhys Gethin was killed, along with Owain's brother Tudur and John Hywel, Bishop of Llantarnam. Glyndŵr's son Gruffudd was captured and died in prison. However, Maredudd, although noted as working for the Bishop of Bangor, led a group of rebels in north-east Wales in 1405, and was outlawed a year later by the king. Maredudd's lands were, like those of his brothers, confiscated by the crown. It may well be that Owen Tudor was orphaned after Maredudd was wounded or died in hiding at this time, possibly after fighting at Pwll Melyn or Usk. There were problems for Glyndŵr in his north-eastern homelands at this time. In

August 1405, the most powerful man in Flintshire, Gwilym ap Gruffydd ap Gwilym, with his brothers Robin and Rhys, and four other Flintshire gentry, surrendered, going to Chester prison. They had joined the rising in 1403.

Bradley writes: 'By 1405 nearly all Wales, with the exception of Anglesey, Carnarvonshire, and Pembroke, lay desolate and bleeding. The mountains were full of stock and booty driven from the harried lordships. But the tide was beginning to turn. Prince Edward and several doughty Barons were stiffening the defence of the Welsh borders. Rhys Gethin, the hero of Pilleth, got badly cut up with a large force by the Prince himself at Grosmont on the Monnow, near Pontrilas. Owen pushed forward to his relief and the combined forces were again defeated in Breconshire by the Prince, and Owen's brother, Tudor, was killed. "All Glamorgan," says an old MS, "now turned Saxon."'

Glyndŵr had held a parliament at Machynlleth, where he was possibly formally crowned Prince of Wales in the presence of envoys from Castile, Scotland and France. His famous Pennal letter to Charles VI of France, recognising the incumbent French Pope at Avignon, survives in Paris:

Most serene prince, you have deemed it worthy on the humble recommendation sent, to learn how my nation, for many years now elapsed, has been oppressed by the fury of the *barbarous Saxons* [author's italics]; whence because they had the government over us, and indeed, on account of the fact itself, it seemed reasonable with them to trample upon us. But now, most serene prince, you have in many ways, from your innate goodness, informed me and my subjects very clearly and graciously concerning the recognition of the true Vicar of Christ. I, in truth, rejoice with a full heart on account of that information of your excellency, and because, inasmuch from this information, I understood that the Lord Benedict, the supreme pontifex intends to work for the promotion of an union in the Church of God with all his possible strength. Confident indeed in his right, and intending to agree with you as indeed as far as it is possible for me, I recognise him as the true Vicar of Christ, on my own behalf, and on behalf of my subjects by these letters patent, foreseeing them by the bearer of their communications in your majesty's presence. And because, most excellent prince, the metropolitan church of St David was, as it appears, violently compelled by the barbarous fury of those reigning in this country, to obey the church of Canterbury, ad de facto still remains in the subject of this subjection. Many other disabilities are known to have been suffered by the Church of Wales through these barbarians, which for the greater part are set forth full in the letter patent accompanying. I pray and sincerely beseech your majesty to have these letters sent to my lord, the supreme pontifex, that as you deemed worthy to raise us out of darkness into light, similarly you will wish to extirpate and remove violence and oppression from the church and from my subjects, as you are well able to. And may the Son of the Glorious Virgin long preserve your majesty in the promised prosperity. Dated at Pennal the last day of March [1406] – Yours avowedly Owen, Prince of Wales.

Also in 1406, writes Bradley, 'the old Earl of Northumberland, whose estates were confiscated after his Shrewsbury outbreak and who had been a refugee in Scotland, turned up secretly in Wales with fresh schemes. At Aberdaron, on the furthest extremity of Lleyn, and the property then of the Dean of Bangor, one of Owen's few clerical allies, Owen, Mortimer and Northumberland met privately and signed the Tripartite Indenture, which Shakespeare has made to antedate the battle of Shrewsbury when it was probably a sort of unwritten understanding. Its details which survive may be roughly summarised as giving to Owen Wales and its border as far the Severn, to Northumberland the northern half, and Mortimer the southern half of England. But the day was past for such a great adventure and the document is of purely academic interest.'

By the Tripartite Indenture, England and Wales were to be broken up into Wales and some of the March, to be governed by Glyndŵr; the North of England, under Northumberland; and the South of England, under Glyndŵr's new son-in-law Edmund Mortimer, who had a better claim to the throne than Henry IV.

In 1406, all three Tudur brothers were outlawed again by Henry IV and Maredudd's estates were now confiscated. Henry fined all of Anglesey's freeholders in response to their actions.

Bradley states:

The siege of Aberystwyth by the Royal forces was the event of 1407. Its Castle, a constant scene of strife in the old wars, had been restored by Edward I in his impregnable fashion. It was now garrisoned by Rhys ap Griffith, one of Owen's best captains. For some reason the siege became a vogue among the English nobles and knights. Foreign campaigns were for the moment in abeyance. All the coast castles were to be crushed and Owen captured. It was to be the final scene and the King was to be present in person. But he wasn't, he had had enough of Wales. Almost everyone else who was anybody seems to have been there, with big scaffolds, wooden towers, and various big guns brought right across England, some of which burst during the siege. But it was all of no use. The heavy-armed mounted warriors could not catch the Welsh in the mountains around and the castle held out till September, when it offered conditions of surrender if unrelieved by a certain future date. The noble company all disappeared, after spending a, perhaps, pleasant summer by the seaside, leaving a few companies to watch the castle. Owen, in the meantime, slipped in with reinforcements, and the coast castles remained to him for another year.

The year 1408 saw widespread disturbances in Glamorgan, as the king's men 'burnt their corn stacks and barns, that the partisans of Owain might not obtain needful food'. Gwilym ap Tudur was still 'at large' in 1408–09, but the rebellion was almost over, with the Welsh-held castles being taken by another two English invasion armies.

Adam of Usk had been with Glyndŵr's forces before 'escaping', and was pardoned in 1411. For 1409 he records:

The wife of Owen (Margaret), together with his two daughters (one of them Catrin, Mortimer's widow) and three granddaughters, daughters of Sir Edmund Mortimer, and all household goods, was taken captive, and sent to London unto the king; and Owen, with his only remaining son Meredith, miserably lay in hiding in the open country, and in caves, and in the thickets of the mountains. To make all safe, and to curb fresh rebellions by means of the king's soldiers and at his costs, the glades and passes of Snowdon and of other mountains and forests of North Wales were held guarded. Mortimer's son, Lionel, was also taken. Owen's family fell into the hands of the English at the capture of Harlech, before February, 1409.

The captives were all soon to die in custody.

Owain Glyndŵr had lost his titles, mansions and estates, his brother, brother-in-law, son-in-law, wife, daughters and grandson, and had only one son of six still alive. Gwilym ap Tudur seems to have asked for pardon in this year, granted two years later. Maredudd was probably dead, but his brother Rhys was still fighting. Glyndŵr now resolved to go on on one last rampage, gathering what support he could. He may have been looking for death in battle, or simply for revenge upon the English who had destroyed his life and his country. Many remaining nobles came to his support, and a contingent of Scots and French who had fought for him in the past landed in North Wales in May 1409. Rhys ap Gruffydd (Rhys Ddu of Aberteifi) was still at Glyndŵr's side, as was Owain's brother-in-law Philip Hanmer. All of his other best commanders had been killed. Glyndŵr started roaming his home estates with a growing warband, causing panic once more in Oswestry, nearby Knockin Castle and Ruthin. Out of nowhere, Glyndŵr suddenly had a major war party. They took no wagons for booty as they next headed into Shropshire – it was an attack of sheer bloody-mindedness, a final effort to make the English suffer.

There was fighting at Oswestry and Shrewsbury, but at Welshpool in 1409 Rhys Ddu and Philip Scudamore were badly injured and captured, with Rhys' head being displayed at Shrewsbury and Scudamore's at Chester. Peniarth MS records: '1409 – The men of Owain made an attack on the borders of Shropshire and there Rhys the Black and Philip Scudamore were captured. The one was sent to London and the other to Shrewsbury to be drawn and quartered. Thenceforth Owain made no great attack until he disappeared.'

The chronicler refers to Rhys Ddu, the defender of Aberystwyth, being tortured to death in London, stating that the badly injured Rhys was 'laid on a hurdle and so drawn forth to Tyburn through the city and was there hanged and let down again. His head was smitten off and his body quartered and sent to four towns and his head set on London Bridge.'

'The xij yeer of king Harri, a squire of Walis called Ris ap Die, that was supporter of Oweyn of Glendore, that did much destruction to the king's people in Walis, was taken and brought to London, and drawn and hanged and quartered.' (*An English Chronicle*, ed. Davies.) Welshpool, Y Trallwng, was given to Lord Charleton, Constable of Welshpool for his services in killing Glyndŵr's only remaining commanders.

Adam of Usk has a different dating: 'A.D. 1411. Meantime, while I there abode, among the other gentlemen of Owen's party, three men of fame, to wit Philip Scudamore of Troy, Rhys ap Griffith of Cardigan, and Rhys ap Tudor of Anglesey, being taken by the captain of the same castle, were drawn to the gallows and hanged; the first at Shrewsbury, whose head is still there set up beyond bridge, the second at London, and the third at Chester.'

Peniarth MS 135 tells us that in '1412 – Rhys ap Tudor of Anglesey and Ednyfed his brother were captured. They were executed in Chester.' The mention of Ednyfed is a mistake, as he died around 1382. Whatever the sequence of events, Rhys Ddu, Philip Scudamore and Rhys ap Tudur were all tortured to death between 1409 and 1412.

However, the Tudur brothers' close relative Gwilym ap Gruffydd was prospering. He had acquired the estates of Rhys and Gwilym ap Tudur in Anglesey and Caernarfonshire, and lived at Penmynydd for a time. The estates of Maredudd ap Tudur were confiscated in 1407, leaving Owen Tudor landless. Gwilym ap Gruffydd married Morfudd ferch Goronwy ap Tudur Fychan of Penmynydd around 1390, gaining lands at Penrhyn and the commotes of Menai and Dindaethwy in Anglesey. Gwilym lived in Penmynydd from 1400, having been Sheriff of Anglesey in 1396–7. His wife's uncles, Rhys, Gwilym, and Maredudd ap Tudur, supported Glyndŵr, and Gwilym ap Gruffydd was forced by his family to join Glyndŵr around 1402. Gwilym made his submission to the king by August 1405, and by November 1407, when he was restored to his forfeited lands, he was granted, in addition, the lands of twenty-seven Anglesey followers of Glyndŵr, who had probably died in rebellion. Both his father Gruffydd and his uncle Rhys died fighting for Glyndŵr. By 1410 he had been granted the forfeited lands of his wife's uncles, Rhys and Gwilym ap Tudur. His brother, Robin ap Gruffydd of Cochwillan, also rebelled but abandoned Owain Glyndŵr before 1408, when he appears as a crown official in Caernarvonshire. Through various circumstances, Gwilym came to own most of the patrimony of the Tudurs of Penmynydd, a major reason for Owen Tudor leaving Anglesey to seek his fortune in London.

The last recorded sighting of Glyndŵr was around 1412 when he captured the loyalist Dafydd Gam of Brecon, later to die at Agincourt, and held him for ransom, which was paid by the king. Before going to France to fight at Agincourt, on 5 July 1415 Henry instructed Gilbert Talbot that he had authority to pardon any rebels who wished to submit, and Talbot went to Wales. He was instructed to receive Glyndŵr and other rebels into the king's obedience, so Owain was believed to be alive at that date, although it is unlikely that he would trust any offer from the English crown that had killed all but one of his extended family.

A recurring tale is that Glyndŵr hid at the mansion of Sir John Scudamore at Kentchurch. At Kentchurch Court there is a medieval tower known as Glyndŵr's Tower, within which a secret passage leads to a room called 'Glyndŵr's bedroom'. It is also associated with the cleric Sion Cent, Jack of Kent, whose portrait is said to be in Kentchurch. Intriguingly, the English believed they had killed Glyndŵr at Usk, but it was his brother Tudur, identified by the fact that he did not have a wart on his cheek. The portrait at Kentchurch shows a cleric with a wart on his cheek. As late as 1430, John Scudamore tried to have Glyndŵr's outlawry reversed so he could claim Cynllaith from John Beaufort, Earl of Somerset. Instead he was dismissed from all his posts as he had married a Welsh woman, Glyndŵr's daughter. The Scudamores also possessed Monnington Court, also placed as the last resting place of Glyndŵr along with seven or eight other sites.

On 24 February 1416 a second commission was given to Talbot to negotiate with Glyndŵr's surviving son Maredudd and to receive Glyndŵr's allegiance and that of any other rebel who sought pardon. There is no mention of Owain in the pardon rejected by Maredudd on 30 April 1417, so some presume that Owain had died by then. Several rounds of negotiation took place between various rebels and the authorities. As no one could speak to the rebels without a commission to do so, Bedford, along with the rest of the Privy Council and the regional commanders in Wales and the borders, would have known who was negotiating with the rebels. Therefore, there were links and connections between the highest echelons of the English government and the rebels. The most obvious conduits were those well-established border nobles who had strong connections with the Welsh, such as the Scudamores. Being married to Alys ferch Owain made John Scudamore useful, and Scudamore is a link between Maredudd ab Owain and John of Bedford. Bedford negotiated with Maredudd or his representatives in 1417, and would have relied on others such as Scudamore to make contact possible. Maredudd ab Owain was known to the Scudamores, and may have joined Bedford.

From February 1415, Gruffydd Yonge and the Hanmers were in Paris attempting to get French intervention. In 1418 Gruffydd Yonge, at the Council of Constance in France, stated that Wales was a nation, and should have a vote in ending the papal schism. Unable to return to Wales, he later went to Scotland, becoming Bishop of Ross and Bishop of Hippo in Africa. Adam of Usk wrote: 'AD 1415 Died Owen Glendower, after that during four years he had lain hidden from the face of the king and the realm; and in the night season he was buried by his followers. But his burial having been discovered by his adversaries, he was laid in the grave a second time; and where his body was bestowed may no man know.' Maredudd ab Owain was not to surrender until 1421. In 1416 he appears to have been in North Wales with a force of Scots, attempting to rally opposition in this area. Even after the death of his father, Maredudd continued to foment rebellion and was almost certainly connected with the Oldcastle plot of 1417. Maredudd was in Snowdonia when he finally accepted a pardon, for himself alone, on 8 April 1421, receiving letters patent granting him pardon for all offences, 'as on the testimony of the Holy Writ, the son shall not bear the iniquity of the father'. Several writers have Glyndŵr's son now going into royal service, serving in France until 1422, but there are no records of it, and he is often confused with another Maredudd ab Owain of Cardigan.

Despite the enormous rewards offered, neither Owain nor his son were ever betrayed. It had been twenty years and six months since Owain Glyndŵr had proclaimed himself Prince of Wales. These two decades of fighting against overwhelming odds, of reclaiming Wales for the British, are neglected in the history books. Glyndŵr had no funeral elegy from the bards – like Arthur, he never died – but in Welsh mythology his disappearance from history, rather than his capture and execution, gave the poets and the nation a hope for the future. Glyndŵr is the Welsh hero par excellence. This is a story of culture, humanity, nobility, treachery, courage, bitter defeat, glorious resurgence and a mysterious finale. It was not until 1948 that a Parliamentary Act declaring Glyndŵr to be a proscribed traitor was repealed.

As late as 1415 Welsh rebels were present in the county of Merionethshire, and in 1420, the sheriffs of Caernarfonshire and Merionethshire appealed for rebels to surrender and be pardoned. There is evidence in the poetry of the bard Llawdden to suggest that some Welshmen continued to fight on, even after Maredudd accepted a pardon in 1421, under the leadership of Owain's son-in-law Phylip ap Rhys of St Harmon, Radnorshire. In 1422 Robert ap Doe was hanged in Welshpool for being a Glyndŵr rebel. The 1430s and 1440s witnessed ambushes and murders of government officials across Wales. It is likely that the area around Dinas Mawddwy never settled, leading in the next century to the *Gwylliad Cochion Mawddwy* (red-haired bandits of Mawddwy), who terrorised the area and killed the Sheriff of Meirionnydd, Baron Lewis Owen.

Many of Glyndŵr's supporters had gone into exile, being unable to trust the English and angry at losing their lands. Henry Gwyn (White Henry) was heir to the confiscated lordship of Llansteffan, but left Wales forever and was to die in the service of France at Agincourt. Against this background of invasion, destruction and desperation, there was no future for Owen Tudor in Wales. He had no possessions or estates, and his father was dead. Some sources believe that Maredudd ab Owain Glyndŵr procured for Owen Tudor a place at court or in the king's service, but this seems unlikely, and is never mentioned in any contemporary sources or by the bards. Wales had been hammered into oblivion. Owen Tudor's missing years could well have been with Sir John Scudamore and his close relation Alys (Alicia) Scudamore.

Every part of Wales had suffered, with Griffith Davies noting that, in Monmouthshire, Rockfield and Troy mills were totally ruined and that the mill at St Maughan's was left derelict and in decay:

The castle, town, lordship and county of Wentllouk [Wentloog, between Newport and Cardiff] and members and the manor of Maghen [Mache] are now of no value because all the same are burnt, destroyed, wasted and annihilated by Oweyn and others of his company... like Grosmont, Trelech never completely recovered from the destruction wrought upon it during the rebellion and both of them, 'dwindled into inconsiderable villages'. What is beyond question, beside the scale of the immediate damage, was the often long lasting effect of much of this devastation. The demesne of St Maughan's near Monmouth, for example, had still not recovered in 1420 and the destruction of the rebel Philip Scudamore's manor house, park and mill at Troy was so complete that it was worth nothing as late as 1433.

With Henry IV's insecurity on the throne following his 1399–1400 usurpation, from the outset of the Welsh wars he followed a deliberate policy of economic destruction, and like the Saxons, Normans and Angevins looted and destroyed sites of religious importance, such as Franciscan Llanfaes and Cistercian Strata Florida Abbey. His son Henry, Prince of Wales, sacked and burnt Glyndŵr's mansions at Sycharth and Glyndyfrdwy, along with those of other Welsh gentry. With six major invasions of Wales, featuring around eleven separate armies, Wales was utterly ruined, its churches smashed and books burnt. Alongside this rapaciousness with the aim to impoverish the nation, after the defeat of Hotspur at Shrewsbury in 1403, Henry IV strengthened the defensive line along the March to contain the disorder.

The 'Iron Ring' of Edwardian castles around Gwynedd was complemented by supply depots based on the great Marcher castles of Chester, Shrewsbury, Ludlow, Hereford, Gloucester and Chepstow. Glyndŵr could hardly supply his volunteer armies, let alone pay them. He took ransoms for Lord Grey of Ruthin and Daffyd Gam, and would have accepted one for Mortimer if Henry IV would have been willing to pay. Along the March there were concentrations of castles, such as those at Skenfrith, the White Castle and Grosmont, as well as fortified manors such as Tretower. Even if he could take these castles that were strangling Wales, Glyndŵr did not possess the resources to permanently man, equip and re-provision them. He never had the access to taxes and loans of the English kings, and was forced to practise the type of guerrilla warfare that gained admiration from later leaders such as Fidel Castro, who described Glyndŵr as one of the greatest freedom fighters of all time. Philip Warner, in *British Battlefields,* called him 'a genius at guerrilla warfare'.

As Prince of Wales, Henry V honed his skills in the Welsh war, implementing the strategy of a scorched-earth policy, and Keith Dockray notes the importance of the Glyndŵr War to the reigns of Henry IV and V, and the acceptance of the House of Lancaster:

Perhaps Wales, galvanised into real nationalistic fervour by the charismatic and dynamic Owen Glendower, provided the most potent challenge to the new Lancastrian dynasty and it was here, too, that Henry of Monmouth spent much of his teenage years. The Welsh revolt broke out in 1400, and, from the autumn of that year, the Prince of Wales was nominally in charge of both the country's administration and the task of regaining control of his own newly granted principality. Early in 1403 he was appointed the king's lieutenant in Wales, and clearly, from then until the fall of Harlech Castle in February 1409 (which finally ended Welsh resistance) he played an active role in the long process of defeating Owen Glendower's challenge to English rule: indeed, the Lancastrian reconquest of Wales firmly established his military reputation.

The scale of the economic and social ruin when the war ended were such that Howell observed that 'the years following the Black Death seem by comparison almost progressive'. While Welsh tactics were of the hit-and-run variety, trying to take weapons, horses and equipment, those of Henry and his son were to 'cry havoc', laying waste to the countryside, much like the aggressive strategy of the Americans in Vietnam, a common policy in medieval warfare to make the populace tired of war and incapable of supporting or supplying their own troops. The military order 'Havoc!' was the command given to English armies to pillage conquered territories and towns and cause chaos, possibly first mentioned in *The Black Book of the Admiralty* (1385). Grose's *Military Antiquities Respecting a History of the English Army* (1801) contains a translation of an Old French text by Thomas De Brotherton, 1st Earl of Norfolk (d. 1338): 'Likewise be all manner of beasts, when they be brought into the field and cried havoke, then every man to take his part.' Shakespeare used 'cry havoc' in several plays, for example in *Julius Caesar*, when after Caesar's murder Anthony regrets his actions and predicts that war is sure to follow: 'Cry "Havoc", and let slip the dogs of war; / That this foul deed shall smell above the earth / With carrion men, groaning for burial.'

As discussed, some sources say that Maredudd ab Owain Glyndŵr Owen Tudor to court after he was pardoned in 1421, but there is no record of this. Other sources state that Owen was taken by his father to court, but his father was probably dead by around 1406, when Owen was around six years old, and had never been pardoned after being outlawed a second time. A recurring claim is that Owen, aged around fifteen, was a squire at Agincourt. 'Squire' had several meanings at this time, referring to a sub-knightly status, but many would be around fourteen to fifteen years old, in attendance upon knights, and hoping in time to be knighted. They would look after the knight's armour and horses, accompanying the knight in any battles, sieges or recesses. A wealthy knight could have many squires and they would all equally try to impress their lord to become a knight, worthy to be dubbed personally by the king, or by one of the dukes or earls when on campaign. They would have been trained in arms from an early age.

Harrison Dwight Cavanagh's view is an example of the Owen-Tudor-at-Agincourt theory:

> In London, Owain became the ward of his father's second cousin, Lord Rhys. At age 7 he was sent to the English court of Henry IV as page to the King's Steward, Lord Thomas Hungerford [this should be Walter], and trained in arms. It is said that he went on to fight in France at Agincourt in 1415, and appears to have reached the rank of squire for his services in the retinue of Lord Hungerford.

Richard Davey believed that Owen fought at Agincourt so well that he became 'Captain of the King's Guard', whereby he met Catherine of Valois. Records are incomplete, but there was an 'Evan' ap Meredith recorded as a man-at-arms serving the Earl of Arundel in Henry V's 1415 expedition to France – this could be an assumed or misspelt name. Chapman notes that a man called Owen ap Meredeth appears as an archer in the retinue of Humphrey, Duke of Gloucester, in 1415. One notable rebel, sometimes confused with Owen Tudor's father, was Maredudd ab Owain of Cardiganshire, who accepted peace and fought at Agincourt. In 1415 another former Ceredigion rebel, Joankyn (or John) ap Rhys ap Dafydd, took out letters of protection for serving overseas in 1415. He had been among the hostages handed over at Aberystwyth Castle in 1407–08, and must have been a wealthy man as he secured his release for £233 6s 8d in 1410–11.

It is notable that many of the Welsh gentry, with everything to lose, had turned to Glyndŵr's cause, and if Owen Tudor had served at Agincourt he will have known many of the Welshmen serving there. The king's brother Bedford was one of the chief negotiators at the end of the Glyndŵr War, trying to persuade the rebels to agree to peace and then also to use their skills in service in France. Bedford will have known of the Tudurs, and Owen Tudor may well have agreed to join the English in France via Bedford. Although the Welsh had no rights, and despite the clampdown in legal restrictions, Brough has noted that evidence over the following generation demonstrates that more Welshmen were elevated to garrison captaincies, allowed to command English (though probably mostly Welsh) forces and given knightoods (two families also rose to earldoms) than in the entire fourteenth century.

The Glyndŵr War had obliged a change of attitude from the military, irrespective of parliamentary proclamations. Making the Welsh captains, leaders and knights tied them closer to the English leadership in terms of loyalty and commitment. More importantly, making the dispossessed Welsh into landowners of French possessions meant that they had to fight the French to retain their new profit-making, reputation-bolstering lordships. This meant they invested in the English project of dominating northern France. Men had flocked to join the expedition to France as, trained in warfare, they had little opportunity to prosper, or even survive, in a devastated Wales. It is, again, not implausible that Owain went to France in 1415 as a squire to Sir John Scudamore, who served in the retinue of Henry V with four men-at-arms and twelve archers. Scudamore's esquire(s) may not have been noted.

An Owen ap Meredeth was also a man-at-arms serving under Lewis Powell under John, Duke of Bedford, on the 1420 French expedition, and Chapman writes:

> ... the retinue of Lewis Powell consisted of twenty-five men-at-arms, all apparently Welsh, and fifty-seven archers appears at first glance to be another selection of men taken from the royal demesne in South Wales and the March. While there is insufficient continuity with other armies to test this properly, the names of one or two individuals might suggest that the shires of North Wales also provided some men ... a man at arms in this company, is recorded as Owen ap Maredudd. It may be that this was Owain ap Maredudd ap Tudor; that is Owen Tudor, grandfather of Henry VII.

Lloyd-Williams states that Owen Tudor was at 'Agincourt, he had tales to tell of the sieges of Harfleur, and of Rouen, he had been in garrison at Cherbourg', but we cannot verify these claims. His first certain appearance in English service is not otherwise until 1420–21, when 'Owen Meredith' joined the retinue of Walter Hungerford, steward of the king's household. Bedford has been associated with being Owen's 'protector', and also may have known him if he served as a man-at-arms.

The website Clement-Jones.com among many others claims that Owen was at Agincourt: 'After Agincourt he was granted "English rights" and permitted to use Welsh arms in England.' There is no record of Owen being knighted, although his son Jasper may have knighted him before the battle at Mortimer's Cross in 1461. It is also difficult to reconcile this information with his actually receiving a patent of denizenship seventeen years later in 1432. There is another Owain ap Maredudd, from Ceredigion, who did fight for Henry V at Agincourt (there were Welshmen on both sides), but this does not preclude Owen from serving there as a young squire, looking after a knight or man-at-arms.

Nothing is definitely known of Owen Tudor from his birth until he appears in the retinue of the great Sir Walter Hungerford, one of the leading men in Britain, but Lloyd-Williams raises an intriguing possibility. She writes that around the time of his father's death, aged six or seven, he was passed into the hands of Sir John Scudamore of Kentchurch, the kinsman of Philip Scudamore of Troy, who was executed for fighting for Glyndŵr. Glyndŵr has always been associated with spending his last days with the Scudamores of Kentchurch or Monnington, and perhaps the two Owains became conflated over time. Lloyd-Williams states that 'Owain ap Maredudd' left the safety of the Scudamores to serve Hungerford, but perhaps he was also the 'Owen ap Meredeth' who served Bedford in 1420 before joining Hungerford in 1421.

The links between the Tudors and Scudamores were strong. Sir John Scudamore I (*c.* 1383–1434), the son of Jenkyn Scudamore, had married Glyndŵr's daughter Alys. Scudamore was the constable and steward of a number of royal castles in South Wales, and Sheriff of Herefordshire. At the start of the war he was in royal service, and in 1403 held Carreg Cennen Castle in Carmarthenshire against a prolonged siege. There is a strong tradition that Glyndŵr ended his days on one of Scudamore's estates, Monnington Straddel in the Golden Valley or Kentchurch. His son and heir, Sir John Scudamore II, was one of the most consistent supporters of the Lancastrian cause in Wales in the Wars of the Roses, fighting alongside Jasper and Owen Tudor at Mortimer's Cross in 1461. He managed to escape with Jasper to hold Pembroke Castle while Henry Tudor and Jasper managed to escape from it. Several close relatives, including his eldest son Henry, were among those beheaded after the battle. Scudamore was among those who, with Jasper, were excluded from the general pardon offered by Edward IV. Although he was promised that he would not be deprived of his property if he surrendered intact Pembroke Castle, his estates were eventually forfeited. Kentchurch and other properties were subsequently restored to the family when Henry Tudor ascended as Henry VII.

The careers of Scudamore, Hungerford and Bedford were conjoined, and we can possibly link Owen Tudor with all three. Scudamore was a 'king's knight' to Henry VI, and Hungerford for a time served Henry VI and his mother Catherine of Valois, as did Bedford. All served in the French campaign of 1415 and in France after that date. For Owen, a 'foreigner' with no rights, to be so readily accepted in the household of Catherine of Valois, he must have been well trusted by Hungerford and Bedford. From at least May 1421, Owen served in France with Sir Walter Hungerford, who was an executor of Henry V's will, and who later became King's Steward to the infant Henry VI, and probably Owen came to court in his service. Sir Walter Hungerford was steward of the young king's household from 24 July 1415 until 13 July 1421, and from 24 April until 16 July 1424.

The *DNB* of 1899 tells us that Sir Walter Hungerford (d. 1449) was the son and heir of Sir Thomas Hungerford, and,

was strongly attached to the Lancastrian cause at the close of Richard II's reign, his father having been steward in John of Gaunt's household. On Henry IV's accession he was granted an annuity of £40 out of the lands of Margaret, duchess of Norfolk, and was knighted... He acted as speaker in the parliament meeting on 29 Jan. 1413–14, the last parliament in which he sat in the House of Commons. Hungerford had already won renown as a warrior... On 22 July 1414 he was nominated ambassador to treat for a league with Sigismund, king of the Romans, and as English envoy attended the council of Constance in that and the following year. In the autumn of 1415, Hungerford accompanied Henry V to France with twenty men-at-arms and sixty horse archers. After diplomatic duties, in 1417 he was made admiral of the fleet under John, duke of Bedford, and was with Henry V in 1418 at the siege of Rouen. In November of the latter year he is designated the steward of the king's household, and was granted the barony of Hornet in Normandy. He took part in the peace negotiations of 1419, and on 3 May 1421 was installed knight of the Garter.

Hungerford was a trusted man and a notable warrior, deep in the heart of government. Owen fought for Walter Hungerford, whose descendant of the same name fought for Owen's grandson, Henry Tudor, at Bosworth six decades later.

Owen was thus very close to the centre of power in the kingdom, being a follower of Hungerford from at least 1420, with Hungerford in 1422 becoming a member of Protector Gloucester's council. According to geni.com,

In 1424 he [Hungerford] was made steward of the household of the infant king, Henry VI, and on 7 January 1425–6 was summoned to the House of Lords as Baron Hungerford. The summons was continued to him till his death. Hungerford became treasurer in succession to Bishop Stafford, when Bishop Beaufort's resignation of the great seal in March 1426–7 placed Gloucester in supreme power. He acted as carver at Henry VI's coronation in Paris in December 1430, but on the change of ministry which followed Henry VI's return from France in February 1431–2, he ceased to be treasurer. He attended the conference at Arras in 1435. He died on 9 August 1449, and was buried beside his first wife in Salisbury Cathedral...

Cavanagh relates:

> After the death of Henry V on 22 August 1422, Owain was appointed
> *Head of Household* (Keeper of the Queen's Wardrobe) for the newly
> widowed Queen Katherine who lived at court with their infant son Henry
> VI but moved to Wallingford Castle early in the new reign, taking Owen
> Tudor with her. Her illicit affair with John Beaufort, Duke of Somerset
> in 1426–27 [actually Edmund Beaufort, later Duke of Somerset] created
> a political firestorm and Henry's regents Prince John, Duke of Bedford
> and Prince Humphrey, Duke of Gloucester (Henry V's younger brothers),
> denied her request to marry John Beaufort as a threat to the child king,
> Henry VI. She allegedly said upon leaving court 'I shall marry a man so
> basely, yet gently born, that my Lords Regent shall not object'. Politically,
> the Regency Council's concern was that John Beaufort was already a
> legitimised Plantagenet second cousin of Henry V, and any children of a
> marriage with the widowed Queen Katherine would immediately become
> strong claimants for the throne. In 1428, in secret, Katherine married her
> *major domo*, Owen Tudor. There is no record of the marriage yet found in
> writing, but it was openly acknowledged as canonically valid by Henry VI.

Let us quickly mention a problem with the above, regarding John Beaufort.
John Beaufort, 1st Duke of Somerset (1403–44) was then Earl of Somerset
and was captured with his younger brother Thomas at the Battle of Baugé in
1421. Thomas was released in 1427, but Somerset was imprisoned in France
for seventeen years, being freed on full payment of his ransom in 1438.
Cavanagh means Edmund Beaufort (1406–55), a younger brother of John
and Thomas, who later succeeded to his titles.

Whenever and however the death of his father occurred, it is difficult to
discover what happened to Owen until the early 1420s when he became
a servant in the dowager-queen's chamber and was possibly at some time
appointed Keeper of the Wardrobe. Originally the 'wardrobe' was the room
where the king's clothes, armour and treasure were stored, but it later came
to describe both its contents and the department of clerks who ran it. The first
known Queen's Wardrobe was that Henry III's queen, Eleanor, which had a
high degree of autonomy, and reported directly to the Exchequer. Henry VI's
Keepers of the Wardrobe, who changed often, were almost always knights.

Owen's service to Bedford and Hungerford in France may well have been
rewarded with some office at court, with several early historians stating that
Owen was keeper of the queen's household or clerk of her wardrobe (at this
time the terms could be interchangeable). The *DNB* of 1899 tells us that:

Glendower's son entered the service of Henry V, and doubtless it was in this way that Owen Tudor came to the court. It is said that he was present · as one of the Welsh band at Agincourt, and distinguished himself so much that he was rewarded by being made one of the esquires of the body to the king; but he seems to have been rather young for such a post at the time. He certainly stayed about the court, and early in the reign of Henry VI he attracted the notice of Catherine, widow of Henry V, who appointed him clerk of her wardrobe.

Strickland relates that Owen was a clerk of the wardrobe, and the Yorkist-inclined Frabcius de Belleforest calls him a tailor. While this has been called anti-Tudor propaganda, there could be an explanation for this: the Frenchman Belleforest probably translated *sewer* (meaning server) as tailor.

Perhaps the earliest reference to Owen holding such a a position is in the chronicle of Elis Gruffudd of Llanasa, Flintshire, which states that the young 'squire of Gwynedd' was a servant and 'sewer' to the queen. Elis Gruffudd (1490–1552), 'The Soldier of Calais', was a Welsh soldier, chronicler, transcriber and translator, best known for his 2,400-page manuscript *Cronicl o Wech Oesoedd* (*Chronicle of the Six Ages*), written in Welsh between 1529 and 1552 and as yet largely untranslated. In 1510 he travelled across the border and joined the English army, fighting in Holland and Spain. He may have been attracted to London because of the Tudor dynasty, whose closest Welsh cousins were the Mostyns, and who offered opportunities for the Welsh. The second part of Elis Gruffudd's *Chronicle*, which discusses the history of England and Wales from the time of William the Conqueror, to 1552, was kept at Mostyn Hall. Gruffydd noted that Owen Tudor was Catherine's sewer, someone who places dishes on the table and serves. After the Glyndŵr War, several Welshmen secured positions at court, and in May 1421 an 'Owen Meredith' joined the retinue of Sir Walter Hungerford. At that time Owen moved to the queen's household; we do not know the date, but it may have been around 1421. Gruffudd is an excellent chronicler for these times, with accurate descriptions of service in the French wars, and his account of Owen being a 'sewer' must be addressed.

Michael Bennett has analysed the career of Sir John Steward, the son of John Steward alias Scotangle (Scot-English), a noted 'sewer' of Owen's time. Steward personally knew Owen, and was later personally interrogated about the marriage to Catherine of Valois. In Scotland they were called stewards, and in England the king's sewer was a trusted gentleman, a high-ranked attendant in charge of serving meals and the seating of guests. Those in the positions of sewer, carver and cupbearer were known as 'Yeoman Ushers of Devotion' and served the king personally. Thus the queen's sewer would be a prestigious position. As Owen is said to have been Keeper of the Queen's Wardrobe when she was living at Windsor Castle, essentially he was in control of the queen's tailors, dressers and anything else relating to her wardrobe room. It was also within his remit to handle all inventories of the dresses and to ensure all clothes that were taken on progresses were satisfactorily accounted for when returned. His presence would also ensure that any jewel thieves were discouraged.

There are several versions of how Owen met the queen. Elis Gruffudd states that Catherine first saw Owen on a summer's day when he and his friends were swimming in a river near the court. As he was handsome, she secretly changed roles with her maid and arranged to meet him in disguise. However, Owen attempted to kiss her, and in a brief struggle the queen received a slight wound on the cheek. The next day Owen served the queen at dinner and realised the identity of the maid from the previous day. He was deeply ashamed but she forgave him. Another tradition first occurs in an ode to Owen by Robin Ddu o Fôn (Robin Ddu ap Siencyn Bledrydd, 'Black Robin of Anglesey'), who wrote an elegy on Owen's death in 1461 which relates that Owen first attracted the queen's attention at a ball at Windsor Castle when, intoxicated, he accidentally fell into the lap of the seated Catherine. Robin Ddu wrote that he, 'on a holiday, clapped his ardent humble affection on the daughter of the King of the land of wine', and that they both fell in love.

The Anglesey poet appears to be our earliest authority for the romance of Owen Tudor and Catherine. He was in close contact with the Tudors and the chief families of North Wales, and it is quite possible that he got his information from Owen Tudor himself, or at least his friends. The version in Stow's *Chronicle*, which is generally accepted, is substantially the same, but of a later date. A similar tale was given by Michael Drayton in 1597:

> When in your presence I was call'd to dance,
> In loftie Tricks whilst I my selfe advance,
> And in a Turn, my footing fayl'd by hap,
> Was't not my chance to light into your Lap?
> Who would not judge it Fortunes greatest grace,
> Sith he must fall, to fall in such a place?

In 1603 the Welsh poet Hugh Holland wrote *Pancharis, containing the first book of the love of Owen Tudor for the Queen*, which tells us:

> Wherefore, as Owen did his galliard daunce
> And grac'd it with a turn upon the toe;

> (Whether his eyes aside he chaunc'd to glaunce,
> And, like the lovely God, became so blind,
> Or else, perhaps, it were his happy chaunce,
> I know not, and record none can I finde)
> His knee did hit against her softer thigh.
> I Hope he felt no great hurt by the fall,
> That happy fall which mounted him so high.

The Italian historian Polydore Vergil wrote, 'This woman after the death of her husband ... being but young in years and therefore of less discretion to judge what was decent for her estate, married one Owen Tyder, a gentleman of Wales, adorned with wonderful gifts of body and minde, who derived his pedigree from Cadwalleder, the last King of the Britons.' Tudor and the widowed queen soon lived together as man and wife. If Sir James Ramsay is right, she had wished to marry Edmund Beaufort but was prevented by Gloucester for personal reasons. At what time exactly the union with Owen Tudor took place, and whether it was a legal marriage, is difficult to determine. The Act that was passed in 1427–28, making it a serious offence to marry a queen-dowager without the consent of the king, is evidence that nothing was then known of the matter – publicly, anyway. The birth of their children can hardly have been concealed.

4

The Early Life of Catherine, Queen of England
1401–1427

Catherine of Valois was the daughter of Charles VI of France and Isabeau (Isabelle) of Bavaria, daughter of Duke Stephen III of Bavaria-Ingolstadt. Catherine was born at the royal palace of the Hôtel Saint-Pol in Paris on 27 October 1401, one of eight surviving children born of the marriage. An older sister, Isabella of Valois, had previously been married to Richard II. Their father, Charles the Mad, was mentally ill, probably suffering from schizophrenia. He experienced delusions, running from room to room until he collapsed from exhaustion, declaring that his enemies had caught him. He sometimes believed he was made of glass and denied he had a wife and children. The 'glass delusion' meant that Charles refused to allow people to touch him, and wore reinforced clothing to protect himself from accidental 'shattering'. The mental problems of the king may have been caused by inbreeding in the Valois dynasty, as many of Charles' ancestors were closely related. Charles' own mother Joan of Bourbon (1338–1377) was slightly unstable, as were her brother, father and grandfather, and she suffered a complete nervous breakdown in 1373 after the birth of her seventh child. Charles' illness is believed to have been inherited by his grandson, Henry VI of England.

As far back as 1393 Charles had suffered attacks of mental debilitation, and as time went on they increased in both frequency and duration. By the time Catherine was three years old the outlook for the king's sanity was dismal, and in 1404 the decision was made that 'for the sake of the kingdom' Charles VI should retire from public life. He was kept securely guarded in the Hôtel Saint-Pol, unaware of what was happening. With assistance from both her brother Louis, Duke of Bavaria, and her brother-in-law Louis, Duke of Orléans, Catherine's mother seized control of the government of France from the rival forces of the king's cousin John, Duke of Burgundy. Isabeau has been called 'an arrogant and ruthless woman... openly unfaithful', but Adams has explained that in her lifetime the queen 'was respected and revered'.

After her death Isabeau was reviled as an incompetent regent, depraved adulteress and betrayer of the throne. Scholars have concluded that the tales of Isabeau's scandalous past are simply scandalmomgers' rumours that evolved after her death in a great political power struggle that lasted decades. With her husband incapacitated by insanity, Isabeau was forced to rule a country ripped apart by feuding, power-hungry factions. Adams argues that Isabeau handled her role astutely in such a contentious environment, preserving the monarchy from the incursions of the king's powerful male relatives. Taking issue with history's harsh treatment of a woman who ruled under difficult circumstances, Adams convincingly recasts Isabeau as a 'respected and competent queen'. Similarly, Marcel Thibault wrote in 1901 that 'the true and complete history of Isabeau of Bavaria has never been written', and only now is she being credited for her actions in a terribly complex situation.

Catherine's elder brother Louis (1397–1415) was the eighth of twelve children, the third son and the second to hold the titles Dauphin and Duke of Guyenne, inheriting them in 1401 at the death of his brother Charles (1392–1401). With Charles VI becoming unstable, control of Prince Louis became vital to the parties wishing to control royal policy. In 1404, John the Fearless succeeded Philip the Bold as Duke of Burgundy. Almost immediately, John accused Isabeau and Orléans of mismanagement of the economy, and demanded money to compensate for the loss of royal revenues after his father's death. He entered Paris with an army in 1405. Orléans and Isabeau fled to the fortified castle of Melun, with her household and children a day or so behind. The queen's brother Duke Louis of Bavaria was ordered to follow them with the royal children. Louis of Bavaria seized the princes and princesses, carrying off the heir to the throne, Dauphin Louis, along with Jean, Charles, Catherine and her sister Michelle.

However, he also took with them the children of the Duke of Burgundy. Philip, the infant son of John of Burgundy, was betrothed to Catherine's sister Princess Michelle, and with his sister lived as a companion to the royal princes and princesses at Saint-Pol. Duke John sent a force of Burgundians to intercept the party, and Louis of Bavaria was forced to surrender the royal children, who were swiftly returned to Paris. He took the Dauphin Louis and his sisters, and returned them to Paris under control of Burgundian forces, but Louis's uncle, the Duke de Berry, managed to take control of the Dauphin on the orders of the Royal Council. Duke John then encouraged Parisians to revolt, and Orléans raised an army. The situation at Saint-Pol was temporarily relieved when Charles unexpectedly regained his senses, resuming his kingship with almost immediate effect. He was lucid for a few weeks, and full-scale war was averted as the Parisians claimed loyalty to the king and Dauphin.

In October, Isabeau became active in mediating the dispute in response to an ordinance from the Royal Council. Despite his temporary recovery, before long the unstable Charles was forced to retreat once more to the sanctuary of Saint-Pol. Catherine's brothers remained at court, and her sister Michelle was given to the care of the Duke of Burgundy, as she was to marry his heir. Because of continuing power struggles at court, it was decided that Catherine should be sent to the convent of Poissy, away from her mother Isabeau's influence. One commentator states that 'Catherine's early years were dismal and impoverished, her only education obtained in a convent at Poissy'. However, according to Isabeau's financial accounts, clothes and toys befitting a French princess were purchased, and religious texts were provided. The queen regularly sent her children gifts, and often wrote them letters. The proximity of Poissy to the capital made it susceptible to outbreaks of plague, and Isabeau ensured that at such times her children were sent to safety in the countryside.

From the twelfth century, Poissy had been a favourite place for the French royal family to stay. In the beginning of the fourteenth century one of its castles was razed to make way for a Dominican priory, erected in honour of St Louis. It was generously endowed and soon became one of the more wealthy abbeys in France. The area of the priory covered more than 120 acres, with 35 acres covered in buildings housing between 120 and 200 Dominican sisters. Apart from the church and the convent there were royal quarters built onto the priory, where the king might stay when in the vicinity.

The poem *Dit de Poissy*, by Christine de Pizan, dates from around 1400, describing her visit to her daughter, who was living there as part of the entourage of Princess Marie, who had entered the community in 1397. It is believed that Christine de Pizan's daughter was endowed by the king at that time. In the poem, de Pizan describes how she and some friends rode from Paris and how a sumptuous meal had been prepared by the prioress. She also gives a long, detailed description of all the wonders – the buildings, the chapel, the gardens and the fountains. De Pizan likened the place to Paradise, but nothing is left of the Priory except the porters' lodge, *la Porterie*.

The Early Life of Catherine, Queen of England

Catherine was not alone, as apart from personal attendants she joined her elder sister Marie in the convent. Marie of France (1393 – 1438) was the sixth of twelve children, eight of them, including Marie, living to adulthood. Isabeau had promised Marie to the Church, possibly hoping that God would cure her husband. Marie took her vows as a nun in 1408 while her surviving siblings were married into royalty and nobility. The prioress was her great-aunt, Marie of Bourbon, and Marie's lodgings were described as befitting a royal princess. In 1405, Isabeau and Catherine's uncle Louis I, Duke of Orléans, visited and asked Marie to leave religious life to marry the son of Robert, Duke of Bar, but Marie declined, saying that only her father (mentally ill at that time) had the power to force her to take a husband. In later years she became prioress of the convent, dying of the Black Death in 1438, being survived by her brother Charles VII.

Catherine was also joined in the convent by her sister Princess Michelle. However, Michelle became engaged in 1404 to Philip of Charolais, the future Philip III, Duke of Burgundy (1396–1467), later known as Philip the Good. They married in 1409, aged fourteen and fifteen respectively. Michelle became melancholic in 1419 following the treacherous murder of her father-in-law, John of Burgundy, by her brother, the future Charles VII. Michelle died aged only twenty-seven, and may have been poisoned. Of Catherine's other sisters, Joan (1391–1433) became Duchess of Brittany in 1396. We have already mentioned Catherine's eldest sister Isabella of France (1389–1409), who married Richard II of England and was widowed three years later, aged ten.

A bloody feud turned into civil war in the French-held territories. On one side, supporting the royal House of Valois, were the 'Armagnacs' led by Louis of Orléans and Louis' father-in-law Bernard of Armagnac. The other great faction was that of the Burgundians under John of Burgundy (the Fearless), followers of the rival House of Valois-Burgundy and allied with the English. Both parties struggled to use the king's illness to seize control of the throne. John the Fearless ordered Orléans' assassination, and on 23 November 1407 hired killers attacked Orléans as he returned to his Paris residence. They cut off the hand holding his horse's reins, and 'hacked [him] to death with swords, axes, and wooden clubs', leaving his body in the gutter. John initially denied involvement, but then confessed that the act was done for the queen's honour, claiming to avenge the crown of alleged adultery between Isabeau and Orléans. His royal uncles, shocked at John's confession, forced him to leave Paris, and the Royal Council now desperately tried to reconcile the Armagnacs and the Burgundians.

Catherine's brother the Dauphin Louis was credited with intervening to bring about peace at Chartres in 1409 and at Auxerre in 1410 and 1412.

By 1411, with the king still frequently incapacitated and the Dauphin not yet of age, open civil war broke out again between the two groups. John the Fearless and the Burgundians first held control of the government, but in 1413 they were forced to flee from Paris. The Armagnacs under the Dauphin came with the intent of defending France against the English, who were trying to capitalise on the civil wars. The Dauphin Louis was fortunately not present at Agincourt (October 1415), remaining with his Charles VI at Rouen on the advice of ministers. However, the Dauphin Louis died in December 1415, possibly of dysentery, and was succeeded by John (1398–1417) as Dauphin. John died just two years later, possibly being poisoned. The surviving brother, Charles VII (1403–61), came to be given the epithet of the 'Victorious' or the 'Well-Served', and was King of France for thirty-nine years from 1422 to his death. When he inherited the throne, England and its ally Burgundy occupied Guyenne and northern France, including France's most important city, Paris, and Reims, where French kings were crowned. In 1420 his father Charles the Mad had disinherited him, recognising Henry V and his heirs as his legitimate successors, but Charles was determined not only to throw the English out of France, but to unite and build the French nation.

Princess Catherine had been recalled from Poissy to court around 1410, aged nine. As the only princess who was neither betrothed nor dedicated to the Church, she was now seen as a valuable asset to her troubled family. From 1410 onwards marriage had been suggested between Catherine and Henry of Monmouth, Prince of Wales, afterwards Henry V. In 1413 Henry IV had again proposed a match between the princess and his eldest son. He had previously made unsuccessful advances towards Catherine's sisters, Isabelle, the widow of Richard II, and Marie, who was by that time a novice in the convent of Poissy. Strickland tells us:

> From time to time Henry IV made attempts to obtain a wife for his heir ... he was, in childhood, contracted to the eldest daughter of Joanna, duchess of Bretagne, afterwards his step-mother. The biography of Isabella of Valois has proved how long and assiduously prince Henry wooed the young widow of the murdered Richard [II], until all hope ended in her marriage with Orléans. Marie, the second daughter of France, was the next object of his choice; but she, who had been devoted to the cloister even before her birth, on being consulted whether she would prefer an earthly spouse and accept the prince of Wales, indignantly reproved her father's envoys for imagining so profane a thought. A daughter of the duke of Burgundy was demanded for the prince, but the negotiation was unsuccessful. At last, both the son and father seemed to have determined on obtaining the hand

of the fair Katherine, the youngest of the princesses of France, and a private mission was confided to Edward duke of York to demand her in marriage for the prince of Wales.

However, all was not well in England, as Strickland continues:

York was absent on this errand at the time when Henry IV was struck with his mortal illness.

Adam of Usk stated he had attended Henry IV's coronation, and for 1413 recorded:

Henry the fourth, after that he had reigned with power for fourteen years, crushing those who rebelled against him, fell sick, having been poisoned; from which cause he had been tormented for five years by a rotting of the flesh, by a drying up of the eyes, and by a rupture of the intestines; and at Westminster, in the abbot's chamber, within the sanctuary, thereby fulfilling his horoscope that he should die in the Holy Land, in the year of our Lord 1412–13, and on the twentieth day of the month of March, he brought his days to a close. And he was carried away by water, and was buried at Canterbury. That same rotting did the anointing at his coronation portend; for there ensued such a growth of lice, especially on his head, that he neither grew hair, nor could he have his head uncovered for many months.

Holinshed explained Henry IV's unpopularity in his *Chronicles of England*: 'By punishing such as moved with disdain to see him usurp the crown, did at sundry times rebel against him, he won himself more hatred, than in all his life time ... had been possible for him to have weeded out and removed.'

It was said that his son had wanted him dead. Henry IV had died while the negotiations for Catherine's hand were pending, in March 1413. In 1414, when Catherine was twelve years old, Henry V renewed his deceased father's negotiations to marry her. Strickland writes:

Henry V renewed his application for the hand of the princess Katherine. At the same time he demanded with her an enormous dowry. If the king of France had been disposed to give him his daughter, it was scarcely possible he could bestow with her two millions of crowns, the bridal portion demanded by Henry, together with the restoration of Normandy and all the southern provinces, once the inheritance of Eleanora of Aquitaine. There was a secret misgiving on the part of the French, lest the ambitious heir of Lancaster should make use of an alliance with one of their princesses, to strengthen the claim of the Plantagenets to the throne of France; yet Charles VI would have given Katherine to Henry with a dowry of 450,000 crowns. This the English hero refused with disdain. Henry desired no better than a feasible excuse to invade France…

The king now borrowed monies to pay an army – his father Henry IV had pawned his personal jewels towards the end of his life to pay for the wars in Wales, and the crown was virtually bankrupt. Strickland was not alone in noting the Plantagenet insolvencies. Edward I had deliberately bankrupted the two leading moneylenders in Europe, Italian banks, in order to pay for his own Welsh wars and then the 'Ring of Castles' in Gwynedd. That king had simply refused to pay his incredible debts. Strickland notes:

The annals of the ancient nobility or gentry of England can bear witness to the extraordinary methods the Plantagenet kings took, to induce their feudal muster to tarry beyond the forty days they were bound to appear in arms by their tenures. Among other possessions of the royal family, the magnificent crown belonging to Henry IV, called 'the great Harry', was pawned; while cupboards and beaufets at royal palaces were ransacked of their rich goblets and flagons, and distributed to the knights and leaders of that expedition, as pledges and pawns that their pay should be forthcoming when coin was more plentiful. Even that stout northern squire, to whose keeping was confided the banner of St George by his warlike sovereign, did not undertake his chivalric commission without a pawn of broken silver flagons.

This latter knight was Thomas Strickland, who bore the banner at Agincourt in 1415. Sir Thomas was to write nine years late, on 14 February 1424 to the Regency Council of the boy king Henry VI, begging for a part repayment of the pawned items:

And that it may please your wise discretions, out of reverence to God and respect to the soul of the late king, grant to your suppliant the said £14 4s 10¼d [almost £11,000 today] in regard for his services, and as part payment of the debt owed him by the late king [Henry V] and that this grant only be sufficient warrant for the discharge of the said suppliant from the £14 4s 10¼d aforesaid; and this for the love of God and a work of charity.

We must remember that Henry V was trying to wed Princess Catherine in the midst of the Hundred Years War, begun because Edward III believed he had a claim to the French crown. There had been a sporadic peace since the 'three-year' truce of Leulinghen of 1389, mainly because of Richard II's problems with nobles before his overthrow by Henry IV in 1399, and then Henry IV's long war with Glyndŵr and hostilities with the Scottish allies of the French. On the French side, the accession of Charles VI aged eleven in 1380, the struggles for power in his minority and his mental instability meant that France was not in a position to resume hostilities and throw the English off the Continent. Skilled in warfare after fighting Glyndŵr for a decade, Henry V had decided to invade France before his accession in 1413, and immediately began asking for loans, collecting weaponry, armour, cannon, gunpowder, bows and arrows ready for the invasion.

In 1414 the new king sent an embassy demanding restitution of all rights settled upon his great-grandfather Edward III in 1360, including half the kingdom of France. The French played for time, busy with feuds between their own nobles and their semi-autonomous duchies, and were so conciliatory that Henry sent a second embassy in 1415 to continue negotiations. Henry did not wish to be accused of waging an unjust war, but asked Parliament and the Church to agree to pay subsidies towards the war even before the second embassy had left England. Henry did not wish to approach Parliament for any loans, just subsidies, but Parliament had been squeezed by his father for thirteen years of campaigning costs, which in the case of Wales brought little reward, the country having been devastated and with rents almost impossible to take. In May 1415 the king sent letters to individuals and towns seeking loans. Mortimer writes that:

> Typically a town would decide on the amount of the loan, and then every citizen would be assessed to contribute even a few pennies to the sum agreed. Royal jewels, plate and regalia were handed out as security for repayment. Not only did this raise a large amount of money, but it meant almost everyone had an interest in the outcome of the French wars. One individual in London who lent money to Henry was Sir Richard Whittington, a rich cloth merchant who was indeed the same Dick Whittington as in the children's story. He was lord mayor of London three times.

Henry's early years as king were not without difficulties. His only real right to the crown was through his father's deposition of Richard II, and his father's illnesses were seen by many as a curse from God, and this made fertile ground for conspiracies to depose the new king. On the night of 9/10 January 1414,

Henry gathered troops in Clerkenwell and charged Lollard rebels. Their leader, Henry's former friend and ally in the Welsh wars, Sir John Oldcastle, managed to escape to the Welsh March. On 10 January, trials were held of eighty rebels who had been captured. Charged with treason and heresy, all but one were supposedly burned at the stake or hanged, and commissions were sent to regions with known Lollard populations, detaining 'heretics' and potential rebels, many of whom were burnt alive, regardless of whether or not they participated in the revolt. Alison Weir tells us the conspiracy was suppressed with 'shocking brutality: seven proven culprits were roasted in chains over a slow-burning fire and another twenty-four were hanged'. The 'Oldcastle Plot' to remove Henry V had failed, but Sir John Oldcastle remained a free man until 1417.

Henry was desperate for money, and had fined the Earl of March, Edmund Mortimer, 10,000 marks (£4.8 million today) for marrying Anne Stafford without his permission. The earl probably had a better claim to the throne than Henry, and this was a disproportionately high fine for the crime of marrying without royal permission. Mortimer would subsequently be the focus of another possible plot, involving the Earl of Cambridge, Lord Scrope and Sir Thomas Gray, in spring 1415. Scrope, a friend of the king who had even shared his bed on occasion, met some plotters to try and find out what they were planning, and on hearing that Scrope had done this Henry took the opportunity to confiscate all Scrope's lands and property. False charges of conspiracy to kill the king were raised against the men whom Lord Scrope was investigating, in order to quickly kill them and raise monies.

They had actually been discussing the legitimacy of Henry's Lancastrian dynasty against that of the aforementioned Earl of March. This was not actually treason as defined by Edward III, but plotting to kill the king was treason, so this became the charge, and Henry made money for his wars through the exposure of the alleged plot. While Grey and Cambridge were beheaded instead of being hanged, drawn and quartered, Scrope suffered the whole horrible torture of a traitor's death.

Throughout his reign, especially with the absurd later imprisonment of his stepmother, Joan of Navarre, and the confiscation of her incomes, Henry V was known to be avaricious to pay for 'God-guided' campaigns. His ships in 1415 bore the motto *'une sanz pluis'* ('one and no more'). The phrase comes from a medieval French version of Homer's *Iliad*, and its arrogance is quite breathtaking: *'D'avoir plusieurs seigneurs aucun bien je n'y vois / qu'un sans plus soit le maistre et qu'un seul soit le roi'* ('As for having several lords, I see no good therein / let one and no more be the master, and that one alone be the king'). Catherine of Valois was being lined up to marry a man of strong disposition, perhaps unlike her second husband Owen Tudor, who will have learned to be flexible as an 'alien' with few legal rights in England.

Assembling his invasion fleet at Southampton, Henry sailed for Normandy with 15,000 troops in August 1415. From the port he sent an envoy to Charles VI, demanding the 'English provinces' and the hand of Catherine of Valois. Charles replied that 'if that was his mind he would do his best to receive him; but as to the marriage, he thought it a strange way of wooing Catherine, covered with the blood of her countrymen'. Henry landed and besieged the fortified port of Harfleur on the wide Seine estuary, downriver from Rouen, the Normandy capital, and Paris. It had well-defended walls and could not be bypassed, and when threatened its defenders could flood the low ground on its landward side. Henry's fleet arrived on 13 August, blockading any supplies or reinforcements from sea, but Henry knew that breaking through its ditches, moats, bulwarks and walls would be a major problem. Henry had experience of besieging and taking Aberystwyth Castle, and had taken scaling ladders, crossbows, cannon and siege engines. He was not able to use his miners to tunnel under the walls because of the water defences. Many died inside the walls of Harfleur from dysentery, as did possibly over 10 per cent of Henry's army. His brother Clarence had to be sent home to restore his health, while his friends the Bishop of Norwich and the Earl of Arundel succumbed.

For five weeks Henry bombarded Harfleur day and night, and it surrendered on 22 September. The sixty-year-old Sir John Greyndour, notable in the fighting against Glyndŵr, served at the siege of Harfleur with ten men-at-arms, thirty archers and 120 miners, the latter probably from the pits in the Forest of Dean. During the siege, some of the reputation of Henry was transmitted in the otherwise semi-hagiographical play *Henry V* when in his address at the city gates to the town the governor states that there will be flames and rape if he does not surrender: 'What is't to me where you yourselves are cause, / If your pure maidens fall into the hand / Of hot and forcing violation?' Henry left Thomas Beaufort, Earl of Dorset, with a garrison of 2,000 men in the town.

After the delay besieging Harfleur the campaigning season was almost over, and Henry decided to march to Calais to return to England. However, the king had borrowed huge amounts of money to invade France and had nothing to show for it but one cannon-battered port. Troops had followed Henry not only because of his fearlessness but because, as the chronicler Jean de Waurin noted, even a rumour of dissent caused him to have men executed. Returning home direct from Harfleur, having lost hundreds of men to sickness, looked like defeat. Some historians believe that because of this Henry informed the

French that they could meet him in a decisive battle. However, it seems that Henry was looking to get back home, diverting his route at least twice before his journey was blocked near Agincourt by a French army said to be around 30,000 men (but probably closer to 12,000 men), 75 per cent of whom were men-at-arms. Henry's army probably numbered around 9,000, of whom only 20 per cent were men-at-arms.

The French decided to use massed cavalry to charge down the English and Welsh archers, but Henry learnt their strategy from a French prisoner a few days before the battle. To counter any charging horses, every archer was to drive a sharpened stake into the ground in front of him on the battlefield. Action began with clouds of arrows from Henry's longbowmen, and the French men-at-arms advanced but were funnelled into a narrower part of the field towards Henry's position. Many died or were disabled by arrows, and those who reached the English ranks were cut down. There was a press of troops trying to climb over a wall of dead and dying on the muddy field, and the wounded or fallen were crushed beneath the weight of those coming behind. Possibly 8,000 French soldiers died, including the flower of the nobility. After the battle, Henry twice gave the order to slaughter his prisoners, suspecting another attack. A soldier reported that the king 'has caused every soldier to cut his prisoner's throat'. The men-at-arms were reluctant to kill their valuable unarmed prisoners, and Henry had to despatch a task force of 200 archers, led by an esquire, to carry out the executions.

Anne Curry says:

The vanguard had little choice but to keep marching into the barrage of arrow fire, an experience for which there could be no prior training. Most were killed or wounded in the melee when they were already helpless, many by a swift dagger in the neck. Their fate dissuaded other French troops from entering the fray. Agincourt was therefore characterised by accusations of cowardice and treason as well as exceptionally high mortality rates for the French along with equally low rates for the English. It is doubtful that the French death rates would have been so high had it not been for King Henry's panic after he had stood his army down. Whether the threat of French regrouping was real or not – and there is no evidence at all that any attack was ever made – Henry's response was to slaughter soldiers who had already surrendered.

English losses were probably in the hundreds, including the Duke of York and the Earl of Suffolk, whose father had died in the siege of Harfleur.

Gloucester was injured. The bodies of the English dead were not given a Christian burial but were heaped into barns and burnt. Henry returned to England and glory with his nobles, but the battered and diseased English army marched to Calais. His soldiers were not given food or shelter but were forced to camp outside the walled port. In exchange for food, the soldiers had to give up their prisoners instead of ransoming them. Many troops were still unpaid in 1418, and the king's brother Bedford was among those in Parliament petitioning Henry to finally pay their wages.

The famous victory did not lead to further English conquests immediately, as Henry's priority was to return to England, which he did on 16 November, to be received in triumph in London on the 23rd. Much like in the present, there seems to have been no plan for what to do after an initial military victory. Henry used the opportunity to ask for more money for another invasion. He brought to England six prisoners of high public standing: Charles, Duke of Orléans (Charles VI's nephew); Jean de Clermont, Duke of Bourbon; Louis de Bourbon, Count of Vendôme; Charles of Artois, Count of Eu; Arthur of Brittany, Count of Richemont (brother of the Duke of Brittany); and the Marshal of France, Jean II le Meingre, known as *Boucicaut*. The victory helped establish the new Lancastrian monarchy, and to finance future campaigns to pursue Henry's 'rights and privileges' in France.

Curry says:

It was Agincourt which transformed him and his kingship. He had invaded in 1415 as the son of a usurper and with his own title insecure. There was even a plot to depose him on 1 August, the very day he had chosen for embarkation from Southampton. He returned with confidence as God's chosen king and warrior. No one could now challenge his royal title or his obsession with France. The English entered one of the most heavily taxed periods in their entire history as well as one of the most militarily demanding. In France, the Armagnacs were sullied by the defeat since their commanders had been captured, whilst the leading Burgundians had died a martyr's death.

Soon after Agincourt, the fragile truce between the Armagnacs and Burgundians fell apart. The Armagnacs had suffered the majority of the senior casualties and were blamed by the Burgundians for the defeat. Within ten days of the battle, the Burgundians had marched on Paris. In December 1415 Dauphin Louis died suddenly and Isabeau's fourth-born son, Jean, became Dauphin. Jean had been raised since childhood in Hainault, in the household of William II of Bavaria. The Dauphin was thus a Burgundian sympathiser, married to Countess Jacqueline of Hainault (who was later to marry Humphrey of Gloucester, the brother of Henry V). Charles VI had appointed Count Bernard VII of Armagnac as Constable of France, and the invading Burgundians plundered Paris after Parisians revolted against another wave of tax increases initiated by Armagnac. William of Bavaria refused to send the Dauphin to Paris, while Armagnac refused to allow Isabeau to reconcile with the House of Burgundy. The king knew nothing of what was happening, and remained in a state of delirium while Paris descended into anarchy and famine.

In April 1417 the Dauphin Jean died, and Isabeau's sixth and last son, the fourteen-year-old Charles, became Dauphin. Married to Bernard of Armagnac's daughter Marie of Anjou, he strongly favoured the Armagnacs. Armagnac imprisoned Isabeau in the palace of Tours, confiscated her personal property, dismantled her household and separated her from her daughter Catherine, her other children and her ladies-in-waiting. She secured her freedom in November 1417 through the help of the Duke of Burgundy. Distrusting Armagnac and his hold over her son, Isabeau maintained her alliance with Burgundy. She declared herself Regent of France, retrieved Catherine and her other children, and set up a court at Troyes, in Champagne, with the support of the Burgundians, to rival the government of her son.

The continuing disorder had given Henry breathing space to better prepare militarily and politically for a more intensive invasion, to finally secure his main objective of becoming king of France – a mission made more acceptable to the French people if he married Catherine of Valois. He would have been in contact with the Burgundians before his invasion. As part of his war preparations, in February 1417 Henry V had ordered all his sheriffs to have six wing feathers plucked from every goose in their jurisdiction and sent to London for fletching arrows. The feathers forced arrows to rotate in flight, increasing both their range and power. In July 1417, Henry V sailed for France with approximately 10,000 men, keeping his destination secret, and on 1 August he landed without opposition at the mouth of the Toques.

He overran the remaining French possessions in Normandy and on 18 August 1417 began to besiege Caen, storming two abbeys in the suburbs and mounting artillery in its towers. Caen refused to surrender, and on 4 September Henry led an assault through several breaches in the walls made by cannon. He attacked from the east side while his brother Clarence attacked from the west. As Mortimer relates,

> The king's brother, the Duke of Clarence, broke the resistance of the townsmen on his side of Caen, and the fighting moved into the streets. When the struggle

was over, Henry ordered that every male over the age of 12 be killed – or so claimed a Venetian chronicler. Eighteen hundred men and boys were put to death. A Dominican friar demanded of Henry how he could justify such killing. Henry replied in perhaps the most chilling tones imaginable: 'I am the scourge of God sent to punish the people of God for their sins.'

In a letter to Charles VI dated 28 July 1415, Henry had recalled Deuteronomy 20, which required those attacking a city to make a final offer of peace but authorised vengeance upon those who did not surrender. He acted according to this same 'law' when negotiating with Harfleur. He called on its garrison to open the gates and surrender to him as the rightful Duke of Normandy. The *Chronique du Religieux de Saint-Denis* claimed that his abuse of the supposed traitors who refused to surrender to him at the siege of Caen in 1417 was unjust because these people were not his subjects. The lower city was taken and a great massacre followed, with at least 2,000 citizens being put to death. The castle held out until 19 September, when it surrendered.

The unforgiving destruction wrought by Henry V in his French wars was first tried out in Wales. At about the same time that Henry had become Prince of Wales, aged thirteen, Owain Glyndŵr had begun his rebellion against the English. Henry IV's policy of attack and withdrawal was unsuccessful against Glyndŵr, and the rebellion rapidly spread across almost the whole country. Later, when Prince Henry was given a freer hand, he altered his father's strategy. He concentrated on taking strategic castles which were then garrisoned and held securely, cutting off supply routes and enabling further advances. Glyndŵr was forced back to two castles on the west coast, Aberystwyth and Harlech. These were not only battered by traditional siege weapons but great cannon as well, possibly for the first time in Britain. Glyndŵr's supporters were starving, and the rebellion ended. Over the next few years, using the same tactics, Henry V conquered Normandy and a large part of northern France.

Weir writes that

...as the war dragged on, the King's reputation for cruelty grew. At the siege of Rouen, his harsh treatment of non-combatants – women, children, and old men – resulted in 12,000 people dying from hunger and exposure. A French monk of the Abbey of St Denis accused Henry of abusing 'the right of kings to punish disobediences'. Anyone bearing arms who refused to surrender to him was put to death, and once Henry had a deserter buried alive before his horrified companions. When Caen fell, 2,000 people were rounded up into the market place and slaughtered, their blood running in rivulets through the streets. Henry himself turned a deaf ear to the cries of the doomed citizens until he came upon the corpse of a decapitated woman with a dead baby at there breast. Only then did he call a halt to the killing, although he allowed his men to continue to plunder and rape. As he rode by on his charger, stern and implacable, hordes of terrified people fell on their knees, crying for mercy.

This was the man to whom Catherine had been promised. With his overwhelming belief in his God-given destiny, he had become accustomed to cruelty. Aged just fourteen years and ten months, he had sat alongside his father in Llandovery marketplace on 9 October 1401 watching the terrible, drawn-out disembowelling of Llewelyn ap Gruffydd Fychan, and since then any semblance of Christian humanity seems to have left him. We cannot excuse Henry V by saying that he was a man of the times – many other monarchs across Europe were different – but he was certainly following the Plantagenet/Angevin/Norman kings of England in his attitudes. If we compare the first Tudor, Henry VII, with his forebears, there is a marked difference – unfortunately, his son Henry VIII returned to the old ways of kingship.

Mortimer continues:

The fact is that the massacre at Caen is just one of many bloody events that mark out Henry V as one of the cruellest and most cold hearted kings that England has had. Caen was not his first massacre – that had taken place at Agincourt in 1415, when he had ordered 200 English archers to cut the throats of a large number of French prisoners. Nor was it his last. Similarly ruthless acts of brutality against the French took place at Pontoise (1419), Melun (1420), Rougemont (1421) and Meaux (1422).

In October 1417 Henry captured Argentan and Alençon, and Bayeux surrendered to Humphrey, Duke of Gloucester without resistance.

Back in England, the hunt was still on for John Oldcastle, the Lollard rebel who had turned his back on his old friend Henry V. His fellow commanders Walter Blake and Sir Roger Acton had been caught and executed. Oldcastle had managed to evade capture with the support of his Welsh comrade John ap Harry, a friend of Jasper Tudor who collected rents from Oldcastle's forfeited estates. Oldcastle was eventually arrested near Welshpool in Montgomeryshire while returning from a meeting with Maredudd, the surviving son of Owain Glyndŵr, who was still at war with the English. Oldcastle was escorted to London and burned at the stake on 14 December

1417 in St Giles's Fields. Before Oldcastle was burnt and thirty-eight of his followers executed in 1417 he had reminded Henry that true Christians did not seek vengeance, telling him that he should show mercy because vengeance was God's alone. Paul Strohm has claimed that Oldcastle was not actually involved in the revolt known as 'the Oldcastle Plot', or was only a peripheral figure. He argues that the Lancastrian monarchy desperately needed to legitimise itself, as Henry IV's claim to the crown rested more on his murder of Richard II than on any dynastic legitimacy. Therefore, the rebellion caused the nobility to close ranks and throw their support behind the monarchy and against the perceived threat to their own interests posed by Lollardy. His belief is that the Lancastrians intentionally allowed, or even helped create, a rebellion which they knew they could easily suppress.

In February 1418 the fortress of Falaise surrendered to the English, and soon Henry's allies the Burgundians recaptured Paris after an uprising. Isabeau had at first assumed the role of sole regent because of her husband's incapacity, but in January 1418 yielded her regency to John of Burgundy. Together they dissolved *Parlement* and began securing control of Paris and the king. Burgundy took control of Paris on 28 May 1418, slaughtering thousands of Armagnacs, and the Dauphin fled the city. Pintoin related that Isabeau tried to reconcile with her son, but the Dauphin refused her invitation to ceremonially enter Paris on 14 July.

In June Henry took Louviers, hanging eight French gunners because their defending artillery hit his royal pavilion. On 20 July he took Pont de l'Arche, on the Seine 12 miles south of Rouen, cutting off the city from reinforcements and supplies. From about 1415, Rouen, the capital of Normandy, had been strengthened and reinforced by the French, and it was the most formidably defended place that the invaders had yet faced. When the English reached Rouen, they faced strong walls with many towers and cannon, lined by an army of crossbowmen (*arbalétriers*) under the command of Alain Blanchard. The city had a population of 70,000, making it one of the leading cities in France, and its capture was crucial to the Normandy campaign. Henry could not leave it intact behind him if he wanted to enter Paris, around 85 miles south-east along the Seine. Owing to a lack of manpower, a 'breach-and-storm' attack on the powerful fortifications was not feasible, so the city was completely surrounded, with the intention of starving out the defenders. On 29 July the king besieged Rouen, building four fortified camps linked by trenches around the city, and arranging for supplies to be shipped from England. By December, the people of Rouen were eating cats, dogs, horseflesh, and even mice. The streets were filled with starving citizens, and to save food the city expelled more than 12,000 of the city's poor, mainly women and children. In the winter of 1418/19, they found themselves trapped in the town ditch.

Henry refused to let them pass through the cordon of the siege. He forced them to stay there without food or shelter, dying in the freezing cold. As far as he was concerned, they were the responsibility of the starving townsmen. As with the people of Caen, Henry thought it right that they should suffer for their countrymen's 'sins'. On Christmas Day, the king allowed two priests to take food to those in the ditch. On 2 January, a delegation from Rouen met with Henry V. He made them wait until he finished hearing Mass, and then berated them for keeping him from his 'rightful heritage'. On 19 January Rouen formally surrendered, and the Vicar-General of Rouen was put in chains for excommunicating Henry from the walls during the siege. The city was to pay 30,000 francs indemnity, and the garrison was allowed to march away without its weapons on the condition that it did not fight the English for a year. Alain Blanchard, captain of the effective crossbowmen on the city walls, was executed. Many of the citizens were so disappointed in the Duke of Burgundy and the Dauphin that they swore allegiance to Henry.

Briefly returning to matters in England, dowager queen Joan of Navarre, widow of Henry IV, was now over sixty. In 1419 Joan was accused of using witchcraft to try to poison the king. It is strongly believed that Henry, desperate for money for wars in France, wished for control of her rich dower of £6,000 a year, over 10 per cent of royal income at the time. The absurd case never came to trial, but she was arrested and her possessions were confiscated. She was imprisoned for four years in Pevensey Castle, Sussex, being denied access to the revenues from her dowry, which Henry took. Her imprisonment was comfortable, and she was allowed to entertain many visitors, including her younger stepson Humphrey of Gloucester. She was then moved to Leeds Castle in Kent.

From February to March 1419, Henry V repaired Rouen's defences while Mantes, Honfleur, Dieppe, Ivry, La Roche Guyon and Fécamp surrendered to his commanders. Henry went on to take all of Normandy apart from Mont St Michel, which withstood an English blockade for over two decades until it was relieved by the French re-conquest. On 7 May, at Vernon, the king authorised Walter Hungerford and Sir Gilbert Umfraville to negotiate a marriage with Catherine of Valois. Perhaps this is the first time that Owen Tudor, probably in the service of Hungerford, saw the queen – it would explain some of the later romances that claim he fell in love with her in France, before her marriage to Henry V. Hungerford and the king's chamberlain, Lord Fitzhugh, were also given full powers to negotiate a final peace between England and France.

Seeming to recognise the real threat to their nation at long last, in the summer of 1419 the Armagnacs, led by the Dauphin Charles, and the Burgundians, led by John of Burgundy, met at Corbeille, agreed a truce and scheduled a fateful second meeting for September. Meanwhile, Sir John Falstolf led raids deep into French territory. On 31 July, John Holland, Earl of Huntingdon, surprised the garrison at Pontoise and took the town, a mere few miles from Paris. John of Burgundy continued to try to impress upon the Dauphin Charles that there was a terrible crisis awaiting France. The second meeting of reconciliation between the Armagnacs and the Burgundians finally took place on 10 September 1419. The Dauphin Charles requested a private meeting with John of Burgundy, promising his personal guarantee of protection. The meeting, however, was a ploy to end the civil war in one fell swoop. On a bridge over the Yonne, at Montereau, the unsuspecting John of Burgundy was hacked to pieces while kneeling to pay homage to Charles. The Dauphin probably gave the signal for the first blow. The break between the Burgundians and the Armagnacs was complete.

On 19 December, Philip the Good, the new Duke of Burgundy, son of the slain duke, formally allied with the English. Charles VI, probably via the device of the pro-Burgundian Isabeau, now disinherited his son. Charles considered his son responsible for 'breaking the peace for his involvement in the assassination of the duke of Burgundy', and wrote in 1420 of the Dauphin that he had rendered himself unworthy to succeed to the throne or any other title. After the Dauphin, Charles of Orléans was next in line as heir under Salic Law, but had been taken prisoner at Agincourt and kept in captivity in London. The way was now open for Henry V to take over Paris and the whole of France.

Strickland informs us that 'before two years had elapsed, the family of Katherine were forced by dire distress to sue for the renewal of the marriage treaty. Henry's career of conquest proceeded with terrific rapidity; he made himself master of most of the towns between Normandy and the French capital, while his brother, the duke of Clarence, and his friend, the earl of March, had already thundered at the gates of Paris. Henry was requested to name his own terms of pacification.'

Isabeau saw a match between Catherine and Henry as the only way to for her family to stay in power. She sent her ambassadors to Henry with a portrait of the attractive 'Catherine the Fair', and asked them to enquire whether so beautiful a princess required so great a dowry. Enguerrand de Monstrelet related:

The ambassadors from the king of France had brought with them a portrait of the princess Catherine, daughter to the king, which was presented to the king of England, who liked it well; but he made too great demands for her marriage-portion, namely, that with the princess should be given him a million of crowns of gold, the duchy of Normandy, of which he had conquered a part, the duchy of Aquitaine, the county of Ponthieu, with other lordships, the whole to be held independent of the crown of France. Nothing therefore was concluded; and the English ambassadors replied to those from France, that their king was not in a situation to form any treaty with, – for the dauphin was not made a party, and it was unbecoming the duke of Burgundy to dispose by treaty of the inheritances of France. On receiving this answer, the cardinal and ambassadors returned to the king and queen of France and the duke of Burgundy, who had lately quitted Paris, and were at Pontoise. They reported to the council all that had passed at Pont de l'Arche; and soon after the cardinal went to Pope Martin at Avignon, for he saw clearly that no peace was likely to take effect between the three parties.

Hungerford and Fitzhugh took great care in arranging a meeting for the respective royals. A truce was obtained and a conference agreed. Isabeau, Catherine and the unstable King Charles arrived at Pontoise in a richly ornamented barge, to be met by the new Duke of Burgundy. Pontoise, 17 miles from the centre of Paris, was a defensive stronghold set up to prevent attacks on the capital. Tents and pavilions were erected, covered with blue and green velvet worked with gold. Henry V arrived with his two brothers and his escort of men-at-arms. 'When the conference was about to commence the queen entered the enclosure from the right side followed by Katherine. The King of England entered from the left, advanced towards the queen, whom he saluted with profound respect, and kissed her as well as the princess. He then took his seat opposite, while the Earl of Warwick made a long speech in French. Some time was spent in discussion, when the parties took leave of each other and separated, leaving everything as unsettled as before.' It was said that Henry fell in love with Catherine at this time, but agreement could not be reached, and the French royal family left overnight. According to Livio in 1513:

And so of all that meetinge and councell ensued nothinge that is worthie of report, except the flame of Love some deale fired the hart of this Martiall Kinge to the sight of this younge Virgine Catherine, daughter to the Kinge and Queene of Fraunce. He [Henry] now loved Katherine more than before, and turning to the Duke of Burgundy, the only member of the royal family of France who was present, he said, 'Fair cousin, we wish you to know that we will have the daughter of your king, or we will drive him and you out of his kingdom.'

According to Strickland,

The duke replied angrily, and many high words passed between the two men before they separated. Henry continued his war in France, conquering at every step, until the royal family were forced to pocket their pride and beg to have the marriage treaty renewed. Henry was even asked to name his own terms. He haughtily replied that 'he had been deceived so often that he would treat with no one but the Princess Katherine herself, who, he was sure, would not try to deceive him'. This message was carried to the queen, who returned a love-letter written by the princess and a request that Henry would come to Troyes for the ceremony of espousal. He consented with pleasure. Henry V had not been modest in his demands, for with the hand of Katherine he was to receive not only the provinces he had named in the first instance, but also the regency of the whole of France, thus disinheriting the older children of the royal family.

As soon as these terms were agreed upon, Henry, accompanied by his brothers Clarence and Gloucester, with 1,600 combatants, mostly archers, advanced to Troyes, where he arrived on 20 May 1420. The Duke of Burgundy, clothed in mourning for his murdered father, met Henry near Troyes, and conducted him in great pomp to the Hotel de Ville, where lodgings were prepared for him. Henry was presented the next day to Catherine, who was with Isabeau in the church of Notre Dame. Before the high altar, the articles of peace were read and signed.

In the absence of an official heir, the Dauphin having been disinherited and Charles of Orléans in captivity in London, Isabeau accompanied the king to sign the Treaty of Troyes. The king's illness meant that he did not know who Henry V was, and prevented him from appearing at the signing of the treaty, forcing Isabeau to stand in for him. Gibbons noted that this gave her 'perpetual responsibility in having sworn away France', and that the treaty 'only confirmed [the Dauphin's] outlaw status'. By the Treaty of Troyes, Henry was to marry Catherine and Charles remained King of France. However, he acknowledged Henry V and his heirs as his only heirs. Henry now had the right to succeed to the French throne after Charles' death, and Isabeau was to reside in Paris. After signing the Treaty of Troyes, Henry V married Catherine in Troyes Cathedral on 3 June 1420. Her father was still too ill to attend. A tournament was planned to celebrate the wedding, but

Henry cancelled it and impatiently left Troyes on 5 June with his new wife plus Charles VI, Isabeau, Burgundy and his captive James of Scotland, and around 4,000 English and 5,000 Burgundian troops.

Catherine was given a new household, almost entirely English. Only three noble French ladies-in-waiting and two French maidservants were allowed to go with her as she left Troyes to campaign, with just one day between marriage and riding to war.

Strickland related:

Thus was the honeymoon of Katherine the Fair passed at sieges and leaguers: her bridal music was the groans of France. Horror, unutterable horror, was the attendant on these nuptials; for the cruel massacre of Montereau took place within a fortnight of the queen's espousals. Yet Katherine was no unwilling bride; for, as her brother-in-law, Philip the Good of Burgundy, expressly declared, 'She had passionately longed to be espoused to king Henry; and, from the moment she saw him, had constantly solicited her mother, with whom she could do any thing, till her marriage took place.' But not a word, not a sign of objection to the cruelties and slaughter that followed her marriage is recorded; nor did the royal beauty ever intercede for her wretched country with her newly wedded lord. Sens received Henry and Katherine within its walls soon after the siege had commenced in form. The king and queen of England entered in great state, accompanied by the archbishop of Sens, who had a few days before joined their hands at Troyes.

This prelate had been expelled from his diocese by the party of the Armagnacs, but he was reinstated by Henry V who, turning to him with a smile as they entered the cathedral, said, — 'Now, monseigneur Archevesque, we are quits, for you gave me my wife the other day, and I restore your's to you this day.' This sad page of history is detailed by Monstrelet. Henry V, exasperated by the desperate defence of this town for its native sovereign, butchered the garrison under pretence of revenging the death of John Duke of Burgundy, with whose death the garrison had not the slightest concern, nor was Henry in the least called upon to avenge it. While the desperate siege of Montereau proceeded, the queen of England, and her father and mother, with their courts and households, resided at Uray-sur-Seine. Here Henry paid frequent visits to his bride. After the tragedy of Montereau, the united courts removed to Corbeil, where Queen Katherine was joined by her sister-in-law, Margaret Duchess of Clarence, and by many noble ladies who had come from England to pay their duty to the bride of King Henry. She was with her mother and King Charles at the camp before Melun.

Catherine's marriage had been under discussion since 1414, and Weir writes, 'She was undoubtedly handsome, if not beautiful, but Henry probably would not have cared if she were otherwise; to him, she represented France. He was never a doting husband, and Katherine seems to have been somewhat in awe of him. Theirs was a dynastic match, and it is unlikely that love played much part in it.' The few months that Henry and Catherine were to spend together confirms Weir's opinion.

With Henry V now the regent and heir of France, Walsingham states that he

turned to those [Armagnac] cities which had rebelled against him and the French crown, with a view to subduing them by force. He first attacked Sens, upstream of Montereau. Henry wished the Parisians to stay loyal, so needed to relieve the city, which had suffered for months from the blockade of its main supply routes. The Dauphin's troops controlled major fortifications on the courses of major rivers in the north, east and south of Paris. The defence of Sens was by 300 men under the command of the Lord of Guitry, and it held out for twelve days until 11 June. Its citizens had desperately wanted the bombarded city to surrender, and the English then held it for nine years. On the day of surrender, its archbishop was officially inducted into Sens Cathedral, witnessed by the kings Henry and Charles, the queens Catherine and Isabeau, and the Duke of Burgundy.

Guillaume de Chaumont, Lord of Guitry, either escaped or was not present, because he was next noted at Montereau. Montereau-Fault-Yonne was an important river port at the confluence of the Seine and the Yonne, downstream from Sens. As at Sens, capture would improve life for the Parisians, who were not only lacking food, but also firewood for cooking. Montereau Castle occupied the confluence of the waterways, controlling bridges over the two rivers, and was surrounded by water because of a moat on its land side. Guitry was its captain and had been present at the assassination of John the Fearless, and had 500 men to hold the two parts of the city. On 23 June the city walls were stormed, but the greater part of its garrison managed to reach safety in the castle. Henry set pontoons on the Seine and Yonne to prevent escape by the rivers. The castle was shelled by artillery and trebuchets but held out despite damage. Henry brought eleven captured prisoners and threatened to execute them if the castle did not surrender, but Guitry refused, and Henry executed the men in the sight of their fellow defenders. Guitry eventually agreed to surrender on 1 July. The garrison were allowed to go free, except those present at Burgundy's assassination, who were executed. Somehow Guitry escaped. The body of

John the Fearless was exhumed and taken to Dijon to be reburied. Again, Catherine was present at the siege.

Henry carried on taking cities that controlled the trade and food routes into Paris. In June he had despatched the Duke of Exeter with Isabeau and a garrison of 500 to Paris. Having received reinforcements of 2,000 archers and 800 men-at-arms, he rode to Melun on the Seine, just 25 miles south-east of the centre of Paris. His combined 20,000-strong army of Englishmen, Frenchmen and Burgundians laid siege to Melun. The garrison of 700, commanded by Arnaud Guillaume de Barbazan, put up a strong defence, blockading the breaches in the walls made by the English cannon and counter-mining the English tunnels. Henry V and de Barbazan were among the fighters in the tunnels, and fought at least once. Feeling himself to be invincible before God, Henry was always involved in fighting. His survival after his near-death experience at Shrewsbury in 1403, when an arrow had to be extricated from near his eye, probably strengthened his belief that his actions were sanctioned from above. At the siege were the kings of England, France and Scotland (the latter being Henry's captive), the dukes of Bavaria, Clarence, Bedford and Exeter, the earls of March, Warwick, Huntingdon, Somerset and so on. The siege lasted fourteen weeks and four days.

From 22 July to 1 November there was violent and almost daily conflict between besieged and besiegers, involving wounding, mutilation and the deaths of many of the besiegers. It is said that more than 1,700 men died, and that all the defenders were killed or wounded. Mining attempts failed to bring down the walls and Henry gave up trying to take the town, instead deciding on a blockade to starve it into submission. The town's motto is *fida muris usque ad mures*, remembering the four-month the siege of 1420 when the citizens had to eat rats, cats and dogs. The Dauphin marched with 12,000 men to raise the siege, but retired without fighting.

By 18 November, its supplies exhausted, Melun surrendered to Henry, who wished to execute Barbazan. However, Barbazan reminded him that, according to the laws of chivalry, since they had fought personally, he could not take this action. Instead Henry placed Barbazan in an iron cage for ten years in the Château Gaillard. Released in 1430, the 'Irreproachable Knight' died fighting for France in 1431, and was buried alongside Charles VII in the Basilica Saint-Denis. Henry also hanged twenty Scottish defenders of Melun for treason. As they were not his subjects they could not have committed treason, so Henry killed them for fighting their own king, who himself was Henry's prisoner. 'He is likewise accused of having violated the capitulation in other respects, in confining the rest of the garrison within prisons and dungeons, where they perished by famine' (*The Field of Mars*, 1781). Catherine of Valois will have witnessed the sieges and killings, in one of the strangest honeymoons in history. It may well be that Henry only married to secure an heir.

With Melun surrounded, Henry had taken time off to ceremonially enter Paris on 1 September 1420. Henry, Catherine, Philip of Burgundy, Charles VI and Isabeau made a magnificent entry before cheering crowds of people who were probably looking forward to a lasting peace, the city having been sacked regularly over the years. The Estates-General ratified the Treaty of Troyes, and *Parlement* declared the Dauphin Charles unfit for the throne because he had committed 'horrible and dreadful crimes', including the killing of John of Burgundy. On 25 December Henry and Catherine kept Christmas at the Louvre, in great state and splendour, while Charles VI stayed at the Hotel de Saint-Pol, abandoned by all his court.

However, in England there was discontent at the idea that France was the king's top priority, and at the implication in the Treaty of Troyes that he or his heirs could rule England as kings of France. Parliament met in December 1420, and the Commons petitioned Henry to return and discuss these concerns, also refusing to grant Henry another subsidy for the war in France. They sent Gloucester to ask him to come to England as quickly as possible to crown his new queen. Henry had been in France for three and a half years, and Parliament saw no point in further contributing to the endless war that he was now waging as Charles VI's regent and heir. Desperate for money as ever, Henry was forced to plan a return to an England increasingly remote from his efforts in France. Many realised that even the great victory of Agincourt had actually achieved nothing but some valuable prisoners. Without Parliament's action Henry might never have returned to England, pressing on with his God-given mission to conquer all of France. On 6 January 1421 Henry and Catherine spent Epiphany at Rouen; Henry had dissolved *Parlement* in Paris, and now held another *Parlement* in Rouen, demanding more money from the Norman estates of his Norman and English subjects. He then had Isabeau proclaimed Regent of France so that he could return to England for Catherine to be crowned, crossing Picardy to embark at Calais at the end of January.

Catherine's beauty was always remarked upon, being tall, slim and fair, and Strickland writes of her coming to England:

The miserably exhausted state of France prevented Katherine from receiving any solid sum as her fortune; but she had an income of forty thousand crowns, the usual revenue of the queens of France, settled on her at her marriage by her father, a few scanty instalments of which proved, in reality, the only property she ever derived from her own country. This circumstance gives an exemplification, by no means uncommon in life, of the manner in which exorbitancy in pecuniary demands often defeats its own ends. Had Henry V required a more reasonable dowry with his bride, Katherine might have been reckoned as the richest of our queens, instead of being, with all her high-sounding expectations, in reality the poorest among them all. The royal pair spent their Christmas at Paris, but at the end of the festival Henry thought it best to pay some attention to the prayer of his faithful commons, who had lately begged 'that he, with his gracious queen, would please to return to England, to comfort, support, and refresh them by their presence.' Accordingly, Henry set out with his queen on a winter journey through France, escorted by the duke of Bedford at the head of six thousand men. Queen Katherine arrived at Amiens on St Vincent's day, and was lodged in the hotel of maitre Robert le Jeune, bailiff of Amiens, and many costly presents were made to her by that magistrate. The royal pair embarked at Calais, and landed at Dover on 1 February, where, observes Monstrelet, 'Katherine was received as if she had been an angel of God.'

R. B. Mowat emphasises Catherine's welcome:

When the king's ship put in at Dover, the assembled barons of the Cinque Ports, regardless of their costly clothes, leaped into the water, and brought the king, and also the queen upon their shoulders, to dry land. There they were met by a great assemblage of clergy, nobles, and people, who enthusiastically cheered both king and queen. But Henry, without delaying long, took his bride on to Canterbury. There he stayed a few days, and then went on to London. Queen Katherine, however, was left at the royal manor of Eltham, while the king went forward to prepare for her reception in the capital. This did not take long; in a few days, as arranged, the queen entered London. Pageantry, magnificent as that of the year of Agincourt, was displayed. The streets were filled with citizens; music was heard, artificial towers and gateways were erected, symbolic statues were placed prominently along the route, masques were held in open spaces.

With a small household including Bedford and Warwick, they arrived at Dover on 1 February 1421 and spent a few days in Canterbury. (Around this time, before her English coronation, the queen must have become pregnant – Prince Henry was to be born on 6 December 1421.) The new queen received a rapturous welcome in London. She was led on foot from Westminster Palace to the abbey between two bishops, and was crowned by Archbishop Chichele on 24 February 1421. There is no record of Henry attending the coronation. Catherine was then conducted to the great hall, where a huge feast was served to the nobility. It is reported that Catherine sat on the King's Bench at Westminster Hall beside her friend James of Scotland at the coronation feast. As Christopher Allmand writes, there is no record of Henry attending either Catherine's coronation or the ensuing feast, and the king would have been recorded if he had been present.

The coronation banquet had to be prepared without meat of any kind, for it was Lent. Where we see meat dishes in the following menu, therefore, they are actually vegetarian or fish dishes concocted to resemble meat. The first course was boar meat with mustard, frumenty with sea bream, pickled lampreys, codling, fried merlin fish, Lombardy pork slices, small pies, eels in sauce, pike, trout, plaice, large crabs and meat en croûte, followed by a special ornate confection, or 'subtlety'. This subtlety would bear a motto implying a political meaning. In the first course it was an image of St Catherine, the queen's patron saint, disputing with doctors and holding a label in her right hand, on which was written *'madame la reine'* (madame the queen). A pelican held an answer in its bill: *'C'est la signe et du roy / Parer tenez joy, / Et tout sa gent. / Elle mette sa content'* (This sign to the king / Great joy will bring, / And all his people. / She [Catherine] will be content).

The second course was galantine (jelly coloured with columbine flowers), white pottage (cream of almonds), bream, sole, chub, halibut, broiled rochet, lobsters, lampreys en croûte, minced chicken, conger eels, mullet, barbell with roach, fresh salmon, baked gurnard, fried smelt, Damascus slices, leche (strained jelly) damasked with the king's motto *une sans plus*, royal pork pie and flampayne 'flourished with a scutcheon-royal, and therein three crowns of gold planted with fleurs-de-lis and flowers of camomile, all wrought of confections, followed by a special confection in the shape of a chef and a lady'. This subtlety was named a *panter* (panther), with an image of St Catherine with a wheel in her hand and this motto: *'La reyne ma fille, / En cette ile, / Per bon reason / Aie renown'* (The queen my daughter, / In this island, / With good reason / Has renown).

The third course was white leche flourished with hawthorn leaves and red haws, compôte of dates, wild carp, mottled cream, tench, gudgeon, fried monkfish, large shrimps, white slices, mixed herbs sauce, turbot, perch with gudgeon, fresh and pickled sturgeon with whelks, roasted porpoise, freshwater crayfish, baked eels and lampreys, and 'meat' en croûte, decorated with four angels, followed by a sublety in the form of a tiger, with St George leading it.

After the feast, Catherine asked her husband to give James I of Scotland, who was a prisoner and had sat at her table, his liberty. Henry consented on condition that he would go with Henry to fight in France, and then left to tour his kingdom. He left Catherine behind – the queen had been crowned only three days before.

Again we hear from Strickland:

After the festivals had concluded, the queen was left by Henry V in her palace of Westminster till Palm-Sunday; when she removed to Windsor, expecting to meet him, as he had promised to pass Easter with her at the castle. Henry, however, found it impossible to return from the north, whither he had gone on progress; he therefore sent for the queen to Leicester, where they celebrated the spring festival: they then continued the progress together, visiting the shrines of all northern saints. Henry was so superfluous in his devotions, and so stem in suppressing all the satirical writings of the Lollards against the clergy, that Reformers gave him the sobriquet of the 'prince of the priests'. The object of the king in this progress was to prepare his people for the extraordinary supplies he meant to request at the ensuing parliament.

For this purpose, he harangued the corporations of every town through which he passed: and showing them his fair queen, as a proof of the progress he had made in the conquest of France, he explained to them, with great eloquence, what forces and funds it would take to complete it. Henry proceeded no further northward than the shrine of St John of Beverley. While he was offering to that popular saint, he left his queen at the royal castle of Pontefract, the fortress where her sister Isabella's first husband, Richard II, had met with his mysterious death, and where that sister's second husband, and her own cousin-german, – the poet duke of Orléans [Charles, captured at Agincourt], was then enduring a strict captivity. It may be inferred that queen Katherine was permitted to see this near relative, or Henry would scarcely have taken her to his place of abode. Katherine returned to Westminster in May 1421, when the king met his parliament. Soon after, the disastrous news arrived of the defeat and death, at the fatal field of Baugy, of that stainless knight the king's best-beloved brother, Thomas duke of Clarence.

On 22 March, Henry's brother Thomas, Duke of Clarence, against the advice of Gilbert Umfraville and the Earl of Huntingdon, set off without his archers, and attacked an Armagnac army at Baugé. Three years before, the Dauphin Charles had made an appeal for Scottish help, Scotland being ruled by Robert Stewart, Duke of Albany, while James I was Henry's captive. Albany had then sent a force of 6,000 volunteers to France, commanded by the Earl of Wigtown and the Earl of Buchan. These Scots now made up by far the largest part of the Franco-Scottish army facing Clarence, with Buchan and Wigtown commanding.

Only a small part of the English army actually took part in the battle, the men-at-arms led by Clarence, with the Earl of Salisbury being left behind to gather together and follow with the archers who were out in foraging parties. The ratio of archers to men-at-arms was at least 3 to 1 at this time, so Clarence, who had missed the 'glory' of being present at Agincourt, went into battle with only around a quarter of his army. Clarence allowed his army to become stretched out on the road to Baugé, and divided by the river. Buchan led his men into view and the two armies met in a confused hand-to-hand melee, with the outnumbered English being virtually wiped out. Clarence was one of the first to be killed. Notable English casualties included the Count of Tancarville, Lord Roos and Gilbert Umfraville. Salisbury, bringing up the rear, rescued what survivors there were and recovered Clarence's body. He managed to escape before the Franco-Scottish army learnt of his presence. Prisoners included the two elder brothers of Edmund Beaufort, who was soon to be associated with Catherine of Valois. French sources tend to support the figure of 1,500 English casualties, mostly dead and captured. The Dauphin Charles made Buchan the Constable of France, and the battle gave major hope to the Dauphinists – the English could be beaten.

Meanwhile, Henry's progress through the country continued. Mowat writes of this royal tour:

So as soon as the coronation of the queen was over, king Henry went on progress, largely for business, partly for pleasure, and also for religious purposes, for he made his tour include many of the holy places of England. He travelled through the Midlands to the Welsh March, as far as Shrewsbury, and gradually worked round again, till at Easter he was at Leicester, where by arrangement he met the queen. For Katherine had not at first gone on the progress, but had remained quietly at Windsor, till the time came for her to go to Leicester to meet the king. Here Henry and his court celebrated Easter, which fell this year on 23 March. Next they proceeded northwards, till they reached York on 2 April. From there the king turned south again, and visited the shrine of St John of Beverley. This was probably on 9 April. It was just after leaving Beverley that he received news of the disastrous battle of Baugé, which was to hasten his return to the labours of the war in France. Baugé was one of the critical battles of the Hundred Years War. Its effects cannot be over-estimated. It decisively checked English influence in France. In the summer of 1421, Henry received word that his brother, Thomas, Duke of Clarence had been killed at Baugé. He abandoned his plans to remain in England until the birth of his heir, held a Parliament and raised money and troops to return to France in June to continue his campaigns.

Strecche gives a slightly different version of the progress, and it is worthwhile here to understand how much time Henry and his new queen actually spent together. Strecche writes that immediately after the celebrations, the king

> visited Bristol, then other towns in the southern and western parts of England. [He was raising loans to return to France.] And then he turned aside to his beloved castle of Kenilworth... And so he progressed to Coventry, then to Leicester, where he waited for a time for the arrival of his queen. She, after leaving Westminster, journeyed via Hertford, Bedford and Northampton to Leicester, where she joined Henry on the eve of Palm Sunday and, in that city, king and queen kept the feast of Easter. When it was over the king set off at once with his followers for the north. First he went to the city of Nottingham, then to the town of Pontefract, and so to the city of York, to Beverley and to Lincoln.

According to Allmand, Henry predictably was focussed on raising money for military actions:

> The king demanded and received from the most powerful men of the realm, such as merchants and bishops, abbots and priors, great loans of money. Henry Beaufort, as usual, contributed hugely, and Enguerrand de Monstrelet commented upon Henry's eloquence in asking everywhere for financial support and troops – 'he very soon collected larger sums than had ever been seen so that they could hardly be counted... he enrolled all the most able in the country, and the most expert in drawing the bow, and, placing them under the command of his prices, knights and esquires, composed as army of full 30,000 combatants'.

While the number of soldiers is a gross exaggeration (Dockray thinks the number was nearer to 4,000), it is absolutely clear that Henry only returned to England to refinance his French war and recruit fresh troops. He had probably been organising this fund-raising progress, sending messengers to towns, immediately after he arrived back in England on 1 February. Just over three weeks later he had set off without his new queen, having missed her coronation and the ensuing celebrations.

It is thought that Henry's constitution had been weakened in his campaigns of 1415 and 1417–20, but he had no time to recuperate. Just three months after returning to England on 1 February, he had called a Parliament for May, which reluctantly voted a tax of a fifteenth, together with a tenth from the clergy, towards his new invasion. Chancellor Langley said that Henry had 'the patience of Job' in not yet avenging his brother Clarence's death, and desperately asked for monies for a new invasion despite Henry being drastically in debt. Henry feared asking for a parliamentary grant as it might be refused, damaging his prestige, and he had to resort to loans, including one for an incredible £17,666 13s 4d from Henry Beaufort.

Miller reflects on the king's debts after Catherine's coronation:

... all was not well with the public mood. Everybody, Nobles, Lords, Bishops and Commons, Clergy and Laity, were heartily sick of the everlasting war which kept their King away for such long periods. They were even more fed up with the expense, and Parliament granted taxes ever more grudgingly. A General Loan was attempted in 1419. Four years earlier, it would have been massively oversubscribed. Now it produced a derisory sum. The expenses of the Agincourt campaign had not been paid off. The wages of the Calais garrison were in arrears to the amount of £28,710, and in 1423 it was to mutiny. Massive sums were owed to private individuals. The Earl of Northumberland was owed £7,000 for the defence of the Northern border country. At the time of his death King Henry V owed his uncle, Henry Beaufort, Bishop of Winchester, the huge sum of £35,630, although Henry probably felt less compunction about this; the Bishop was notoriously acquisitive, and pumping some of his ill-gotten gains into the War Chest could have been regarded as just and fair. Some writers have estimated that the annual deficit was no less than £30,000, which may have been about right; their estimate of the private debts, however, at £20,000 must be a substantial under-estimate. The credit of the Crown was not what it was. In 1415, the City had been happy to advance £6,000. Now the most it would lend, and grudgingly at that, was £2,000. As ever undismayed by money matters however gloomy the news, Henry decided to go off on a fund raising tour of his kingdom. Ostensibly it was to introduce Queen Catharine to her new subjects, but its ulterior motive was to extract loans from his people. In the wake of the royal couple, there came the officials with their hands out. It met with considerable success, and altogether

£9,000 was raised. Whilst Henry was at Lincoln during the spring of 1421, the news of the disaster of the Battle of Baugé reached him...

On 10 June Henry drew up a will, and a few days later he landed in Calais. The pregnant Catherine was left in the care of his brother John, Duke of Bedford. With 4,000 troops, which may well have included Owen Tudor, Henry marched to Paris to relieve the Duke of Exeter, with Dauphinists blocking the duke's roads out. He sent many of his own men with Burgundy to relieve Chartres. Gloucester, assisted by James of Scotland, took Dreaux after five weeks. Henry marched south to Beaugency trying to lure the Dauphin into a fixed battle. He captured Beaugency and Vendôme in September and camped for three days outside Orléans. Without a strong enough force to take it, Henry next marched north, taking Nemours, Villeneuve-le-Roy and Rougemont in September 1421, where the surviving defenders were all either hanged or 'callously drowned in the nearby river', says Dockray.

Rougemont was burnt to the ground. With the failure to take Orléans, the king began to understand that the French refusal to meet him in fixed battle would mean an end to his campaigning. He would have to take castle after castle, and in each he would have to leave men, and his lines of communication would be increasingly stretched. His success in Wales was against a poor country barely 35 miles across and studded with massive English-held castles, with easy access to provisions from the Marches and by sea. France was a different proposition entirely. Henry was also frustrated by sickness among his men and lack of provisions. As his lines of communication grew, he lost food, baggage, horses, carts and military equipment.

On 6 October the king laid siege to the great Armagnac stronghold of Meaux. Apart from those who died in the continuous assaults, around a sixth of the English army died of rheumatic fever, dysentery and other illnesses. Henry fell ill, with doctors being sent for from England in late December 1421. Over the period of Christmas 1421 and Epiphany 1422, a Parisian commentator (quoted in Dockray) noted that Henry V 'had his men pillaging all over Brie', and people were unable to plough or sow their crops in the spring.

Back in England, while Henry V was falling ill, Catherine gave birth at Windsor to Prince Henry on 6 December 1421. The birth was assisted by a precious relic renowned for aiding barren women and women in labour. This was 'Our Lord's foreskin', brought on Henry V's orders under armed guard from Coulombs Abbey, later returned to Sainte Chapelle in Paris and then to the Abbey of St Magloire.

The godfathers at Prince Henry's christening were Henry Beaufort, Bishop of Winchester, and John, Duke of Bedford, the eldest of Henry's brothers. The godmother was Jacqueline of Hainault, Countess of Holland and Zeeland, who had recently left her husband, the Duke of Brabant, and had taken refuge at the English court. Here, she attracted the attention of the king's brother, Gloucester. She may have become close to Catherine, another new foreign noblewoman in the English court. At the confirmation of Prince Henry, shortly after the christening, Henry Chichele, Archbishop of Canterbury, also stood as godfather.

Stickland tells us:

No regular English dower was at this time settled on Katherine, but it is evident that the revenues of the unfortunate queen-dowager Joanna of Navarre were confiscated for her use, as her maids were paid from that source. Her damsels were Joanna Belknap, Joanna Troutbeck, and Joanna Coucy, besides Agnes, who has no surname. 'These ladies,' says Henry, 'the demoiselles of our dear companion, are to receive ten livres a-piece out of the funds of queen Johane, (Joanna of Navarre). Guillemote, damsel of the bedchamber to his said dear companion, is to receive one hundred shillings from the moneys of queen Joanna'. Not very honest of the valiant Henry, to pay his wife's servants with another person's money. These gifts are declared to be in consideration of the 'costages and expenses the beloved demoiselles are incurring, by following the said dear queen and companion to meet me, king Henry, in France.' Likewise an annuity of twenty livres per annum, 'for that dear doctor of philosophy, maister Johan Boyers, because of his office of confessor to queen Katherine.' The revenue of the unfortunate dowager was likewise taxed for the maintenance of Katherine's guest Jaqueline of Hainault, to the enormous amount of a hundred pounds per month. This princess had eloped from a bridegroom whom she hated, and had taken refuge at the court of Katherine, with whom she lived on great terms of intimacy. Jaqueline was in hopes that the pope would dissolve her forced marriage, and consent to her union with Katherine's handsome brother-in-law, Humphrey duke of Gloucester. Henry directs the treasurer of his exchequer to pay to his dearly beloved cousin, *dame Jake* duchess of Holland, such moneys from the profits of the dower of Joanna, late queen of England.

During the siege of Meaux the ailing Henry was told of his son's birth, and in tradition he asked, 'Where was the boy born?' When told 'at Windsor', he was angry, repeating the prophecy: 'I, Henry, born at Monmouth, / Shall small time reign and much get; / But Henry of Windsor shall long reign and lose all; / But as God will, so be it.'

While Henry weakened, Meaux was being bombarded day after day, with Henry's troops also suffering from artillery fire. Sir John Cornwaille was standing next to his seventeen-year-old son when a gunstone beheaded the boy. The injured and devastated father, before returning to England, is said to have stated that Henry should have been satisfied with Normandy instead of trying to take all of France. Meaux was indeed the 'worst' of all Henry's sieges. On 9 March 1422 the town surrendered to Henry, but the garrison withdrew into the Market, a fortified suburb, and held out. On 10 May the garrison surrendered to Henry. Its commander, the Bastard of Varus, was hanged with three others, and his brother was taken to Paris and executed. The cornet player who had sounded defiance from the walls of Meaux was also hanged for the delight of the ailing king. Henry V could now return to Paris, but he remained gravely ill.

As a Frenchwoman in a foreign court, Catherine was isolated. In spring 1422, she wrote to Henry 'declaring that she earnestly longed to behold him once more'. The king wrote to her to join him in France. When Prince Henry was five months old, Catherine left him at Windsor in the care of his nurse Elizabeth Ryman and the Duke of Gloucester, and rode to Southampton. Accompanied by the Duke of Bedford and a small body of troops, she embarked on 12 May, taking part in a planned visit whereby Bedford would replace his brother Gloucester in France. Catherine and Bedford landed at Harfleur and proceeded to Rouen, and from here she went to meet her parents at Bois de Vincennes. On 25 May she was joined there by her husband for Whitsun, and both kings and queens entered Paris to keep Whitsuntide.

Livio recorded:

And the xxx day of May, in the x yeare of his most victorious raigne, which was the Fryday next before the holy Sunday of Penticost, the two Kings of England and of Fraunce and there Queenes departed Bois de Visceinte [Vincennes] and went to Parris in much royall estate. The King of England and his Queene were lodged in the Castle of Lowre [Louvre], and the Kinge of Fraunce and his Queene were lodged in the pallace of S' Paule; in which two places these two Kings solemnized the feast of Penticost, everie of them severally by himselfe. And the proper day of Penticost the Kinge of Englande and his Queene satt together at there table in the open hall at dynner, marvelouslie glorious, and pompiously crowned with rich and precious diadems; Dukes also, Prelatts of the Church and other greate estats of England and of Fraunce, weere satt euery man in his degree in the same hall, where the Kinge and Queene kepte there estate. The feast was marvelouslie rich and abundant in sumpteous delicate meats and drinks. That day the Court was open to all that woulde come to the feast; the cittizens and commons of Parris resorted in greate number...

Henry had never really recovered from the illness he suffered at Meaux. Pained, feverish and emaciated, he was unable to sleep properly. However, he would not stay and rest in Paris. Burgundy sent for assistance as the Dauphin was attacking his castle at Cosne on the Loire. The sick king donned his armour, left Catherine with her parents and prepared to join his ally. The Dauphin, with Scots help, had attacked Cosne on the Burgundy border, and Henry sent his force on ahead, boosted by the 1,000 or so troops Bedford had brought with him. Here was his opportunity to take France once and for all in a pitched battle by killing the Dauphin. However, en route to Cosne-sur-Loire, he was in too much agony to ride. He was transported by horse litter to Corbeil, and could go no further. Henry sent Bedford and Warwick forward to Cosnes to attack the Dauphin, and then he was carried to the castellated palace at Bois de Vincennes, which he reached on 10 August. Knowing he was dying, the king summoned Bedford, Warwick and Exeter to his bedside. His final hours were almost exclusively preoccupied with establishing a protectorate for his infant son Henry VI. Close to death, his intestines, genitalia and lungs were in a state of putrefaction. On 26 August he added codicils to his will and appointed his brother John, Duke of Bedford, as provisional Regent of France (provided that Philip the Good did not want it) and guardian of the young Henry VI, and made his other brother, Gloucester, Regent of England. Just 30 miles away in Senlis, perhaps five hours' ride, Catherine was not called to the dying king, and was not given any particular role under the provisions of his will.

It is surprising that Henry did not call for Catherine at the end of his life, and it gives weight to the hypothesis that Henry was simply not interested in women. The stories that he was a wild youth, sowing his oats, are later additions to his life that cannot be corroborated. There were no mistresses and no illegitimate children, though these were extremely common in royal and noble circles. Catherine may have been the only woman with whom Henry had relations, and possibly cursory and essential ones at that. In his dying hours, he is stated to have said to Bedford: 'Comfort my dear wife, the most afflicted creature living.'

France was less than half won, and England was now exposed to the dangers of a very long minority regin under Henry VI. The king died at the castle of Vincennes on 31 August 1422, just before his thirty-fifth birthday. The twenty-year-old Catherine was with her parents in Senlis. With the huge influence of Shakespeare Henry V has achieved cult-like status, but he almost bankrupted the nation (a recurring problem for warring kings), and, as Carter declares, 'his wars had won him great glory but they conferred no permanent benefit upon England and they brought many troubles in their train'.

According to Livio:

The Kings disease dayly increased, untill that most Christian Kinge yealded his soule to God, departed this life in the Castell of that is called Bois de Vistenne not farr from Parris; where at that time was present Kinge Charles and the two Queenes. But tofore his death this most prudent Kinge in his Testament disposed the care and garde of the younge Prince, his sonn, and the defence of the Realme of Englande, to his most deere brother, Humphrie, Duke of Glocester, who faithfullie defended that noble Prince Henrie, and governed and protected this his Realme in all peace and good obedyence, untill he was passed the state of childhoode and of abilitie to see and provide for the governance of his Realme. But the custody of the bodie of the younge Prince the Kinge committed to his unckle the Duke of Excester, to endoctrine him in all good manners. And the revenews of the Dutchie of Normandie the Kinge bequeathed to his right puissant brother John, Duke of Bedforde, for the governance and defence of the same Dutchie and of the Realme of Fraunce.

Around 200 years later, Baker wrote:

Some say he [Henry] was poisoned, which Polydore Virgil saith, was much suspected. The Scots write that he died of the disease called Saint Fiacre [venereal disease], which is a Pallieand a Cramp: Enguerant saith that he died of St Anthony's fire [erisypela]: But Peter Basset Esquire, who at the time of his death was his Chamberlain, affirmeth that he died of a Pleurisy, which at that time was a sickness strange and but little known. Being dead, his body was embalmed and closed in lead; and laid in a Chariot Royal richly apparelled in cloth of Gold, was conveyed from Bays de Vincents to Paris, and so to Roan [Rouen], to Abbevile, to Callice [Calais], to Dover, and from thence through London to Westminster, where it was interred next beneath King Edward the Confessour; upon whose Tomb Queen Katharine caused a Royal Picture to be laid, covered all over with silver Plate gilt, but the head thereof altogether of mostlie silver: All which at that Abbeys suppression were sacrilegiously broken off and transferred to prophaner uses. He died the last day of August, in the year one thousand four hundred twenty two, when he had reigned nine years and five months, lived eight and thirty years though some say, two years fewer... Henry was but eight months old when his Father died... Then Henry the Fourth had four Sons, of so Heroical Disposition all, that you might know them all to be his Sons, only King Henry the Fifth to be his eldest. And now that in him the Heroical nature was come to the height, it degenerated again in King Henry the Sixth, which must needs be attributed to the Mothers side; who though in her self she was a Princess of a noble Spirit, yet being the Issue of a crazy Father, what marvel if she proved the Mother of a crazy Issue? And yet even this Issue of hers, a Prince no doubt, of excellent parts, in their kinde, though not of parts kindely for a Prince; in a private man praise worthy enough, but the Sword of a King required a harder metal than the soft temper of King Henry the Sixth was made of.

Catherine travelled with the body back to England. Shortly after her arrival in England she received word that, after many years of illness and suffering, her father Charles VI had passed away on 21 October 1422. This was less than two months after Henry V had died in pain. For those who accepted the Treaty of Troyes of 1420, Henry VI, only ten months old, became the first (and only) king of both France and England. However, the so-called 'final peace' of Troyes had created two nations, one loyal to an English dynasty and one to the French Dauphin Charles, uncle of Henry VI. Catherine was left a widow and Dowager Queen of England.

According to Strickland:

The queen made all the funeral arrangements herself, and they were conducted with great pomp. The body was laid on a chariot drawn by four black horses. Above it was a bed on which lay a figure made of leather, and painted to resemble the dead king. On the end of this figure was a crown of gold and precious stones, and around the body a purple robe lined and trimmed with ermine. In the right hand was a sceptre, in the left a globe of gold with a cross rising from it. The face was uncovered, and a canopy superbly decorated was held above it. The King of Scots and a number of princes, lords, and knights followed in deep mourning. Four hundred armed knights rode around the car with their lances pointing downward, and these were followed by a company of men clothed in white bearing lighted torches. The queen with her retinue came about a mile behind. When the procession reached London it was met by fifteen bishops, a score of abbots, and a vast crowd of priests and people. They proceeded along the streets chaunting hymns for their dead king. After his burial Katherine raised a magnificent tomb to his memory.

It was reported that the sight of their grief-stricken queen 'greatly edified the people'.

Davey writes that Owen Tudor ('M. Tidder', according to the *Histoire de Boulogne*) led the queen's procession on a white horse through Montreuil-sur-Mer to Boulogne and Calais to embark for England. If true, this makes sense of the stories that Owen knew Catherine well before 1427–28. On 5 November the funeral cortège of Henry V arrived in London, including the executors of his will, magnates of the realm and members of his household. Attending a council of Lords later in the day, they determined that the Duke of Gloucester's wardship of the realm had ended with Henry V's death, but that he could open the forthcoming parliament with the council's permission. This was a rebuff to Gloucester's claims as Regent of England, and he challenged the ruling, although unsuccessfully.

On 7 November Henry was laid to rest in Westminster Abbey. Henry Beaufort arranged for the chantry chapel that Henry had requested around his tomb, and Catherine paid for Caen stone for his new chapel and a Purbeck marble tomb topped by wood, an effigy of Henry and silver ornamentation. Henry Beaufort had the arduous task of paying the all king's debts, which Henry had requested in his will to clear his conscience. Beaufort himself was owed thousands of pounds lent over the years. Debts dated back to Agincourt in 1415 and the reign of Henry IV, and the task of repayment took twenty years. Even ships and royal jewels intended to be left to Henry VI had to be sold.

After the funeral Catherine retired to Windsor Castle, reunited with her son, now Henry VI. The young king now ruled England and France, but his uncle the Dauphin Charles was fighting for his kingdom. The widows of French kings often served as regents during royal minorities, but regency powers in England were vested in the council of magnates. The regency in France had thus been assigned to John, Duke of Bedford, and there was no way that Henry V's brothers would allow a Frenchwoman, an enemy of England, to be involved in the Regency Council during her son's minority.

Revenues from the Welsh estates at Hawarden, Montgomery, Builth, Flint, Coleshill, Mostyn, Englefield, Caldicot, Newton, Talybolion, Lleyn, Maltraeth, Menai, Cemmaes, Newburgh, Beaumaris and Aberfraw were assigned to Queen Catherine on the death of her husband; the last eight of those estates were in north-west Wales and Anglesey, the Tudor heartland.

Henry's first parliament provided for royal household expenses of 10,000 marks a year, but the Regency Council decided that a child's household only needed 3,000 marks, devoting the rest towards urgent military expenditures until July 1424. Elizabeth Ryman and Joan Astley were the infant king's nurses on £20 a year, doubled in 1424, and Agnes Jakeman his chamberwoman. Margaret Brotherman was his laundress, and the infant king had other personal attendants, Margaret Brekenham and Rose Chetwynd. For the first few years of her widowhood Catherine spent most of her time with her son, remaining in charge of him until he was seven years old. She was sometimes called upon to take part in state processions, and contemporaries describe how often on such occasions 'the infant king was seated on her lap'. She spent Christmas of 1423 at Hertford in the company of her good friend James of Scotland, whose marriage to Lady Joanna Beaufort she had the pleasure of witnessing not long afterwards. She was then moved from Windsor to Baynard's Castle, a palace on the Thames near Blackfriars.

The temporary Regency Council, in the absence of those fighting under Bedford in France, consisted of Bishop Langley; John Stafford, Keeper of the Privy Seal), William Kinwolmersh, Treasurer of England for just seven days before his death in December 1422; Bishop Morgan of Worcester, the Welsh cleric in whose palace Jasper Tudor was born when Morgan was bishop of Ely; Richard Fleming, Bishop of Lincoln; Edmund Lacey, Bishop of Exeter; John, Lord Talbot; James Butler, Earl of Ormond; Lord Clinton; and Lord Poynings. On 9 December 1422 the Regency Council was formally established by the House of Lords, consisting of Archbishop Chichele, Henry Beaufort, Bishop Morgan, Bishop Wakering, Bishop Kemp, Gloucester, the Duke of Exeter, the Earl of Norfolk, the Earl of Northumberland, the Earl of March, the Earl of Warwick, Baron FitzHugh, Baron Tiptoft, Baron Cromwell, Sir Walter Hungerford (Owen Tudor's employer) and Sir Walter Beauchamp. A quorum of four councillors, plus the three officers of state, was required for small matters, and a majority of the councillors was required for important matters of state. This council was presented to the House of Commons, who were satisfied – on the condition that either the Duke of Bedford or the Duke of Gloucester was to be consulted in those matters where the king would ordinarily have taken part.

In the second year of Henry VI's reign, Catherine's dower was settled by Act of Parliament. As part of the Treaty of Troyes it had been arranged that in the event of Catherine's widowhood she would receive an annuity of 20,000 crowns, but instead she was settled with 40,000 crowns. Henry had also settled on Catherine an income from his personal Lancastrian estates, as well as from the Bohun inheritance of his mother. As a princess of France, she might have been able to retire to her homeland as dowagers had done before. However, with her son declared King of France and her brother fighting against the English occupation, a return to France was untenable.

Bedford was required in France to complete its conquest, and Henry V's younger brother, the far less capable Gloucester, was in charge of administration in England as Lord Protector to his nephew Henry VI. While the reliable thirty-three-year-old Bedford was a warrior, statesman and diplomat respected by the French, according to Mabel Christie his 'wayward' brother' Gloucester was ambitious and self-serving:

Utterly wanting in public spirit or statesmanship, during Bedford's lifetime he heedlessly imperilled the all-important friendship with Burgundy by his schemes of personal aggrandisement, and after his death, regardless of the plight of the country and the hopeless condition of affairs in France, he so inflamed the war-spirit and false pride of the English that he drove them into rejecting offers of peace against the better judgment of the King's other advisers. At home, by his quarrels with his uncle of Winchester, and later with the Queen and her ministers, he undermined by dissension the position of the House of Lancaster, ruined himself, and hastened the ruin of his master. His private life [his marriage to Eleanor Cobham] so scandalized the people of London that it became at one time the subject of an expostulation to Parliament. Yet in spite of all he was very popular, and was even – most undeservedly – called the 'good Duke Humphrey.'

The guardianship of Prince Henry was entrusted to the Duke of Exeter, Thomas Beaufort, a half-brother of Henry IV, as he was the son of John of Gaunt and Catherine Swynford. Beaufort had been captured at Baugé with his elder bother John, Earl of Somerset, and had only just been released from captivity, but Somerset would remain a prisoner until 1438. Exeter was assisted in his duties by Lord FitzHugh and Sir Walter Hungerford. Hungerford employed Owen Tudor, and this remains the most likely way that Tudor came to know Catherine of Valois. Exeter's brother, Henry Beaufort, Bishop of Winchester and afterwards cardinal, was ambitious, energetic and capable and was also the richest man in England, gaining a fortune through the wool trade. His arrogance constantly clashed with that of his nephew Gloucester. The Beauforts always supported the Lancastrian dynasty, and Henry Beaufort funded both Henry V and Henry VI in times of financial crisis. According to Christie, 'there seems to have been considerable affection between him and the young Henry VI as he grew up'. Along with Gloucester, Thomas and Henry Beaufort, respectively Duke of Exeter and

Bishop of Winchester, were the most powerful nobles in the absence of Bedford, and their animosity to Gloucester did not help the young Henry VI in any way.

When Parliament met on 9 November 1422, four months after the death of Henry V, Catherine passed through the city of London with her son on her lap, on a throne drawn by white horses, surrounded by all the nobles of England. According to Christie:

> The Lords did not look upon Gloucester with favour, and, knowing his ambition, realised that it was necessary to put some check upon him. The Beauforts, meanwhile, had had time to organise the opposition. Accordingly, on 5 November [1422], Gloucester was authorised by the Council to open and dissolve Parliament only 'by assent of the Council,' and not in his own right as Warden of the Realm. The Duke strongly objected to this insertion, protesting that the words were unusual and likely to prove prejudicial to his rank. In spite of his protest, however, the Lords replied that 'considering the King's age, they could not, ought not, and would not otherwise consent, but that these words, or others having similar import, should be inserted for the security of the aforesaid Duke, and of themselves in time to come,' and to that Gloucester had to submit.

Catherine hardly appears in any records, but in 1423 she was asked to try to end the feud between Humphrey of Gloucester and Philip of Burgundy. They had argued over Gloucester's controversial marriage to Catherine's childhood friend Jacqueline of Hainault. Their marriage caused outrage in Europe, and Catherine's intervention seemed to resolve the affair. Sir Walter Hungerford, appointed by Henry V to attend on his son, was excused from his office on 18 February 1423, with the young king remaining under his mother's care. It may be that Owen Tudor, in the service of Hungerford, stayed with the queen's household at this time, possibly with instructions to guard the young king, rather than being in charge of the queen's wardrobe.

On 20 October 1423 Henry VI was brought from Windsor and shown to his second parliament at Westminster, which dissolved on 18 February 1424. The council insisted that the king had to take a personal part in public functions even before he was four years old. Strickland relates that in 1423

> Katherine left Westminster with her infant, and retired to Waltham-palace, November 26th, and from thence to Hertford-castle, where she kept her Christmas with her friend James I of Scotland, whom she soon after had the pleasure of seeing united, at St Mary's, Southwark, to the lady

he passionately loved, and whose happiness she had kindly promoted. Katherine's dower was not settled by act of parliament until the second year of her infant's reign. She appears to have been put in possession of all the ancient dower-palaces belonging to the queens of England, with the exception of Havering-Bower and Langley, where resided the queen-dowager [Joanna of Navarre], widow to Henry IV. In the third year of the reign of Henry VI was granted to his dearest mother Katherine, all that inn, or hospitium, in the city of London, where his dear cousin the earl of March, lately deceased, used to reside; and that she may have possession of it during the minority of his dear cousin, Richard duke of York, on condition that she keeps in good repair all the buildings and gardens, and is at all charges concerning them. There is reason to suppose that this was Baynard's-Castle. This year, Katherine and her mother, Isabeau of Bavaria, were entreated by Parliament, on behalf of England and France, to act as mediators between Humphrey duke of Gloucester and Philip duke of Burgundy, who had challenged each other to mortal combat. Duke Humphrey insisted on retaining, as his wife, Jaqueline of Hainault, the heiress of Holland, who had formerly thrown herself on Katherine's protection. Katherine, being the friend of all the parties, succeeded in preventing the duel.

In 1424, Gloucester, calling himself Count of Hainault, Holland and Zeeland, had taken his wife and an army to conquer his 'inheritance'. However, Philip of Burgundy challenged him to a duel instead of partaking in slaughter. Gloucester unexpectedly returned to England to prepare for the single combat in early 1425, but Burgundy's ally Bedford persuaded Parliament to refuse to finance Gloucester, and the Pope also forbade the fight.

On 16 January 1424 Joan Astley, wife of Thomas Astley, was appointed Henry VI's nurse with a salary of 40 pounds a year, a similar sum as was paid to a Privy Councillor. On 23 April 1424, the council decided that Henry needed a governess to train him in discipline, courtesy and other elements necessary for a royal person. Dame Alice Butler (Boteler) was selected to attend Henry's person, with licence 'to chastise us reasonably from time to time'. She also received £40 annually, soon increased by forty marks, making a salary of around £67.

Initially, the English prevailed in the ongoing war with France. Victories at Cravant in July 1423 and Verneuil in southern Normandy in August 1424 opened the way south, with Le Mans, the capital of Maine, being taken in August 1425. Heading south once more, Beford's army took much of the Duchy of Anjou.

In April 1425 Catherine brought the three-year-old king in procession through London to open the third parliament of his reign. Gloucester lifted Henry down from his litter. He was 'led upon his feet between the lord protector [Gloucester] and the Duke of Exeter unto the choir [at St Paul's Cathedral], whence he was borne to the high altar'. Fabyan recounts that then he was 'set upon a fair courser and so conveyed through Chepe and the other streets of the city'. Waurin relates that during the parliament Henry was at 'sundry times conveyed to Westminster, and within the parliament chamber kept his royal state'.

The king's third parliament lasted two sessions in 1425, between 30 April and 14 July. The Regency Council agreed that the king be brought up with boys of his own age, decreeing that all nobles in royal wardship should accompany Henry at court, so that the court became an 'academy for the young nobility'. Catherine still had an active role in her son's life until around this time, and Owen Tudor was probably still in her service. Catherine's presence as a young and attractive woman was a problem for the council, as another marriage could spell disaster for either France or England. In 1425 it was decided that the king should be removed from his mother's care into a separate household, and Catherine seemed to accept this, apparently content with her role.

Drayton writes that Catherine first saw Owen Tudor at Windsor and that he had known her in France:

> First saw I *Henry*, clad in princely Armes.
> At pleasant Windsore, there these eyes of mine,
> Judg'd *Tudor* first, for wit and shape divine.
> *Henry* abroad, with puissance and with force,
> *Tudor* at home, with courtship and discourse;
> Hee then, thou now, I hardly can judge whether
> Did like me best, *Plantaginet* or *Tether*.
> A march, a measure, battell, or a daunce,
> A courtly rapier, or a conquering Launce.
> His princely bed advaunced my renowne
> And on my temples set a double Crowne;
> Which glorious wreath, (as *Henries* lawfull heire,)
> *Henry* the sixt upon his brow doth beare.
> At Troy in Champayne he did first enjoy
> My bridall-rites, to England brought from Troy;
> In England now, that honour thou shalt have,
> Which once in Champayne famous *Henry* gave.
> I seeke not wealth, three kingdoms in my power,
> If these suffice not, where shall be my dower...

However, concerns were growing over Catherine's romantic attachment to a different man. Bennett relates:

> Given the rivalry over policy, patronage and precedence between Humphrey, duke of Gloucester, the late king's youngest brother, and Henry Beaufort, bishop of Winchester, the senior member of a cadet line of the house of Lancaster, [Catherine's] future political stance could prove decisive. In October 1425, open conflict between Gloucester and Beaufort prompted the hurried return to England of the Duke of Bedford. Bedford became Protector directly he set foot upon English soil, as his brother Gloucester only held the office during his absence, and seems to have arrived in London towards the end of December, for during the Christmas kept by the royal household at Eltham in 1425/1426 it is stated that he gave the king a ruby set in a gold ring. A concern in the crisis was the issue of the queen's remarriage. Rumours of a romance between the queen and Edmund Beaufort, Bishop Beaufort's nephew, raised the probability of an alliance that would consolidate or perpetuate Beaufort influence in the royal household.

On 18 February 1426 Henry opened his fourth parliament, the 'Parliament of Bats', in the Great Hall at Leicester Castle, where Bedford tried to mediate between his brother Gloucester and Beaufort. Attendees were not allowed to carry swords, so some armed themselves instead with clubs or bats. During the proceedings, Henry Beaufort was permanently removed as Lord Chancellor. On Whitsunday 1426, Bedford dubbed his nephew Henry VI a knight at the nearby St Mary de Castro Church. Gregory recounts that a number of young nobles afterwards received knighthoods from the 'gracious hands' of the boy king. Bennett writes:

> A petition in the parliament at Leicester in spring 1426, requesting that the queen be permitted to marry again, added to the tensions. Bedford successfully arbitrated between Gloucester and Bishop Beaufort, with the cardinal resolving on a pilgrimage to Rome. A compact between Bedford, Gloucester and Catherine in November 1426 to safeguard the young king and advance his interests acknowledged the importance of the queen's stance for the stability of the realm.

This petition for the twenty-six-year-old Catherine of Valois to be allowed to remarry asked the chancellor 'to grant to king's widows permission for them to marry at their will'. There was no direct reference to Catherine, but it could hardly have referred to anyone else, as the only other queen was

Henry IV's widow Joan of Navarre, born around 1370. Joan's remarriage was not considered important – she and the king had not produced children. The petition was deferred by the chancellor for 'further consideration', but at the next parliament, which opened in Westminster in autumn 1427, a definite response was to be given.

Henry kept court at Christmas 1426 and New Year 1427 at Eltham Palace, and among his presents were coral beads that had once belonged to Edward III. As he grew up he was present each year at the opening of parliament, and when he reached the age of seven the Earl of Warwick was appointed his tutor. Thomas Beaufort, Duke of Exeter, a son of John of Gaunt, had been responsible for the king's upbringing, but died around New Year's Eve 1426. Thus the Earl of Warwick was also given the king's guardianship. The king was almost five years old, and in 1427 John Somerset, a monk in the service of the Duke of Gloucester, was appointed as a master to teach him English and French, inspire him with Christian fervour, and, as Weir puts it,

...teach him to recite all the divine books by heart. Many books were bought for the boy, including devotional treatises, Bede's *History of the English Church*, and a work entitled *On the Rule of Princes*, which set out how a king ought to behave and how he should set a moral example to his people. Henry was not the only boy to benefit from such instruction, for each of the royal wards in his household was appointed a schoolmaster of his own, thus forming an exclusive and privileged school.

According to his chamber treasurer's accounts, the young king took portable organs on his travels. He had lived mainly at Windsor Castle, Eltham Palace and Hertford Castle, but also made use of Kennington, Kenilworth Castle and the royal hunting lodge at Woodstock. At Christmas 1426 he and Catherine were at Eltham, being entertained by John Travaill's London Players and the Jews of Abingdon.

On 13 October 1427 Henry opened his fifth parliament. In 1427 the young king was finally taken from the care of women, and from here on saw his mother less and less. As a French princess, Catherine was removed to prevent the king developing French sympathies as his lords were trying desperately to fight off a French resurgence into their territories. Not yet six, Henry now began to reside mainly in the royal castle-palaces of Windsor, Berkhamsted, Hertford and Wallingford. Henry VI had been born at Windsor Castle, and was later to be buried there. Berkhamsted is in Hertfordshire, and had been a favourite castle of the Black Prince. Hertford, also in Hertfordshire, stands on the River Lea. John of Gaunt, Duke of Lancaster, used it as his main country home in England. Richard II had installed the eight-year-old Isabella of France, his new wife, at Hertford after taking it from John of Gaunt after his death.

Henry VI's parents had been together at Hertford in 1421, and he may well have been conceived there – it was the habit of royals to leave London in the 'plague season' of the summer. When Henry V had died, Catherine had made Hertford Castle her home with her son. He thus spent a great deal of his infancy there and later kept his court there, and on his marriage to Margaret of Anjou in 1445 he gave her the castle; Edward IV would later give it to his wife, Elizabeth Woodville.

Wallingford Castle is on the Thames in Oxfordshire, and was a powerful medieval fortress. On Henry's marriage to Catherine in 1420, the castle and honour of Wallingford, with the honour of St Valery, formed part of her dower. Catherine would hold it until her death. It is said that Henry VI received much of his education at Wallingford, and in some accounts Catherine is supposed to have first met Owen Tudor here. Considerable repairs were undertaken in 1424 with a view to making the castle more suited for a queen's residence, and in 1428 it was appointed as a summer residence for the young king Henry VI.

5

The Marriage of Owain and Catherine, and the Births of Edmund and Jasper Tudor 1428–1436

In spring 1428 the king was still in the care of his mother, but arrangements were now made to assist his development into kingship. In 1427 he already had his own doctor, and Easter 1428 may have been one of the last occasions he was with his mother in an unofficial capacity. They spent time with the court at Hertford Castle, watching French players and dancers, and then nine days at St Alban's Abbey. The king was almost seven. His new guardian, Richard Beauchamp, Earl of Warwick, was one of the leading warriors of the era, with a reputation for chivalry. He had been a close friend and comrade-in-arms of Henry V. On 8 May 1428 Warwick was described as the king's 'master', and on 1 June 1428 a Great Council officially appointed him governor to the young king, taking the boy further from Catherine's proximity. Warwick was ordered 'to be about the king's person', and directed to 'teach him to love, worship, and dread God, draw him to virtue by ways and means conveyable, lying before him examples of God's grace to virtuous kings and the contrary fortune of kings of the contrary disposition, teach him nurture, literature, language, and other manner of cunning, to chastise him when he doth amiss, and to remove persons not behovefull nor expedient from his presence'. Henry was given four Knights of the Body and four Esquires of the Body, the knights receiving a salary of 100 marks and the esquires 50 marks. Each knight was given board and lodgings in the king's household and two personal esquires. The boy king now had sixteen men surrounding him at all times, and they were all under the command of Warwick.

Fluent in French, Warwick had sole responsibility for the king's upbringing and education, with orders to instruct him in courtesy, manners, letters and languages. Warwick also taught Henry horsemanship, tilting, swordsmanship and military strategy. Henry was provided with a small suit of armour and a sword at around this time, and his military education began, presumably in company with the other young wards that were kept at court. Alice Butler, Henry's 'mistress', had been authorised to chastise the young sovereign for misbehaviour or sloth, and Warwick was instructed likewise not to spare the rod. Warwick had made a pilgrimage to Jerusalem, being named 'the Father of Courtesy' by Emperor Sigismund, and predictably he instilled piety and courtesy into his young charge. However, soon Warwick was formally complaining to his fellow members in the Regency Council that Henry was reluctant to submit to his wishes.

Meanwhile, in 1427, Gloucester, angered by his failed attempt to secure his wife Jacqueline of Hainault's lands in Europe, began to hear rumours that Catherine intended to make a match with Edmund Beaufort, a cousin of Henry V and an heir to the Earl of Somerset. Gloucester thus influenced the Regency Council to instigate a parliamentary statute relating to the remarriage of the queen, prohibiting any person from marrying her without the consent of the king and council.

Professor Griffiths rediscovered in Leicester this 'missing statute of the realm', dating from the Westminster parliament of 13 October 1427 to 25 March 1428. Ashdown-Hill notes the specific clause threatening death and dispossession upon any who dared marry a queen without royal permission:

> ...it is ordered and established, by the authority of this parliament, for the preservation of the honour of the most noble estate of queens of England, that no man of whatever estate or condition make contract of betrothal or matrimony to marry himself to the queen of England, without the special licence and assent of the king, when the latter is of the age of discretion, and he who acts to the contrary and is duly convicted will forfeit for his whole life all his lands and tenements even those which are or which will be in his own hands, as well as those which are or which will be in the hands of others to his use, and also all his goods and chattels in whosoever's hands they are, considering that by the disparagement of the queen the estate and honour of the king will be most greatly damaged, and it will give the greatest comfort and example to other ladies of rank who are of the blood royal that they might not be so lightly disparaged.

Giles's Chronicle relates that 'the lords of the king's council would not agree to her marrying anyone during the king's minority, because she [Catherine] wished to have the Lord Edmund Beaufort, count of Mortain; but the duke of Gloucester and many other lords objected, ordaining that whoever presumed to marry her, against the Council's letters would be punished in the forfeiture of all goods and in the death penalty as a traitor to the king'.

Griffiths and Thomas relate that from autumn 1427 constraints had been placed upon the queen additional to those forbidding her to remarry. However, she was still officially in her son's household on 14 February 1431, and possibly as late as 24 May that year. They write that during this period of over three years, 'she and her *familia* [household, her close servants, generally of noble birth] were accommodated within the king's own household, where she would be under more vigilant control by councillors and household servants alike. Her receiver-general paid £7 a day to the treasurer of Henry's household to meet the additional expenses involved.' Given how close she was kept, it is all the more surprising what occurred between Catherine and Owen Tudor. Lloyd-Williams picks up the story:

It was now 1428. Katherine, who was twenty-seven or eight, was obliged to acquiesce outwardly [to Gloucester refusing to let her marry Edmund Beaufort], but inwardly she was rebellious… Just at this moment Sir Walter Hungerford returned from France and was re-appointed Steward of the King's Household. Among his retinue came one Owen Tudor, a young man whom we have met before. Such a handsome good-natured young man, who had been through the whole of the French wars, he had even been at Agincourt, he had tales to tell of the sieges of Harfleur, and of Rouen, he had been in garrison at Cherbourg, and knew all about those horrible new cannon which, so it was said, were completely to revolutionise warfare and make it a dull affair even for men. Presently one of Katherine's maids-in-waiting came and told her that this delightful young man was paying her more attention than she liked. The Queen was at Windsor and was looking out of the window over the river, watching the men of the Household swimming and performing other gymnastic exercises, and at first appeared to be taking little notice of the girl's complaints. However, it seemed that she had taken some notice, for after a time she pointed to one of the young men who was fairer in complexion than the others and who excelled them in their sports. Is that the man you say is so much in love with you? said she. 'Yes,' said the girl, 'at least he says he is. And I really think it must be true, for he follows me about everywhere…'

Catherine then fell in love with Owen, according to Lloyd-Williams.

Owen had been in Catherine's service possibly as early as 1423, but more likely from 1425 onwards. There is no contemporary record of how Owen and Catherine met, but there are many later traditions. Elis Gruffudd claimed that the young Owen was appointed *yn wasanaethwr ac yn sewer* ('servant and sewer') to the queen, who took a fancy to him when she saw him swimming in a river near the palace. Ieuan Gethin claims that the two fell in love 'on a feast day' and that the event had been 'energetic' or 'passionate', which accords with an account given in later English sources that Owen fell accidentally into the queen's lap whilst demonstrating his prowess at dancing during a feast.

However they met, it appears that they had soon married. *Baker's Chronicle* tells us:

This illustrious princess, regarded as dowager-queen both of France and England, by reason of her husband having borne the title of King of both realms, was destined ere long, in her turn, to bow at the conquering shrine of personal attractions. She became so enamoured with Owen ap Tudor, a Welsh gentleman, of moderate fortune, though ancient family, who was attending the court at Windsor, that unmindful of her high estate, and following only the impulse of attachment, she was privately united to him, on her son's entering his seventh year.

This alliance excited great indignation, as well as astonishment; that a brow that had been graced with the lily and crowned with the rose could disregard the regal circlet, and condescend to become the bride of a private individual – a mere soldier of fortune. To the princes of the realm, who ruled during the minority of the young king, the marriage was so offensive that a law was forthwith passed, enacting severe penalties on any person who might presume to espouse the Dowager-Queen of England, without the license of the reigning monarch. But the slenderness of Ap Tudor's fortune, and the mean extraction imputed to him by his enemies, was more than counterbalanced, in Queen Catherine's estimation, by his noble bearing and extraordinary personal endowments.

We simply do not know for certain when Owen Tudor married Catherine of Valois, but the marriage seems always to have been accepted as legal. The Act passed early in 1428 had made it a serious offence to marry a dowager-queen without the consent of the king, and the lack any reaction at this time is evidence that nothing was then known of the marriage, at least publicly.

Almost definitely physical relations did not begin until they married, although their love affair had probably begun at some stage after Henry V's death in 1422, while she was in Windsor Castle. The consequences of an illegitimate birth to a queen of England, in a deeply Catholic society, would have been devastating. We can add the complication that her son Henry VI's forces were fighting those of her brother to bring France under English rule, and that the French were hated by nobles and commons alike.

Giles's Chronicle records that Catherine deliberately chose a landless commoner, so that the council 'might not reasonably take vengeance on his life'. To later justify her marriage, she seems to have produced Owen's lineal descent, claiming that he was no common Welsh squire. *Giles's Chronicle* tells us of the young Catherine's 'carnal passions' regarding Owen Tudor, and Belleforest states that Catherine brought dishonour to her blood and her rank by having an affair with her 'tailor'.

Regardless of whether or not the marriage was kept secret, the birth of Catherine's sons by Owen Tudor around 1430 and 1431 can hardly have been concealed. Catherine had stopped living in the king's household and moved to Hertfordshire, and here she gave birth to the boys, half-brothers to the king. They were named Edmund and Jasper. She went on to have at least two more children.

It would be extraordinarily difficult to conceal four royal pregnancies and four children. As Monmouth, translating Biondi, stated, 'it is not to be supposed that the Court could be hoodwinked in four great bellies'. Biondi added that although the marriage must have been known, yet it was 'winked at by reason of her husband's birth, which though it was not answerable to her present condition, yet to be tolerated in respect of his forefathers, for nobility doth not lose its privileges for want of fortune and want of worth, which he wanted not'.

The notion that Owen Tudor was low-born is interesting. *Caxton's Chronicle* describes Tudor as 'Owayn, a squyer of Wales, a man of lowe byrthe', but Polydore Vergil described him as 'a gentleman of Wales, adorned with wonderfull giftes of body and minde'. It was written that 'Queen Catherine being a French woman born, knew no difference between the English and Welsh nation', but she had lived in royal circles for a decade, and must have known that her father funded a French invasion in 1405 to support Glyndŵr, and she must have been aware of the almost 'pariah' status of the Welsh. There were oppressive penal laws even before those of Henry IV in 1402 forbidding Welshmen from owning property, convening public meetings, wearing armour on the highways or holding royal office. Welsh castles could only be garrisoned by pure-blooded Englishmen, Englishmen were placed in Welsh religious offices, and the older, far more enlightened Welsh laws were suppressed. Englishmen could not be convicted of a crime on the testimony of a man of Wales, and these laws, among others, also applied to Englishmen who married Welsh women. The mingling of impure British blood and respectable French and German blood was not allowed. Catherine must have known this, bringing the risk of disgrace, but still married Owen.

Halstead says:

> Owen ap Tudor, however, though the victim of calumny and prejudice, was not unworthy of alliance with the British empire. He could justly boast of two royal descents, and claimed higher lineage even, than that of the Fleur-de-lys of France, or the Planta-Genista of England. Accumulated reverses had greatly reduced his parents from the dignified station, which was nevertheless their birth-right; for in virtue of their ancestry, he claimed uninterrupted descent from the aboriginal princes of Britain, through Arthur and Uther Pendragon, the grandsons of Constantine the Great, whose British dominions (A.D. 310.) were united to the empire of Rome, of which he was the first Christian emperor. In proof of his direct descent from Cadwallader, the last British prince, and first King of Wales, (A.D. 678.) he bore a dragon as his device, that being the ensign of the above-named ancient monarch, and was consequently displayed by the grandson of Owen ap Tudor, King Henry the Seventh, on his victorious standard at the battle of Bosworth Field. Leaving it to antiquaries to decide the merits of this lengthened pedigree, it will be sufficient here to state the fact, that, in 1428, the beautiful Queen Mother, the Princess Katherine of France, became the acknowledged wife of Owen ap Tudor; and many ludicrous tales are still extant arising from this incongruous union.

Belleforest claims that it was actually in order to legitimise Jasper and Edmund that Catherine married Owen, suggesting a different chronology. *Hall's Chronicle* notes that the queen,

> ...being young and lusty, folowyng more her owne appetite, then [than] frendly counsaill, and regarding more her private affeccion, then [than] her open honour, toke to husband privily, a goodly gentilmin, & a beautyful person, garnished with many Godly gyftes, both of nature & of grace, called Owen Teutiier, a man brought furth and come of the noble lignage, and ancient lyne of Cadwaleder, the laste kyng of the Brytons, by whoine she conceyved and broughte forthe. iii. goodly sonnes, Edmond, Iasper, and

another, whiche was a monke in Westmynster, and lived a small tyme, and a doughter, which in her youth departed out of this transitorie life:

After whose deathe kynge Henry, because they were his bretherne of one wombe deseeded, created Edmonde, erle of Rychemonde, and Iasper, erle of Pembroke, whiche Edmond engendered of Margaret, doughter and sole heyre to John, duke of Somerset, Henry, which after was king of this realme, called king Henry the seventh, of whom you shal heare more hereafter. Thys Owen, after the death of the Quene his wife, was apprehended and admitted to ward, because that contrary to the statute made in the. vi. yere of this kyng, he presumptuously had rnaried the Quene, without the kynges fcspeciall assent, and agrement, out of which pryson he escaped, and let out other with him, and was agayne apprehendyd, & after escaped agayne.

The reference to 'lustie' refers to the belief that women were more prone to carnal lust than men, and female 'virtue' was associated with the ability to control strong sexual urges. Catherine's mother Isabeau was roundly abused for being a nymphomaniac, on unproven grounds, by her enemies. It was an easy way to destroy a woman's reputation, and unfortunately some of today's historians repeat such assertions as facts. Medical belief in the West, coming down from the Greeks, was that wombs were cold, needing 'to be filled constantly with hot sperm if women were to be happy and healthy. The Greek word *hyster* refers to the womb, and the term "hysteria" is born from the assumption that women's wombs cause them to have uncontrollable emotions,' according to De Lisle.

Sir John Wynn of Gwydir wrote that:

Queen katherin beinge a frensh woman borne, knewe noe difference between the Englishe and Welshe nation untill her marriage beinge published Owen Tuders kynred and countrey weare objected to disgrace him, as most vile and barbarous... the opposition to her unione made her desirous to see some of his kinsmen, whereupon he brought to her p'sence John ap M'edyth and Howell Ll'in ap Howell his neere cozens men of goodly stature and p'sonage, but wholley destitute of bringeinge upp and nurture, for when the Queene hadd spoken to them in div's languages and they weare not able to answere her, shee sayed they weare the goodliest doombe creatures that ever she sawe.

There is no record of when or where the marriage took place, but its legality was never challenged, either in Owen's time or in later Yorkist proclamations and manifestoes against his son Jasper and grandson Henry.

There has never been any question of the validity of the marriage or of the legitimacy of the children of Owen and Catherine. Richard III in one of his proclamations against Henry Tudor describes his grandfather Owen as a bastard but says nothing about his marriage. Few people knew about it until after Catherine's death, with the *The Great Chronicle of London* recording, 'Unwyting [were] the comun peple tyl she were dede and beryed.' Henry Beaufort stayed with Catherine over the Christmas period in 1430, at her manor of Waltham, and must have known about her marriage – she may have been pregnant at this time.

Bennett believes that the life of one John Steward is key to pinning down a date for the birth of Edmund Tudor. He relates the tangled history of Steward, described as the 'son of Scotangle', who in his September 1447 will requested burial in the mother church of Calais. He left a ship called *Grace de Dieu*, given him by Bedford, the Regent of France. 'Other bequests included a gold goblet given him by Queen Catherine at her coronation and a diamond ring given him by Eleanor Cobham, duchess of Gloucester, while she was in his custody.' Steward assigned the tutelage of his eldest son to Sir Thomas Kyriel and also appointed him his executor. (Interestingly, in the Wars of the Roses Kyriel would be 'executed in retaliation for the execution of Owen Tudor and his companions'.)

Steward was assigned to Queen Catherine's service and knighted at her coronation in February 1421. According to the family history, he was brought up by Bedford after his father's death, won a place in the service of Queen Catherine through his patronage, was knighted at her coronation, and served as cupbearer at the feast. However, in tracking his movements Bennett notes Catherine's absence from Henry VI's coronation in France in 1431:

> His absence from Rysbank makes it probable that he was the knight who served as master of the king's horse in 1430 and led a company in the expedition accompanying Henry VI to his coronation as king of France. His experience as the queen's master of the horse would have stood him in good stead for what was, after all, very much a reprise of his role in 1421–2. It was perhaps originally assumed that Queen Catherine, who attended her son at his coronation in Westminster in November 1429, would take part. In April 1430 the royal host arrived in Calais, and over the following months proceeded to Rouen and Paris, where Henry was crowned in Notre Dame.
>
> … It is likely that Queen Catherine's absence from her son's coronation in Paris had some connection with her affair with Owen Tudor. The queen's morganatic marriage to a Welsh gentleman in her service is a most obscure episode in British history. There had been some discussion of her

possible remarriage in 1426, and indeed rumours of a romantic attachment to Edmund Beaufort. The parliament of 1427–8 passed an Act declaring that the dowager queen could only marry with the permission of the king when he came of age and laying down that anyone marrying her without permission would suffer forfeiture of his property. It has been reasonably assumed that the queen's liaison with Owen Tudor arose from this impasse. [As noted, *Giles' Chronicle* indeed claimed that the queen's choice of a husband with little to lose was in response to this statute.]

The chronology of the relationship, however, can only be inferred from the fact that Queen Catherine had three or four children before she became ill in 1436 and died at the beginning of 1437. The most plausible inferences are that the elder sons, Edmund and Jasper, were born around 1430 and 1431. Recent speculation that Edmund may have been the queen's son by Edmund Beaufort, and that the marriage to Owen Tudor may have been a cover for the affair, adds further layers of uncertainty. All in all, the queen's personal circumstances, which did not become public knowledge until after her death, must have precluded her full participation in the coronation expedition. Sir John Steward may have been among the first to know something of her new condition. He was well acquainted with Edmund Beaufort and *would probably have known Owen Tudor as a colleague* [author's italics].

Bennett has discovered a 1560s transcription of Steward being interrogated by the council as to what he knew of Catherine's marriage. His answers were discreet, telling the lords that he had promised Catherine that he would keep her counsel private. Indeed, in matters that did not relate to the crown, dignity and estate of his sovereign, he would never broadcast her secrets 'to the perpetual shame of his name and estate'.

[Steward] denied having any dealings in the affairs of Owen Tudor and the queen other than that which was fitting for a loyal knight. He declared that he knew nothing of their intentions prior to their marriage and was actually serving in the king's wars in France at the time of the ceremony... Scholars have tended to assume that no formal investigation took place until after the queen's death. This statement makes it clear that the queen was alive at the time of the interrogation, and that *the fact of the marriage and when it took place were known* [author's italics].

Steward stated that he was in France at the time of the wedding between Owen and Catherine, and Bennett believes, assuming that Catherine gave birth to Edmund in 1430, that she married when Steward was in his first term at Rysbank, between November 1427 and November 1429. Steward was asked by the council what Sir Thomas Kyriel knew about the marriage. Kyriel does not seem to have been in the queen's service, but was in the retinue of Edmund Beaufort from 1429, and perhaps his enemies in the council suspected Beaufort of being the one to impregnate Catherine. Guthrie, in his *General History of the World*, wrote that Gloucester was annoyed to find out about Owen's marriage: 'The High spirit of the duke of Gloucester could not brook this match; neither the beauty of Tudor's person, nor his genealogy, deduced from British Kings, could prevent both him and the queen from a sharp prosecution as soon as the marriage was declared.' This may have led to Steward's interrogation. Steward remained in Queen Catherine's service and was master of the king's horse at 20 marks a year. In May 1434 he was among the lords and knights who came before the council to witness the reconciliation of Bedford and Gloucester.

The most likely explanation is that the young Catherine, upset at both the council's and Parliament's ban on her remarrying, decided to take a husband who was a not a threat to the great magnates. Owen possessed no rights to rank and property, so the threat of legal ruin meant very little. While it was thought that their marriage was contracted in secret, possibly while most of the court was abroad for her son's French coronation in Paris in 1431, from the evidence of John Steward it was far more likely to have been between June 1428 and November 1429. From 1430 the queen ceased to live with her son, and Edmund Tudor could have been born around September 1430, conceived in wedlock, and Jasper about eleven months later in August 1431. (Royal and noble women employed wet nurses, to enable a faster reproduction rate.) The households of Catherine and Henry VI became formally and financially separated in early 1431, never to be reunited. She described herself in letters as 'Catherine, queen of England, daughter of King Charles of France, mother of the king of England, and lady of Ireland', but now travelled on her own itinerary, joining the court only on ceremonial occasions. For Gloucester, Bedford and the great lords, it was a case of the less French influence in affairs the better, as they were in constant warfare with her brother, Dauphin Charles. With Catherine out of the king's household, it would have been easier for her to live with her children by Owen.

Back in France, by 1428 the English had approached Loire, having to cross the river to strike deep into the Dauphin's territory. However, first the strategic city of Orléans needed to be taken (its lord, Louis, was still in captivity after Agincourt). Thomas, Earl of Salisbury, besieged it in late September 1428, but in December was killed by debris lifted by a cannonball. Jeanne d'Arc, with others, lifted the Siege of Orléans on 29 May and destroyed the English army at Patay on 18 June 1429, with Talbot being captured. In July 1429, after a fast advance north-eastwards, when many towns had opened their gates to her army, Jeanne d'Arc brought the Dauphin to Reims for his coronation as king of France. With the French pushing further into English and Burgundian lands, the people of Reims had switched their allegiance, opening the city gates to the Dauphin for his coronation at the traditional place for kings of France. The twenty-six year-old Charles de Valois was crowned Charles VII in Reims upon 17 July 1429.

Meanwhile, in England, Henry VI had his coronation at Westminster Abbey on 6 November 1429. This early coronation was a response to defeats in France, and was suggested by Henry's English and French advisers. There had been widespread resentment at the course of the French wars, and Henry VI, not quite eight years old, was crowned at Westminster Abbey by his great-uncle Cardinal Henry Beaufort, Bishop of Winchester. Traditional English rites were modified to incorporate French practice, demonstrating to the nation that this was merely the precursor to the boy's coronation as King of France. Lydgate's poems were read to stress the king's dual inheritance of England and France, linking Henry to his grandfather Charles VI. In parallel, a painted pedigree showed Henry's descent through Catherine to St Louis. Cardinal Beaufort carried out the coronation. Every opportunity was taken, by the use of symbolism, to show Henry as the 'Enherytoure to the flowredelysse, the man Borne by dyscent and tytylle of ryght Justely to raygne in Ingelonde and yn Fraunce'.

Henry's English coronation had already been postponed for seven years, and after the Dauphin's coronation, Bedford now also strongly recommended a French coronation for Henry in Paris, to confirm his claim to the French crown. There was no longer any reason to further postpone either coronation until he came of age. Bedford believed that the king's coronation in Paris would cancel out the victories of Jeanne d'Arc, and the shock of the Dauphin being crowned. Military support was needed in France in the face of French advances, loans were raised, and in December 1429 Parliament voted subsidies to pay for 5,000 men to cross to France in 1430. Three bishops, John Stafford of Bath and Wells, William Alnwick of Norwich and Philip Morgan of Ely, once Chancellor of Normandy, accompanied Henry VI. Morgan's palace at Hatfield may soon have been occupied by Owen and Catherine.

On 23 April 1430, the nine-year-old Henry VI sailed from Sandwich to Calais, and in July moved to Rouen, the administrative centre of the English possessions in France. Allmand relates of the young king: 'He stayed at the castle [Calais] until July, when he moved to Rouen, the journey being undertaken by road with a large company of men-at-arms accompanying the King to ensure his safety.'

Once at Rouen he probably stayed at its castle, the administrative centre of the English dominion in France, where his uncle John, Duke of Bedford, Regent of France, resided with his staff. Probably on account of the very uncertain military situation in the Seine valley between Rouen and Paris, Henry was to stay in Rouen until November 1431, a period of some sixteen months.

A valuable source of information for part of his stay is the Household Book of the Earl of Warwick, which covers a year and four days from 15 March 1431. Each page of this volume gives a daily account of expenses, and is headed by a list of those who had dinner, and sometimes supper. The first name every day is that of 'Madame Talbot', Margaret, Warwick's eldest daughter, who was wife of John, Lord Talbot, later to be created 1st Earl of Shrewsbury and one of the outstanding military commanders of his day. The list of diners on Wednesday 14 March 1431 included two royal valets whose duty is revealed by the list for the next day, which describes them as being valets *corone regis*, probably guards for the crown that was to be used for the French coronation. There were some eight valets with this duty, and the daily list of diners includes them in varying numbers. Occasionally, as on 19 May 1431, the king came to dinner with the Earl of Warwick and others; he was always well escorted, and on this occasion came with sixty others.

On 24 May 1430, Jeanne d'Arc had been captured by the Burgundians at the Siege of Compiègne and handed over to the English. On 27 May 1431 a large company of guests, including many French and English nobles and important councillors, dined with Bedford, Regent of France, and the king, some of them having been involved in the trial of Jeanne d'Arc. Tried for heresy by a court composed of pro-English French clergy, she was burned at the stake on 30 May 1431 in the marketplace, just a few hundred yards away from the king's residence. Henry stayed in Rouen for sixteen months, until November 1431. The route to Paris now being open, Bedford having recovered the towns between Rouen and the capital that had gone over to the French, Henry was taken to Paris by Bedford and Warwick to be crowned. On 2 December 1431, Henry VI, riding a white horse, made his entry into Paris for his coronation on 16 December. Riding with him were the dukes of Bedford and York, the Earl of Warwick and a large company of nobles. Allmand relates:

Two aspects of the ceremony in particular emphasised the cult of monarchy. Henry rode a white horse (*une haquenée blanche*), a deliberate choice since white was often regarded as a symbol of sovereignty, which the king was now claiming in France. But perhaps even more significant was the use of the canopy to escort Henry once he had made his entry into Paris, and the emphasis placed upon such a canopy in the tableau of himself which had greeted him once he was in the capital. The use of such a canopy was a well-recognised mark of rank and honour, probably eastern in origin, certainly known to the era of the Roman Empire and to the Byzantine world of the end of the first millennium. By the end of the thirteenth century the social importance of a person might be judged by whether the bed on which he or she slept had a canopy or not. By the early years of the fourteenth century the canopy had become a necessary part of the bed of the *seigneurial* class, a symbol of *seigneurie* as well as of honour. In the course of the fourteenth century, in both England and France, with the growing popularity of the Corpus Christi procession during which the Host was carried under a decorated canopy, the idea of God's sovereignty over man had been increasingly widely expressed in this way. The practice was soon to be taken up and developed by those who wished to emphasise the power and authority of monarchy and its 'imperial' pretensions through the expressive use of symbols.

The actual ceremony took place at Notre Dame Cathedral on 16 December. The funds necessary for the coronation had to be advanced by the incredibly wealthy Cardinal Beaufort, a solid source of royal funding, and Beaufort insisted that he carry out the crowning. Reims was the traditional place of coronation but was occupied by the king's uncle, the former Dauphin, Charles VI. Paris, in the midst of winter, was depopulated and starving, and officials provided numerous splendid pageants in the streets. The events were meant to create an impression and revive French loyalty, but were ominously unpopular. Allmand writes:

After the ceremony, a great feast followed. But the organisation of it left much to be desired, and the food was said to be very poor, having been cooked three days before, 'which', one Parisian wrote, 'seemed very odd to the French'. [French dismay at English cuisine is nothing new.] Equally prone to contemporary criticism were the celebrations which followed the feast, condemned by the same Parisian as quite inadequate since they failed to bring to the tradespeople the profits which they had a right to expect. In spite of the welcome given to the King at a moment of considerable poverty and at a most unfavourable time of year, by the day he came to leave nobody, it was said, had a good word to say for him since neither he nor the English had given much in return. Perhaps not surprisingly Henry stayed little more than a week in Paris before setting out on the journey which was to bring him back to the French coast by way of Rouen and Abbeville.

The French coronation committed England to the military defence of Henry VI's right as King of France, but a major reason for his unpopularity over the years was the steady loss of French possessions in constant warfare that drained the country of scarce resources. Both Henry IV and Henry V had almost bankrupted the nation taking foreign loans to pay for war. (Indeed, most of Henry V's fleet had been sold off, and loans had to be raised to ship Henry VI to his French coronation.)

As discussed, in this period of twenty-one months of the king's absence, from April 1430 to February 1432, Catherine may well have given birth to both Edmund and Jasper without her son's knowledge. Equally, she may not have wished to attend the coronation as she would have seen her son crowned in opposition to her brother Charles. Finally, she may have been excluded on the grounds of her indiscretion in marrying a Welsh commoner who did not have the rights of an English citizen – it is unclear who knew what at this point.

Edmund was probably born at the Bishop of London's summer palace, outside the church in Much Hadham in Hertfordshire. Now called Much Hadham House, it was originally established as the home of the bishops of London before the Norman Conquest, and had become the home of Owen Tudor and Catherine of Valois. William Grey was Bishop of London from 1426, being translated to Lincoln on 30 April 1431. (His brother Sir Thomas had been executed in 1415 for his part in the Southampton Plot against Henry V.) Grey was a spiritual advisor to Catherine of Valois, and it is inconceivable that he did not know about the birth happening on his property. Grey was succeeded by Robert FitzHugh as Bishop of London from 1431 until his death in 1436. FitzHugh was a distinguished ambassador, civil servant, prelate, councillor and courtier he must have known the queen, or at least something about her private life. Only one nearly contemporary source has survived to give us information on the dowager queen's movements in this time: *Giles' Chronicle*. It may have been written by one of the masters of St Leonarde's Hospital in York, and Bishop FitzHugh held that post from 1415 until 1431.

It may be that Owen and Catherine did not wish their second child to be born at Hadham, and before FitzHugh took it over moved to the Bishop of Ely's palace at Hatfield, now called Bishop's Hatfield, also in Hertfordshire. The Welshman Philip Morgan was Bishop of Worcester from 1419 to 1426 and Bishop of Ely from 1426 until his death in 1435. Ely was among the smallest dioceses in terms of size or duties but was the fifth wealthiest see in England, a terrific reward for a trusted prelate. Here Jasper Tudor was born, probably in 1431, when Morgan was with the king's court in France. Owen and Catherine had deliberately chosen retreats independent of the main court that were run by servants dependent upon their local masters, in these latter cases the bishops of London and Ely. Like Bishops Grey and FitzHugh, Bishop Morgan of Ely and his servants kept quiet about the birth of Jasper. Loose-fitting clothing would have concealed Catherine's pregnancies, and was often used to disguise the birth of an illegitimate child. Almost certainly some of the main councillors, supporters of the Beauforts and enemies of Gloucester and York, knew of Catherine's pregnancies and her morganatic marriage, but until their later ennoblement the Tudor brothers were known as Edmund de Hadham and Jasper de Hatfield.

Like Bishop FitzHugh, Bishop Morgan will have known the queen since he had been Chancellor of Normandy and was an experienced diplomat and expert in French affairs. The Welshman had had held church offices in Aberedw, Llanfeugan, Abergwili and Llandegley. From 1414 onwards he was employed almost constantly upon foreign missions, playing a prominent part in peace negotiations with France. He could have conversed in Welsh with Owen Tudor, and was probably deep in the confidences of Owen and Catherine. He had been a Privy Councillor since 1419, and as a bishop he was unusually vigilant in putting down clerical abuses, which makes it virtually certain that he knew that the couple were legally married – he may even have been the one to officiate at the wedding. He died at Bishop's Hatfield on 25 October 1435.

John Ashdown-Hill, in *Royal Marriage Secrets*, claims that Edmund and Jasper Tudor were the sons of Edmund Beaufort. Following the death of her husband Henry V, Catherine of Valois was only twenty-one and was generally disliked for the simple reason of being French. Ashdown-Hill believes that the coats of arms of Edmund and Jasper, which owe nothing to the arms of Owen Tudor, were derived from the arms of Edmund Beaufort:

> The blue and gold bordures of Edmund and Jasper Tudor were simply versions of the blue and white bordure of Edmund Beaufort... The whole purpose of medieval heraldry was to show to the world who one was. And the coats of arms of Edmund and Jasper Tudor proclaimed, as clearly as they could, that these two 'Tudor' sons of the queen mother were of English royal blood, while their bordures suggest descent from Edmund Beaufort. The only possible explanation seems to be that Beaufort was their real father.

However, there is also a strong resemblance between the Tudor brothers' arms and that of their half-brother Henry VI. Also, the splendid website europeanheraldry.org states that both the Beaufort arms and the Tudor arms simply show their close relationship to the royal house. *Bordures* are a method of creating a new version of arms already used by a family (in this case the royal arms). There are also other ways of showing this, and the only fact that can be derived is that the people concerned are in some way related to the person who uses the full arms. 'The coincidence of the arms of the Beauforts and those of the Tudor earls has nothing whatever to do with any Beaufort connection. Richard II simply gave his half-brothers royal arms with augmentations, i.e. a border for difference. The *fleurs de lis* reflect their Valois blood and the martlet was a device used by Owen Tudor.'

In a proclamation of June 1485, Richard III described Henry Tudor as 'descended of bastard blood both of father side and of mother side, for the said Owen the grandfather was bastard born, and his mother was daughter unto John, Duke of Somerset, son unto John, Earl of Somerset, son unto Dame Katherine Swynford, and of their double adultery gotten'. There is no denial of the marriage between Owen and Catherine, and it is almost impossible to credit that the bishops of London and Ely would allow their palaces to be used for producing illegitimate children.

Colin Richmond repeats the theory of G. L. Harriss that Edmund Tudor may have been the child of Catherine of Valois and Edmund Beaufort, and that Catherine, to avoid the penalties of breaking the statute of 1427–28, secretly married Owen Tudor: 'By its very nature the evidence for Edmund "Tudor's" parentage is less than conclusive, but such facts as can be assembled permit the agreeable possibility that Edmund "Tudor" and Margaret Beaufort were first cousins and that the royal house of "Tudor" sprang in fact from Beauforts on both sides.'

It was certainly public knowledge that Beaufort had some sort of 'dalliance' with Catherine, often being seen in her company. The Lord Protector to the young king, Gloucester, knew that Beaufort being Henry VI's stepfather would weaken his own influence. The Beaufort family had a bitter and personal feud with both Gloucester and Richard of York. It is very doubtful that Beaufort would have risked everything – his life and estates – by making Catherine pregnant. Later, though, when Duke of Somerset in the 1450s, he was seen to have a psychological hold upon the 'child-like' Henry VI, which may date from his closeness to Catherine.

Richard III himself did not question the legitimacy of Henry Tudor, nor of his father Edmund; instead he proclaimed that 'the said rebels and traitors have chosen to be their captain one Henry Tydder, son of Edmund Tydder, son of Owen Tydder'. As Richard, in his short two-year reign, was the first English king to use propaganda to disparage his enemies, the Yorkists would have used claims of illegitimacy if they had reason to suspect it. Also, we have Owen Tudor's acknowledged illegitimate son, Sir David Owen, born in 1459. If Ashdown-Hill's theory was correct, and Edmund Beaufort fathered Jasper and Edmund, David Owen would have no ties to either Edmund or Jasper Tudor, but in his will David ordered masses for the souls of 'King Henry VII, Edmund, sometime Earl of Richmond, Jasper Duke of Bedford, my father and mother's souls, my wife's and all Christian souls'. Why would David Owen have remembered Edmund, who died before David Owen was born, if he was not his half-brother?

Owen and Catherine still stayed away from Henry's court, and probably had two more children. Their youngest son, Owen, was born at Westminster Abbey in 1432. Catherine was visiting the king at Westminster when her waters broke prematurely, forcing her to seek the help of the monks at the abbey. It may be this event that brought her marriage and children to the young king's knowledge. Their son Owen seems also to have been named Thomas or Edward Bridgewater, and was taken from Catherine and raised by the monks, according to Polydore Vergil. This 'Owen Tudder' became a monk, being given an award of £2 on 30 July 1498 out of his nephew Henry VII's Privy Purse. By 1501 this third son was dead, as the churchwardens of St Margaret's, Westminster, paid 6d for 'the knell of Owen Tuder with the bell'. On 18 June 1502, Morgan Kidwelly was paid £3 1s 2d 'for burying Owen Tudder'. A daughter of Owen and Catherine, variously called Jacina, Tacine, Tomasina, Jacinta or Pacina, is supposed to have married Reginald, 7th Baron Grey of Wilton (1421–93). Grey fought for the Yorkists at Towton and Mortimer's Cross. However, Jacina was probably an illegitimate daughter of John Beaufort, Duke of Somerset. John Beaufort was the father of Margaret Beaufort, the last in the royal line of that family, who married Owen's eldest son Edmund. There is mention of a daughter of Catherine and Owen whom Vergil states became a nun, but little is known of her.

By early February 1432 Henry VI was back in England, and he would never return to his French kingdom. Later in February he made his entry into London with ceremony not unlike that with which he had been greeted in Paris some weeks earlier. Allmand and Styles pick up the story:

Again the King was met by members of the London guilds, formally dressed. Whereas in Paris Henry had been greeted by the nine male and nine female worthies, the emphasis in London was to be upon figures representing the kingly virtues, strength (leading to victories over enemies) being prominent among them… In spite of the differences, seemingly similar ideas had been running through the minds of those who had designed the tableaux in the

King's two capitals. Henry was now something extraordinary, the twice-crowned king of two kingdoms, in theory united through him, in practice at war with each other. The coronation in Paris was to make the matter of peace and reconciliation between them difficult, if not impossible. Henry's long visit to France (in all it lasted over twenty-one months) at an impressionable age must have made him feel that he was the legitimate king of France, now formally received and crowned.

Certainly the coronation could and would be used to strengthen his legal claim, with the effect that in future English negotiators, when pressed to abandon Henry's title to the French crown, could point to the events of December 1431 and reply that they could not 'un-king' their king. Any concession which might be made by Henry or, worse still, by anyone acting on his behalf, had to take this fact into account. The coronation in Paris had made it almost impossible for the English to make any face-saving diplomatic concession. More than that, it committed them to the military defence of their king's right. As events were to prove, only a French re-conquest, achieved by force of arms, could effectively resolve the impasse once and for all.

Henry VI possibly learned about his half-brothers after his return from France in February 1432. 'Oweyn fitz Meredyth', his mother's new husband, was suddenly granted letters of denizenship in May 1432 by the ten-year-old king. This was a public and formal event, but it is unknown if it happened just before or during the parliament that met on 12 May. Leland believes that this was the occasion upon which Catherine presented Owen's 'noble pedigree' before the Lords in Parliament, 'the which thing was then approbate and taken for excuse of her marriage'. It may be at this time that the statute forbidding her marriage disappeared, no longer being considered valid, but there is also no record of its repeal. It seems odd that no comment was made at this time by Gloucester, who would have been informed of such an unusual occurrence. Henry IV's laws had limited the rights of Welshmen, and it was still illegal for a Welshman to own a property in England or to marry an Englishwoman, but fortunately for Owen Tudor he had married a Frenchwoman. Denizenship was granted by letters patent to give a status similar to today's 'permanent residency', a legal status giving most of a citizen's rights to an alien. It was only granted to high-ranking Welsh subjects who had proved their value to the crown in the wars against the French, but Owen was still barred from becoming a burgess, a freeman or representative of a borough. He was officially restricted from holding a crown office in any city, borough or market town, but was given permission to acquire land, bear arms, marry an Englishwoman and run a marital household.

Indeed, Owen was still denied several of the rights of a full citizen, which H. T. Evans thought rather mean on the part of the regency government:

In 1432 the franchise [denizenship] was bestowed upon Owen ap Meredith, who was probably the romantic Owen ap Meredith ap Tudor, better known as Owen Tudor. There is a forbidding leanness about this grant which betokens flagrant insincerity or intriguing suspicion. He could not become a citizen or a burgess, nor hold a Crown office in any city, borough, or market town. By a process of elimination we infer that he could bear arms, acquire land, intermarry, and serve on a jury. He might hold a household appointment, a fact of outstanding significance in his particular case. As we shall see, he was already the husband of Queen Catherine, though the fact was not generally known... Intermarriage with Welshmen was contrary to law, and Owen did not receive denizenship till 1432. The date of this grant, and the unusually stringent conditions attached to it, suggest that the marriage was known to a limited circle of courtiers who were not averse to shielding Owen while Catherine lived.

It was possibly around this time that Owen shed his old name, Owain ap Maredudd, and became known as Owen Tudor, or at least began to be unofficially referred to as this. We are unsure when it happened, but Catherine is thought to have established the lineage of her husband, and had it presented it to Parliament. John Leland (*c.* 1503–52), in his *Itinerary*, quotes a pedigree of Henry VII which was shown to him by Sir Thomas Brudenell of Deene in Northamptonshire. Leland records that 'this Linial Descent was shewid by thaforesaide Quene Catarine, and by her Counsel openly in the Kinges Courte of Parlement before the Lordes, the which thing was there probate and taken for excuse of her marriage'.

The father of Thomas, Sir Robert Brudenell (1461–1531), was a successful barrister, and by 1503 had attracted the favourable notice of Henry VII. He was a protégé of Lady Margaret Beaufort, and looked after the affairs of that king's mother. As a King's Serjeant, he worked with the king's inner group of councillors. In 1506 he was appointed judge to the King's Bench and became Lord Chief Justice of the Court of Common Pleas. On Henry VII's death he attended the crowning of Henry VIII, who knighted him in 1516/7, and he was sworn in as a Privy Councillor. Brudenell could well have had access to information about Margaret Beaufort's mother-in-law, Catherine of Valois.

As statute had forbade Catherine to marry without the consent of her son and she had done so, some doubts could have been cast on the legitimacy of the succession of her grandson Henry Tudor as Henry VII. This author's suspicions are that Henry VII ordered the statute's removal from the books, as he did with *Titulus Regius* in his second Act of Parliament upon his accession in 1485. *Titulus Regius* had ratified the bastardisation of Edward IV's children on the grounds of the invalidity of the marriage to Elizabeth Woodville, owing to a mythical pre-contracted marriage with Eleanor Butler. This was one of the devices by which Richard declared himself the true king, along with accusing his own mother of adultery, thereby accusing his brother Edward IV, and by extension his sons, of being illegitimate. However, Henry was not wary of legitimising Edward IV's sons, 'the princes in the Tower', as pretty much everybody believed they had already been killed by Richard III. The repeal also allowed Henry to marry their sister, Edward IV's eldest daughter, Elizabeth of York, now the legitimate heiress of the House of York. *Titulus Regius* has survived, but one of the first acts of Henry VII's reign had been to not only repeal it but to remove it from the statute book, with all copies to be destroyed under pain of punishment, 'so that all things said and remembered in the said Bill and Act thereof may be for ever out of remembrance and also forgot'. Henry wished to wipe out the dubious claim of the illegitimacy of his prospective wife as her legitimacy as the eldest heir of Edward IV served to strengthen his claim to the throne. Ricardians have described the attempt to eradicate all records of Richard's 'king's deed' as 'sinister', whereas some might see it as common sense.

The Tower Rolls show that Catherine procured for Owen a hundred marks a year, and Stowe says that he had much good land after, while the Recognizance Rolls of Chester give an entry showing that on 11 March 1434 Catherine granted Owen the wardship and marriage of the heir of John de Conway of Bodrhyddan in Flintshire, which was a valuable grant. Bodrhyddan Hall, near Dyserth, even now is in the hands of the Conway family, who supported Henry VII on his march through Wales in 1485. The grant of interests in the queen's lands in Flintshire reflected his family's ancient authority in North Wales. However, although Owen Tudor enjoyed a degree of protection from the law, his security was completely in the hands of his wife. She may have also given him presents of plate, as later silver to the value of £ 137 10*s* 4*d* was found in his possession.

Back on the Continent, Burgundy had now moved away from supporting England and was negotiating peace with Charles VII. Towards the end of 1434 the Duke of Burgundy wrote to Henry formally breaking the English alliance, and Henry is said to have cried when he read that he was no longer addressed as King of France. Riots broke out in London, and Flemish traders and merchants, the subjects of Burgundy, were hanged in the streets. Even the common people seemed to be aware that France would be lost without Burgundy's assistance. By 1434 the ailing Bedford, knowing that England did not have the resources to support the war in France, wished to negotiate an honourable peace, but he was blocked by his brother Gloucester, who bullied the Regency Council. He knew that Bedford's return to England would remove him from power, and the growing influence of the king's favourite, Suffolk, King's Steward since 1433, was also a cause of concern to him. Cardinal Beaufort and others on the council argued for a peace, but Gloucester was firm in the belief that England needed to follow the ambition of his brother Henry V and take France.

Bedford died in 1435, making Humphrey of Gloucester heir presumptive to the English throne. Gloucester also claimed the role of regent, previously occupied by his brother. Gloucester's claims were strongly contested by the lords of the king's council, and in particular his half-uncle Henry Beaufort. Henry V's will, rediscovered at Eton College in 1978, actually supported Gloucester's claims. Christie tells us:

> The proposals for peace were abandoned, Gloucester's proposition for the renewal of the war was carried in Parliament, and Bedford returned to his hopeless task in France. He never saw England again, for in the following year, worn out by his ceaseless labours, he died at Rouen on 15 September, 1435. By his death England lost her only able administrator, and the only man who could have hoped to quiet the factions that were so soon to play havoc in England. Gloucester and the other self-seeking statesmen who from time to time found themselves in power were left without a check, while the former now occupied the position of heir presumptive to his nephew the King.

There is little to relate about Owen's career at this time, but in 1436, when Edmund Tudor was six and Jasper was about five years of age, Catherine was again expecting a child. It seems that she realised that she was dying, possibly from cancer, and went to Bermondsey Abbey to be nursed by the sisters there. It was a Benedictine foundation on the south bank of the River Thames, directly opposite the Tower of London, that regularly helped the sick and wounded. Some sources state that she was forced to go there by Gloucester and allied members of the king's council, angered by her marriage. Strickland tells us:

> The only notice that occurs of Katherine from the third year of her infant's reign till 1436 is, that her son, then in his seventh year [1428], by the advice of his governess, Alice Boteler, presented his mother, for a New-year's gift,

with the ruby ring given him by his uncle, the duke of Bedford... 'The high spirit of the duke of Gloucester,' says one of our historians, 'could not brook her marriage; neither the beauty of Tudor's person, nor his genealogy deduced from Cadwallader kings, could shield him or the queen from a sharp persecution as soon as the match was discovered.' The children, to whom queen Katherine had previously given birth in secret, were torn from her by the orders of the council, and consigned to the keeping of a sister of the earl of Suffolk ...

Surely Gloucester knew of Catherine's marriage and children, but it seems unlikely that he would have moved against Owen while the king's mother was alive. If she died, Owen Tudor would be in serious trouble.

6

The Death of Catherine and the Imprisonment of Owen Tudor

1437–1444

By 1 January 1437, Catherine had written her will and given birth to a short-lived daughter, possibly named Margaret. In the will she spoke of her long illness:

Right high and mighty prince, and my full [re]doubted lord, and full entirely beloved son, in due humble wise, with full hearty natural blessing, I commend me to your highness. To the which please to be certified, that before the silent and fearful conclusion of this *long, grievous malady* [author's italics], in the which I have been long, and yet am, troubled and vexed by the visitation of God, (to whom be thanking and laud in all his gifts!) I purpose, by the grace of God, and under your succour, protection, and comfort, (in whom only, among all other earthly, stands all my trust) to ordain and dispose of my testament, both for my soul and my body.

And I trust fully, and am right sure that, among all creatures earthly, ye best may, and will best tender and favour my will, in ordaining for my soul and body, in seeing that my debts be paid and my servants guerdoned, and *in tender and favourable fulfilling of mine intent.*' [Author's italics: Strickland believes this is an allusion to Owen and her children, noting 'Here some intent, supposed to be known to the king, is implied – a mysterious clause evidently distinct from the previously enumerated portions of the sentence – viz, obituary and burial; paying her debts and rewarding her servants'. It refers in a guarded manner to an intent known only to her son, 'in tender and favourable fulfilling of mine intent' is thought to refer to her wishes which may have been revealed to him before her confinement in Bermondsey.]

Wherefore, tenderly I beseech you, by the reverence of God, and upon my full, hearty blessing, that to my perpetual comfort and health of soul and body, of your abundant and special grace (in full remedy of all means that in any wise may amnentise [impede] or deface the effect of my last purpose and intent) grant, at my humble prayer and request, to be my executor; and to depute and assign such persons to be under you or your servants, or of mine, or of both, as it shall like you to choose them, which I remit fully to your disposition and election. Beseeching you, also, at the reverence of our Lord God and the full entire blessing of me your mother, that, this done, ye tenderly and benignly grant my supplication and request, contained particularly in the articles ensuing. And if tender audience and favourable assent shall be given by so benign and merciful a lord and son to such a mother, being in [at] so piteous point of so grievous a malady, I remit to your full, high, wise, and noble discretion, and to the conscience of every creature that knoweth the laws of God and of nature that if the mother should have more favour than a strange person, I remit [refer or appeal] to the same.

Strickland believes the will to be an indication of her desire to protect Owen Tudor and her children by him:

From the perusal of this solemn exhortation, a conclusion would naturally be drawn that it was the preface to the earnest request of Katherine for mercy to her husband, and nurture for her motherless infants; yet the articles or items which follow contain not the slightest allusion to them. All her anxiety seems to be centred, – firstly, in the payment of her creditors, (without which she seems convinced that her soul will never get free); secondly, in obtaining many prayers and masses for her soul; and thirdly, in payments being made and rewards given to her servants. If Catherine, by this mysterious document, really made any provision for her helpless family, it is all comprised in the dark hints to her son of acting 'according to his noble discretion and her intents;' her real intent, perhaps, had been confided to the young king in some interview that had taken place previously to her imprisonment. There is no enumeration of property in the items that follow, excepting the portion of income due at the day of her departing. She declares that her soul 'shall pass as naked, as desolate, and as willing to be scourged, as the poorest soul God ever formed'. This piteous exhortation to her son was written, or dictated, a few hours before her death; yet, even at her last gasp, she evidently dared not break regal etiquette so far as to name to her son her plebeian lord, or her young children. Whilst this pathetic document was in course of preparation, the dying queen received a token of remembrance from her son, on New Year's Day, consisting of a tablet of gold, weighing thirteen ounces, on which was a crucifix set with pearls and sapphires: it was bought off John Pattesby, goldsmith, and was sent to Catherine at Bermondsey.

Lloyd-Williams relates that:

There is a letter from Katherine to Henry among the Cotton MSS. begging him to come and see her and a copy of her will. But she does not dare to mention her husband or children except in vague terms as to her son's 'fulfilling mine intent' and a prayer that he would either act as her executor himself or appoint one of his or her servants, perhaps indicating her husband. Henry could do nothing. Gloucester and Cardinal Beaufort acted as executors when Katherine a very short time after this died and was buried, as the chroniclers tell us, at Westminster, having been taken thence from 'Powlys' [St Paul's] and laid in a tomb of marble.

In Bentley's list of the New Year's gifts presented by Henry VI in 1437 is a present to his mother, who died three days later, followed by gifts to the queen consort Joan of Navarre and other nobility:

First, delivered by your gracious commandment and appointment to send to Quene Katine for her yerisgifte [year's gift] on New Year's day, she being at Bermondsey, 1 tabulett of gold with a crucifixe garnized with sapphire and pt weighing about xiv ounces of gold, and was bought of John Patteslee goldesmyth for the sum of x pounds... Item, delivered by your said commandment to send to Quene Jane for her yerisgyfte, she being at Langeley, on that same day, a tabulett of gold garnized with iv bat viii pt and in ye midst a great sapphire of entaille weighing vi ounces i qrt'n di, the which tabulett some time was given the Kynge by my lady of Gloucestre.

Henry then gave presents in the following order to Cardinal Beaufort at his palace in Esher; 'the Duke of Gloucester at Greenwich; the Duchess of Gloucester; the Earl of Warwick in Wales; Warwick's mother Lady

Stafford; the Bishop of Norwich, being with the king at Estham; his dean Richard Peaty; his wardrober Robert Rolleston; etc.' Finally, tragedy struck. Holinshed tells us that:

About this season, queen Katherine, mother to the king of England, departed out of this life & was buried by her husband, in the abbey of Westminster. This woman, after the death of king Henry the fifth her husband, being young and lusty, following more her own wanton appetite than friendly counsel, and regarding more private affection than princelike honour, took to husband privily, a gallant gentleman, and a right beautiful person, endowed with many goodly gifts, both of body and mind, called Owen Teuther, a man descended of the noble lineage and ancient line of Cadwallader, last king of the Britons. By this Owen she brought forth three goodly sons, Edmund, Jasper, and another that was a monk in Westminster, and lived a small time; also a daughter, which in her youth departed out of this transitory life. King Henry, after the death of his mother, because, they were his brethren of one womb descended, created Edmond, earl of Richmond, and Jasper, earl of Pembroke: which Edmond of Margaret, daughter and sole heir to John, duke of Somerset, begat Henry, which after was king of this realm, called king Henry the seventh, of whom you shall hear more in a place convenient. This Owen, after the death of the queen his wife, was apprehended and committed to ward, because that (contrary to the statute made in the 6th year of this king), he presumptuously had married the Queen, without the king's especial assent, out of which prison he escaped, and let out other out with him, and was again apprehended, and after escaped again. Polychronicon saith that he was a squire of low birth and like degree, the same author also reported that he was commanded to Newgate by the duke of Gloucester then lord protector of this realm; out of which prison he broke by the help of a priest that was his chaplain. Nevertheless he was apprehended afterwards by the lord Beaumont and brought again to Newgate, whence (when he had remained there for a while) he was delivered and set at liberty.

Catherine of Valois died on 3 January 1437. When the news was brought to Henry VI, then just fifteen years old, he was on his throne presiding in Parliament. Henry Beaufort, Bishop of Winchester, and Humphrey, Duke of Gloucester, were the executors of Catherine's will. From Bermondsey Abbey, near Southwark Cathedral, her body was taken along the Thames to the church of her patroness, the Collegiate Church of St Catherine, near the Tower of London. On 8 February her funeral procession passed through London from St Catherine's to St Paul's Cathedral. Her hearse was draped with red cloth of gold, stitched with golden flowers, on top of which lay her wooden effigy, dressed in a mantle of purple satin. Its head was painted with blue eyes and red lips, surmounted with real light-brown hair, and bore a crown of silver gilt. Its arms crossed the body, holding a royal sceptre. Catherine lay in state at St Paul's until 18 February, and was then taken to Westminster Abbey. Her coffin was carried under a canopy of black velvet, hung with bells that tinkled as it moved. Catherine was buried in the Lady chapel, close to the tomb of Henry V. We have no knowledge as to whether Owen attended or watched his wife's funeral. He may have been imprisoned; he may have been trying to flee London. Perhaps he had been told that he was in danger and was preparing to ride to Wales.

The inscription around the ledge of the tomb platform of Henry V can be translated as: 'Henry V, hammer of the Gauls, lies here. Henry was put in the urn 1422. Virtue conquers all. The fair Catherine finally joined her husband 1437. Flee idleness.' Henry VI erected an altar-tomb to his mother's memory, upon which was engraved a Latin epitaph. The long monumental inscription, once on the tomb of William de Valence, half-brother to Henry III, is also given by Camden, and Keepe says it was around the verge of the tomb. It is preserved in the *Annales rerum Anglicarum* of William of Worcester (*c.* 1415–*c.* 1482), which Strickland translated thus:

> Death, daring spoiler of the world, has laid
> Within this tomb the noble clay that shrined
> Queen Katherine's soul; from the French king derived
> Of our fifth Henry, wife; of the sixth
> Henry, mother: – as maid and widow both,
> A perfect flower of modesty esteemed.
> Here, happy England, brought she forth that king,
> On whose auspicious life thy weal depends.
> And reft [bereft] of whom, thy bliss would soon decay.
> Joy of this land, and brightness of her own,
> Glory of mothers, to her people dear,
> A follower sincere of the true faith;
> Heaven and our earth combine alike to praise
> This woman, who adorns them both e'en now, –
> Earth, by her offspring; by her virtues heaven!
> In the fourteen hundred thirty-seventh year.
> First month's third day, her life drew to its close,
> And this queen's soul, beyond the starry sphere
> In heaven received, for aye reigns blissfully.

Strickland tells us that 'when the peculiar circumstances of Katherine's second wedlock are considered, the epitaph becomes of no little importance, for, instead of acknowledging, it tacitly denies her second marriage'. She believes that 'this original epitaph ... implied the fact that Katherine died a widow, and not a wife ... it occasioned the demolition of the tomb under the reign of her grandson [Henry VII]'. However, Henry VII did not 'demolish' her tomb, as we shall see later.

Mottley's edition of *Stowe's London* relates an epitaph written by the poet John Skelton (*c.* 1463–1529) in the time of Henry VIII. The capitalisations and italics of the poet Skelton (also known as Shelton) have not been altered. A tutor to the young Henry VIII, he referred to himself as the poet laureate:

Some Years later when her Grandson King *Henry* VII pulled down that [the Lady Chapel] in order to build a sumptuous Chapel, her Body was taken up, and the Coffin being decay'd, it was put in a wooden Chest, and placed near her Husband's Tomb at the East End of the Fryars (as *Stow* calls it) where it has ever since continued to be seen, the Bones being firmly united, and thinly cloth'd with Flesh, like Scrapings of tanned Leather; a view fit to us to represent the End of Beauty, Greatness, and what else sublunary things we boast. Near which Chest, on a Tablet, *Latin* Verses were formerly legible, written in King *Henry* VIII's Time, and, as it is supposed, by *Skelton*. And on the same Table, these wretched Rhimes, by way of Translation [the verses no longer exist]:

> Here lies Queen Katherine, clos'd in Grave,
> The *French* King's daughter fair;
> And of thy kingdom *Charles* the Sixth,
> The true redoubted Heir.

> Twice joyful Wife in Marriage match'd [in London and Paris],
> To Henry Fifth by name;
> Because thro' her he Nobled was,
> And shin'd in double Fame [as King of both England and France].

> The King of *England* by Descent
> And by Queen KATHERINE'S Right;
> The Realm of *France* he did enjoy,
> Triumphant King of Might.

A happy Queen to *English* Men,
She came right grateful here
And four days Space they honour'd GOD
With Mouth and reverend Fear.

HENRY the Sixth this Queen brought forth
In painful Labours plight,
In whose Empire a *French* Man was,
And eke an *English* Wight.

Under no lucky Planet borne,
Unto Himself nor Throne;
But equal to his Parents both,
In pure Religion.

Of *Owen Tiddor* after this,
Thy next Son *Edmund* was,
Oh KATHERINE! a renowned Prince
That did in Glory pass.

HENRY the Seventh, a *Britain* Pearle,
A Gem of *England's* Joy,
A Peerless Prince was *Edmund's* Son,
A good and gracious Roy [king].

Therefore a happy Wife this was,
A happy Mother pure;
Thrice happy Child, but Grandam she,
More than thrice happy sure.

Catherine's wooden effigy still survives, now dressed only in her painted red undergarment, and was for many years in the Undercroft Museum at Westminster Abbey. It will go back on display when the Jubilee Galleries open in 2018. However, Henry VII disinterred his grandmother from the Lady chapel during extensions to build his wife Elizabeth's tomb and his own. Her body, loosely wrapped in lead from the chapel roof, was placed near Henry V's tomb monument, intended as a temporary arrangement as the chapel was not completed until his death. Indeed, Henry VII had given Catherine's presence in the Lady chapel as a major reason for choosing to be buried there. Some modern historians have written that he deliberately desecrated her tomb in order to hide his humble Tudor origins in their continuing attempts to blacken his reputation. This 'destruction' described by Strickland and others has passed into anti-Tudor lore, but the facts are that his orders were ignored by his son Henry VIII. Like the spectacular King's College Chapel built by Henry VI and Henry VII at Cambridge, work upon Westminster's Lady chapel, now known as the Henry VII Chapel, was nowhere near complete upon the deeply religious Henry VII's early death in 1509, and was only finished in 1526.

Work had begun on the chapel in January 1503. It was intended to be a shrine for Henry VI, whom the king wished to have canonised. Henry VI was not elevated to the sainthood, however, so Henry and his wife were interred in the tomb instead. Henry VII also wished to build a more glorious chapel to the Virgin Mary, and a royal mausoleum for his new dynasty. He would have felt that such a building at Westminster Abbey would enhance the legitimacy of his heirs. Henry spent more than £14,000 on its construction between 1503 and his death in 1509, and allocated more funds for its completion after his death, the final cost being around £20,000. With the chapel incomplete on his death, he was not around to ensure Catherine's body was properly interred. His own tomb was not begun until 1512, three years after his death, and the altar was built between 1517 and 1526, but like the chapel's stained glass it was destroyed by Puritans during the Restoration of the Monarchy.

For two hundred years after her death Catherine of Valois lay in a coffin above ground, covered by loose boards which exposed her embalmed body from the waist up. Her corpse became a tourist attraction. On 23 March 1669 the diarist Samuel Pepys kissed the long-deceased queen:

> Up; and to the Office, where [I worked] all the morning, and put a mouthful of victuals in my mouth; and by a hackney-coach followed my wife and the girls, who are gone by eleven o'clock, thinking to have seen a new play at the Duke of York's house. But I do find them staying at my tailor's, the play not being today, and therefore to Westminster Abbey, and there did see all the tombs very finely, having one with us alone, it being Shrove Tuesday; and here did we see, by particular favour, the body of Queen Katherine of Valois; and I had the upper part of the body in my hands, and I did kiss her mouth, reflecting upon it I did kiss a Queen: and this my birthday and I thirty-six years old, that I did kiss a Queen.

During the eighteenth century her body was still exposed, being described as 'thinly clothed, with flesh like scrapings of tanned leather'.

Catherine's body was eventually buried in 1778 in a vault, and in 1878 Dean Stanley removed her remains for permanent burial under the altar in Henry V's Chantry Chapel. The inscription for her on this altar reads: 'Under this slab (once the altar of this chapel) for long cast down and broken up by fire, rest at last, after various vicissitudes, finally deposited here by command of Queen Victoria, the bones of Catherine of Valois, daughter of Charles VI, King of France, wife of Henry V, mother of Henry VI, grandmother of Henry VII, born 1400, crowned 1421, died 1438.' Her death date is a year late in the inscription. Henry V's Chantry Chapel is above the king's tomb at the east end of the abbey and is not open to the public, but special tours were available in 2015, on the anniversary of Agincourt. It was built on the orders of Henry V within the shrine of Edward the Confessor, and is one of the smallest of the abbey's many chapels, measuring about 23 by 10 feet. Entrance to the chapel is via narrow spiral staircases of uneven steps, worn down through centuries of use. Henry's tomb had an effigy head, hands, sceptres and other regalia, all made of silver, with silver-gilt plates covering the figure of the king. Catherine of Valois made the major contribution to the costs. Some ornaments were stolen between 1467 and 1479, and all the rest of the silver was stolen in 1546. In 1971 a new head, hands and a crown for the effigy were modelled in polyester resin. The saddle, helmet, sword and shield of Henry V, which once formed part of his funeral 'achievements', will be displayed in the new Westminster Abbey Museum. They were carried at his funeral in 1422 and later suspended on the wooden beam above the Henry V Chantry Chapel until 1972, so were too difficult to steal.

With Catherine dead, Owen was in trouble. He had only been safe while the queen was alive to shield him. His stepson Henry VI was not to come of age until 6 December 1437, at which point he could form a king's council. Until this time, the Regency Council would effectively rule the nation, and it was dominated by Gloucester.

Lloyd-Williams cannot believe that Gloucester only found out about Catherine's marriage upon her death, and again brings up the intriguing prospect of Owen and Bedford knowing each other, probably from Owen's service in France: 'The Duke of Bedford seems to have been Owen's protector. He himself had married for love, and slightly beneath him, when he married Jacquetta of Luxembourg, and while he lived Katherine and her husband were at peace.' However, the extremely capable and loyal Bedford had died fifteen months before Catherine of Valois. Without his restraining influence, Gloucester saw himself as the leading man in England after his nephew the king. The Regency Council, led by Gloucester, probably mistrusted the Welsh commoner, and, lacking estates or wealth, he was at the mercy of the great lords.

Regardless of who pursued Owen Tudor and when, is clear that after his wife's death he had packed all his belongings, most of them gifts from Catherine, and headed to Anglesey by the fastest route out of London. After all, he had married the dowager queen in violation of a recent parliamentary statute and fathered half-blood relatives of the king.

Finding Owen had fled London, Gloucester despatched men led by his servant Myles Sculle to quickly capture and return Owen to the capital. (One wonders whether Myles Sculle was Robert Lord Willoughby of Eresby, who succeeded to the barony in 1409 and died in 1452. His badge of 'the Mill Sail', or rather mill rind, was derived from his ancestors the Beks of Eresby.) Owen had reached Daventry in Warwickshire, riding along Watling Street, still the quickest route from London to North Wales, when the council's messengers caught up with him, 70 miles north-west of London.

Owen was handed a summons to the royal palace of Westminster to appear before the Regency Council, with Gloucester's assurance, delivered by Sculle, that he should 'freely come and freely goo' (as recorded in the council's proceedings of 15 July 1537). However, Owen refused to accept the validity of this verbal promise of safe conduct from Gloucester's servant. He refused to come, 'saying that the said grant so made sufficed him not for his surety, less than it were sent him in writing'. Owen was rightly suspicious of Gloucester's motives. He also stated that he 'would not so come without that it were granted and promised him on the king's behalf that he should more freely come and freely go'. Gloucester reminded the king that Owen had committed a felony, 'to mix his own blood with the royal blood of kings'. We are informed by Strickland that 'the high spirit of the Duke of Gloucester could not brook her [Catherine's] marriage. Neither the beauty of Tudor's person nor his genealogy, descended from Cadwallader Kings, could shield him or the Queen from sharp persecution as soon as the match was discovered.'

The reluctant Owen was eventually escorted to London, but he headed immediately into sanctuary at Westminster, where the monks had brought up his third son Owen since 1432. He stayed there 'many days, eschewing to come out thereof', although 'divers persons assured him of friendship and fellowship to have come out'. Unsuccessful efforts were made to entrap him by trying to induce him into a tavern nearby, and several weeks passed before Owen decided to leave sanctuary to defend himself before the council. He had discovered that Henry VI was 'evilly informed of him' by his councillors, and that reports of disloyalty were being circulated against him, forcing him to come out of sanctuary. Henry was now almost sixteen, and Owen realised that the king might make his own decisions, overruling Gloucester.

The meeting with the king and council took place in the Chapel Chamber in Kennington Palace on 15 July 1537. Present were Tudor's enemy Humphrey, Duke of Gloucester; William de la Pole, Earl of Suffolk; John Stafford, Bishop of Bath; John Kemp, Archbishop of York; William Alnwick, Bishop of Lincoln; Henry Percy, 2nd Earl of Northumberland; Lord Walter Hungerford; Sir John Lord Tiptoft, Treasurer of England and Keeper of the Privy Seal; and Sir William Philip, Privy Councillor and King's Chamberlain.

Owen took the offensive, boldly protesting that he had done nothing to offend the king, and declared his willingness to 'byde the law'. It appears that the king bore no hostility towards his stepfather but that events had been stage-managed by Gloucester. However, Hungerford was Owen's former employer, and had been Steward of the King's Household from 1417 to 1421 and 1424 to 1426, and may well have argued his case. He had fought at the siege of Harfleur, had been with Henry V at Agincourt and had been as a guardian to his son, now the king. He had probably also accompanied Henry V back to England for the coronation of Catherine of Valois, and this is when Owen may first have met the queen. Hungerford had been a member of the Regency Council from 1422, and would later become a member of the King's Council from 1437 until his death in 1449.

Owen Tudor must have been nervous, appearing before the king and the greatest lords in the land. The record of Owen's meeting with his stepson and the council opens thus: 'The King not longe agoo, that is to say soon after ye deeth of (noble memoir) Quene Katherine his moder whom God assoille [her soul] desired, willed that on Oweyn Tidr the which dwelled with the saide Quene sholde come to his presence...'

This seems to be one of the first times that Owen was addressed with the surname of his grandfather. It was fairly obvious that 'Oweyn Tidr' had lived with Catherine of Valois for at least the last ten years, since around 1427, and that the members of the council would have known this, despite some believing that Gloucester did not know about it. Owen's response was that he had done no wrong, and that he was the king's 'true liege man' no matter what any man should say against him. This seems to be a calculated attack upon Gloucester taking him to London. Owen would have known that some members of the council, such as Suffolk, were enemies of Gloucester, and that Henry VI and Hungerford would not be overly happy to see Owen imprisoned. Would the fifteen-year-old Henry VI want to imprison the man who had been his stepfather for ten years? To do so would place a stigma on his stepbrothers, the only close family he possessed except his uncle

Gloucester. Owen pleaded in front of the king (spellings modernised): 'He affirmed and declared his Innocence and his truth, affirming that he had no thing done that should give the king occasion or matter of offence or displeasure against him, offering himself in large ways to answer as the king's true liege man should to all things that any man could or would submit upon him or say to him.'

Some writers believe that Owen was in Newgate before his council trial. Wherever he was held, he was released, probably because of the wishes of Henry VI. At this time, any deadlock in council could be decided by the king. The only condition was that Owen would appear before the king whenever summoned. He pledged to do so, and was promised a safe conduct to return to Wales. Owen gathered what few portable possessions he could take on horseback and left, but was soon arrested in Wales on the spurious grounds that he had broken the king's safe conduct. However, Owen had never accepted the safe conduct, so could not have broken it. Nevertheless, he was thrown into Newgate (probably for the second time) with his servant and priest. Robin Ddu publicly admonished those responsible for the imprisonment and called Owen 'neither a thief nor a robber; he is the victim of unrighteous wrath. His only fault was to have won the affection of a princess of France.' On 19 August 1437 Gloucester was granted the king's 'declaration of his worship', and found innocent of breaching any verbal promise of safe conduct he had made to Owen despite this having been broken by his imprisonment in Newgate.

Along the great walls of London were several gates: Aldgate, Bishopsgate, Moorgate, Cripplegate, Aldersgate, Newgate and Ludgate. Two of the gates, Ludgate and Newgate, were used as prisons. Furthermore, the body parts of traitors who had been hanged, drawn and quartered were displayed over the gates as a warning. The wealthy gentleman-poet Ieuan Gethin's contemporaneous poem opens with a complaint that Owen is imprisoned in London (Caer-ludd), and specifically at Newgate (Niwgad), 'where he is chained to the wall'. It is unknown whether Ieuan Gethin was informed by his aristocratic connections, but according to fourteenth- and fifteenth-century sources, all prisoners held at Newgate 'wore irons unless they could afford to pay for the privilege of going without them'. Ieuan Gethin would have known of the circumstances of Owen's imprisonment, and possibly writes that he was chained for dramatic effect. As Owen was later placed in Newgate again, it could have been either imprisonment he is referring to. As an alien Welshman, Owen had absolutely no rights at this time and could well have been treated more harshly than his status as the husband of a queen deserved.

Owen notes:

Ieuan Gethin does not understand why Owain has been arrested, let alone imprisoned: Owain, he maintains, has not been accused of theft or treason, he has not stolen a horse and has no debts, indeed he can see no legal reason for Owain's apprehension. His crime, quite simply, was that 'on a feast day, he fell in love ... with the daughter of the king of the land of wine'. But Owain did not take advantage of the queen, because she was completely in accord with his feelings, and furthermore there had been no sexual relationship between them before her first husband had died and also they had married. The fact that God had subsequently blessed them with children proved the validity of the union. Ieuan Gethin does not reveal directly who he believes arrested Owain, but at the end of the poem he appeals directly to the Duke of Gloucester for his release, wisely dedicating a few lines of praise for the duke, the 'splendid black stag' Is it likely that Ieuan recognised the duke's hand in this. With the aid of his priest and servant, he made his first escape from that prison, presumably heading to relative safety with relatives in Gwynedd and Anglesey, until he felt safe.

Extortion was rife in the prison, with gaolers supplementing their meagre incomes by charging an extortionate price for privileges and even basic comforts such as food, bedding and candles. Nobles were usually kept in confinement in far better conditions in the Tower of London, with their own apartments, but in Newgate there were very few decent rooms with lavatories and chimneys. For prisoners who could afford the necessary bribes, they had access to a chapel and a flat roof above the main gate, where exercise could be taken. However, most parts of the prison, the dungeons known as the 'less convenient chambers', were unlit, cramped and full of rats and diseases. No one drank London water, so the prisoners were given a ration of 'small beer' (weakened ale, given to the old and children) to survive.

Underground water channels, along with Newgate's close proximity to the open 'City ditch', the main sewer, caused a noxious stench, which became far worse in times of dry weather and drought. In 1419 Ludgate Prison was closed and the prisoners moved to Newgate after its status as a prison for freemen was invalidated by the admission of 'false persons of bad disposition'. Christine Winter tells us that 'within months of the relocation many of the transferred prisoners had died, their deaths blamed on the "fetid and corrupt atmosphere" at Newgate, and Ludgate was reinstated as a prison'.

A light on the condition of Newgate around this time is given by an entry in the City of London records that Richard Whittington (c. 1354–1423), the moneylender and mayor of London in 1397, 1406 and 1419, recommended the restoration of the debtors' prison at Ludgate. In his will he left monies to rebuild Newgate. Gaol-fever (typhus) was rife in the prison, as would have been the flux (dysentery), cholera and smallpox.

Newgate was in a decrepit state, and in May 1423 Whittington's executors were granted permission to demolish both the existing gaol and gate and erect a new gaol. However, it was not long before the prison was again being described as having 'fallen into disrepair', with the security of the prison perhaps being compromised. Peter Ackroyd, in *London: The Biography*, states that Newgate was 'almost from its beginning, an emblem of death and suffering … a legendary place, where the very stones were considered "deathlike" … it became associated with hell, and its smell permeated the streets and houses beside it'. With its overcrowded squalor, lice-ridden dungeons and corrupt and sadistic governors and keepers, many prisoners did not even make trial. By the mid-fifteenth century, Newgate accommodated roughly 300 prisoners.

Leaving Owen in prison for the time being, matters for his stepson Henry VI had deteriorated rapidly. The council was so divided that it could no longer rule effectively, with Suffolk and Henry Beaufort leading a faction committed to peace with France. Beaufort hoped that with peace he could start retrieving some of the loans he had made towards the wars. There was inefficiency and corruption in government across the kingdom, and this was feeding growing unrest. Henry VI was in effect bankrupted by the war, and by the end of 1437 owed £164,815 to his creditors, with no savings to fall back upon. His annual income was only £75,000. As king, if he was insolvent there would be unrest and he would be deposed. Edward I had advoided his debt problems twice by simply refusing to repay foreign loans (making foreign banks and lenders wary of financing English kings), but nearly all of Henry VI's debt was internal.

In France, York had driven the French from Normandy with the help of John Talbot, Earl of Shrewsbury, who had fought with his brother Gilbert from 1404 against Glyndŵr. Shrewsbury was widely acknowledged as Henry VI's finest general in France. However, York had refused council's request for him to stay in France from April 1437 as the government could not pay the monies it owed him, and he simply could not afford to go further into debt. York actually had to ask his own tenants for loans.

The king was almost sixteen in November 1437, when he officially assumed his royal powers, but he had begun to take a positive role in government before this date. Apart from tantrums noted by his governor Warwick, there seemed to be no hint of the later mental instability that would lead to his catastrophic decline in 1453. According to the *Polychronicon*, Owen was committed to Newgate by Gloucester as Protector, and it was from there that Owen, his priest and servant escaped in January or early February 1438.

Owen was known to be tall and strong, and with his priest and a servant, says the *London Chronicle*, 'he brak out of Newgate ayens nyght at serchynge tyme and went his wey hurtynge foule his kepere'. However, they were quickly recaptured by John, 6th Baron Beaumont, with the aid of Thomas Darwent. On 24 February, Lord Beaumont paid to the Exchequer £89 which he had found on Owen Tudor's priest.

The three prisoners were committed to Newgate again in March 1438, but it is noticeable that there was no suggestion of putting Owen to death. Apart from Beaumont being well rewarded for capturing Owen, his lieutenant Thomas Darwent was granted the office of porter at Pontefract Castle for life, with a daily wage of 4*d*.

The inventory taken from Owen, mainly silverware, revealed just some of the wealth that he had been able to accumulate, probably given by Catherine, including 'first a douszein gilt cuppes chased writhen', valued at £32 3*s* 4*d*. Owen also possessed 'an olden lowe gilt guppe covered', a gilt chalice, six enamelled silver salt-cellars, a silver ewer, various silver cups and flagons, several candlesticks and basins, two spice-plates and 'a paxbrede of silver and gilt with an ymage of Seynt Cristofre'. (A 'pax-board' or 'paxbrede' was a small plaque of metal, ivory or wood, generally decorated with a pious carving and provided with a handle, which was first brought to the altar for the celebrant to kiss at the proper place in the Mass and then brought to each of the congregation in turn at the altar rails. Perhaps these were claimed to be Church items, in the possession of Owen when he tried to escape.) Several of the pieces were broken, possibly to fit into saddlebags, and the whole collection was valued at the considerable sum of £137 10*s* 4*d*. Perhaps there had been an accusation that this had belonged to the crown via Henry V's widow, Catherine. Goods and jewels which had belonged to Owen, presumably seized at the time of his arrest, were not handed into the Treasury until 15 July 1438 by William Milrede, mercer, sheriff, MP and alderman of the City of London. One week later, on 21 July 1438, possessions were all handed over by the Treasury to William Estfield of London, one of the many creditors of the government. On 26 November 1438, however, Estfield bought the silverware from the government for the same sum, presumably another 'loan' to the king, and the Treasurer was ordered to deliver the money to John Kemp, Archbishop f York (later of Canterbury) for his expenses in going on the king's business to Calais.

Owen was now handed over to the Earl of Suffolk to keep safely and surely 'at our Castle of Wallingford', his priest and servant with him. It was a place Owen knew well, as it had been one of Catherine's possessions. Strickland tells us:

> The lord constable of England, Beaumont, was paid twenty marks [£13 6s 8d] for the expenses he had incurred in catching and keeping Owen, his priest, and servant. The place where the privy council met to arrange this business is rather remarkable; it was transacted in the secret chamber belonging to cardinal Beaufort as bishop of Winchester, in the priory of St Mary's Overy. There were present, in this secret conclave, the lord cardinal [Henry Beaufort], the lord chancellor [John Stafford, Bishop of Bath and Wells, later Lord Chancellor], the earl of Suffolk [William de la Pole], the treasurer, Lord Hungerford, and John Stourton, knight [Baron Stourton was to fight in France and become Treasurer].

Leland wrote that 'it was the pride of the king's uncles alone which sought to cast scorn on Owen's birth' and that 'Owen escaped by aid of the priest'. There is a curious secrecy surrounding this affair, but Gloucester's absence may explain it. Hungerford, Beaufort and Suffolk, the latter two committed enemies of Gloucester, will have probably been friendly to Tudor, and the other two members of the panel were staunch in their support of Henry VI.

Paul Remfry has translated some findings of the meeting as recorded in *Rymer's Foedera*:

> Concerning the escape and recapture of Owain ap Tudor.
> Henry &c. to, our dear and loyal cousin, the Lord Beaumont, Salutations. We wish, of the advice and assent of our council, that the guard of Owen Tudor who recently Escaped out of our Newgate prison, after which escape he was taken and brought for you to guard at our pleasure, the which Owen by our commandment you have delivered to our council, & by the advice of the same you have delivered to our treasurer and loyal cousin the Earl of Suffolk, constable of our castle at Wallingford, for him to safely and securely guard within our castle, and also of the guarding of the priest and servant of the said Owen, who had assisted in his said escape, and likewise put with him and bring to you

for guarding, which we command you to deliver before our council and for advice and instruction of them, deliver to our sheriff of our city of London for the safe and secure guarding within our prison of Newgate, you are discharged and quit towards us for all days, in addition, we command you and yours that the eighty and nine pounds, which was found with the said priest, which you have in your hand, you may take them by indenture, deliver through our Treasurer and Chamberlains of our Exchequer, by which indentures and through these we wish that, of the region of the Somme, you will not be discharged to us through all our days.

Donn. &c.

Apart from the noted handing over of the £89 found on Tudor's priest, there is also mention of the payment of 20 marks to Beaumont:

Henry, the treasurer and chamberlains etc, greetings.
We wish, with the advice and assent of our council, and order you that, for the charges, costs and expenses, which, our dear and loyal cousin, the lord of Beaumont to sustain for the guarding and also the conducting to our council of Owain ap Tudor, the prisoner taking to our prison of Newgate, out of which he Escaped and was taken through the love of our said cousin, and also for the guarding and conducting to our said council of the priest and servant of the said Owain, who were knowing and consenting of the escape of the said Owain, you must pay our Cousin from our Treasury, 20 marks, to have for the Causes above.

Given etc Dorset [is this Edmund Beaufort, Earl of Dorset?], 25 day of March, in our 16 year [of rule] in the *secret* [author's italics] room of the lord Cardinal, in the priory of St Mary of Overhey, London. Conceded and agreed through the lords of the king's council, who were all there by the warrant of the Lord Beaumont and the treasurer and chamberlain, according to the tenor of the underwritten. Then present there – Lord Cardinal and Lord temporal, [Henry Beaufort], Lord Chancellor [John Stafford, later Archbishop of Canterbury], the Earl of Suffolk, Treasurer [Ralph de Cromwell], Hungerford, and Sir John Stourton.

Baron Cromwell (*c.* 1393–1456) is surprisingly missing from accounts of this secret meeting, but he was Treasurer of England from 1422 to 1443, with a one-year gap in 1432–33 owing to Gloucester's enmity before Bedford returned from France and restored him. From 1433 he was paid 200 marks annually for attendance at council. In 1443 he resigned the post to become Chamberlain of the Exchequer until 1455. He was also Chamberlain of the Household for Henry VI from 1425 to 1432 and from 1450 to 1455 after Suffolk's murder. Cromwell was always trying to reign in the king's spending and introduce financial reforms, but the French war ensured that the crown debt significantly increased. Cromwell had fought at Agincourt and at Caen, and was one of the commissioners at Troyes. He will have known Catherine of Valois from 1421 – and by implication would have known Owen Tudor. He sided with the Beauforts, hence Gloucester's ousting him in 1432.

The rest of the attendees were close to the king and more inclined to the Beaufort faction than to Gloucester. None of the Gloucester faction attended this meeting. St Mary Overy was an Augustinian priory on the south side of the Thames opposite Westminster and is now called the Cathedral and Collegiate Church of St Saviour and St Mary Overie at Southwark, or simply Southwark Cathedral. Henry Beaufort had rebuilt it after a fire in the 1420s, and probably constructed a 'privy chamber' for his own use.

On 29 July 1438 William Hales and William Chapman, sheriffs of London, were pardoned for Owen's escape from Newgate. The Calendar of Patent Rolls in 1438 indicates the king's pardon 'for the escape of Owin ap Tuder, esquire':

PARDON [given at] Dogmersfield
Concerning the pardon upon the escape of Owain ap Tudor
The king to all etc, greetings.
Know that with Owain ap Tudor, alias the said Owain ap Tudor Armiger, formerly in our Newgate prison under the custody of our beloved liegemen William Hales and William Chapman, our sheriffs of the city of London, detained for certain reasons from that same prison by deceit and subtlety he escaped, the said William and William knowing nothing of such, We, for the said W&W who submitted themselves to our grace humbly in this cause, willingly desiring for us in this cause to provide especially of our grace special pardon, remission and release for the aforesaid W&W and by whatever names they are appraised, both our suit as to all escapes, evasions, offenses, contempts, impeachments, transgressions, forfeitures, fines and amercements, which from us against them alone or with others in this part pertains or may pertains in such manner, Let it be known that the same W&W, their heirs or executors, for the forgoing reasons through us or our heirs, justiciars, escheators, sheriffs or any other of our bailiffs or ministers whatsoever, will have occasion to molest or discomfort in anything, or

anything else occasioned by it, molest in anything or discomfort; but then towards us and our heirs we will make no mention forever.

Owen was not beaten yet; he attempted to escape again. Lloyd-Williams writes:

> Owen laid his plans so successfully this second time of breaking out of Newgate, that he was not retaken, but fled with his faithful adherents to the fastnesses of North Wales, where he waited for better times. It is, perhaps, not too much to infer that the priest thus connected with Owen was the person who secretly performed the marriage ceremony between him and Katherine, and that the servant was witness to wedlock. The *London Chronicle* vindicates the honour of the queen in words not very complimentary to her spouse: in this year, one Owen, a man neither of outline or livelihood, brake out of Newgate at searching time; the which Owen had privily wedded queen Katherine, and had three or four children by her, unknown to the common people till she was dead and buried.

All three men made their second escape from Newgate, and this time it may have been with the secret connivance of those in authority. Once again Owen was captured and returned to Newgate, and soon after he was brought to Windsor Castle where Edmund Beaufort was the newly appointed constable. Robin Ddu, the Anglesey bard, describes Owen as anxious about his children at this time, as one of the *Claus Rerum* records describes him as *Prisoner Notabilis* at Windsor, and perhaps it was in an attempt to see his children that he was recaptured. According to Dan Jones, 'it was not until July that Owen's friends, represented by none other than his late wife's one-time sweetheart [Edmund Beaufort], secured his transfer to the more salubrious surroundings of Windsor Castle, where he was put under the watch of Walter Hungerford, the captain under whom he may have served in France two decades previously'.

Owen remained at Windsor for a year, being released in July 1439 under a mainprise (similar to bail) of £2,000, a massive amount. A writ of mainprise was directed to the sheriff when any man was imprisoned for a bailable offence and bail has been refused, or when the offence or cause of commitment was not properly bailable. It commanded the sheriff or relevant royal official to take sureties for the prisoner's appearance, commonly called mainpernors, and to set him at large. Mainprise was granted, on condition that Owen appeared before the king on the following 11 November and at any other time deemed necessary by the king. Owen must have attended on 11 November, as on 12 November he was pardoned all offences committed before 10 October 1439, even though these 'offences' were not stated. His mainprise was cancelled, and all processes against him annulled, on 1 January 1440. This may have been a New Year's gift from Henry. The king may have regretted the treatment his stepfather had suffered, and could have blamed Gloucester for it. This pardon of all charges seems to relate to the fact that Henry VI was now almost eighteen, and his King's Council had replaced Gloucester's Regency Council.

At last, after three years of being chased, being imprisoned and escaping, Owen Tudor was accepted in public by his stepson, which protected him from Gloucester. In 1440 Henry VI granted his stepfather an annual pension of £100 from his own Privy Purse and other gifts by 'especial favour', and was to treat him favourably for the rest of his life. Restored to his freedom, goods and lands, Owen now began living on the periphery of court life, within the king's household but never central to it. (The king's expensive and bloated household contained around 1,200 persons in 1442.) Having been formally pardoned by royal sanction, he soon received a further grant for life of £40. Henry VI had reasons for leniency beyond his religious leanings; he had no parents and no close family. He was seventeen, and a stepfather and two stepbrothers aged eight and nine had come into his life.

Lloyd-Williams writes of Owen:

He appears, in spite of his stepson's favour, to have retired to his home at Glan Conwy, with occasional visits to London. The Devon Issue Rolls mention his £40 grant being paid in money (1442) into his own hands, when Owen must have been near the king's presence. We have no record of Owen visiting his sons in Barking Abbey ... Presently his residence there [Glan Conwy] and his influence in Wales were to prove very useful to his sons and to his stepson, for amid the numerous changes of the Wars of the Roses Owen's loyalty to the Lancastrian party never wavered, and he was fully able to arouse in North Wales that clan enthusiasm that his father and uncles had used so successfully for Glyn Dwr. The bards indeed unquestionably regarded the Tudors as successors to Glyn Dwr. Robin Ddu speaks inaccurately of Owen as a Prince of the blood of Edeyrnion, and when Henry of Richmond was born at Jasper Tudor's castle of Pembroke in January, 1457, forestalled the prophecy of Henry VI that the son of Edmund Tudor and Margaret Beaufort would be King of England.

Edmund and Jasper Tudor, and perhaps a sister, had been placed in the care of the Duke of Suffolk's sister, Katherine de la Pole, the abbess of Barking

Abbey in Essex. The boys, aged around six and seven at the time of Owen Tudor's arrest, possibly with an unknown daughter, were placed under Pole's care until considered old enough for their education to be continued by priests. They were known to be at Barking by 27 July 1437, remaining there until at least 6 March 1442. The richly furnished abbey was set around the large church of St Mary and St Ethelburga, enclosing one of the richest and most prestigious nunneries in England. Here the abbess supervised around thirty nuns, assisted by a staff of male servants and priests. It was a place for daughters and widows from the nobility and higher gentry to live or retire, following the strict Benedictine rule in prayer, charity and scholarship. Its links with the higher classes had brought Barking Abbey prestige and wealth, with its abbess holding the same precedence as a baron (after dukes, marquesses, earls and viscounts). Katherine de la Pole received the revenues of at least thirteen manors, plus incomes from estates in several counties, and the hundreds of acres surrounding the abbey alongside the Thames. It was less than a day's ride from the centre of London.

It is unclear when Henry VI became aware of the existence of his half-brothers; perhaps his mother told him before her death in Bermondsey Abbey. It was only after her death that he would begin to care for them, but perhaps Gloucester had ensured that he kept his distance beforehand. Henry would eventually raise them to the peerage by making them the premier earls in the land. Owen's sons had been taken from their father and had lost their mother. Until they were around ten and eleven they were probably not in contact with their father Owen, who had his own difficulties. At this time the boys were called 'Edmond ap Meredith ap Tydier' and 'Jasper ap Merediyth ap Tydier', among other spellings – Tudor had not been adopted as a surname as yet. The abbey was peaceful, a sanctuary from the dangerous intrigues of the court, and the children would not receive the knightly training of boys of rank, as in royal or noble courts.

However, for hundreds of years Barking's abbesses had regularly stood as godparents for high-ranking children who had been placed there for the early stages of their education. The boys would learn Latin and French under the nuns, as well as English, which was being used for the first time in official documentation since Henry IV took the crown. There was an excellent library, and Owen's sons would have had a deeply religious upbringing, paralleling that of their pious half-brother, the king. When they became his wards in 1442, on being removed from Barking, the king continued this emphasis. According to John Blacman, Henry VI's biographer and chaplain, writing around 1485, 'and like pains did he apply in the case of his half-brothers, the Lords Jasper and Edmund, in their boyhood and youth;

providing for them most strict and safe guardianship, putting them under the care of virtuous and worthy priests, both for teaching and for right living and conversation, lest the untamed practices of youth should grow rank if they lacked any to prune them'.

It cost the abbey a great deal, 13s 4d a week, to pay for food for the brothers and their servants, quite apart from the cost of their lodging, education, clothing and entertainment. Over the years that followed, the abbess would have to write on many occasions to the Royal Exchequer asking for huge sums to recompense her for Edmund and Jasper's upkeep. A £50 warrant in Katherine de la Pole's favour was sent to the Exchequer on 14 March 1439 and she was eventually paid on 16 July, but it needed periodic requests on the part of the abbess to secure further payment for the Tudor expenses. In November 1440 she had to petition the king for payment of £52 12s 0d owed to her for the costs of keeping 'Esmond ap Meredith ap Tydir', and his brother Jasper and their servants. Another warrant was sent to the Exchequer in February 1443 for a further payment of £55 13s 4d to the abbess, covering expenses from 1 November 1440 until 6 March 1442. The warrants were not honoured until 4 July 1443. However, on 20 February 1445 the abbess was granted a tun (around 1,100 litres) of red Gascon wine annually for life by the king for her good service. After 1443 the abbess's records with regard to Jasper and Edmund disappear, so we may assume that they were with her until March 1442 and then joined the court. Lloyd-Williams wrote that 'Henry paid her [Katherine's] account with the money obtained by the sale of Owen Tudor's plate. It was not very generous of him, but the Lancastrian Kings were not too well off, and he had married a penniless wife. After 1440 [actually in 1442] he delivered his mother's children to discreet persons [probably priests] to be brought up.'

Strickland, echoing Blacman, tells us of the brothers:

They were wholly neglected by the court; for, till the abbess supplicated most urgently, no money had been paid for the sustenance of these neglected little ones after the death of the mother. Soon after the abbess had drawn the attention of Henry VI to the existence of the children of his unfortunate mother, he placed them under the care of discreet priests, to be brought up chastely and virtuously.

Strickland also notes that

the tutelage of the king himself had, at this time, ceased by the laws of England. If Katherine [de Valois] had survived till this period, she would have been differently treated, for more than one old historian asserts that Henry VI never forgave his uncle Gloucester the harsh usage his mother had experienced. As soon as the young king attained his majority, he allowed Owen Tudor an annuity of £40 per annum, which, for certain causes him moving, he gave him out of his privy purse by especial grace.

(This author cannot source the origin of the statement that Henry VI never forgave Gloucester.)

In 1440, Owen and two others gave bond to Sir James Ormond (*c.* 1418–97), the illegitimate son of the Earl of Ormond and Princess Margaret of Thomond. Ormond was a grandson of Turlogh O'Brien ('the Brown'), King of Thomond (counties Clare, Limerick and part of Tipperary), and later became Henry VII's loyal supporter in Ireland, being knighted and appointed into the Irish peerage by the king. Owen Tudor was also present with distinguished knights to witness a charter that was signed in the favour of the Duke of Gloucester in July 1440, demonstrating Owen's belated acceptance in court circles.

In 1440, Gloucester was involved in a land dispute on the Isle of Wight with John Whithorne. According to Patent Roll 25, Henry VI: 'Humphrey Duke of Gloucester… caused the said John Whithorne… to be brought to Pembroke Castle and there imprisoned in so dark a dungeon and in such misery and lack of food and clothing for seven years and more, that he lost the sight of his eyes and suffered other incurable ills.' The bleak basement of the dungeon tower at Pembroke is one of the few surviving authentic mediaeval gaols, accessible only through a trap door, and built about 1260.

Upon the death of Henry V in 1422, Humphrey had become Lord Protector to the young Henry VI. He also claimed the right to the regency of England following the death of his elder brother, John, Duke of Bedford, who had been Regent, and this also made Humphrey heir-presumptive to the crown. Humphrey's claims were strongly contested by the lords of the Regency Council, and in particular his half-uncle, Cardinal Henry Beaufort. Henry V's will, rediscovered at Eton College in 1978, support Humphrey's claims. However, he annulled his marriage to Jacqueline of Hainault in 1428 and disinherited her to marry his mistress, Eleanor, daughter of Lord Cobham, in the same year. Eleanor consulted astrologers to try to divine the future. The astrologers, Thomas Southwell and Roger Bolingbroke, were said to have predicted that Henry VI would suffer a life-threatening illness in July or August 1441. The king's men arrested Southwell and Bolingbroke on charges of treasonable necromancy. After interrogation, Bolingbroke named Eleanor as the instigator, so she too was arrested and tried. The charges against her were possibly exaggerated to curb the ambitions of her husband. Eleanor Cobham was arrested and tried for sorcery and heresy. She was convicted of practising witchcraft against Henry VI in an attempt to retain power for her husband. Eleanor denied most of the charges but confessed to obtaining potions from Margery Jourdemayne, 'the Witch of Eye', to help her conceive. Bolingbroke was hanged, drawn and quartered, Jourdemayne was burnt at the stake and Southwell died in the Tower, possibly killing himself.

Humphrey's wife Eleanor Cobham had to carry out public penance in London and divorce her husband and was condemned to life imprisonment. In 1442 she was imprisoned, then moved to Kenilworth Castle, then the Isle of Man, finally dying in Beaumaris Castle in 1452. Gloucester's power had thus been broken by his enemies, and he retired from public life for some years. (However, he himself would be arrested on a charge of treason in 1447, dying three days later, perhaps of a stroke but possibly by poison. The hated Suffolk was blamed for the 'murder' of the popular 'good Duke Humfrey'). Owen Tudor, for one, would have been happy to see Gloucester removed from political influence. Meanwhile, the capable Richard, Duke of York, fighting alongside Lord Talbot, the Earl of Shrewsbury, had been appointed lieutenant for all France, operating from Normandy. With Gloucester disgraced, Edmund Beaufort's elder brother, John, Duke of Somerset, in April 1443 declared himself captain of Aquitaine and Captain-General of Guyenne. Somerset led an army into Gascony and Maine, achieving nothing, and was paid £25,000 by the king while York struggled with massive debts. Somerset's death in 1444, possibly from suicide, was followed soon after by that of his uncle, Cardinal Beaufort, and the Beaufort influence on the king was for a time replaced by that of William de la Pole, Duke of Suffolk. However, Edmund Beaufort was to return the family to influence after succeeding as Earl and then Duke of Somerset, and the York–Somerset feud became even more bitter.

As for the Tudors, around March 1442 young Jasper and Edmund were taken from Barking by Henry VI, into his household to attend court. It was to be over a decade before the brothers were elevated to positions of importance. Their father was granted another £40 in addition to the £100 annual pension from the king, possibly to allow him to dress in accordance with his status of being father to the king's half-brothers.

Owen had received back the lands in North Wales granted by his wife, and on 25 August 1442 Owen and others were granted land in Surrey by Robert Asshwell, son of John Asshwell, formerly King of Arms. On 20 October 1442, Henry VI granted £40 in cash from his Privy Purse '*a notre ame Oweyn ap Tuder'*. Further personal payments from the king's Privy Purse, each of £40 cash, were given to 'oure welbeloved squier' on 12 February, 20 July and 18 September 1444, when the cash rewards ceased. For the king to call his stepfather 'our friend' (*ame*) and 'well beloved squire' indicates personal warmth, to be reciprocated by Owen in loyalty and duty. Leading the life of a gentleman, and now generously treated by the king, Owen was probably part of his stepson's household until at least the late 1450s, if not until his death. An Owen or 'Owyn' Meredith was in the royal household from at the latest 1444 to 1453, which must be him. As 'Owen ap Maredudd', Owen was in the court party that went to France in 1444 to bring back the young Margaret of Anjou, the king's new queen.

Owen had little to do with his sons' upbringing, which was being supervised by the king. While the brothers grew up Henry kept them close to him at court and, according to Blacman, personally protected them from any sexual temptation by keeping 'careful watch through hidden windows of his chamber'. Very few accounts survive of these early years of Edmund and Jasper's lives or of their father's life at this time. Until very recently we knew little of Owen's whereabouts over the next fifteen years, and it was thought that he was tending to his estates, possibly in Wales. However, on 15 January 1449 the Chancellor was ordered to authorise the payment of £18 4s 0d to Owen for his expenses in France recently incurred, and we can trace him to Normandy in 1445–49 in the next chapter. There is a mention of Owen fighting at Rhodes, which could have been around 1440–41 or before he met Catherine in the 1420s. There were calls across Europe at the time for men to go on Crusade, and defending Rhodes against the Egyptians counted as such.

Their half-brother Henry VI took a special interest in the welfare of Jasper and Edmund Tudor. The ascetic Henry arranged for the best priest to educate them intellectually and morally. John Blacman, his confessor and biographer, wrote of Henry VI:

> For before he was married, being as a youth a pupil of chastity, he would keep careful watch through hidden windows of his chamber, lest any foolish impertinence of woman coming into the house should grow to a head, and cause the fall of any of his household. And like pains did he apply in the case of his two half-brothers, the Lords Jasper and Edmund, in their boyhood and youth: providing for them most strict and safe guardianship, putting them under the case of virtuous and worthy priests, both for right living and conversation, lest the untamed practices of youth should grow rank if they lacked any to prune them.

The brothers also received military training, and later were given military positions.

While Edmund and Jasper were growing up, the minority of Henry VI had led to factional struggles among the magnate and gentry classes, and the government of the realm had begun to deteriorate. Richard, Duke of York, was a direct descendant of Edward III, and the Duke of Exeter also had a claim to the crown. The continuing enmity of York and the Somerset family led to a series of crises. Throughout Henry VI's reign, the gains made in France under Henry V were slowly being lost. Small English garrisons, with irregular supplies, were unable to prevent constant attacks by the French. Towards the middle of the fifteenth century England had lost nearly all of its new lands in France, which led to fury among nobles and commoners alike. After the fiasco of Somerset's aimless expedition England needed peace, and Suffolk was despatched to France early in 1444. Suffolk was increasingly in the favour of Henry VI, and organised a marriage for the twenty-two-year-old king, selecting a niece of Charles VII, Margaret of Anjou, then just fourteen years old. Suffolk stood in for Henry and married the girl by proxy in front of the French king, queen and court, at Tours on 24 May 1444. Returning to England having agreed a two-year truce, Suffolk was created a marquess and in 1448 was to be promoted to a duke. The marriage was part of a plan to bring peace so that England could begin to repair its finances.

The match caused public outrage, with Gloucester being particularly angry that Henry intended to ignore a contracted union to the Duke of Armagnac's daughter. Gloucester had helped arrange that marriage, and now reappeared in public life to complain. Grafton wrote: 'Humfrey Duke of Gloucester, Protector of the realme, repugned and resisted as muche as in him lay, this newe alliaunce and contrived matrimone: alleging that it was neyther consonant to the lawe of God nor man, nor honourable to a prince, to infringe and breake a promise or contract.' Chroniclers later related that Suffolk was to murder Gloucester, and be murdered himself. Basically, the marriage was a flawed attempt to pacify the French, thereby decreasing English expenditures in France. The sister of Margaret's father René of Anjou had married Charles VII of France, and Henry and Suffolk hoped that the marriage would help stabilise affairs.

In 1445, accompanied by Owen Tudor, Suffolk returned to France to escort Margaret back to England, landing in Southampton on 9 April. Owen was in the party escorting her to London, which to some extent demonstrates how far he had risen in the ranks of those at court. On 23 April 1445, Margaret of Anjou, just fifteen, married the twenty-three-year-old Henry VI at Titchfield in Hampshire. Henry still claimed the Kingdom of France and controlled various parts of northern France. Charles VII agreed to the marriage of his niece to his rival for France on the condition that he would not have to provide the customary dowry. Instead, he would receive the lands of Maine and Anjou from England. This agreement was kept secret from the English public, and when discovered it was to prove disastrous for the king. Also, with her new husband often incapable, Margaret of Anjou was to have considerable and increasing influence in the running of English affairs, angering nobles and commoners alike for her links with France.

It was necessary for Henry to produce an heir, otherwise the crown would pass to Henry V's three brothers and their heirs. However, by this time Clarence and Bedford had died without issue. Gloucester had married twice, but only fathered an illegitimate daughter and son. He was also fifty-five years old and in disgrace following the Eleanor Cobham affair. Henry VI was the only surviving grandchild of Henry IV. After him, if he had no son, were at least four great families that could claim descent from Edward III, Henry VI's great-great-grandfather. The main family was that of Richard of York, whose own father Richard of Cambridge had been beheaded for plotting against Henry V in 1413. At the time York was the richest layman in England, his enemy Cardinal Henry Beaufort being the wealthiest individual apart from the king. Richard was also the greatest landowner after Henry VI, but his constant loans for the wars in France had severely depleted his finances.

On 15 and 25 December 1449, Edmund of Hadham and Jasper of Hatfield respectively were knighted, both having reached the age of eighteen, but there is no record of their father Owen being thus honoured. He will have recently returned from four years' service and a siege in France. Although the king had been married for seven years by 1452, he still had no children, and the death of Duke Humphrey of Gloucester in February 1447 removed his last surviving uncle from the scene. With Gloucester's death, the king's immediate family consisted solely of his wife, Margaret of Anjou, and his half-brothers Edmund and Jasper Tudor. The future security of the country seemed to be in jeopardy, and in November 1450 Thomas Young, a Bristol lawyer, MP and protégé of Richard, Duke of York, petitioned for the latter's recognition as heir presumptive, for which he served a term of imprisonment. The Tudor brothers were not thought of as potential heirs to the throne as others, such as York and Exeter, had far better claims.

Here, we must quickly consider the background to the finances of the king. The subject of the king's powers and finances had been a problem since the reign of Henry IV (1399–1413), the Lancastrian usurper who confiscated great estates, especially from leading Yorkists. During his son Henry V's brief reign from 1413 to 1422, his nobles were busy profiteering from plundering France, but under the boy-king Henry VI, unrest had grown among nobles and commoners. As Bishop of Winchester, Henry Beaufort held the richest see in England, and this made him invaluable to a Lancastrian crown perpetually short of money. Both Henry V and Henry VI often had to resort to borrowing money from Beaufort. At the same time, many royal lands reverted to the crown on the deaths of Lionel, Duke of Clarence (1421); John, Duke of Bedford (1435); Queen Catherine of Valois (1437); and Humphrey, Duke of Gloucester (1447). However, between 1437 and 1449 Henry VI had granted many estates into the hands of his non-royal favourites, and almost the whole income from what he did retain was enjoyed by members of his household.

7

Owen in the Hundred Years War in France 1445–1449

From December 1444 until at least 1453, an Owen or 'Owyn' Meredith was in the royal household, and this must be our Owen. To discover his whereabouts between 1445 and 1449 we must look to Regnéville Castle, or the Château de Regnéville, south-west of Coutances in the Manche department in Normandy, and its role in the Hundred Years War, which raged from 1337 to 1453.

The castle dates back to the twelfth century, and was built to protect the important dry harbour of Regnéville-sur-Mer and guard the approaches to Coutances. The English, French, Dutch, Scots and Spanish all at times dried out their ships on its sands. Owing to the large tidal range, the whole port dries out for more than six hours in every twelve, so it is known as a 'drying port'. There were no docks at this time, so ships arrived at high water, and could unload and load their cargoes directly onto horses and carts at low water. The ships could then float off and leave the port as the tide came back in. Also there are no rocks, so the wooden ships were less likely to be damaged when grounding. Among other towns and castles in Normandy, it had been inherited by Charles the Bad, King of Navarre.

After the invasion of the Cotentin Peninsula (also known as the Cherbourg Peninsula) in 1346 by Edward III in the Hundred Years War, Charles the Bad sided with the English. The English retreated, leaving Charles the Bad engaged in civil war with Charles V of France. The Norman castles were difficult to take and a peace was negotiated. Regnéville Castle at this time consisted of an upper courtyard in the east, and a large tower. In the west, facing the harbour, the lower courtyard was originally the royal residence of Charles the Bad. The castle was strengthened during the truce. However, in 1378 the aging Charles V attacked again, destroying sixteen castles on the Cotentin Peninsula. Regnéville was one of the only six castles preserved in the area, strategically placed to prevent more invasions from English possessions in France. England was not to retake it until 1418.

Arthur de Richemont (1393–1458), Lord of Parthenay, was the second son of John IV, Duke of Brittany, and his third wife Joanna of Navarre. He was given the English title of Earl of Richmond (later to be held by Edmund Tudor and then Henry Tudor) by his older brother Duke John V in 1399. Their widowed mother, Joanna of Navarre (1370–1437), had married Henry IV of England in 1403, re-establishing Brittany's connection with the English crown. Henry Bolingbroke had resided in the Breton court when banished from England, before his return to murder Richard II and become Henry IV, and must have admired the duchess at that time. In 1413 Henry IV died, succeeded by Joanna's stepson Henry V. Joanna of Navarre initially had a very good relationship with Henry, who even entrusted her with the post of Regent of England during his absence in France in 1415. Upon his return from Agincourt, however, he brought her son Arthur of Brittany, wounded and captured in battle, to England as a prisoner. Joan unsuccessfully tried to have him released, which may have damaged her relationship with the king. In 1419, she was falsely accused of hiring two magicians to poison the king. Her large fortune was confiscated to help pay Henry V's war debts, and she was locked up for four years in Pevensey Castle. She was only released upon the orders of a guilty Henry V on his deathbed in 1422.

Arthur de Richemont fought for the Armagnacs in the ongoing feud with Burgundy. He also became the close friend of the Dauphin Louis, son of Charles VI. Richemont had been wounded and captured at Agincourt in 1415, after which Henry V and his Burgundian allies attempted to unite England and France. Richemont was held prisoner in England until 1420, then released on parole to support Henry V. He was extremely influential in persuading his brother John, Duke of Brittany, to back the 1420 Treaty of Troyes, by whichHenry V was appointed 'Heir of France'. Henry V rewarded Richemont with lands in France, and in 1422 made him Duke de Touraine.

Richemont's support for the alliance between England and Burgundy was further strengthened by his marrying Margaret of Burgundy, widow of the Dauphin Louis, in 1423. The marriage made Richemont the brother-in-law of both Philip, Duke of Burgundy, and John, Duke of Bedford, the English Regent of France. Richemont's star was rising, but there was an unexplained quarrel between him and Bedford, and he deserted the English cause, returning to his former French allegiance. An extremely capable warrior and general, he was appointed Constable of France by Charles VII in March 1425, and began to mould France's unreliable troops into an effective fighting force. However, Richemont lost popularity because of his insistence in driving back the English at all costs, and the young Charles VII was controlled by incompetent favourites who resented Richemont's successes. A treaty between his brother John V of Brittany and Bedford in September 1427 caused Richemont to be expelled from the French court.

In 1429 Richemont allied with Jeanne d'Arc at Orléans, winning several battles against the English, but the king's favourite, General La Trémoille, again forced him out of the French army. At this time, the uncle of Jacquetta of Luxembourg, John II of Luxembourg, Count of Ligny (1392–1441), joined Philip, Duke of Burgundy, in besieging Compiègne in 1430. Although the siege was unsuccessful, the Bastard of Vendôme, one of John's company, captured Jeanne d'Arc, and John kept her at Beauvoir as a prisoner. His aunt Jeanne, the Demoiselle de Luxembourg, showed kindness to her, and pleaded with John not to sell her to the English, but died shortly after. Under pressure from England and Burgundy, John sold Jeanne d'Arc to the English for 10,000 livres, thus causing her death, noted earlier.

However, Richemont was able to bring Brittany and Charles VII together once again in the Treaty of Rennes in March 1432. In June 1433 La Trémoille was overthrown, and Richemont returned to court and resumed the war against the English. In September 1435, mainly as a result of Richemont's diplomacy and his Burgundian connections, the Treaty of Arras was signed between Charles VII and Duke of Burgundy. This was the 'hinge factor' in England's eventual defeat – without the argument of Bedford and Richemont, it is quite possible that France and England would be one country today. Richemont was now in a position to strongly suppress warbands of soldiers and peasants, known as *routiers* or *écorcheurs*, which were operating across France. The *écorcheurs* ('flayers') were armed bands who terrorised France in the troubled reign of Charles VII, stripping their victims of everything, often including their clothes. Many were mercenaries without employment after the Treaty of Arras ended the fighting between Armagnacs and Burgundians. *Routiers* were mercenary soldiers, organised into bands or *routes*. Also known as 'free companies', they had desolated the French countryside throughout the Hundred Years War. They were usually called 'Englishmen' by their victims, but they were mainly Gascons, from south-west France, then considered a distinct people from the French.

In April 1436 Richemont marched into Paris as the city rose against the English garrison, but he had little support from Charles VII and was forced to lead frequent expeditions against the *routiers* and *écorcheurs* rather than fight the English. The great magnates serving in English-held Normandy were Edmund Beaufort, Earl of Dorset; Edmund's older brother John Beaufort, Earl of Somerset; and the Lords Talbot, Fauconberg and Scales. Somerset had only been released from seventeen years' imprisonment in France in 1438, and was appointed in place of Suffolk as captain of Regnéville Castle, sailing to Normandy at the end of May 1439.

John, Earl of Somerset was nominated by council to administer the Duchy of Normandy for the king. Somerset took over a number of important captaincies: Cherbourg from his uncle the cardinal, and Avranches, Tombelaine, Sainte-Suzanne and Regnéville from Suffolk. These, the most important fortresses on the western side of the Cotentin Peninsula, were a special area of military responsibility, no doubt decided on in council before Somerset left for France. Cherbourg, one of the major ports in Normandy, was handed over to Somerset on 15 July. He had taken possession of the others earlier. Regnéville, guarding the approaches to Coutances, was occupied by Somerset's lieutenant on 27 May, and Avranches and Tombelaine by 1 June. Tombelaine, near Regnéville, had been constructed on a rock a couple of miles north of Mont-St-Michel to keep a watch on the French garrison there. These captaincies were to occupy much of Somerset's attention over the next two years. He was styled captain of Avranches, Tombelaine and Cherbourg in a *quittance* dated 6 June 1439. Although actual garrison duties were delegated to lieutenants, there were more general problems to be dealt with. The surrounding area suffered badly from the activities of the French at Mont-Saint-Michel and the incursions of raiding enemy troops. Tombelaine was only 2 miles north of the French-garrisoned Mont-St-Michel, which was often sending raiding parties into the area, with troops from the castles held by the Duke d'Alençon, Laval, La Gravelle and La Guerche in the Breton marches. Henry Barton was Somerset's lieutenant at Regnéville, which with Avranches suffered from a lack of money and provisions caused by the invading French in 1439.

Enguerrand de Monstrelet (and d'Escouchy) gives us a French perspective on this period, with interesting descriptions of subterfuges and siege tactics, and describes the changing fortunes of the Hundred Years War. In 1441 Charles VI besieged Pontoise. It was relieved by the Duke of York and Talbot, Earl of Shrewsbury, but then Charles VI captured it. He knighted Jean d'Estouteville (of whom more later) with his brother Robert. In 1442 the king's army took Tartas, then Saint Serere near Cognac. De Monstrelet records that he 'conquered the place by storm, putting to death abut 800 English, with the loss of 20 to 30 of his own men'. The French army then took Marmande-sur-Garonne, La Reole, and Mailly in Picardy. In early

1443 Charles assembled a large army to march into Normandy and relieve Dieppe, and they drove herds of cattle into the walled port. Somerset retaliated by marching into Anjou, laying waste to villages, and then entered Brittany, taking La Guerche, which belonged to the Duke of Alençon. Remaining there, he sent raiding parties into Anjou and Touraine. He then took Beaumont-le-Vicomte; posting garrisons along the Normandy frontier, he then returned to his capital of Rouen. The Duke of Burgundy next took Luxembourg and its castle, but hostilities were to die down.

The Treaty of Tours in May 1444 led to a truce lasting almost five years. Its terms saw the marriage of Charles VII's fifteen-year-old niece, Margaret of Anjou and Henry VI, with a twenty-one-month truce (later extended) between England and France. In exchange for the marriage, Charles asked for the return of the province of Maine, sometimes known as southern Normandy. (After the 1424 Battle of Verneuil, England had possessed Maine, with John of Lancaster taking the title Duke of Maine.) Aged twenty-three, Henry married Margaret in April 1445. However, he did not give up Maine, despite Charles sending envoys and threatening to break the truce. The Treaty of Tours was seen as a pathetic match by the dukes of Gloucester and York. Margaret was indeed a relative of the French king, but by marriage rather than blood, and wed without a dowry, which should have been around 20,000 *livres*.

Margaret's father was the impoverished René of Anjou, and Henry even had to pay for the wedding. The Treaty of Tours furthered the antagonism between the followers of Gloucester and York towards the court's Beaufort faction, and was a major contributing factor to the outbreak of the Wars of the Roses. Vale wrote that 'the truce of Tours (1444) had left the English war suspended for twenty years. This was further cemented by the marriage of Henry VI and Margaret of Anjou. The English administrations of Normandy, Maine and Guyenne thus survived... Charles VII's military ordinance of June 1445 had created a standing army picked from the ranks of the unoccupied men-at-arms, without employment because of the truce. The problem of utilising this potentially anarchic force again plagued the king and his advisers.'

De Monstrelet records:

With the king [Charles VII] were René king of Sicily, and numbers of great lords and knights, the queens of France and Sicily, the dauphiness, and the daughter of king René, whom the earl of Suffolk had come with a splendid embassy to demand in marriage for the king of England. After a few discussions, everything was agreed on; but before their departure

with the new queen, a magnificent tournament was held, in which the
kings of France and Sicily, the lord Charles d'Anjou, the counts de
Foix and de St Pol, the lord Ferry de Lorraine, and several other great
lords, tilted. These feasts lasted eight days, – and the ladies were most
splendidly dressed. The kings of France and of Sicily escorted the queen
of England two leagues from Nancy, where the king took leave of his
niece with many tears, and recommended her to the protection of God:
their grief was so great that they could not speak. The king returned to
Nancy; but her father, the king of Sicily, accompanied her as far as Bar-le-
Duc, where he and her mother took their leave of her, with floods of tears,
and prayers for her welfare.

Owen Tudor was with the party that took Margaret of Anjou to England for
her wedding to Henry.

The truce with England was England's initiative. However, it gave the
aggressive and effective Richemont the capability to finally carry out his
proposed large-scale reorganisation of the army. Along with his total reform
of the French army, he modernised the financial structure of France to
provide the necessary revenues. At last supported by Charles VII, he was
given regular revenues from taxes upon hearths and salt. He reorganised
the French cavalry into the first standing army in Europe, ready for action
at any time, with well-drilled and professional *gens d'armes d'ordonnance*.
He created the *compagnies d'ordonnance*, and began organising a militia
of French archers, having personally witnessed the success of the Welsh
longbowmen at Agincourt. These regular companies enabled Richemont to
renew the war with a massive force in 1448–49.

Against this background, shortly after the Truce of Troyes, Owen Tudor
had been appointed captain of Regnéville in 1444. The garrisons defending
this important castle were always small, with an average of five or six armed
men and fifteen armed archers, under the command of a captain. The small
number of defenders indicates that there were uninterrupted walks around
the curtain wall:

The defence of the castle in the Middle Ages. The garrisons defending
the castle of Regnéville always remained modest: an average of 5 or 6 to
15 armed men archers or archers, under the command of a captain. The
numerical weakness of this party assumes a certain concentrated layout of
the castle's defences, [with] round uninterrupted paths around the curtain
[wall]. Contracts of commitment were concluded between the sovereign
and the captains. The balance of the garrison of professional soldiers

was provided by the overlord, King of France, King of Navarre or King of England according to the times. In the early fifteenth century, three guns are manufactured for the castle. These small guns, called culverins, projected balls of stone weighing four pounds. The castle gradually lost its military role in the second part of the fifteenth century. The Hundred Years War left the castle in bad shape and Roulland Gourfaleur in 1582 began restoration work.

In Luce we read:

The retinue of Owain Tudor, a mounted man-at-arms, the captain of Régnéville and the garrison of the said castle composed of 4 men-at-arms on foot and 15 archers. There was one mounted man-at-arms and for on foot with the foreign archers in the garrison of Renierville castle under the noble man Owain Tudor, captain of the said place, himself included, taken during this present quarter ending next Christmas, coming via us, John Simon, lieutenant general of the gentle and wise man Sheriff Piers Osber, viscount of Coutances, and William Goulet, the chief officer of the said garrison, the 22nd day of December, the year 1445, as well as if after following. And firstly the lances [cavalry], Captain Owain Tudor, a mounted man-at-arms, 4 foot men-at-arms and the archers. And firstly. Lances: Captain Owain Tudor, mounted man-at-arms, Guillaume Thorp, Guillaume Goulet, Richart Robert, Thoumas Browe, 4 men-at-arms on foot. Archers: Jouhan Templier. Jouhan Creston. Jouhan Handoyn. Jehan Warde. Davy Flyngth. Thoumas Breton. Clement Ovreton. Emesfrey Guyton. Jouhan Grynelef. Rogier Bryd. Jouhan Allecot. Guillaume Portier. Richart Conq. Richard de Ver. Thoumas Wentewarde.

All those above named, lances and archers, we certify that they are all fully mounted, armed and dressed well and sufficiently, each according to their estate. This is witnessed by our own signature by hand the said 22nd day of December in the above said year 1445, by Simon Goulet. The indenture under which Henry VI instituted Owain Tudur or Tudor, esquire, protector and captain of the castles, place and stronghold of Regneville, is dated at Rouen the 20th of December 1444. William Mineurs, esquire, who had agreed to give up this captaincy in favour of Owain Tudor, received as compensation the sum of £300 Tournais. (Translated by Paul Remfry)

The *noble homme* attribution italicised above could describe men as eminent as dukes, but could also be applied to knights and even sometimes esquires.

We are unsure if Owen had been knighted at this time, or indeed if he was ever knighted in English-occupied France

Captains like Owen and their retinues were also in attendance on the governor, Somerset. They operated in shifts, serving garrison duty and then around Somerset personally. The duke was also accompanied by secretaries, heralds and a number of messengers, constantly being dispatched with his instructions.

Owen was placed in a deteriorating situation, close to the north-east border of the Duchy of Brittany. English-held castles across Normandy were repaired and strengthened during Owen's tenure, but Richemont's efficient reorganisation of the French army was to be the death-knell for the English possession of Normandy.

Mont-Saint-Michel was the last French bridgehead in English-held Normandy. The Mont, located at the mouth of the Couesnon River, is nowadays part of the Normandy region, but this was previously a matter of dispute as the Couesnon River marks the border between Normandy and Brittany. This cone-shaped granite islet in the Gulf of Saint-Malo is now connected by a causeway with the mainland, and can only be accessed at low tides. There are huge tidal ranges here, of up to 46 feet, and Victor Hugo described the tides as changing 'as swiftly as a galloping horse'. During the Hundred Years War the Mont became a one of the strongest fortresses in Europe. Towers and battlements were built all around it, adding to its natural protection – apart from the tides, the granite rock it stood upon was almost impossible to mine and so its walls were almost indestructible. The abbey itself was fortified, especially its entry, where towers and successive courtyards were built to create a barbican. After Agincourt in 1415, Normandy was conquered by Henry V and his brother Bedford, and they had gained the support of the Mont's abbot to take the fortress, but the monks refused to follow his orders and remained loyal to Dauphin Charles, the future Charles VII.

Matters became particularly critical for Mont-Saint-Michel after Agincourt. The English were determined to capture and/or destroy the fortress, which had resisted their assaults for years. In 1423–24 they had besieged it, stationing troops and a wooden fortress on the mainland while ships formed a blockade on the water. It was far easier to starve it into submission than storm it. However, a Breton maritime expedition from St Malo broke through, enabling desperately needed supplies to reach the defenders by sea.

After his coronation in Reims, Charles VII began to reclaim his kingdom and in 1425 had appointed the redoubtable Louis d'Estouteville, Lord of Valmont and Sieur d'Ausebecq (1400–64) as captain of Mont-Saint-Michel's garrison. Charles was to also appoint him Governor of Normandy and Rouen after its conquest in 1449.

For nine years, d'Estouteville held on grimly to the last French possession in Normandy, occasionally sending out raiding parties. In 1433–34, Sir Thomas Scales, 7th Baron Scales, Seneschal of Normandy, again attacked the Mont. The English partially destroyed the battlements and lit a fire in the village, then used siege engines to open a breach in the wall, allowing 20,000 soldiers (according to the French) to invade the streets. A French source relates that d'Estouteville led 118 knights who swore, like him, to hold the Mont for the King of France or perish under its debris. The Mont's garrison resisted, and the English army was forced to retreat with 2,000 dead, according to French sources. As a souvenir, the garrison kept two massive wrought-iron English cannons, *Les Michelettes*, which are today displayed near the outer defensive wall.

In 1439 Henry VI ordered Scales to build a fortress and walls at the port of Granville, just 12 miles south of Regnéville, to isolate the Mont prior to another attack, and in 1440 work began. To further protect Granville, situated on its own headland, Scales had a ditch dug between the peninsula and the mainland so that the sea and the waters of the River Boscq made his new castle an island. However, on 8 November 1442, by a ruse, d'Estouteville took over Granville and its new defences – they then remained permanently in the hands of the French. Charles VII decided to make Granville a fortified town, and signed a charter in 1445 granting arms and exempting its residents from tax. D'Estouteville was also to be involved in the taking of Tombelaine, Saint James and Avranches, and later, in 1449, Coutances, Saint-Lô and Pont-Give.

Edmund Beaufort, now Duke of Somerset on the death of his brother, was appointed Governor of Normandy in 1448. Based in Rouen, he despatched instructions to all English-held garrisons and towns. Aged around fifty, despite inheriting the massive wealth of his uncle Cardinal Beaufort, the chronicler Thomas Basin, who knew him personally, noted Beaufort's 'great avarice' and its disastrous consequences. There were increasing breaches of the truce across the lower Seine region by the French, much more disciplined and confident after Richemont's reforms, which Somerset seemed to be unable to stop. De Monstrelet wrote, 'On the first of April, in the year 1447, the truces between the kings of France and England expired, but were prolonged until the first of April in 1449, and thence until the first day of June ensuing, in the hope that a general peace might be concluded in the mean time.' Owen Tudor was unaware of what was to come, probably spending his days drilling his men and attending meetings in Rouen with Somerset, the former suitor of Catherine of Valois.

However, the English had been planning a reprisal attack for the imprisonment of their ally Gilles of Brittany. Francois de Surienne (*l'Aragonais*), captain of Verneuil, had visited London in 1447 to plan the attack with Suffolk and Somerset. In autumn 1448 Somerset appointed de Surienne to review troops in lower Normandy, including Owen Tudor's garrison at Regnéville. On 15 January 1449 the Chancellor was ordered to authorise the payment of £18 4s to Owen for his expenses in France.

Troops were gathered around de Surienne's captaincy at Verneuil, while scaling equipment was stored near Avranches, closer to the target. On the night of 23 March 1449, de Surienne's English raiders captured the rich Breton wool town of Fougères on the Normandy frontier in a surprise attack. There was little resistance as there was a truce in place and the town was not properly defended, and it was heavily plundered, with the takings being estimated as high as 2 million *ecus d'or*. De Surienne was created a Knight of the Garter, and was granted a pension and the castle of Porchester in Hampshire. The Duke of Brittany made an immediate protest regarding Fougères to Somerset, who basically lied about his involvement and refused to apologise. The French delayed their reaction for over a month, carefully preparing for war. Although Charles VII had sent an embassy to Rouen from 7 to 22 April to discuss other infringements of the truce, the matter of Fougères was never officially raised. Charles VII had been preparing his ground carefully and did not wish for arbitration, a matter made easier by Somerset's obtuseness. In April 1449 the captain of Evreux almost took the English-held Mantes. By the time of the duke's first formal protest and demand for reparation on 13 May, full support had already been promised to the Bretons by Charles.

In May 1449, because of the imminent danger of war, in England it was decided that Somerset was to be provided with an additional force of 100 men-at-arms and 1,200 archers. However, there were problems of recruitment, and only 55 men-at-arms and 408 archers mustered at Winchelsea, and not until 31 July. They were not to arrive in France until it was too late. Somerset held a meeting of the Estates in May 1449. The reorganisation of the French army and their superiority in artillery, combined with the poor general state of the Normandy fortresses, was causing Somerset considerable concern. The Estates complained that they could no longer carry the burden of taxation, and that substantial aid must be provided by England. On 13 May 1449 news arrived that French troops and Breton partisans had seized Pont-de-l'Arche and captured Lord Fauconberg. Mayenne and Juliez in

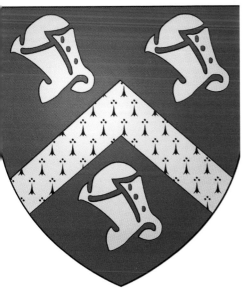 

Above left: Coat of arms of Ednyfed Fychan (*c*. 1170–1246), Seneschal of Llywelyn the Great and the direct male ancestor of Owen Tudor. The heads represent three Franco-English lords killed in battle. Courtesy of Sodacan.

Above right: Ednyfed Fychan's arms are represented in those of his descendant, Dorothy Wynn, in the plasterwork of Plas Mawr, Conwy, Britain's best-preserved Elizabethan town house. Author's collection.

Llys Euryn, the site of a Tudor mansion on their Rhos estate, sits near an Iron Age fort on Bryn Euryn, overlooking the sea, and was probably sacked by Owain Glyndŵr around 1409. Courtesy of Paul Remfry.

Aberlleiniog Castle was a motte-and-bailey castle first built in 1088 by the Norman, Hugh of Chester, and taken by Gruffydd ap Cynan in 1094. It was held by Ednyfed Fychan, resting on a steep hill just above the Tudor coastal estate at Trecastell, Llangoed, Anglesey. Courtesy of Heledd Haf Williams.

Aberlleiniog Castle was just 2 miles east of the great Edwardian fortress of Beaumaris, and controlled a landing beach on the Menai Straits. Its reduced walls date from the seventeenth-century Civil War. Courtesy of Heledd Haf Williams.

The Church of St Gredifael, Penmynydd, is on a sixth-century site with a holy well (Ffynnon Gredifael). It is mainly fourteenth century, with a north chapel (the Tudor Chapel) dating from the early fifteenth century. Courtesy of Heledd Haf Williams.

Penmynydd Church, Anglesey, holds the magnificent 1385 alabaster effigy tomb of Goronwy ap Tudur, the uncle of Owen Tudor and his wife, Myfanwy. The pew ends have the *fleur-de-lys* symbol, representing the marriage of Owen Tudor to Catherine de Valois. The tomb has been extensively chipped to use for medicinal purposes. It was removed from the Franciscan friary at Llanfaes when the friary was destroyed. Courtesy of the Gwynedd Archaeological Trust.

Beaumaris Castle, adjacent to the Tudor Anglesey estates, was built between 1295 and 1330 by Edward I as one of his Iron Ring of castles, and is now a World Heritage Site. Courtesy of Paul Remfry.

Above: Plas Penmynydd, a Tudor site since Ednyfed Fychan's time, and the possible birthplace of Owen Tudor. It was rebuilt in 1576 by Richard Owen Tudor, and the private residence is Grade 2* listed. Courtesy of Heledd Haf Williams.

Left: Doorway to Plas Penmynydd, showing Owen Tudor's coat of arms of three helmets. Opposite is a Saracen's head, indicating the story that Ednyfed Fychan went on Crusade. The father of its builder, Owen Tudur Fychan, was Esquire of the Body of Henry VII. Courtesy of Heledd Haf Williams.

Above: Caernarfon Castle, one of the Iron Ring of castles, next to Tudor lands, was built to subdue Gwynedd. It was sacked, along with its walled town in the 1294 Madog ap Llywelyn rebellion, and besieged by the Tudor brothers in the Glyndŵr War of Independence of 1400–21. Courtesy of Jeffrey L. Thomas at castlewales.com.

Right: The coat of arms of Owen Tudor (*c.* 1400–1461) is almost identical to that of Ednyfed Fychan, but probably included martlets (heraldic swallows), like the arms of his son Jasper. Courtesy of Sodacan.

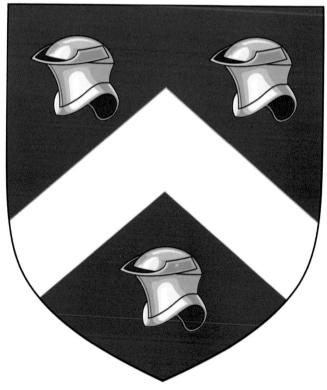

The Iron Ring fortress of Conwy Castle was captured in 1401 by the Tudor brothers Rhys, Gwilym and Maredudd, the latter the father of Owen Tudor. Courtesy of Jeffrey L. Thomas at castlewales.com.

The massive fortifications show how Conwy Castle could be held by the Tudor brothers and a few dozen men against an English army for six months in 1401. Courtesy of Jeffrey L. Thomas at castlewales.com.

Right: Catherine de Valois, widow of Henry V, mother of Henry VI (1421–71), who secretly married Owen Tudor and was the grandmother of Henry VII. Author's collection.

Below: Wallingford Castle, one of the homes of Catherine de Valois. Owen was said to have married her at Wallingford, on the River Thames in Oxfordshire. Courtesy of Bill Tyne.

Left: Coat of arms of Edmund Tudor, Earl of Richmond, eldest son of Owen Tudor. It is based upon the arms of lions and *fleur-de-lys* of his stepbrother Henry VI, but surrounded by a *bordure of fleur-de-lys* representing Catherine de Valois and martlets representing Owen Tudor. Courtesy of Sodacan.

Below: Berkhamsted Castle, Hertfordshire, one of the several homes of Owen and Catherine de Valois. It was granted to her by Henry V, and used by Henry VI, but soon began falling into disrepair. Courtesy of Paul Remfry.

Right: Coat of arms of Jasper Tudor, Earl of Pembroke, the second son of Owen Tudor, distinguished from that of his brother Edmund Tudor by having all martlets in the *bordure*. Courtesy of Sodacan.

Below: The impressive Carreg Cennen Castle stands on a rocky crag in Carmarthenshire, and was taken by Owen's son Edmund, Earl of Richmond, from the Yorkists in 1456. Author's collection.

Carmarthen Castle gatehouse. Edmund Tudor was imprisoned here by Yorkists in 1456, dying shortly afterwards of unknown causes, three months before his son, who was later crowned Henry VII, was born. Author's collection.

Tomb of Edmund Tudor in front of the high altar of St David's Cathedral, removed from Carmarthen Greyfriars Priory in 1540, during the Dissolution of the Monasteries. Author's collection.

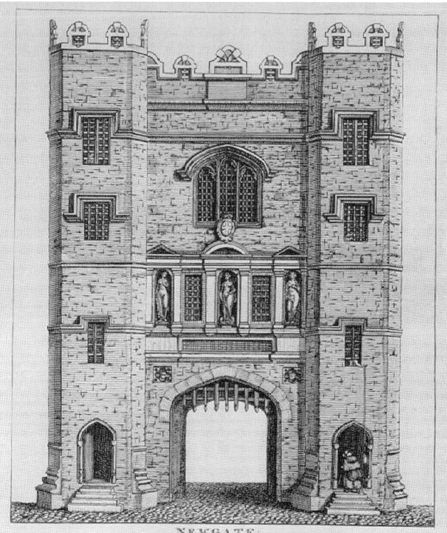

NEWGATE:

Chamberlains Gate, a most miserable Dungeon, was rebuilt by Rich.ᵈ Whittington, in the style here represented and from its meanness called ... Newgate, from which Newgate Street was named. Against the street front were four emblematical figures viz. Liberty, Peace, Security, & Plenty, and on the East front were three figures Justice, Fortitude & Prudence, this Building was destroyed in the Conflagration, was again rebuilt 1672 with great magnificence though nearly on the same plan as appears by the views given in Maitlands London. At the entire demolition of this Gate, four of the figures were put up on the south wing of the present useful structure.

Old Newgate Gaol, where Owen was held at least twice, in 1437 and 1438. Normally high-ranking prisoners would be placed in the Tower of London, in comfortable quarters, but according to bards Owen was chained to a wall. Author's collection.

Denbigh Castle and town walls were built by Edward I. It was besieged by Owen and Jasper Tudor in 1460 and only taken after a six-month siege. Jasper tried to take the castle from the Yorkists again in 1468, but only succeeded in getting over the town walls and burning the town. Courtesy of Paul Remfry.

Owen held the castle at Regnéville-sur-Mer, on the Cotentin Peninsula, Normandy, from 1444 in the Hundred Years War. He surrendered it after six days of fighting on 19 September 1449. The remains are shown here with church and *lavoir* (wash-house). Author's collection.

Mont-St-Michel, the nearest French-held fortress to Owen's garrison in Normandy, was never taken by the English despite several attempts over the decades of the Hundred Years War; raiding parties often left from here to go into English-held Normandy. Author's collection.

Looking towards Mortimer's Cross from York's great stronghold of Wigmore Castle, where Yorkist troops gathered before battle with the Lancastrians under Jasper, Wiltshire and Owen Tudor. Author's collection.

The double tomb of Walter, 1st Baron Hungerford (1378–1449) in Salisbury Cathedral, for whom Owen fought in France, and probably through whom Owen entered Catherine's service. Author's collection.

Maine soon surrendered to the French. A Gascon noble took Cognac on the Charente and Saint-Maigrin for the French. In May, Conches and Gerberoy in Normandy were also surprised and recaptured. Robert de Flocques, bailiff of Evreux, took Conches, and De Monstrelet relates that Gerberoy 'was taken by Scalado, by the lord de Mouy, governor of that country; and all the English within it, to the number of thirty, were put to the sword.'

Against this background of continued success, France next signed a formal alliance with Brittany on 17 June, promising all-out war with England if the matter of compensation for Fougères was not resolved, and on 31 July, the date of the Winchelsea muster, France formally declared war. A furious Somerset was unable to undertake any major effort to regain Pont-de-l'Arche, fearing that the French would attack Rouen in his absence. Somerset claimed (falsely) that the taking of Fougères had been without his knowledge or consent, playing for time for reinforcements from England. However, some English troops in a raiding party from Fougères were captured and admitted that they were following Somerset's orders. Collection of the *aide* had now broken down across Normandy, so the English captains could not pay their troops, which included mercenaries, or even adequately provision their fortresses. The great warrior Mathew Gough even had to extort forced loans from the clergy in Bayeux to pay his soldiers' wages. Owen Tudor at Regnéville would have faced similar problems in paying his men and securing provisions, as did all the English castles on the Cotentin.

In his castle and palace at Rouen, Somerset had built up stockpiles of munitions and supplies, strengthening the city's defences during June and July at the expense of the outlying garrisons. However, full-scale war had already started on the Breton marches, with Breton troops entering Normandy to support France. Expecting an attack from Richemont in the east, and the Bretons from the west, Somerset kept his main force at Rouen, unable to send reinforcements to the castles on the Cotentin Peninsula. Owen Tudor could do nothing but wait and hope at Regnéville, possibly expecting Somerset to meet the advancing armies in a pitched battle. However, on 19/20 July 1449 the French under Dunois took the fortified city of Verneuil, near where Bedford had smashed the French army in 1424. It was the first step in the reconquest of the Duchy of Normandy. Jean Bertin, a miller, had been mistreated by the garrison, and was said to have been beaten up while carrying out his bread rounds. His mill was next to the walls of the castle, and the day after the French army arrived, he part-emptied the castle moat, allowing the French access to storm the walls. The castle was valiantly defended, with 120 men killed or captured and the rest retreating to the 'impregnable' *Tour Grise* (Grey Tower), separate from the castle, surrounded by water ditches.

Jean de Dunois, Charles's army commander, and Pierre de Brézé, seneschal of Evreux, led the French. Somerset, isolated in Rouen, had to resort to dubious financial methods to pay his troops, but managed to send a messenger to Verneuil promising a relief force, and troops under Talbot and Mundeford left on 21 July. The English army had reached Breteuil, a few miles north of Verneuil, on 31 July, but instead of attacking the larger army of the Bastard of Orléans and Dunois, who was still trying to take the *Tour Grise*, Talbot turned north. Dunois left some men to carry on with the siege and hastened after Talbot. The two armies faced each other at Harcourt on 2 August 1449. Talbot chose a strong position, and sited his artillery to deter an immediate French attack, but under cover of the night he quick-marched his troops back to Rouen, which he reached on 4 August. Talbot had probably received a message that a new army of 300 lances (mounted men-at-arms) and 1,500 archers, under the counts of Eu and Saint Pol, had almost taken Somerset's capital by surprise. Upon Talbot's arrival the French retreated to Pont-Saint-Pierre.

Owen Tudor would have been informed of ominous events. Including the Count of Eu's army, there was a royal French army in eastern Normandy. Richemont had taken Breton and French troops into the Cotentin Peninsula from the east, and partisans led by the Duke of Alençon had entered lower Normandy. He would soon be surrounded, and would have heard that the Duke of Brittany was on his way from the west with an even larger army. There were four armies converging on the Manche, and he had only a few dozen men. It would be unfeasible to hold the curtain walls, so Owen would have desperately attempted to stock the keep with provisions and beverages (he could not stock water as it carried diseases). He could hold the keep until cannon were brought up to relieve him.

In early August 1449, Somerset summoned an emergency meeting of financial officials and captains in Rouen, which would have included Owen, to discuss how to provide payment for troops and defences. On 6 August Charles VII crossed the Loire to take command of the French southern army. The French under the counts of Eu and Saint Pol, with a few hundred horsemen, surrounded and took Talbot's château of 'Nogent-Pré' on 9–10 August. Many were killed and wounded, but de Monstrelet writes that 'on the Saturday the place surrendered between eleven and twelve o'clock, on condition that the garrison should march away in safety unarmed, except the governor who was to wear his sword. They deposited all their effects in the church of St Peter, whence they afterward came to seek and carry them away whither they pleased. The conquerors, perceiving on the Sunday that the place was not tenable, decamped, but not before they had set fire to it and burned it to the ground.' Owen Tudor at Regnéville may have heard of the capture, with its significance for a peaceful surrender. This event caused Talbot's force to return to Harcourt. This is east of the Cotentin, in the Eure department.

On 6 August a company of some 500 troops had left Rouen under Eyton and Mundeford to stiffen the garrison at Pont-Audemer, a major target necessary for the French to taken Normandy. Pont-Audemer was strategically situated on the routes from Caen to Rouen via Pont-l'Eveque and Lisieux, and its capture would block any aid to Rouen, of men or supplies, from lower Normandy. Knowing the strength of Rouen, the French may have realised that it would have to be starved into submission. Ignorant of the fresh troops under Eyton and Mundeford in the town, a first detachment under de Brézé and Floques, which reached Pont-Audemer on 10 August, made an assault on the walls, which was comfortably beaten off.

On 12 August, the Bastard of Orléans joined his force of 2,000 men with that of the counts of Eu and Saint-Pol to surround Pont-Audemer, 35 miles west of Rouen, near Pont-l'Évêque. The full French contingents under Dunois deployed for a full-scale attack on Pont-Audemer. The counts of Eu and St Pol took up position on the westward side of the town, towards Caen, with Dunois on the eastern side. A fire started in the town spread rapidly, distracting the defenders, and the French assault broke through the palisades on 12 August, capturing both Eyton and Mundeford and taking 420 prisoners. Pont-Audemer was taken after serious fighting, with twenty-two men being knighted.

Here de Monstrelet writes in his account of the battles: 'It was evident that Heaven was against the English, – and they were deserving of it; for it is a fact that they have always encroached on their Christian neighbours, as well in the kingdom of France as in Scotland, Ireland, Wales, and elsewhere.'

Around 20 miles from Fougères, Saint-James-de-Beuvron neighboured Mortain and was next to surrender, after a siege lasting from 18 to 22 August. This was in the Manche, just to the west of the Cotentin.

On the 12th of August the king of France came to Vendôme, grandly accompanied by men-at-arms, as well as lords, knights and esquires, and others. He remained there until the 18th; and during this time the lord de Lohéac, marshal of Brittany [Lohéac was one of Richemont's captains at Patay and fighting for Jeanne d'Arc, and was also at the battle of Castillon in 1453 which ended the Hundred Years War]... and others, attacked the town of St Jacques de Beuvron with great vigour, from nine in the morning until night, and, with heavy and small artillery, kept up a continual fire on the walls. It was, however, gallantly defended; but on the morrow the English capitulated for its surrender, on being allowed to march away in safety with their effects. On the 23d of the said month the king of France entered Chartres; and on the next day the garrison of the tower of Verneuil surrendered themselves prisoners. They were but thirty, of whom the greater part were renegade French.

On 25 August the remaining starving garrison at Verneuil surrendered, and on that same day Saint-Guillaume-de-Mortain fell.

Eu and St Pol marched on Pont-l'Eveque, while Dunois and a larger force went to Lisieux. Both towns quickly surrendered, Bishop Basin negotiating an agreement with the French commanders at Lisieux.

Joachim de Bohault, with these lords who had gained St Jacques de Beuvron, took, after an attack of ten hours, the town of [Saint-Guillaume-de-] Mortaine. The count de Dunois, with the count de St Pol and those who had been at the capture of Pont Audemer, marched to lay siege to the city of Lisieuz ; but when those within the city observed the great force brought against it, and which it was impossible for them to resist, – fearing also, that, should it be taken by storm, they would lose everything, they held several conferences together, and, by the advice of their bishop, offered to surrender the place to the king of France. The bishop managed so honourably and ably that not the smallest damage was done to any individual, but each peaceably enjoyed his property as before the surrender.

Dunois and his captains decided to avoid the major garrisons of western Normandy such as Caen and Falaise. Instead the remaining garrisons in eastern Normandy were to be reduced systematically before a general advance on Rouen. In Rouen itself, the situation was growing increasingly serious. On 24 August, the army of Dunois moved south to lay siege to Mantes. De Monstrelet relates:

The counts de Dunois and St Pol arrived with five or six hundred combatants, the same day, before the town of Mantes, and summoned the inhabitants to return to their obedience to the king of France. They at first refused, from fear of the garrison, although in their hearts they were well inclined to obey the summons; and the lieutenant-general ordered preparations for an immediate attack. The inhabitants noticed this, but were fearful that the English garrison, amounting to two hundred and sixty men ... would make a defence.

The French army arrived unopposed, but news had also come of boats gathered at Paris laden with engines of war in readiness for a bombardment. On 26 August the citizens of Mantes took the tower and gate, forcing the garrison to surrender. On 27 August there was the ceremonial entrance of Charles VII into Verneuil. Every week, three or four English castles were being taken or surrendering to massively superior forces. Owen Tudor, aged around forty-nine at this time, had to decide whether to surrender or fight. He knew that Somerset could not call in his garrisons to help strengthen Rouen, as it was 125 miles east, and the French had taken possession of virtually every town on the way except Caen. Even worse, he would have been receiving less and less information about the situation as the French controlled more and more roads and river crossings. Apart from escape by sea – and certain disgrace at home – he had no option. Even if he requisitioned a ship, there was a potential death penalty for captains who deserted their posts.

The surrender of the boundary town and castle of Vernon to the army of Dunois quickly followed the fall of Mantes. Robert de Flocques, bailiff of Evreux, was initially sent to ask for Vernon's surrender. Then it was attacked by the counts of Saint Pol and Eu, with a strong body of archers. After fighting between 28 and 30 August, the 'town and castle of Vernon were surrendered, – in which were twelve score English, under the command of the [wounded] son of the earl of Ormond. They marched away in safety with their baggage, and the inhabitants remained peaceably in the town, without losing an article of their effects.' Dunois was given the town and castle, which had been in English hands since 1415. Vernon is in the Eure near Giverny, straddling the Seine, around halfway between Paris and Rouen.

At the end of August, the seneschal of Poitou took a force and gained the castle of Logny (Loigny), held by an esquire of Normandy for its owner, Sir Francis de Surienne, 'the Aragonian'. The mercenary de Surienne, captain of Loigny, arranged for the castle to be taken, not wishing his property to be destroyed. He accepted a bribe of 12,000 *ecu* from Pierre de Brézé to let 200 French into the keep, capturing its defenders, including foreign mercenaries. De Surienne then accepted the captaincy of Loigny from Charles VII. De Surienne was not alone in changing sides. Richard Merbury was to give up the powerful fortress of Gisors in October, in exchange for the ransom-free liberation of his sons, captured at Pont-Audemer. He was made captain of Saint-Germain-en-Laye by Charles, and allowed possession of his French wife's territories. His lieutenant, 'Reynfoks', possibly Raynforth, had followed Matthew Gough in 1444, but was given 687 *livres tournois* by Pierre de Brézé for his part in the surrender.

Barker's *Conquest* is invaluable for seeing the events unfolding around Owen Tudor and his garrison. The castle of Anjou surrendered to the governor of Pontoise. At the end of August Charles VII rode to congratulate the garrison of Evreux, and by the beginning of September the valuable Vernon castle and town (mentioned above), Dangu Castle, Harcourt, Gournay, Roche-Guyon and Gourlay had fallen. Most had delayed surrendering expecting Somerset to lead out an army from Rouen. Dangu Castle lies on the course of the Epte, one of two castles in Dangu, in the Eure department, built in the twelfth century. Little survives of the first, and the other dominated the village from a hill on the west opposite the church of Saint-Jean-Baptiste. Located between Gisors and Château-sur-Epte, it faced the French castles of Courcelles and Boury.

De Monstrelet says that the Count of St Pol laid siege to Gournay:

On his march he was met by some of the townsmen, who came to make an offer to yield up the place, which was under the guard of William Harper, lieutenant to William Coram, an Englishman. The lieutenant, fearful of the event of a siege, and knowing also how the tide of war was turned, – and that all the towns and castles were surrendering to the French' gave the castle to St Pol. The count d'Eu now crossed the Seine to besiege Harcourt...

The lord de Jalognes, marshal of France, and the lord of Roche-Guyon, marched a large body of men-at-arms to conquer the castle of La Roche-Guyon. To effect this, they detached about thirty men by water, well suppijed with cannon and ammunition, who approached the place as if intending to besiege it, making as much noise as though they had been two hundred, and remained before it for three days, constantly skirmishing with the garrison; but although this garrison did not consist of more than sixteen men, the French gained no advantage over them. On Thursday the 3rd of September, the lords de Jalognes and de la Roche-Guyon appeared before it with their forces; and when John Howel, the English governor, saw so numerous a body that it would be vain for him to oppose it, at the same time fearing the event of a siege, and considering the right the king had to reconquer his kingdom, entered into a treaty with these lords conditionally to surrender the castle, unless he should be relieved by the king of England, or his lieutenant in Normandy, within fifteen days; and that he and his men should have free liberty to march away with their baggage whither they pleased.

Intelligence of this was sent to the duke of Somerset, lieutenant of Normandy, in Rouen, who tampered with the messenger to introduce four-and-twenty English into the castle, and put Howel to death. On his return, he attempted to gain over some of the garrison to his purpose, of admitting the twenty-four Englishmen to execute his damnable design; but knowledge of this plan coming secretly to the ears of Howel, he sent in haste for the lord de la Roche-Gnyon, who had withdrawn himself and his forces until the fifteenth day should arrive, to whom he surrendered the place. The garrison marched away, under passports, with their effects; but Howel was so indignant at the plot formed against his life that he became a Frenchman, and took the oaths of allegiance, on condition that he should enjoy the landed property of his wife, who was a native of France – and the lord de la Roche Guyon continued him in the government of his castle.

However, there is a slightly different version given by Vale in his biography of Charles VII, stating that in September 1449 at La-Roche-Guyon, its Welsh captain, John Edwards (not Howel), was persuaded by his wife to accept a payment of 4,500 *livres tournois* to change his allegiance to Charles VII. The castle was taken undamaged. Nonetheless, De Monstrelet goes on to say:

About the middle of September it was resolved, in the councils held at Louviers, that, considering the great body of French chivalry, it would be necessary to form two divisions: the one under the command of Charles d'Artois count of Eu, Louis de Luxembourg count of St Pol, and other captains, having with them from three to four thousand combatants, were ordered to besiege the new castle of Nicorps [in the Manche], which was held by the captain, Adam Illetont, an Englishman. The French army came before it on Tuesday the 12th day of September, and took the town by storm on the following Thursday. The castle was then besieged, – and surrendered on capitulation fifteen days afterward. The other division was under the command of the count de Dunois, lieutenant-general, having with him the counts de Clermont and de Nevers, with four thousand veteran soldiers. On leaving Louviers, they marched to lay siege to the castle of Chambrais [Chambray, on the Eure] on the 18th of September, of which an Englishman, called William Crinton, was governor, and had under him two hundred men for its defence. After seven days' siege it surrendered on capitulation with the count de Clermont, – and thus was it restored to the obedience of the king of France.

Mortimer accounts for the fast destruction of English resistance in Normandy, describing how the Duke of Brittany and his brother Richemont, 'falling into the Cotentin with an army of Bretons, reduced Coutances, Valognes, St Lo [15 September], Torigny, Carenton, Gavré and Pont d'Euve [Pont d'Oue], with all lesser places in those parts held out six weeks: Fougeres, indeed, held out six weeks, but at last was taken by assault'. According to Mortimer, in just a few weeks Charles's army had taken

> Nogent, Chateau Gaillard, Pont l'Eveque, Neufchatel, Gisors, La Roch Guyon [la Roche Guyon on the Seine was said to be 'almost impregnable'], Fecamp and Harcourt… The Duke of Alençon, with his body of troops, took Fresnay; and, entering Normandy on the side of Maine, surprised Condé, and reduced Alecon, the capital of his own dominions, together with Belesme, Epay and Yimes, with the adjoining county. But no-one appeared more zealous in this war than Regnier, king of Sicily, Margaret of Anjou the queen of England's father, and her brother John, duke of Calabria; they brought a gallant body of troops to the assistance of the French, and, having acted with the duke of Alençon in some of his enterprises, joined Charles' division with his forces, who, thus strengthened, resolved to form the siege of Rouen, the capital of Normandy.

Talbot now advised Somerset to make a great stand in Rouen, much as Bedford had done in Paris. Winter was approaching, and armies hardly ever campaigned during that time because of the attendant hardships. However, Charles wanted Normandy to fall as quickly as possible.

Somerset did not know what to do, remaining at Rouen with the majority of his troops and leaving other towns and fortresses to their own resources. It had been decided that the French armies should again separate, the counts of Eu and St Pol operating in the Pays de Caux, and Dunois on the left bank of the Seine. Gournay and Neufchatel fell to the former while Dunois captured Harcourt (14 September), Chambrais (20 September), Exmes and finally Argentan. Harcourt was the first castle to put up major resistance, with a garrison of eighty men, and it endured a siege lasting fifteen days with both sides using artillery. The Bastard of Vendôme had a particular grievance against Robert Frogenhall, its captain, for breaking his oath not to take up arms against the French.

At the end of the month, the siege of Gaillard was opened under the direction of Charles VII himself. Fécamp fell. Meanwhile, in the west, the Duke of Brittany had crossed into Normandy with a large army early in September, and by October he had captured Coutances. In September the

Bretons besieged Avranches and took most of the Cotentin Peninsula and Saint-Ló, Torigni-sur-Vire and Carentan. Matthew Gough had to surrender Carentan and Bellême, the latter he was holding with 200 men. Château-Gaillard was besieged. Partisans of the Duke of Alençon had made further gains, capturing Essay and Alençon itself.

Meanwhile, the army commanded by Francois I of Brittany, and led by his uncle Richemont, was progressing and taking the English-garrisoned castles in Normandy one by one. At this point, French armies totalling over 30,000 men were facing 6,000–8,000 English and their allies in scattered garrisons. Possibly unknown to Owen Tudor, every castle around him was falling. It would have been dangerous to send out riders to scout the area or contact other garrisons, as Regnéville was already undermanned. De Monstrelet dispassionately describes the sequence of events thus:

About the same period of this year, the duke of Brittany, his brother the count de Richemont, constable of France, with other nobles and men-at-arms from his duchy, amounting to a thousand or twelve hundred lances, entered lower Normandy, to restore it to the obedience of the king of France from the dominion of the English (the ancient enemies of the realm,) who had usurped the government of it for nearly thirty-two years. They first advanced to the town of Mont St Michel; and the nobles and men-at-arms were quartered in the villages of upper and lower Les Pas, Courtis [both in Avranches], St George en Gaine, Postulbanch, and thereabouts. The duke, on quitting Brittany, had left his brother, the lord Peter, on the frontiers, near to Fougeres and Avranches, for their defence, with three hundred lances.

On the morrow, the duke and the constable formed their van-guard under the command of Sir James de Luxembourg lieutenant to the constable, the marshal and admiral of France, of five hundred spears, who that day marched to Coutances [capital of the Cotentin], and lay before it, – while the duke and the main army, consisting of five or six hundred lances, remained that night in and about Granville [the seaport a few miles south of Regnéville]. On the morrow, the constable advanced the main army toward Coutances, and halted opposite to the hospital but they were not there a day before the English in the town marched away, and the inhabitants continued in the same peaceful state as before this renewal of war. The duke of Brittany next marched to lay siege to St Lo, and ordered his van to advance and take up their quarters on one side of the town, – while he followed with the army on the next day, and posted himself on the opposite side. Sir William de Poitou commanded in the place, with a garrison of two hundred men, – but, notwithstanding these numbers, he made no resistance, but capitulated with the duke for its surrender, on being allowed to march away with his men whither he should please. The duke and the constable, during their stay at St Lo, won the following towns, villages, and castles, namely, le Hommet [near St Lo], Neufville [near Alencon], Torigny [near Coutances], Beuseville, Hambie [a market town near Coutances], La Motte l'Evêque [a barony and castle near Coutances], la Haye-du-Puy [a market town near Coutances], Chanteloup [near Coutances], L'Aunay and many other small places round St Lo, in which city, at well as in those captured places, strong garrisons were posted. The van was now detached to the town of Carentan, and followed by the main body; but the garrison held out only three days before they surrendered, and then marched away with staves in their hands, – and those in the town were reinstated in their possessions.

The marshal and the admiral of France now separated from the duke and the constable, and came before Pont d'Oue [Pont d'Ouilly, a market town on the Vire in Normandy],which having taken by storm, they overran all the country of Coutantin, without meeting any resistance. The government of it and Carentan was given to Joachim Rohault. [Caentan had surrendered to the Duke of Brittany on 30 September. Mathew Gough shared command with Sir William Herbert, who had been in France since around 1440.] From Carentan, the above lords returned to Coutances, and thence, in the month of October, detached a party to Gavrey [on the Seine, near Coutances]. On the morrow, the duke and the constable came to Coutances, where the duke stayed that day, and before the constable could arrive at Gavrey, the bulwark had been won by storm; and on the morrow, Sir Geofirey de Couvren, who directed the siege, having made great approaches by his mines, attacked the castle with such vigour that the English garrison, of about six score men, demanded a parley, and concluded a treaty with the constable for its surrender, on being allowed to march away in safety with their effects.

As Captain of Regnéville, Owen Tudor may have heard of the great Richemont's advance, via escapees by boat from Granville. On 12 September Richemont took nearby Coutances, and immediately besieged Owen's garrison:

A detachment is charged to regain the castle of Regnéville. Regnévillais farmers fill the moat to facilitate the assault. The battle will be fierce and the castle is severely damaged. The French prevail. On 19 September 1449, the fortress was taken from the English by the Constable of Richemont with the army of the Duke of Brittany and with a hundred citizens of Coutances and peasants of Regnéville. The assault desolated the fortress by the sea. The following year, in 1450, following the Battle of Formigny, between Isigny and Bayeux, the English are driven from Normandy. Three years later ended the Hundred Years War.

Renneville, on the Eure, captained by 'Griffith ap Meredith, Welshman', surrendered soon after this.

By the end of the year Richemont had retaken the whole of the Cotentin Peninsula, and Regnéville Castle was said to be severely damaged after a siege. (The castle was razed in 1637, the four-storey keep having been filled with gunpowder. In the remaining two walls, the thickness is over 10 feet.) The *Annnuaire de l'Enseignement Primaire de la Manche, 1* (1897) dates the surrender of Regnéville as 19 September 1449. The original source for Owen Tudor having been still captain of Regnéville when it fell in 1449 is the *Chronique de Mathieu d'Escouchy*, which says that the garrison was then commanded by a *'cappitainne un nomme Avain'*: *'Vers 1415, le château de Regnéville tomba aux mains des Anglais et resta en leur possession jusqu'en 1449. Après six jours de siège, le Gallois Owen Tudor, qui le commandait, le rendit à l'amiral de Coëtivy, commandant des troupes ...* (*Revue des Questions Historiques*, 92, 1912). It tells us that towards 1415 the castle fell into the hands of the English and remained in their possession until 1449. After six days of siege, Owen Tudor surrendered it to the admiral of Coëtivy, commander of the army. However, Owen Tudor still held the post as captain of the castle as late as 22 December 1449.

Bicheno writes that 'hardly any of the smaller fortified towns put up a fight. In most, the inhabitants opened their gates and welcomed the French armies, or, as at Verneuil, helped them scale the walls. Most of the English garrisons which prevented this were persuaded to surrender on generous terms. One such was Regnéville, a port on the coast of the Cotentin peninsula near Coutances, where the king's stepfather Owen Tudor surrendered to the Bretons after six days. He was permitted to take ship to England with his men, their dependants and possessions.'

However, nearly all French sources comment upon the 'fierce battle' at the castle at this time, with the sea walls and side walls being badly damaged. 'Towards 1582, Roulland de Gourfaleur modified the castle, which was badly damaged by the battles of the Hundred Years War and the lack of maintenance for a century. He modernized it by opening windows in the dungeon.' It appears that Owen, after initially resisting, came to an agreement to surrender in order to save the castle from destruction. Certainly, there was no punishment or disgrace involved in his men sailing back to England. Richemont could now complete the conquest of the Cotentin Peninsula, before overcoming all of Normandy. More than anything else, Owen's posting to a strategic castle in Normandy may have meant that he commanded respect in action in war. The old Welsh tales about him being at Agincourt may well have been true, and his service under the renowned warrior Hungerford will have helped his cause. It may well be that Henry VI had given Owen this fairly prestigious posting to keep him out of England and the intrigues at court, but it could not have come about if Owen was not experienced in warfare.

Somerset's situation in Rouen was now desperate. There was no sign of the promised army from England, and the city prepared itself for the inevitable siege.

After the disaster at Pont-Audemer, those soldiers that had managed to return to Rouen were sent to reinforce Gisors. Troops of the Somerset's own personal retinue were also despatched to strengthen the besieged Château-Gaillard. Assisting these two castles, both strongly sited and fortified, offered some chance of holding up the enemy advance. However, the French encirclement continued remorselessly, Caudebec being taken in early October. Cut off from any support, Somerset was forced to go to the local moneylender to raise cash for his troops. By the beginning of October the armies of Dunois, the counts of Eu and St Pol and the duke of Alençon were converging on Rouen, and on 19 October there was a major rising in the town. The English were driven to the three main fortresses – the castle, the palace and the barbican on the bridge – and French troops entered Rouen. Somerset's position was hopeless, and on 20 October he was forced to abandon the barbican.

On 22 October a full-scale bombardment of the castle and palace began, and on 23 October Somerset opened negotiations for surrender. His surrender was seen as shameful or even treasonable in England. The news was conveyed to York in Ireland, and *Hall's Chronicle* records how it 'kindled so great a rancour in his harte and stomack, that he never left persecuting of the Duke of Somerset'. York still held the captaincy of Rouen during Somerset's governorship, and used the surrender to try and lessen Somerset's hold on the king and increase the influence of his own faction. To surrender a town without siege was a treasonable offence if there was opportunity for reasonable defence, and York wanted Somerset imprisoned and taken to court, but Somerset was never put on trial.

Victor Duruy summarised the campaign leading to the fall of Rouen:

Charles felt himself strong enough to bring matters to a conclusion with the English. An Aragonese adventurer in the service of England, failing to receive money from the government of Henry VI., attacked in time of peace a rich town of Brittany, and gave it to his men to plunder in compensation for their arrears of pay. Immediately the king of France and the Duke of Brittany demanded reparation and indemnity from the English governor of Normandy. As the indemnity was not forthcoming, the French proceeded to take it themselves. Dunois entered the province with a strong army. Lisieux, Mantes, Vernon, Evreux, Louviers, and Coutances were taken, or delivered up by the citizens without striking a blow. England was then upon the verge of the War of the Roses, and troubled herself little about Normandy. The governor, Somerset, instead of concentrating his forces, scattered them in twenty garrisons: in negotiation he showed equal want of skill. Good order and ability were now on the side of the French, and victory passed over to them. In October, 1449, they appeared before the walls of Rouen. In a moment all the bourgeoisie of Rouen was in arms; but against the English, who withdrew into the castle, and were compelled to surrender, delivering to the king of France, with Rouen, the whole lower course of the Seine.

8

Owen's Sons and the Wars of the Roses 1450–1460

From *The Union of the Two Noble and Illustre Families of Lancastre and Yorke*, commonly called *Hall's Chronicle* (spelling modernised), we read:

When foreign war and outward battles,were brought to an end and final conclusion the domestic discord and civil dissension began to renew and arise within the realm of England; for when the care of outward hostility (which kept the minds of the princes in the realm occupied, and in exercise,) was taken away and vanished, desire of sovereignty, and ambition of pre-eminence, suddenly sprang out so far, that the whole Realm was divided into two several [separate] factions, and private parts. For king Henry, descended from the house of Lancaster, claiming the crown from Henry IV his grandfather, first author of this division: and Richard duke of York, as heir to Lionel, the third son to king Edward the third: wrestled for the game, and strove for the wager. By reason whereof, the nobles as well as the common people were into parts divided, to the destruction of many a man, and to the great ruin and decay of this region. For while the one part studied to vanquish and suppress the other, all commonwealth was set aside, and Justice and equity clearly exiled.

In January 1450, French defeats and royal incompetence led to Adam Moleyns, Lord Privy Seal and Bishop of Chichester, being lynched by a mob of unpaid soldiers in Portsmouth. He had been an active partisan of the deeply unpopular Suffolk.

William de la Pole, the first Duke of Suffolk, was a commander in the 100 Years War and had been a king's favourite, although he lost many French possessions and York had managed to have him briefly imprisoned for 'treason'. Suffolk was disliked by the people, and from him we get the term 'jackanapes'. At the time it was slang for a monkey, derived from 'Jack of Naples' with 'of Naples' being rendered 'a Napes' in vernacular. Monkeys were one of many exotic goods from Naples exhibited in Britain, and the nickname 'Jack a Napes' acquired the meaning 'upstart person', from its use as Suffolk's nickname. He was one of first *nouveau riche* nobles, risen from the merchant class and despised by the older houses. His family used a collar and chain on its coat of arms, and as this was more associated with monkey leashes, leading to the insult of 'Jack a Napes' for the duke.'
(Breverton, *Jasper Tudor*)

The king's favourite, and a close ally of Carinal Beaufort, the Earl of Suffolk had been made a marquess in 1444, and a duke in 1448.

After Cardinal Beaufort's retirement in 1443, Suffolk had become Henry VI's chief adviser. He dominated Henry and the government, and he set about enriching himself, giving himself the lucrative posts of Chamberlain of England, Captain of Calais, Warden of the Cinque Ports and Chief Steward of the Duchy of Lancaster, among other profitable offices. Some felt that he and Margaret of Anjou had been responsible for Gloucester's death, and he came to be 'the most despised man in England'. Suffolk was suspected of being a traitor, secretly meeting Jean, Count de Dunois, several times in 1448 in his London mansion. Dunois was the successful French general at the Siege of Orléans. Suffolk was said to have passed him council minutes, possibly in exchange for not paying the ransom of £20,000 he owed to Dunois. Meanwhile, Ralph de Cromwell, Lord Treasurer, was trying to make Suffolk pay heavy taxes that he owed. England lost Maine and Anjou through Suffolk's negotiations for the marriage between Henry VI and Margaret of Anjou, and the loss of nearly all English possessions in northern France led to his arrest on 28 January 1450. His downfall came after the English treacherously captured Fougères in March 1449 with his approval, reopening a war which England could not win. Suffolk was arrested, and impeached in Parliament, where the Commons blamed him for the defeat at Formigny and the loss of Normandy. He was charged with treason, but the king intervened to protect his favourite, reluctantly banishing him for five years, beginning on 1 May 1450. Suffolk was forced to leave his London mansion for his country manor at Wingfield by rioting crowds.

On 1 May Suffolk embarked for Calais, but a huge ship of the royal fleet, *The Nicholas of the Tower*, intercepted him. In the *Paston Letters*, William Lomner wrote to John Paston on 5 May that men from the *Nicholas* boarded Suffolk's ship and 'the master badde hym, "Welcom, Traitor," as men sey'. Suffolk's fate is described:

> ...and thanne his herte faylyd hym, for he thowghte he was desseyvyd [deceived], and yn the syght of all his men he was drawyn ought of the grete shippe yn to the bote; and there was an exe, and a stoke, and oon of the lewdeste of the shippe badde hym ley down his hedde, and he should be fair ferd wyth, and dye on a swerd; and toke a rusty swerd, and smotte off his hedde withyn halfe a doseyn strokes.

His headless body washed up on a Dover beach. The king had suddenly lost his Lord Privy Seal, Moleyns, whom he had known since childhood, and his closest advisor, Suffolk, both by violence. Matters were to worsen.

Owen had returned to the king's household from Normandy, where the important fortified ports of Harfleur and Honfleur on the Seine estuary were lost in January 1450. This gave France complete control over the Lower Seine. The Duke of Brittany now handed over to France the castles that his army had taken in Normandy. Dissent was rife in England, and Duruy reports that the king sent Thomas Kyriel with 6,000 men into Normandy. On 15 April 1450, near the village of Fourmigny, Richemont and the Count of Clermont attacked. Kyriel was defeated and left 4,000 men on the field in what would prove to be the penultimate major battle of the Hundred Years War. (Castillon in 1453 is regarded as ending the English effort to conquer France.)

Vire, Bayeux, Avranches, Caen, Domfront, and Falaise fell by the end of July. Cherbourg, the great port on the top of the Cotentin Peninsula, finally capitulated after a month's siege on 12 August 1450. All of Normandy had been acquired in a single year by Richemont, who for the next six or seven years defended it from sporadic English attacks.

The Hundred Years War had constantly depleted the Treasury, and heavy taxation was the direct result. Because there was no proper administration of the tax system, royal officials were known to make money at the expense of merchants, gentry and the working classes. Jack Cade led an uprising against the unpopular policies of Henry VI's advisors in May 1450, followed by peasants and small landowners from Kent. They were objecting to forced labour (via the Statute of Labourers), corrupt courts, heavy taxation, the seizure of land by nobles and the loss of royal lands in France. The minor gentry and churchmen involved had different priorities to the peasants. They did not wish for social upheaval, but wanted the removal of certain of Henry's councillors, the return of royal estates that had been granted to them (making the king poorer and thus unable to finance the wars), the removal of the 'traitors' who surrounded the king, and fairer taxation. The rising was not against the king, but his councillors and advisors.

The rebels defeated a government force sent to disperse them at Sevenoaks and entered London, where at first the Londoners supported Cade. The king fled to Warwickshire with his household, which included Owen Tudor and his sons. The rebels stormed the Tower of London, but just failed to take it. They beheaded Sir James Fiennes, Baron Saye, Henry's Lord High Treasurer, after a mock trial but the violent behaviour of some of Cade's men turned the Londoners against the rebels, and there was a skirmish on London Bridge. In Wiltshire, a separate group of rebels killed William Ayscough, Bishop of Salisbury, on 25 June. He was the king's personal confessor, one of the most influential men in the kingdom, and had married Henry to the unpopular Margaret of Anjou. In the first few months of 1450, four of the king's closest advisors had met violent deaths.

John Kemp, Archbishop of Canterbury, was Lord Chancellor and took action in the vacuum left by the king's flight, issuing pardons and offering redress of complaints. In an arranged truce Cade presented a list of his grievances to royal officials, who assured him that the demands would be met, and Cade handed over a list of his men so that each could receive a royal pardon. Cade's manifesto represented not only the grievances of the people but those of some MPs, lords and magnates. The document included fifteen complaints and five demands to be brought before the king for scrutiny and dictated the causes of the revolt. The rebels then returned home. Although pardons were issued to Cade and his followers, after their dispersal Henry, probably on the advice of his hated council, voided all pardons because they had not been created or approved by Parliament. A reward of 1,000 marks was promised to anyone who would deliver Cade to the king, dead or alive. On 12 July, in a skirmish, Cade was mortally wounded. His corpse was hanged, drawn, and quartered, and his head placed on a pole on London Bridge. His limbs were sent throughout Kent on display. Some of his followers were executed, as were those behind a smaller rising in Sussex in 1450.

Somerset was an extremely unpopular figure after his return from France, as under his rule Normandy had fallen in little over a year. However, he had resumed his seat on the King's Council by the middle of August 1450. Unfortunately for Henry VI, he retained complete trust in Somerset's abilities, creating him Constable of England, and Somerset replaced Suffolk in the king's affections. In France, matters kept deteriorating. Bordeaux had been captured in 1451 by Charles VII, and the Hundred Years War appeared to be at an end. However, after 300 years of English rule, the citizens of Bordeaux still felt themselves to be subjects of the English king, and sent messengers demanding that he recapture the province. In October 1452, Talbot landed near Bordeaux with a force of 3,000 men, and with the co-operation of the townspeople, Talbot easily took the city. The English took control of most of Western Gascony by the end of the year. The French had expected an expedition to come through Normandy, and Charles VII prepared his forces over winter, and by spring of 1453 was ready to counter-attack with three armies.

The siege of Castillon-sur-Dordogne (now Castillon-sur-Battaille) in Gascony began in July. John Talbot, Earl of Shrewsbury, was surrounded, and decided to attack, not realising the strength of the French force. He was the only Englishman who remained mounted in the battle, and did not wear armour. After being taken in Normandy, he had promised not to wear armour against the French. He was killed, with his son, the Lord Lisle. His horse was hit by a projectile, with Talbot being pinned under it, and he was axed to death. Duruy relates:

> Talbot hastened to attack them; but their artillery, skilfully managed by the brothers Bureau, mowed down the English ranks, and Talbot himself was slain. Then the French advanced from their fortifications and fell upon the disconcerted English, of whom they killed four thousand men. Two days after, Castillon surrendered, and other strong places soon after. The royal army closed around Bordeaux, francs archers overran the country; the vessels lent the king by La Rochelle and Brittany blockaded the mouth of the Gironde. Bordeaux, threatened with famine, was obliged at this time to accept such conditions as the king was willing to grant. He deprived the town of its privileges, exacted an indemnity of a hundred thousand crowns, and ordered the banishment of twenty ringleaders, with confiscation of their goods, and also the construction of three citadels commanding the town. In October, 1453, Charles VII made his triumphant entry into Bordeaux: the Hundred Years War was finished. The English no longer possessed anything in France but Calais and two small towns near it.

Although the king had been married for seven years by 1452, he still had no children, and the death of Gloucester in 1447 removed his last surviving uncle. His immediate family consisted of his wife, the widely disliked

Margaret of Anjou, and his Tudor half-brothers. Somerset's power had grown since York had attempted an unsuccessful coup earlier that year, and Somerset wished to bolster the small royal house of Lancaster against York's desire to become Henry's heir and king. Evans suggested that Edmund Beaufort, now Duke of Somerset, had a 'flash of Athenian acuteness' and was responsible for the two Tudors being ennobled during the Christmas holidays in 1452. The *DNB* of 1899 tells us that Edmund of Hadham was summoned to Parliament on 30 January 1452 or 1453, and created Earl of Richmond and premier earl of England upon 6 March 1452 or 1453. Jasper of Hatfield became Earl of Pembroke on 23 November 1452. They were noted as the 'premier earls', with only dukes in precedence (there were no marquesses at this time). Griffiths and Thomas write that the 'titles are significant. They were the titles held by the two uncles whom King Henry could remember, John, duke of Bedford, and Humphrey, duke of Gloucester.' The next two stages of ennoblement did not follow immediately, probably delayed because Henry VI was out of London and Parliament was not in session. There was also the situation of the two new earls being the king's half-brothers. Henry and Somerset would have wished, as Thomas writes, 'to elevate them in the most solemn and dignified way available to him, and so the second stage of creation, belting with the sword, was held over until the end of the Christmas holidays at the beginning of 1453'. In preparation for this, at Christmas 1452 the new earls were given velvet garments, cloth of gold and furs, and expensive trappings and saddles for their horses. Owen Tudor, that penniless Welsh adventurer, now had two sons almost at the very height of English nobility.

Henry and Margaret spent Christmas at Greenwich, returning to their palace at the Tower of London for the investiture of the new earls. In the Tower on Friday 5 January 1453, the eve of Epiphany, the two young men were knighted in company with four others. On 6 January Henry formally created the Tudor brothers as earls, and they were summoned on 20 January to their first Parliament, which opened on 6 March. The third and final stage of their creation took place in the parliament that opened at Reading on 6 March 1453. On that day they took their seats as premier earls and the Commons presented a petition that begged the king to recognise them as his legitimate uterine brothers, to release them from liability under any statute because their ancestors were not English, and to confirm the letters patent which Henry had previously granted to them. Much of the petition is taken up with ensuring that the brothers did not suffer from the punitive legislation of Henry IV, despite the fact that their father had himself been granted letters of (partial) denizenship in 1432.

Thus in the parliament of 1453 Edmund and Jasper Tudor were formally declared legitimate. Griffiths and Thomas note that Henry and Margaret of Anjou had produced no children after eight years of marriage, and in the deteriorating conditions and uncertainty the capable Richard of York seemed to many to represent stability and hope for the future. They write: 'In these circumstances, King Henry looked to his small group of relatives – the Beauforts, the Hollands, the Staffords and the Tudors – with a view to buttressing the aristocratic basis of his rule and buttressing his dynasty.' Indeed, the Tudor brothers were the only close relatives the king had left.

By March 1453 the two Tudor brothers stood on the steps of the throne itself. Thomas writes, 'No earl, however, especially a member of the royal family, could sustain the high estate which he enjoyed without a very substantial income, and so it was essential for the king to endow his penniless step-brothers with extensive and profitable lands. Fortunately for the two new earls, the king and Parliament had reached a successful compromise over the Act of Resumption of 1450 and the crown now had large tracts of land available for fresh alienation' to pass on to the new earls. The earls had asked the king to release them from any statutory disabilities arising because their father was not English, which Henry did, along with granting Jasper the estates of the earldom of Pembroke.

Edmund had already received the estates of Richmond as they had been available previously. The honour of Richmond included lands down the east side of England, from Yorkshire to Norfolk, plus lordships in Lancashire and Westmorland. Jasper, as well as Pembroke, had the adjacent lordships of Cilgerran and Llansteffan (Llanstephan). Edmund was given the fortified Baynard's Castle, on the Thames, and Jasper and his councillor Sir Thomas Vaughan were given a house in Brook Street. Henry made the formerly penniless Edmund and Jasper more large grants of land and entitlements to build up to an earl's necessary revenues, particularly in 1454, and Edmund's name occurs alongside Jasper's as being exempt from the operation of Acts of Resumption. In a household memorandum of 30 March 1453, Edmund was appointed great forester of Braydon forest.

Jasper was given an identical retinue at court, described by Williams:

In an old memorandum of the household of Henry VI, in November 1454, the Earle of Richmond and the Earle of Pembroke are prominently named, each with his retinue of i chaplein, ij squiers, ij yomen, ij chamberleins.' But their father is not included in the household at all.

These earls entirely dropped the coat-armour of the Tudors, and used the royal arms of England with a difference; thus, Jasper Tudor, Earl of

Pembroke, bore: Quarterly, France and England; a bordure azure charged with eight martlets *or*. This appears to have been the coat carved on an ancient bedstead once at Penmynydd. All the old books of arms ascribe to Owen Tudor himself the arms of his house: 'gules, a chevron ermines between three close helmets argent'. Sometimes, even in his case, the chevron is argent; but prevailing opinion seems to be that, after his union with the royal family, Owen Tudor bore the chevron ermines, and not plain as before.

Jasper Tudor's coat of arms was to parallel his brother Edmund's royal coat of arms, but with the martlets of his father added. (The martlet appears like a legless swallow, which accounts for some references in poetry to Owen as a swallow.)

It was now necessary to find a suitable (i.e. wealthy and well-connected) bride for each of the new earls, and as a first step, on 24 March 1453 they were jointly granted the wardship and marriage of one of England's richest heiresses, the Lady Margaret Beaufort, only surviving daughter and heiress of John Beaufort, Duke of Somerset. She was the neice of the duke's only surviving son, Edmund Beaufort. Edmund had already been given the wealthy estates of his uncle Cardinal Henry Beaufort. When John, Duke of Somerset, died on 27 May 1444 his daughter was a little under a year old, but she was soon married to John de la Pole, son and heir of the Marquess (later Duke) of Suffolk. Her Beaufort inheritance was already estimated at £1,000 per annum, and her 'acquisition' was probably part of Suffolk's known greed. Lady Margaret was a rich prize as a bride, not merely owing to her incredible riches but also because of her prominent position in one of the greatest magnate families of England. Around March 1453, the king allowed the ten-year-old Margaret Beaufort to divorce John de la Pole, the son of the deceased Suffolk, with a view to a potential marriage with a Tudor.

We may here mention the position of Richard, Duke of York, regarding the new earls. He would have undoubtedly been one of the better kings of England, which admittedly is not extensive praise, but he always seemed to want to do what was best for his nation. York's strength did not lie in military attributes, but in being an excellent and efficient administrator who did his best to restore a derelict economy. He tried to build bridges, and certainly was respected by the Tudor brothers and other Lancastrians, who followed his leadership when the king was not able to rule. His wife, Duchess Cecily, and his mother, Anne Mortimer, daughter of the Earl of March, were both from magnate families with huge estates, giving him kinsmen as allies. Apart from undoubted qualities of leadership, his economic worth was incredible, allowing him to build a great following among the nobility. Ross writes:

> Richard of York was also the greatest English landowner of his day. In England proper his estates, chiefly inherited from Edmund of Langley, extended into more than twenty shires. In Yorkshire he had wide estates in the West Riding centred around his castle of Sandal near Wakefield.
>
> Fotheringhay Castle in Northamptonshire was the focus of substantial estates in the east midlands. Further south another concentration lay in Hertfordshire, Essex and Suffolk, and he had other valuable properties in Berkshire, Hampshire, Wiltshire and Somerset. But his greatest strength lay in the inheritance of his mother, Anne, heiress of the powerful Mortimer earls of March. A chain of great lordships stretched through eastern Wales and the Marches from Denbigh in the north to Caerleon and Usk in the south, and was flanked by others in the adjoining English border counties, especially Shropshire, where Ludlow Castle formed the administrative headquarters of the whole. As Earl of Ulster, York was also a leading Anglo-Irish landowner. These estates together yielded the duke nearly £7,000 a year gross (£40 million today in labour value), and perhaps about £5,800 net.

His control of the Marcher territories gave him the great support of the invaluable Herbert, Devereux and Vaughan families, and his estates were worth possibly five times as much as those of Edmund and Jasper Tudor. Against such an ambitious and capable man, with royal heritage and powerful family connections, a weak king with a widely disliked French wife faced growing problems.

There is a vexing problem of whether Owen was knighted or not. Angharad Llwyd is in no doubt. Owen's sons were recognised as the premier earls in England by their peers, so one would assume that Henry VI may have granted his stepfather the award, but there is no record whatsoever.

The website thepeerage.com's entry for Owen begins: 'Sir Owen Tudor was born circa 1400 at Plas Penmynydd, Wales.' It calls Owen 'Squire of the body to Henry V and Henry VI, Clerk of the wardrobe of the Queen-Dowager Catherine of Valois.'

The website *geni.com* agrees that Owen was knighted, and his *Wikitree* entry reads: 'Henry VI in due time gave his two oldest Tudor half-brothers the rank of Earl though, as a signal recognition of their rank, they ranked above Marquesses and immediately below non-royal Dukes. Henry VI also issued an edict that the legitimisation of his two Tudor half-brothers was unnecessary. Henry VI knighted his stepfather Owen, made him Warden of Forestries, and appointed him a Deputy Lord Lieutenant. Prior to his creation as a Knight Bachelor, Owen, though excused from duty, was appointed an Esquire to the King's Person. Ironically, many years later, in order that he could command Henry VI's forces at Mortimer's Cross, Owen was made a Knight Banneret.'

Mirehouse gives us a rough date of knighthood: 'In 1458 Earl Jasper strengthened the walls of Tenby, making them six feet wide all round; he knighted his father, Owen Tudor, about this time, and fought stubbornly against Edward of York.'

Collins' *Baronettage* calls him 'Sir Owen Tudor, Kt., who marry'd Catherine, Daughter to Charles, the Simple king of France, and widow to H5 King of England...' Glover calls 'Owen Theodore the issue male of Kennan son of Coel, King of Brittaine, and brother of Helen, mother of Constantine the Great'.French's ancestry of Queen Victoria notes: 'Sir Owen is said by Thierry to have been an equerry in the palace of Henry V...', and footnotes that 'Queen Catherine is fifteenth in descent from Hugh Capet.'

However, the French writer Thierry does not entitle Owen, the relevant section making interesting reading:

Owen Glendower, the last man who legitimately bore the title prince of Wales, by the election and will of the Welsh people, survived the overthrow of his people and died in obscurity (A.D. 1416). His son Meredith ap Owen capitulated [not until 1421 or after], went to England, and there received the king's pardon, the other leaders of the insurrection received it likewise; and offices and titles at the court of London were given to many of them and their families on condition that they should no longer inhabit Wales, which, indeed, was no longer inhabitable for Welshmen, on account of the redoubled vexations of the agents of the foreign authority (A.D. 1416–1485). Among these Cambrian emigrants through necessity or through ambitions was a member of the family of the sons of Tudowr, named Owen ap Meredith ap Tudowr; who during the whole reign of Henry V, lived with him as an equerry of his palace; giving great satisfaction to the king, who granted him great favour, and vouchsafed to call him *Nostre cher et foyal*.

His manners and fine countenance made a deep impression on the queen, Catherine of France; who, having been left a widow by Henry V, privately married Owen ap Tudowr, or Owen Tudor as he was called in England. By her he had two sons Jasper, and Edmund; the second of whom, having arrived at man's estate, married Margaret daughter of John de Beaufort, earl of Somerset, sprung from the royal line of Plantagenet.

This took place when the branches or scions of that house were *slaughtering each other* [author's italics] for possession of the kingdom conquered by William the Bastard... The order of hereditary succession was peaceable during the continuation of the direct line of Henry II; but when the inheritance descended to the collateral branches, there arose a greater number of claimants in virtue of hereditary right; there were more troubles, factions and discords than had ever anywhere been occasioned by the practice of election. There now broke out the most dreadful and disgraceful of civil wars – that of kindred against kindred, and of men against infants in the cradle.

For several generations, two numerous families slaughtered each other, either in the field of battle or in cold blood, to maintain their legitimacy, without either of them being able effectually to destroy the other; for some member was continually springing up to fight against and dethrone his rival, and to reign until he himself was dethroned. There perished in these quarrels, according to the historians of the time, sixty or eighty princes of the royal house, almost all in the flower of their youth; for, in the princely families of York and Lancaster, few of the males attained to length of years. The women indeed lived longer, to see their sons butchered by nephews, and these by other nephews or by uncles, who themselves were murdered by near relatives.

Thierry then mentions that Richard III 'was indebted for his crown to the perpetuation of many murders' and described Henry Tudor taking the crown from exile in France, being assisted by Louis XI with loans. However, he notes sadly that Henry VIII

treated the mass of the [Welsh] people, like all his predecessors, as a conquered nation, to be feared and disliked. He studied to destroy the ancient customs of the inhabitants of Cambria, the remains of their social state [including laws], and even their language... The English authorities attacked about the same time the manuscripts and historical records, more numerous at that time in Wales than in any other country in Europe. Many noble families which had preserved their archives were obliged strictly to conceal them, whether to secure court favour, or to preserve them from the perquisitions of the royal agents.

Thierry expands on the theme, but it is worth noting that thousands upon thousands of records and manuscripts will have been burnt and lost during over a millennium of continuing foreign attacks upon Wales.

The Castillon disaster occurred on 17 July 1453, with John Talbot, Earl of Shrewsbury and his son both dying, as mentioned earlier. Talbot's death, and the subsequent recapture of Bordeaux three months later, effectively ended the Hundred Years War. Henry would not have heard of the loss until the first week in August. On 31 July, Henry and his court were at Kingstone Lacy in Dorset, and by 5 August were at Clarendon, a royal hunting lodge near Salisbury, on the return route to London. He received the kiss of homage from Sir William Stourton here on 7 August, and may have heard the news of the devastation of his army. He had a complete physical and mental breakdown, remaining in a semi-comatose depressive or schizophrenic stupor for eighteen months. (Other near-contemporary sources state that the king lost his mind after the loss of Bordeaux on 19 October 1453.) It may be that apart from the loss of Gascony, his deeply religious convictions had been shaken and that he now understood that York had been correct in his analysis of the hopeless French situation.

The area of mental illness is deeply complex, but Henry VI suffered from a major and recurring depressive disorder, characterised by catatonia, delusions and other symptoms, which Bark terms DSM-IV schizophrenia. Bark seems to favour a genetic causation: 'On his father's side were strong ruthless characteristics with no known psychosis but possible dementia in old age. His mother died at the age of thirty-six [actually thirty-five] having "lost her wits" [this author cannot find the original reference, but it is known that she was in great pain] in her terminal illness. His father, Charles VI of France, had forty-four episodes over thirty years of psychosis, mania and depression. Charles's wife, Henry's grandmother, was timelessly dissolute [this canard regarding Isabeau had been dealt with earlier in this book]. Henry's maternal great-grandmother was perhaps psychotic.'

Ashdown-Hill states that 'it has long been questioned whether Edward of Westminster was truly fathered by Henry VI', and relates that Margaret of Anjou became pregnant while Henry VI was mentally ill.

Costain, in *The Last Plantagenets*, places the king's breakdown on 6 July 1453. *Giles' Chronicle* places it on 7 July, but both are too early. Most historians relate that the king suffered his massive breakdown after hearing of the defeat at Castillon, which took place over a week later.

Henry's son Edward was born at Westminster on 13 October 1453. Using this date, Ashdown-Hill's time frame for an illegitimate birth would not fit. He also states that Isabeau of Bavaria 'enjoyed the reputation of being something of a nymphomaniac', possibly misunderstanding that this was propaganda bruited by Valois opponents after her death. Henry's condition was hidden for eight months, but the death of his Chancellor, Archbishop

John Kemp in March 1454, and the inability to use the Great Seal, forced its revelation.

Some have suggested that the grant of the earldom of Pembroke to Jasper gave offence to Queen Margaret of Anjou, who had formerly possessed it, pushing Jasper into York's faction, but Thomas tells us that 'this interpretation cannot be accepted, partly because the grant of the honour to Jasper Tudor was made with the queen's full knowledge and assent. Moreover, the absence of any bad feeling between Queen Margaret and Jasper is amply demonstrated by the fact that only a month after his ennoblement, on 20 April 1453, the earl and his elder brother Edmund accompanied the queen to Norwich, where they were entertained and presented with gifts by the city father.' Apart from this occasion, neither earl as yet seems to have been associated with the queen in any way since their ennoblement. Instead, they were considered members of a loose association of lords focussed around the real centre of power, the Duke of York.

Edmund Tudor was busy attending to affairs in Wales when a council was held on 15 March 1454, but in attendance were the archbishops of Canterbury and York, the bishops of Winchester, Durham, Ely, Worcester, Norwich, Hereford, Lincoln, Coventry and Lichfield, and the Prior of St John's. The lay peers present were the dukes of York and Buckingham, the earls of Pembroke, Warwick, Oxford, Devon, Salisbury, Shrewsbury and Wiltshire, and the Lords Graystoke, Fauconberg, Clinton, Stourton, Bourchier, Welles, Scrope of Bolton and Fiennes, Lord Say. Along with Jasper, Earl of Pembroke, only five of the sixteen were later to be loyal to the king – Buckingham, Oxford, Wiltshire, Shrewsbury and Lord Welles. The king had suffered his mental and physical collapse the previous year, and it would last for seventeen months; during this time Charles VII was slowly taking Aquitaine from the English, lords were fighting in Devon and Yorkshire, and York and Margaret were struggling over control of the government.

At this council it was decided that a commission should be given to three physicians and two surgeons to attend the king and prescribe remedies for his malady. They found the king far worse than they had expected, and on 27 March 1454 Jasper and other peers agreed that York should become Protector, albeit with several careful restrictions. (Some remembered that Richard of York's father, Richard of Cambridge, had been beheaded in 1415 for his part in the Southampton Plot against Henry V.) York proved himself an efficient and effective administrator, and he was supported by Jasper. York brought both stability and justice to the government of the kingdom, and both Edmund and Jasper were summoned on 29 May 1454 to attend a Great Council on 25 June. Both brothers, especially Jasper, were associated with

York and Warwick at this time, and were Privy Councillors for their step-brother Henry. During the November 1454 Great Council, action was taken to cut back on court and royal household expenditures as York attempted to grapple with the king's great debts. Jasper and Edmund were usually present in the household, and agreed to the economies. The entourage of each at court was reduced to a chaplain, two esquires, two yeomen and two chamberlains, a retinue only matched by that of Henry's spiritual confessor.

Unfortunately for York's hopes, after being utterly incapacitated since August 1453, Henry VI recovered his senses on Christmas Day 1454. He now learned for the first time that he had a year-old son, that York was Protector of the Realm, and that his favourites had some of his grants confiscated from them. His closest advisors, Somerset and Exeter, had been placed in custody by York for misgovernment. The king's recovery destroyed any prospect of order and good governance, and Margaret of Anjou and her party now plotted vengeance on York and his followers, and Somerset was released on bail on 5 February 1455, to the despair of York and his allies. Briefed by Margaret, Somerset complained at a council meeting on 4 March that he had been held for over a year without any charge being preferred against him. The king declared that his friend Somerset was his 'faithful liegeman', who had done him 'right true... service'. All Yorkist ministers were swiftly purged from office. York's other great enemy Henry Holland, Duke of Exeter, was soon released from Pontefract Castle on 19 March, after nine months' captivity. York was dismissed as Protector of the Realm, and summarily stripped of the profitable Captaincy of Calais, which was restored to the less capable Somerset.

The Prince of Wales, Edward of Lancaster, was not yet two years old, and Queen Margaret knew that York wished for a Yorkist dynasty to replace the Lancastrians. York saw little future with a newly healthy Henry, a new Prince of Wales and a vengeful queen again backed by his great enemies Somerset and Exeter. Margaret effectively restored all of Henry's former friends and advisors to power, in a group headed by her uncle Edmund Beaufort, Duke of Somerset. York, the Earl of Salisbury and Salisbury's son Warwick swiftly withdrew from London, returning to their estates. (Salisbury was York's brother-in-law, and Warwick was Salisbury's son Richard Neville, later to be known as the 'Kingmaker'.) Edmund and Jasper Tudor had to decide whom to support – their semi-sane Lancastrian half-brother, or the capable, efficient and honest Duke of York. Jasper Tudor was one of the main peers who tried to bring the factions together, possibly foreseeing the bloodshed to come. War was not in the interest of either Jasper or Edmund. They had come from nothing into wealth, unlike the great magnates, and had more to lose. Parliament met and attempts were again made to try and improve royal finances. Jasper was recorded as now swearing an oath of allegiance to Henry along with other lords, but again, Edmund does not appear to be as involved in proceedings as his brother, likely busy on the king's business in unsettled Wales. Owen seems to have been with Edmund, assisting through his experience of the families of north Wales.

Now the queen and the king's confidantes saw the opportunity of finally getting rid of York. In May 1455 a Great Council was summoned to meet at Leicester 'for the purpose of providing for the safety of the king's person against his enemies'. The summons implied that York and his supporters were 'mistrusted persons' against whom action must be taken. York, Salisbury, Warwick and their adherents were not invited to attend the council, which was ominous for York. The Yorkists had given no provocatin for any such proceedings, as they had been living quietly on their estates since their dismissal from office. York, Salisbury and Warwick were not invited to attend as councillors, but instead summoned to appear 'before' the Great Council. They obviously feared Margaret and Somerset's retribution; they thought they would be charged with subversion. York was in the north at Sandal Castle, and sent a fast messenger to Salisbury to bring a force and meet him. They marched south, hoping to gather allies, but only Warwick and Lord Clinton joined them, forming an army of around 3,000 men, nearly all from Yorkshire. The Duke of Norfolk gathered men to join them but lagged behind.

York's force was travelling too quickly for Norfolk; York was trying to face the king's army before it was joined by the forces of other lords, and the Yorkists were already massively outnumbered. Somerset summoned the king's allies to march to Leicester, but York swiftly bypassed the East Midlands on his way from York, instead heading directly for London, where he had great support because of his honesty in government. Jasper and Edmund were on very good terms with York, Salisbury and Warwick, and had been ennobled as earls at the same time as Warwick. They had supported York at the council meeting when he received the Protectorship during the king's illness. However, York needed more allies among the great lords. The Tudors' loyalty lay with their half-brother, but his illnesses, his inability to lead and his inclination to allow himself to be led by favourites such as Somerset meant the country had drifted towards power struggles. While Protector, York had displayed true qualities of leadership, offering a more effective and widespread government.

The twenty-four-year-old Jasper accompanied Henry's small force from London, but Edmund and Owen were now dealing with unrest in Wales.

Jasper had closely co-operated with Richard of York when he was Protector, and probably hoped that there would be no battle. A battle was certainly not expected by the king's party, with his lords expecting to parley to come to an agreement. Henry's army had fewer than 3,000 archers and billmen. Although a quarter of the peerage was present, most had only their small London retinues in attendance. Some had gone directly from their estates to Leicester after Somerset's call to arms, heading away from the action. Somerset, alongside the king, led the army out of London, accompanied by his nineteen-year-old son, the Marquis of Dorset. The army bivouacked for the night at Watford, and was just reaching St Albans en route to Leicester when they were surprised with the news that York had his force nearby. This was Somerset's failing – he should have sent scouts out days previously to track York's force.

St Albans was undefended, with no walls or gates; it was merely a large village that straddled the main road north out of London. Somerset swiftly barricaded all its outlets, and drew the royal army under cover of the line of houses that formed the eastern part of the town. Seeing York's army slowly advancing from the east, around seven in the morning Henry sent Buckingham to ask why York had brought an army with him. On 22 May 1455, during the long parley, York answered that he was truly loyal, but demanded that Somerset should be arrested and tried for treason. Talks broke down, probably owing to Somerset's intransigence and the fact that he had not passed on York's letters of loyalty. Somerset's use of narrow barricades meant that York's archers could not be used effectively, but York could not delay an attack, fearing that more lords would rally towards the king and that some of his troops might defect as well. York decided to attack, targeting the barricades that blocked the three roads into St Albans from the east with three columns of infantry. The attack failed, with many Yorkists dying under a hail of arrows as the Lancastrians had a clear field of fire while the Yorkists did not.

Warwick saw what was happening, and found an unguarded dirt track to the south-east of the royalist army. Bursting through the back doors of the houses, his soldiers ran out into the main thoroughfare of the town, cutting the Lancastrian line in two. They charged the Lancastrians from the town side of the barricades. The royalists turned to face them, allowing Yorkists to pour over the barricades. There was ferocious fighting for around thirty minutes, during which Somerset, Northumberland and Clifford were killed. Henry VI stood passively beneath his standard throughout the battle, and received a very slight wound in the neck from an arrow. Emerging victorious, York, Salisbury and Warwick knelt before Henry on the dirt floor of a tanner's house where he was having his wound dressed, swearing their allegiance and begging forgiveness. Henry forgave them, although saying, 'Forsothe, forsothe, ye do fouly to smyte a Kygne enoynted so.' The royal army threw down its weapons and the uninjured were allowed to escape with few losses. However, nobles and knights, weighted with heavy mail and plate armour, were caught and cut down. It seems that Warwick had ordered his men to spare the common soldiers and slaughter the nobles, Somerset being particularly targeted as having to die. It may well be that Warwick, who became increasingly noted for his savagery towards the captured, killed Somerset himself. Of forty-eight bodies buried by the abbot, only twenty-five were those of unknown common soldiers, the others being lords, knights, squires, and officers of the king's household. In this first battle of the Wars of the Roses, there seemed to be no killing of fugitives or prisoners. That horror was yet to begin, after the Battle of Wakefield in 1460.

Buckingham, Devon, Dorset, Fauconberg, Roos, Percy and Stafford were all wounded and captured, the only unwounded prisoner of note being Dudley, who was sent to the Tower. Wiltshire fled the field early, giving him a reputation for cowardice that he was to confirm again later. We do not know if Jasper was captured or escaped the field. If captured, his former friendship with York and Warwick would have probably saved him. It was Jasper's first experience of battle, and seems to have left him with a lasting wish for peace. He certainly tried, until his own life was at risk, to reconcile the opposing factions, especially seeing an opportunity now the implacable Somerset was dead. York did not press his own claims to the throne, preferring to come to an agreement to succeed Henry as king. For this to happen York needed more support from the peerage, and the Tudor earls had showed no animosity towards his plans. Neither saw themselves as having any claim to the crown – they probably felt extremely fortunate to be accepted in the royal household. York escorted the king to London, telling its citizens that the king had been saved from his real enemies: his advisors. London was to be a Yorkist stronghold during the coming wars.

Throughout recent years, York had repeatedly stated that all he had ever wanted was the dismissal of the inefficient and incapable Somerset and his corrupt officials. He constantly reinforced his desire simply for competent and honest persons in government, not the usurping of the king. The birth of Prince Edward meant that Richard of York was no longer first in line to succeed Henry VI. The Tudor brothers had been formally recognised as the half-brothers of Henry VI, all of whose uncles and other possible heirs were dead by this time. However, few except some Welsh bards saw the Tudors as potential rulers. To Queen Margaret's chagrin, York replaced the dead

Somerset as Constable of England. Margaret now departed for Hertford Castle with the king and her child Prince Edward. The battle had upset Henry's mental stability once more, and he had been advised to recuperate in the countryside. Jasper remained associated with the Yorkists despite St Albans. Along with the earls of Buckingham and Shrewsbury, Jasper was a moderate, willing to work for either side of government, and all three tried to solve the issues between Lancastrians and Yorkists.

On 26 May 1455 writs were issued for a parliament to meet at Westminster in the following July, with both Tudor brothers being summoned. The king remained in Hertford, still unwell. Jasper remained in London rather than attend the king's court at Hertford, and on 4 June he and Richard of York, with Warwick, Bourchier and Fauconberg, attended a council meeting at St Paul's. Two days later Buckingham and Worcester renewed their association with York at another council meeting. York was still looking for support from such moderate peers such as Buckingham, Worcester, Shrewsbury, Jasper of Pembroke and Edmund of Richmond. As a result of the deaths of men such as Somerset and Northumberland at St Alban's several public offices were vacant, and on 2 June 1455 Richard of York was appointed constable of the castles of Aberystwyth, Carmarthen and Carreg Cennen for life, positions formerly held by Somerset. This was to be ominous for Edmund Tudor.

Parliament opened at Westminster on 9 July 1455 in the presence of Henry, to whom the lords, including Jasper, swore allegiance. Measures were yet again undertaken to repair the nation's finances. In this parliament, a committee consisting of Marcher lords and the crown's legal advisers was set up to investigate means of establishing 'restful and safe rule in Wales'. All again looked prosperous for Edmund and Jasper, as they were accepted in both Lancastrian and Yorkist circles. As Earl of Pembroke Jasper had considerable landed interests in south Wales, but his estates were far wider, for he held jointly with his brother the profitable wardship of Margaret Beaufort and valuable properties in the Midlands, as well as several English estates in his own right. Jasper and Edmund each maintained a small household within the greater royal household of their half-brother, and it is possible that they normally lived at court with Henry. It was customary for magnates, both lay and ecclesiastical, to have town houses or inns in London, such as Earl Edmund's establishment at Baynard's Castle, and on 15 November 1456 Earl Jasper and Thomas Vaughan, esquire, one of his councillors, were jointly granted a house in Brook Street, Stepney, called 'Le Garlek' or the 'Garlek-House'.

Both Tudor brothers were absent from the second session of the parliament, which lasted from 12 November to 13 December 1455. At least thirty-five lay and thirty spiritual peers also absented themselves, possibly not wishing to discuss new demands that York should once again be appointed Protector. Just one week after the parliament opened, York was again appointed Protector. It was argued that only York, or someone like him, could undertake the restoration of proper law and order. Edmund, however, was in Wales, probably on York's direct orders, and Jasper may well have been with him, in his earldom of Pembroke. However, they were firmly ordered to appear at the third session of this parliament, which was scheduled to open on 14 January 1456. Jasper's attention was soon to be directed away from the centre of political life at court to Wales, a region with which he would be closely associated for the next three decades.

Wales had never settled since the fourteenth century. Because local disorders were a perpetual issue throughout Wales, during his second protectorate York decided to prioritise peace in the country. Even before the Glyndŵr War of 1400–21, Wales had experienced frequent outbursts of local and national violence. Absentee magnates in the Marcher lordships, and absentee royal officials in the Principality of Wales, had given over the administration of their estates to local families, the *uchelwyr* (high men). As long as they successfully collected incomes, these men had been largely allowed to do as they pleased. Absenteeism led to more power in the hands of resident Welshmen, with ancient rivalries flourishing. With lack of supervision and a weak central government, local officials abused their powers for their own ends, so the quality of royal and Marcher government in Wales was on the decline.

York seems to have chosen Edmund Tudor to re-establish royal government in the principality and Marcher estates across south Wales. From the late autumn of 1455 Edmund intervened by direct action, leading to enmity with Gruffydd ap Nicolas. It was previously thought that Edmund was acting for Queen Margaret as a rival to York in the region, but he had probably been directed by York all along.

Around this time, on 1 November 1455, the marriage of Margaret Beaufort to Edmund Tudor took place. It had been almost definitely arranged by Henry VI. As Margaret was the deceased John Beaufort's only child, her marriage to Edmund would easily solve the financial problem of how he could live in the style of an earl. Edmund and Margaret wed at Bletsoe Castle, Margaret's birthplace. She was around twelve years and five months old, and Edmund probably twenty-five. Also in this month, Edmund's presence was recorded in south Wales. Neither Edmund nor Jasper attended the November parliament as they were probably in Wales to keep the king's peace.

By the end of November, Edmund and Margaret were staying in Wales at Lamphey Palace in Pembrokeshire, a palace of the bishop of St David's, only a few miles east of Jasper's huge castle at Pembroke. It is said that Henry Tudor was conceived here at this time, but Jasper's Caldicot Castle also claims this distinction. Edmund regularly stayed at Lamphey when on state business in south Wales.

While Edmund, his new wife and presumably Jasper were concerned with affairs in Wales, by February 1456 the court party, increasingly dominated by Queen Margaret, felt strong enough to move against York, and he was relieved of his post as Protector. York's influence and authority was again in decline. Edmund was asked to re-establish the king's control in south Wales, and had growing success. At a time when the queen and York were both trying to build a greater power base, Edmund's victories enhanced the position of the royal family and the king's government against York.

While Edmund was fighting in Wales, Jasper was back in London. Late in April, and for much of May 1456, London was seriously disturbed by anti-alien riots, the Lombards in particular being persecuted. On 30 April 1456, Jasper, with Exeter and Buckingham and a number of others, had been given a commission of oyer and terminer to restore order the city and its suburbs. On 6 June Jasper and others were given a similar commission to deal with disturbances in Kent and Sussex, while from January 1457 until 1458 Jasper was appointed a Justice of the Peace for Middlesex. Jasper seems to have spent time in personal attendance on the king. Jasper was, in fact, the only lord in attendance on Henry at Sheen Palace, Richmond, in June 1456 according to the *Paston Letters*. In July Henry was at Sheen and Windsor palaces, but in August he travelled to Coventry to be with his queen, and probably Jasper accompanied him.

The greatest official in west Wales was Gruffydd ap Nicholas of Newton and Dinefŵr, who had accumulated offices and land in Carmarthenshire, and also dominated royal government in south Wales. Despite attempts to lessen his power, his position in west Wales was unrivalled by the time that Jasper Tudor had become Earl of Pembroke in 1452. Gruffydd, his sons and his grandson are integrally important in the story of Owen, Edmund, Jasper and Henry Tudor.

York himself had attempted to discipline Gruffydd ap Nicolas during both his protectorates, and his attempts had met with utter failure. Now, Edmund was faced with an increasingly hostile situation. Gruffydd ap Nicolas had not given in to York, and neither would he acquiesce to Edmund, and by

June 1456 both were 'at werre gretely in Wales'. Although York had been appointed constable of the castles of Aberystwyth, Carmarthen and Carreg Cennen on 2 June 1455, following Somerset's death at St Albans, Gruffydd ap Nicolas and his sons were still in active control of these fortresses, and preparing to defend them and Cydweli against Edmund. Edmund was no longer a representative of York as Protector – he was now a representative of the king.

Edmund was eventually victorious in the struggle, and took possession of the Welsh castles that had belonged to York, earning his enmity. Despite York's grant, Edmund took over his castle at Carmarthen and probably acted in Pembrokeshire as the representative of his brother Jasper. In the lordship of Kidwelly the clash between Edmund and Gruffydd threatened to disrupt the administration, as in the autumn the bailiffs of Carmarthen felt it necessary to send men to escort the Duchy of Lancaster auditors, with their books, over the mountains from Monmouth. Edmund was now described as Carmarthen Castle's 'custodian', and set about imposing royal government in the principality shires of Carmarthen and Cardigan. However, York was still officially constable of Carmarthen Castle, and knew he had to move against Edmund or lose face.

Thus York determined to reassert his power by acting as the legitimate constable of the castles of Carmarthen, Aberystwyth and Carreg Cennen, thereby neutralising any rivals in the principality. He knew that if Edmund Tudor returned Carmarthen and its lands to Henry VI rather than himself it would be a massive blow to his prestige. In April 1456, York's followers Sir Walter Devereux and his son-in-law Sir William Herbert of Raglan decided to make their move and gathered a force, despite Herbert having been one of Jasper's inner council. Herbert, Devereux and members of the Vaughan family joined forces, their stated intention being to fully assert York's authority, and headed for west Wales. The justification for the attack was the grant of major Welsh castles to York in 1455. On 10 August, 2,000 men from Herefordshire and the neighbouring Marches set out for Carmarthen Castle, where Edmund was based. The record of indictment makes it clear that this was a well-armed force, led by more than thirty prominent gentlemen and esquires, several of whom were kinsmen or associates of Herbert and Devereux. With his younger brother Richard Herbert of Coldbrook, 'esquire of Abergavenny', Sir William enjoyed the support of his half-brothers Roger Vaughan, 'esquire of Tretower' and Thomas ap Roger Vaughan, 'esquire of Hergest'. Also involved were Herbert's cousins William and Meredith ap Morgan ap Dafydd Gam, 'gentlemen', of Raglan and Crickhowell respectively. Similarly, Sir Walter Devereux was accompanied by James

Baskerville, 'esquire of Eardisley', who was, like Sir William Herbert, a son-in-law of Devereux.

The Yorkists seized Carmarthen Castle and put Edmund in its gaol in September 1456. Edmund was possibly released, but apparently contracted an illness, perhaps plague, and died there on 1 November 1456. Lewys Glyn Cothi called Edmund 'brother of King Henry, nephew of the Dauphin [Charles VII] and son of Owain'. It seems that no one was accused of directly causing his death and it is possible that he always suffered from ill health. Government records show he was absent from many more meetings than Jasper. He was buried in a fine tomb at *Cwrt y Brodyr*, Greyfriars Priory in Carmarthen, but the tomb was moved after the Dissolution to St David's Cathedral. Lewys Glyn Cothi wrote an elegy to Edmund, describing his father Owen's great sadness, the desperate loss felt by Jasper and the consequences of Edmund's death for Wales: 'Owain Tudur – pining / For his son he is.' Edmund was described as a lover of peace who died in the prime of life. Glyn Cothi does not blazon Edmund's shield, saying only that it was charged with *fleurs-de-lis*, the three helmets of the line of Ednyfed Fychan, three birds and a bull.

Cardigan, in the hands of a constable sympathetic towards York, was bypassed as the Yorkist force moved north to take Aberystwyth Castle, successfully reasserting York's power. From Aberystwyth they moved through west Wales. While we do not know Owen Tudor's whereabouts at this time, he was known to be at Jasper's great castle of Pembroke soon after, and was quite possibly caring for his young daughter-in-law Margaret Beaufort during Edmund's captivity. H. T. Evans writes of Elis Gruffydd's belief:

William ap Griffith was a chieftain of North Wales. Deeply disappointed by the death of Edmund Tudor, earl of Richmond, before a son had been born to him, he threw his bard, Robin Ddu, into prison, exclaiming angrily: 'You made me believe that a scion of the House of Owen would one day restore us the crown of Britain. You now perceive that your prophecy was false, for Edmund has left no son to succeed him.' Soon it became known that the duchess was about to give birth to a child. Robin Ddu was immediately set free and despatched to Pembroke. A son was born, and they called his name Owen, by which name young Henry Tudor was for many years known among the Welsh.

Jasper must have considered York to be a better ruler than his half-brother the king, but Edmund's death ensured his lifelong support for the House of

Lancaster. Jasper had stayed close to the king, but on the news of Edmund's death, he was sent to replace him in Wales and to care for Edmund's pregnant window at Pembroke. Jasper quickly came to a rapprochement with the powerful Gruffydd ap Nicolas and his sons, who henceforth sided with his forces. After Edmund's death, the government began the process of reorganising the Richmond and Beaufort inheritances. Edmund's wife and his posthumous son, Henry, were both minors, which complicated matters. On 28 January 1457, Margaret Beaufort gave birth to Henry Tudor, Earl of Richmond, at Pembroke. A small room in the east end of a tower on the northern wall of the fortress, which in Leland's time contained a 'chymmeney new made with the arms and badges of King Henry VII', is still shown as Henry's birthplace.

After having been a widow for almost three months, the thirteen-year-old Margaret Beaufort and her child were lucky to survive the childbirth. The care of the infant Henry fell to his uncle, Jasper, who was possibly twenty-five when the child was born. Henry was supposedly taught by the monks at nearby Monkton Priory. Jasper soon took up residence at Pembroke Castle, probably with his father, and took over the task that had been intended for Edmund of organising a strong base in south-west Wales for the Lancastrian cause. Jasper's income rose as high as £1,500 per annum at this time, as they had jointly owned a number of properties.

In January 1457, Jasper was summoned to a Great Council that was to be held at Coventry on 14 February. Attempts were made to condemn the Devereux/Herbert upheavals that caused the death of Edmund Tudor, and having dismissed York's allies from the government, the queen needed to get rid of York himself. The Great Council agreed to this on 6 March 1457. Thus York was re-appointed Lieutenant of Ireland, to hold the office for ten years, virtually exiling him from England.

In March 1457, shortly before the court moved to Hereford, Jasper stayed with Duke Humphrey of Buckingham at Greenfield Manor, in his lordship of Ebbw near Newport, to present to Buckingham his widowed sister-in-law Margaret. Buckingham and Jasper probably felt an affinity, having been moderates between the two great houses in the preceding years. It was agreed that Margaret would marry the duke's second son, Henry Stafford, thus helping to consolidate both families' interests. The marriage would lessen Jasper's incomes, but would help secure the safety of Jasper's nephew Henry.

York's attempt to control west Wales had failed. On 21 April 1457 he is recorded as agreeing to surrender the constableships of Aberystwyth, Carmarthen and Carreg Cennen to Jasper in return for a paltry £40 per annum. With great foresight, Jasper strengthened Pembroke and Tenby castles and walled towns to act as his headquarters in west Wales. He travelled on the king's business across south and west Wales, bringing his dead brother's attackers to trial. On 29 November 1457 Jasper and the other peers were summoned to another Great Council, to be held at Westminster on 27 January 1458. The king hoped to reconcile the partisans of the queen and those of York. A 'love-day' was held on 25 March 1458 to mark the alleged new-found affection between the sides. However, the queen and York quickly forgot the king's ideals, and prepared for collision. Jasper had moved into the very inner circle of the court party, and was to be of great assistance to the queen in the coming conflict.

In 1458 Owen was back in Pembroke, for he had an illegitimate son around 1459, Dafydd (David) Owen, born in Pembroke. The illegitimacy is shown in David's arms, which include 'overall a bendlett sinister argent'. He would feature in the later fighting.

Alphonso V, King of Aragon and Naples, had died on 28 June 1458, and sometime before 23 April 1459 Jasper was elected to Alphonso's stall as a knight of the Garter. On 2 May 1459 he was granted a tower in the palace of Westminster where he could hold council meetings and keep his legal records and papers. He had occupied the tower by royal licence, but was now granted it for life, thereby enjoying the position of neighbour to the queen, since she held a similar tower nearby in the palace. Jasper seems to have concerned himself increasingly with Welsh affairs, and on 1 March 1459 a commission was directed to Jasper and Owen Tudor, together with Thomas and Owain, the sons of Gruffydd ap Nicolas, to arrest and bring before the king seven Welshmen, one of whom, John Gruffydd, was described as a servant of John Dwnn, the principal supporter of York in the area. About the same time, the garrisons of Carreg Cennen and Kidwelly were strengthened on Jasper's orders, after a force of York's retainers had descended on the lordship. Jasper had become the commanding figure in Lancastrian Wales.

York had returned from Ireland, and the summer of 1459 was punctuated with minor clashes as York and the Lancastrians prepared for war. On 23 September Margaret's army sent men under James Tuchet, Lord Audley, to intercept Salisbury and prevent him from joining York's army. At Blore Heath, near Market Drayton, Staffordshire, the Lancastrian force was defeated, and Audley, the chamberlain of south Wales, was killed. Seeing that his army was outnumbered, Salisbury quickly left the battle site and marched south to join York, Warwick, Devereux and others at Ludlow. However, a far greater army had been mustered for the king at Worcester, and moved south towards York's men. York and his allies issued a manifesto protesting their loyalty to the king, but Henry replied by offering a pardon to all who would join his standard within six days. By 12 October the armies were facing each other at Ludford Bridge, just outside the walled town and mighty castle of Ludlow. Many of the professional soldiers Warwick had brought over with him from Calais deserted overnight to the king, and York was also deserted by the main part of his army, which preferred a royal pardon to fighting against overwhelming odds. To fight one's king was believed to be treason, not only in the eyes of royalty but also in the (admittedly biased) opinion of the Church.

York, with his second son Edmund, Earl of Rutland, fled across Wales, 'and breke downe the bryggys aftyr hym that the kyngys mayny schulde not come aftyr hym'. While York and Rutland sought safety in Ireland, Warwick and Salisbury escaped to the Continent. Before Ludford Bridge, the king had summoned Parliament to meet at Coventry on 20 November 1459, and Jasper arrived late, on 6 December, 'with a good feleschip', probably including Owen. There is no record of them at Ludford Bridge, but it is likely that they were either present or close to joining the king's forces, having marched from Wales. Jasper's delay in arriving at Coventry may have been caused by the pursuit of York and others. After the battle of Ludford Bridge Jasper is said to have dubbed Owen a knight, but he is always called *armiger* in the documents referring to him.

On 20 November 1459 there was held the so-called 'Parliament of Devils' at Coventry, which passed a Bill of Attainder blaming York for the political strife of the previous decade. York and his sons, March and Rutland, together with Salisbury and Warwick, and their chief allies and retainers, men like Devereux, Lord Clinton and Sir William Oldhall, were all attainted and stripped of all their estates. Future stability was supposedly ensured by yet another oath of loyalty to the king and Prince Edward, sworn and signed by all the peers present, including Earl Jasper. Owen was also present and he, with Jasper, stood at the king's side and swore undying loyalty to his sovereign lord and stepson.

With York and his sons forced into exile, and the leading Yorkists attainted, there was now bounty to be shared out. On 19 December 1459, the day before Parliament was dissolved, Owen Tudor was granted for life a £100 annuity from six manors forfeited by John, Lord Clinton. These were Folkestone, Walton and Benstead (Kent); Blakenham (Sussex), and the lordships or manors of Shustoke and Bolehall (Warwickshire). On 12 May 1460, Owen took out a lease for seven years, running from the previous 19 December, at a rent to be agreed with the Exchequer, of the lordships or manors of Folkestone, Millbroke, Benstead and Huntingdon (Kent), and of

Blakenham and Hamsey (Sussex), all of which also had been forfeited by Lord Clinton. Owen Tudor was now a wealthy man, rewarded for his loyalty and service to the king. Earl Jasper was also rewarded with fresh estates, including York's castle and estate at Newbury in Berkshire.

For Owen Tudor, life could not be much better. He probably had a mistress in Pembroke, a young son, a great income, and properties and estates. His son was the premier earl in England and close to the royal family, and his grandson Henry Tudor would assuredly grow up with great wealth. The Lancastrian cause seemed secure – all the leading Yorkists were in exile. On 5 February 1460 Owen was given by the king an important 'charge for life', that of 'Wodeward and Park Keeper' over various parks in Denbighshire. This was a profitable appointment, as it included all dues and also all tolls levied at fords, etc., across a large part of north Wales. It was granted to him partially due to complaints made at the Coventry parliament that Englishmen who held these offices were extortionate and overbearing. Strickland states: 'Owen Tudor himself was taken into some sort of favour, but never graced with any title, or owned by Henry as his father-in-law; as may be plainly seen by a deed dated so late as 1460, just before the battle of Northampton, where the king declared, "that out of consideration of the good services of that beloved squire, our Owinus Tudyr, we for the future take him into our special grace, and make him park-keeper of our parks in Denbigh, Wales". This was granted when the king was in a distressed state, and the old warrior, his father-in-law, had drawn his Agincourt sword in his cause.'

Again we have a reference to Owen being at Agincourt, but as stated previously, it was possibly another Owain ap Maredudd. Owen Tudor could now use Jasper's Denbigh Castle as his headquarters, but it was still held by Yorkists.

According to Thomas Pennant, in 1283 Edward I had given Prince Dafydd's lordship, Denbigh

...to Henry Lacy, earl of Lincoln, who built the castle, and inclosed within a wall the small town he found there. Among other privileges, he gave his vassals liberty of killing and destroying all manner of wild beasts on the lordship, except in certain parts reserved out of the grant; I suppose for the purpose of the particular amusement of the lord; for I find, in the reign of Henry VI the names of five parks in this lordship, viz. Moylewike, Caresnodooke, Kylford, Bagh, and Posey, of which the king constituted Owen Tudor, ranger. On the death of Lacy, the lordship passed to Thomas earl of Lancaster...

On 5 January 1460 Jasper had been appointed for life constable, steward and master forester of the lordship of Denbigh in north Wales, formerly one of York's estates, and in May he was granted the farm of York's forfeited lordship of Newbury for seven years. The Yorkist leaders had fled, but there were still pockets of resistance. York's supporters would not give up the walled town and castle of Denbigh, so Jasper laid siege, with the sixty-year-old Owen in his retinue. By 16 February Jasper had informed the king of what he needed to take Denbigh. He requested a commission to raise men in Wales to help subdue the castle, and the power to pardon the rebels who were prepared to submit. However, those who surrendered or were outlawed or attainted were to be kept in prison until they could give sureties of good behaviour. He then requested authority to execute rebels at his discretion and a grant to himself of all the moveable goods belonging to the men in the castle, to reward people who had assisted him. Finally, he asked for commissions of muster to be directed to three groups of men to provide him with a besieging force.

Henry VI wrote urgently to his Chancellor ordering the swift execution of Jasper's requests, and on 13 March Jasper was awarded a sum of 1,000 marks to support the cost of reducing Denbigh, and other castles in Wales and the Marches held by Yorkist rebels. Denbigh Castle was not captured easily, but it must have been taken by May 1460, for by 25 May Jasper had left Denbigh and was at Pembroke, probably with Owen organising defensive measures there.

In 1460, Owen may have been briefly captured. In an undated guidebook, *Rambling in Monmouthshire: A Historical Walking Guide to the Trails and Paths of Wales*, we read that 'southern Monmouthshire was strongly Yorkist in the Wars of the Roses and at Newport Castle, Owen Tudor, a Lancastrian Welshman, was imprisoned; later he married Henry V's widow'. James Matthews claims that Owen Tudor was held prisoner within the castle in 1460. Thomas relates a similar tale:

Reinallt ap Gryffydd ap Bleddyn, of the Tower, with five other gallant Welsh captains, defended Harlech Castle against Pembroke, Edward the fourth's general. Dafydd ap Ieuan ap Einion, another of the party, observed, after battling, for a long time, Pembroke's assault, 'I held a tower in France, till all the old women in Wales heard of it, and now the old women of France will hear of how I defended this castle'. Owen Tudor was also a partisan of the Lancastrian party; he was made prisoner by the Yorkists, and *confined in Uske castle*. [Author's italics. Usk was held by the Herberts for York, but could it be Newport on the Usk?] His cousin John ap Maredudd, and a hundred or more of his countrymen, feeling for the confinement and misfortunes of his kinsman, repaired to Uske. On his return, within two miles of Caerlleon, being beset by a party, favourers of the house of Yorke, and supposing destruction inevitable, he harangued his companions, and begged them to remember, at that time, the support of the honour, prowess and credit of their ancestors; Let it never be said, that there a hundred North Welsh gentlemen fled, but that the spot should be memorable and pointed out as the place where a hundred North Welsh gentlemen were slain. So, assuming courage from despair, he so arranged his small detachment, placing Hywel ap Llywelyn ap Hywel, and some others (who were the only sons of their fathers, and as such were to succeed in their name and inheritance) in the rear, and out of the brunt of the attack, whilst all his own sons were drawn out in the van, headed by himself to death or victory. The onset was tremendous; he opened a passage with his sword; the party was defeated. A scar of honour, from a wound in the face, caused him to be called 'Squier y Graith', to his dying day.

Whether Owen was imprisoned at Newport or at Usk, if at all, this will have occurred before the Battle of Mortimer's Cross. An intriguing part of the story concerns the two named leaders of the rescue party for Owen, members of the family of Gwydir. These were the compatriots whom Owen chose to reach Catherine. 'They could not speak anything but Welsh; and so John ap Meredith and Howell ap Llewelyn had the honour of being characterised by the Frenchwoman, Queen Catherine, as "the goodliest dumb creatures she ever saw".'

On 26 June, Warwick landed at Sandwich with his father Salisbury, his uncle Fauconberg, his nephew Edward, Earl of March, and his new ally John Tuchet, 6th Baron Audley (the son of James, killed at Blore Heath). Before landing the Yorkists had published a manifesto, complaining of the weak governance of the kingdom, the exclusion of the king's relatives from his council, their cruel oppression by the queen's favourites, the loss of France, the 'murder' of Gloucester, the diversion of the king's revenues of the realm into the pockets of his courtiers, and the collusion of the king's ministers with the French and Irish. Their complaints resonated with the people of London and the south-east, and Kent rose in Warwick's support, led by Archbishop Bourchier and Baron Cobham. By 30 June, Warwick was at the gates of London, and the following day the archbishop's herald summoned the city to surrender. The Lancastrian nobles Robert Hungerford (son of Walter), Thomas Scales and John Lovel tried to resist but were driven by Londoners into the Tower on 2 July. Warwick's army was welcomed into the city.

Warwick set up a siege force under Salisbury and Cobham around the small Lancastrian force defending the Tower of London, and marched north to attack the Lancastrian army. The court had been in Coventry, but on learning of the Yorkist advance the king moved to Northampton and camped in a meadow just south of the town. Before the Battle of Northampton, 10 July 1460, Henry VI was said to have knighted ten men, including Thomas Stanley (later to marry Margaret Beaufort) and the five-year-old grandson of the Duke of Buckingham. Sources including Davey state that Owen Tudor was knighted at Northampton. If so, it must have been at this time – the king was about to be captured.

Warwick sent heralds and bishops to the Lancastrian camp to negotiate, maintaining they did not want to fight. Henry's commander Buckingham allegedly declared that 'the Earl of Warwick shall not come to the King's presence and if he comes he shall die', to which message Warwick replied, 'At 2 o'clock I will speak with the King or I will die.' This seems to be the last time that any negotiations preceded a battle. Warwick ordered his troops to spare Lord Grey's Lancastrian soldiers, whose symbol was the black ragged staff.

Yorkists attacked the town of Northampton, pillaging and burning the town as they passed through it, then advanced on the defensive position of the Lancastrians. It was the only time a fortified camp was assaulted during all thirty-seven years of the Wars of the Roses, signifying that Warwick knew that there would be a weakness. Heavy rains seem to have rendered the Lancastrian cannon useless. Edward, Earl of March, reached the defences, and his frontal attack was repelled. However, Lord Grey of Ruthin's men on the Lancastrian left flank helped the Yorkists into the camp. As well as Lord Grey, the Earl of Kendal, Lord de la Warre and Jean de la Foix betrayed the king and went over to Yorkists. (Grey was well rewarded, becoming Treasurer of England in 1463.)

Now, with the Lancastrians being attacked on both sides, many fled and the battle resolved into the great nobles defending the king's tent. Lancastrians killed included Humphrey Stafford, Duke of Buckingham; Sir John Beaumont, Viscount Beaumont (England's first viscount); Sir John Talbot, Earl of Shrewsbury; Thomas Percy, Lord Egremont (son of the Earl of Northumberland); Sir Thomas Vernon; and Sir William Lucy (killed after the battle, having arrived late). Henry VI, too befuddled to escape, was captured and led back to London in procession. The Lancastrian garrison in the Tower of London under Hungerford, Lovel and Scales surrendered on 18 July for want of food. Lovel took no further part in the war, dying in 1464, but Hungerford was executed after the Battle of Hexham in that year. Scales was hated by the Londoners, so went by water after dusk to seek sanctuary at Westminster. However, he was recognised and murdered by boatmen, who left his corpse on the Southwark shore. William of Worcester wrote that he saw Lord Scales' naked corpse lying by the porch of St Mary Overy Church (now Southwark Cathedral). Richard of York soon returned from Ireland again, but this time he laid claim to the crown, symbolically laying his hand on the throne in the Council Chamber on his arrival on 10 October 1460.

After Northampton, Margaret of Anjou fled from Coventry, where she had been waiting for Henry's army, and joined Jasper and Owen at Pembroke. Gregory says that she first made for Harlech, not taken by the Yorkists until 1468, 'and there hens she remevyd fulle prevely unto the Lorde Jesper, Lorde and Erle of Penbroke', probably sailing from Harlech to join Jasper at Pembroke Castle. Jasper's works at Harlech enabled him to use it several times as an escape port in his travels to Scotland, Ireland, France, Brittany and Flanders during the ensuing decades of war. He knew that Milford Haven was the only Welsh harbour equally accessible from France, Ireland and Scotland, and built up the fortifications of Pembroke Castle to make it a stronghold for bringing men and supplies into Wales. Margaret was not only Jasper's sister-in-law but was also a distant cousin, and they now planned to regain the king and expel the Yorkists from government. Owen was with Jasper at this time, possibly in the company of his mistress and son David Owen.

An ode to Jasper by Lewys Glyn Cothi, dated 1460, was probably written shortly after the Battle of Northampton. It seems to have been composed to rally the Welsh under the banner of Jasper as Earl of Pembroke. At the time, Jasper was gathering a Welsh army. The plea was written, according to the manuscript note, when Lewys Glyn Cothi was in hiding. Professor Adrian Lewis translated some lines relevant to Owen Tudor:

I IASPAR IARLL PENVRO -	TO JASPER EARL OF PEMBROKE -
Irion wiail o ran Owain	Young scions from Owain's side
Edn a gywain, dawn i gywir,	A bird who garners, a talent to a staunch supporter,
Ei waed rhial hyd Darywain	His royal blood up to Darywain
Ac o Owain ni wna gohir.	And from Owain he does not delay.
Tŵr o Owain â 'r gwayw trahir	Tower of Owain with with the very long lance

Jasper was to lead an army from Pembroke against the Yorkists in the middle Marches of Wales. James Butler, Earl of Wiltshire and Ormond, a favourite of the queen, was to be his second-in-command. Wiltshire had been widely scorned for fleeing from the First Battle of St Albans in 1455 (an accusation that was not levelled at Jasper, indicating the earl may well have fought there and been captured and released by York). Wiltshire had also savagely pillaged Newbury, a town belonging to York, who named him, with Shrewsbury and Beaumont, 'oure mortalle and extreme enemyes'. Shortly after, with the Yorkists landing in Kent, Wiltshire had quickly fled to Holland, escaping the killings of Shrewsbury and Beaumont at Northampton. Hodges believes that 'while in Holland he received orders from the Queen at Pembroke, to ask for French and Breton reinforcements, and to arrange for a contingent of his own clansmen to be ready at Waterford or Wexford. This would account for the French, Bretons and Irish whom he is reported to have brought to Mortimer's Cross. Pembroke Castle, well sheltered up its river on Milford Haven, would appear to be the obvious place for the disembarkation of these foreign troops.'

On 9 August 1460, the Yorkist parliament ordered Jasper and his kinsman Roger Puleston, deputy-constable of Denbigh, to hand over Denbigh Castle, and similar orders were sent to the constables of the Lancastrian-held castles at Beaumaris, Flint, Conway, Hawarden, Holt, Ruthin and Montgomery. On 17 August Sir Walter Devereux, Sir William Herbert and Roger Vaughan were empowered to take all castles that were illegally garrisoned by Lancastrians. The Act of Accord was passed by the new Yorkist parliament on 25 October 1460, three weeks after Richard of York had laid his hand on the throne. Under the Act, the virtually imprisoned Henry VI was to retain the crown for life, but York and his heirs were to succeed. The inept Henry was forced to agree to the Act, which excluded his son, Edward of Westminster. (This has a resonance with the mentally unstable Charles VI agreeing for the Dauphin, later Charles VII, to be disinherited in favour of Henry V.) In the same parliament, on 31 October, York was made Prince of Wales, Earl of Chester, Duke of Cornwall and Lord Protector of England. Of course, this was unacceptable to Margaret, who had sailed to Scotland from Pembroke.

Early in December, York and his eldest son, Edward, Earl of March, left London. York took a force to suppress the Lancastrians in the north of England, and Edward of March headed west to defeat Jasper. On 30 December 1460 York met a Lancastrian force near Sandal Castle, Wakefield, and was defeated and killed. O'Flanagan, in 1870, wrote of the fate of York's seventeen-year-old son Edmund, Earl of Rutland:

Urged by his tutor, a priest named Robert Aspell, he was no sooner aware that the field was lost than he sought safety by flight. Their movements were intercepted by the Lancastrians, and Lord Clifford made him prisoner, but did not then know his rank. Struck with the richness of his armour and equipment, Lord Clifford demanded his name. 'Save him,' implored the Chaplain; 'for he is the Prince's son, and peradventure may do you good hereafter.' This was an impolitic appeal, for it denoted hopes of the House of York being again in the ascendant, which the Lancastrians, flushed with recent victory, regarded as impossible. The ruthless noble swore a solemn oath: 'Thy father,' said he, 'slew mine; and so will I do thee and all thy kin;' and with these words he rushed on the hapless youth, and drove his dagger to the hilt in his heart. Thus fell, at the early age of seventeen, Edmund Plantagenet, Earl of Rutland, Lord Chancellor of Ireland.

Edmund was thus executed on the orders of the Lancastrian Lord Clifford, or by some accounts, by Lord Clifford himself. His head was displayed on the gates of York, England, along with those of his father and of his uncle, Richard Neville, 5th Earl of Salisbury.

York's other sons, George, Duke of Clarence (later to be executed by his brother Edward), and Richard, Duke of Gloucester (later Richard III) were too young to fight. Edward of March, now Duke of York, had now lost his brother and father, and his main ally, Warwick, had lost his father.

Margaret had probably sailed from Pembroke to Scotland about mid-October 1460, accompanied by Exeter. She had entered negotiations with the Scottish Queen, Mary of Guelders, widowed since the death of James II at the siege of Roxburgh Castle in August. Scotland then provided troops for Margaret's northern army, in exchange for the cession of the border towns of Roxburgh and heavily defended Berwick. Queen Margaret ordered Somerset and Devon to bring further reinforcements from the West Country, to join her Lancastrian northern army at Hull, early in December 1460. While gathering Scots troops, Margaret heard of York's defeat and death at Wakefield. With her Scots soldiers, Margaret now joined the Lancastrian northern army at the start of 1461 and began marching south.

Jasper gathered associates and servants whose loyalty had already been proven, such as Thomas and Owain ap Gruffydd ap Nicholas, Philip Mansel, Sir Thomas Perot and, of course, Owen Tudor. Other men followed the Earl of Pembroke's cause, some of whom remained staunchly loyal to him in the next few years, despite a multitude of defeats. Thomas Fitzhenry (or Fitzharry) of Monnington and Eton Tregoze (Herefordshire) was a lawyer by training, and deputy-justiciar of the Principality in South Wales at various times. In 1460–61, he was acting as Chamberlain of South Wales, and deliberately destroyed the records of the county courts and Petty sessions of Cardiganshire for that year, in order to embarrass the new Yorkist government.

Another ally was Sir John Scudamore of Ewyas Lacy and Kentchurch, who was accompanied by his two sons, James and Henry, as well as his brother Sir William Scudamore, with thirty men of his own. Scudamore had married Maud, daughter of Gruffydd ap Nicholas of Dinefwr and Newton, so was thus connected with one of the most prominent families of west Wales, and was in Jasper's service in September 1461, acting as constable of Pembroke Castle. Owen Tudor, now aged around sixty-one, was given a command in Jasper's army.

9

The Battle of Mortimer's Cross and Owen's Execution 1461

While his father had marched north to meet the Lancastrian army and died at Wakefield with his son the Earl of Rutland, Edward of York had been sent to contain Jasper and the Lancastrians after the Yorkist rout at Ludlow. The Act of Accord of 25 October 1460 had made Richard of York heir to Henry VI, and under the Act, Edward, now Duke of York, was heir to the throne upon Henry VI's death. Edward of York was now informed by his 'scurriers' (mounted scouts who 'scoured' the countryside) that the Lancastrian northern army was being joined by Margaret of Anjou with a force from Scotland to march south for London.

Edward, busy raising men in Shrewsbury, wished to join Warwick to oppose the Lancastrian march south but was threatened more immediately in the west by Jasper Tudor and the arrival in Pembroke of a foreign army under James Butler, Earl of Wiltshire and Ormond. Lewys Glyn Cothi, who was with Jasper around this time, believed that Jasper had been sent overseas to raise troops. The *Short English Chronicle* also hints at this, but it is more likely that Wiltshire, with estates in Ireland and some experience of the French wars, was responsible for bringing French, Breton and Irish support. Margaret of Anjou's father René had supported the French in the Hundred Years War, and Charles VII of France was Jasper Tudor's uncle through Catherine of Valois. The pro-French Lancastrian regime was thus more acceptable to France than a Yorkist regime that was unwilling to abandon the Plantagenet claim to the French throne. This would help account for the French and Bretons whom Wiltshire or Jasper is reported to have brought to Pembroke Castle.

Hall's Chronicle calls Owen a knight. Some accounts place Owen Tudor as not only a Knight Bachelor but an Esquire to the King's Body, although excused from duty. An Esquire of the King's Body was one of the sovereign's closest attendants and also his shield-bearer, expected to bear arms and fight close to the king. The *Liber Niger* states that the Esquire of the Body should be 'attendant upon the king's person, to array and unray [undress, from un-raiment] him, and to watch day and night' and to be ready to help the king because 'no man else [is] to set hands on the king'. It was considered a great honour and a position of considerable influence. Thomas Daniel was one of Henry's VI's esquires, and in the *Paston Letters* (letter CLIV) it is noted that 'an esquire of the king's body was a position of great trust, lodged near, and during the night all messages, &c were delivered by him in person to the king'. Sir John Trevilian (Trevelyan), a supporter of Suffolk, was also one of Henry VI's esquires, expected to travel everywhere with him, as were Sir John Nanfan and Sir John Norreys, but this author can find no record of Owen serving the king in such a capacity.

It is important to reflect whether and when Owen was knighted. Henry VI was in custody in the lead-up to the approaching Battle of Mortimer's Cross, but as a great noble Jasper could act for the king before, during and after battle. In order to command a battle of the king's forces (armies were usually divided into three battles, with a vanguard, central 'battle' and rearguard), Owen had to be made a knight banneret. This was conferred, nearly always by the king, and usually on a battlefield, to a knight or esquire who ahd proved his worth in battle and could be trusted with a position of leadership. A knight banneret, sometimes known simply as banneret, was 'a commoner of rank' who led a company of troops during time of war under his own banner. His banner was square-shaped, in contrast to the tapering standard or pennon flown by lower-ranking knights, and bannerets were eligible to bear supporters on their heraldic devices. The military rank was higher than that of a knight bachelor, who fought under another's banner, but was lower than an earl or duke. In this engagement Jasper commanded one battle, Wiltshire another and Owen the third, so Jasper probably conferred the honour of knight banneret upon Owen in the name of Henry VI.

Wiltshire's foreign troops may have been late, held off by bad weather, which would explain the delay of nearly a month between Jasper's hearing the news of Wakefield (perhaps a week after the event) and the Battle of Mortimer's Cross. The march from Pembroke Castle to Mortimer's Cross is only around 110 miles, around six days' march. It looks as though the invasion force arrived in Pembrokeshire after the middle of January, and the news of its landing would have reached Edward well before the coming battle.

Jasper probably marched through Carmarthen and headed up the Tywi Valley to Llandeilo and Llandovery, then took the road to Brecon in the Usk Valley. From Brecon, they would have followed the Wye past Glasbury on the Leominster road into Herefordshire. He may have wished to link with the queen's army at Coventry, but it was a midwinter march, outside the normal campaigning season. He needed to requisition food for thousands of troops and followers, and forage for hundreds of horses. In view of the apparent delay, Jasper had every possible reason for haste.

Edward's main army was possibly stationed around the huge Wigmore Castle, 4 miles away from Mortimer's Cross. Wigmore had not been maintained since around 1424 and the fall of the Mortimers, but recent archaeological excavations suggest that building work was carried out there in the mid-fifteenth century. Edward's men probably also used Croft Castle at Yarpole, Herefordshire, as an advance base in the final stages of the campaign. (One owner, Sir John Croft, had married a daughter of Owain Glyndŵr). Only 2 miles from Mortimer's Cross, Croft Castle has outstanding views across north Herefordshire to the Black Mountains and any approaching force.

The Yorkists would have been mustered and waiting in a prepared position when Jasper was within two days' march. The tradition is that they were waiting in ambush, as recounted a century later by the Elizabethan poet Samuel Daniel. Edward's army was full of capable soldiers, experienced in war. Jasper had little chance, with men tired from marching for five or six days, many seemingly with little battle experience, facing an entrenched, well-fed army of hardened troops strengthened by archers. There was also a difference in the quality of commanders. Owen, leading another battle, had seen service in France and accompanied Jasper on his siege of Denbigh, but was over sixty years old. Wiltshire, meanwhile, would not inspire confidence.

Edward had moved south from Shrewsbury Castle, mustering support from the lords of the Marches. Among his army was Warwick's rival for Edward's confidence, Sir William Herbert. Herbert was Jasper's enemy, and was responsible for the death of his brother Edmund five years previously. Edward knew the area very well from his youth, and would have hunted in the woods at Aymestry, Shobdon, Lingen and Wigmore. His estate included Wigmore Castle, which was managed for him by the Devereux family of Weobley Castle. Devereux, with most of Herefordshire's noblemen, would fight for York at Mortimer's Cross. Attending were Lord Grey of Wilton near Ross, John Lingen (buried in Aymestry Church), Richard Croft of Croft

Castle (buried in Croft Church) and Roger Vaughan of Hergest Court near Kington (buried in Kington Church). The great families of the Herberts and Vaughans were related, and Edward's local popularity gained him an army of local men who knew the area extremely well. Herbert was supported by his warrior brother Lord Richard Herbert of Coldbrook, his half-brother Roger Vaughan of Tretower, and his brother-in-law Sir Walter Devereux (whose father Sir Walter had died in 1459). Sir Richard Croft, Henry ap Gruffydd and Sir John Lyngen had been indicted for their part in the west Wales expedition of 1456, and several of York's followers had been servants of his father. It was a tight-knit army of experienced soldiers.

The Dwnn family were also committed Yorkists, as were two brothers of Roger Vaughan who are not named (like the Dwnns) at the battle but were present, Watkin Vaughan of Bredwardine and Thomas Vaughan of Hergest. Members of the Dwnn family of Kidwelly either assisted York to muster men or were themselves present at the battle, for Jasper blamed them, together with March and the Herberts, for the events that would follow.

Edward of York was thirsting for vengeance after the death of his father and brother. His army probably contained around 5,000 local troops, with a select force of household retainers. Many were Welsh, or raised in Herefordshire, and the latter would naturally fight all the harder for their homes and estates.

Evans writes:

Against this compact, homogeneous force, the Lancastrians brought a motley body of Welsh, Lancastrian Irish, French and Bretons, under the leadership of Jasper, earl of Pembroke, and the earl of Wiltshire and Ormond (James Butler). With them were Jasper's father, old Owen Tudor, Sir John Skydmore, who had a personal bodyguard of thirty men; Sir Thomas Perot of Haverfordwest; two of the sons of Griffith ap Nicholas, Owen and Thomas; Lewis ap Rhys of Carmarthen; Philip Mansel and Hopkin ap Rhys of Gower; Rheinallt Gwynedd of Harlech; Lewis Powys of Powysland; Hopkin Davy of Carmarthen; Thomas Fitzharry; James Skydmore and Sir Harry Skydmore, sons of Sir John Skydmore; Sir William Skydmore, his brother.

Apart from Wiltshire and Jasper, Sir John Scudamore had experience of war, as, perhaps, had his brother Sir William, who brought thirty men to join Jasper's army. Sir James and Sir Henry were sons of Sir John, and the four Scudamores of Kentchurch fought for Jasper, described by Worcester as 'knights in arms in France' and 'knights for Queen Margaret'. Some of the Scudamore family had assisted Glyndŵr almost six decades previously, and may well have supported Owen Tudor when he was young. Another Englishman, John Throckmorton of Tewkesbury, had supported William Herbert but had been pardoned and had joined the court party. Jasper was also accompanied by Hopkyn ap Rhys of Gower, and Lewis ap Rhys esquire and Hopcyn Davy esquire from Carmarthenshire; all would serve him for several years. Rheinallt Gwynedd brought troops from Harlech. Jasper's army contained men speaking five different languages, but we know nothing of the numbers, quality or leadership of the foreign troops, except for Wiltshire, who 'fled the field at the start of battle' according to Worcester. Jasper's Welshmen were probably his best troops, but apart from Sir Thomas Perot of Haverfordwest and Owen Tudor, they were led by esquires of Pembroke, Carmarthen and Gower who may have lacked military experience.

Jasper's forces seem to have been relatively ill-equipped and inexperienced, though they were strengthened by foreign mercenaries. Edward of York had spent some years with his brother Rutland at Ludlow Castle, so knew most of these local lords well. John Milewater of Stoke Edith had been receiver for Richard of York in the Marches, and had been rewarded, like Herbert, for his neutrality at Ludford. Other veterans of the French war were Sir William Mytton, of Weston-under-Lizard in Staffordshire, and Philip Vaughan, described by Worcester as captain of Hay Castle, and 'the most noble esquire of lances among all the rest'. Lord Grey of Wilton, Herefordshire, Lord Audley from Cheshire and Humphrey Stafford of Southwick had probably accompanied Edward from London to Shrewsbury. Audley (who had succeeded his father, who was killed at Blore Heath) and Stafford had become Yorkists recently, after being captured while serving with Somerset in his attempt to take Calais. John Radcliffe, Lord Fitzwalter, fought for York but was to die two months later at the Battle of Ferrybridge.

A former Lancastrian supporter, Sir Richard Croft of Croft Castle, on whose estate the battle was fought, was one of the most celebrated soldiers of his times. Worcester refers to him at Mortimer's Cross as 'Sir Ricardus de Croft, Castell de comitatu Heref., Chevalier'. There is a letter from Edward, then Earl of March, and his brother the Earl of Rutland, to their father the Duke of York, written about 1456, when they complain of Croft and his brother's 'odious rule and demeaning' when they were entrusted to his custody. Sir James Baskerville of Eardisley, Herefordshire, had fought at St Albans on the Yorkist side and in 1456 was involved in the Yorkist invasion of south Wales, being denounced at the Coventry parliament in 1459. He was sheriff of Herefordshire at the time of the battle, and joined Edward's force. Sir Thomas Monnington of Sarnesfield, Herefordshire, had fought with his brothers for York against Edmund and then Jasper Tudor in Wales, and was MP for Herefordshire. William Knylle was Lord of Knill, Herefordshire. Worcester refers to him as 'Sir William de Knylle, Chevalier de comitatu Heref'.

Reginald (Reynold), 7th Baron Grey of Wilton (*c.* 1421–*c.* 1494), whose Wilton Castle was on the river near the English side of Ross-on-Wye, had married Tacine, or Tacinda, likely an illegitimate daughter of John Beaufort but thought by some to be Owen Tudor's daughter. John Tuchet, Baron Audley, was the son of Baron Audley who had been killed fighting for the Lancastrians at Blore Heath in 1459 by Roger Kynaston. Tuchet himself changed sides to join the Yorkists, fighting for Edward at Mortimer's Cross and thereafter. Humphrey Stafford, Earl of Devon, was another former Lancastrian. Sent to Calais with Audley to take it off Warwick, they were persuaded to join York's cause and came with him to England. William Hastings, 1st Baron Hastings, was Edward's closest companion. John Wenlock, 1st Baron Wenlock, had fought in France and initially fought for the House of Lancaster at St Albans in 1455, but his friendship with Warwick led him to change sides, and at Blore Heath in 1459 he had fought for York.

Mortimer's Cross is roughly 6 miles north-west of Leominster and deep in the heartland of the Mortimer/York family. Some historians believe that Jasper intended to attack the nearby castles Wigmore and Ludlow, but Wigmore is up a steep slope and Ludlow is a walled town with a great castle. Jasper would not have brought cannon or siege engines across Wales, and it was in his interest not to delay but to join Margaret's army. However, Jasper's quick defeat was the Yorkist priority, and the account in the *Brut Chronicle* records: 'This time, the earl of March being in Shrewsbury, hearing the death of his father, desired Assistance & Aid of the town for to avenge his father's death; & from thence went to Wales, where, at Candlemass after, he had a battle at Mortimer's Cross against the earls of Pembroke & of Wiltshire.' An appendix to the chronicle refers to 'the bateyle of Wygmore'.

Stowe's account of the Battle of Mortimer's Cross is as follows:

When the Earl of March was setting forth against the Queen (Margaret) and his father's enemies, news was brought him that Jasper and James Butler Earle of Ormonde and Wiltshire had assembled a great number of Welshmen and Irishmen suddenly to take and surprize him; he, being therewith quickened, retired back and met with his enemies in a faire plaine neere to Mortimer's Crosse beside Ludlow, not far from Hereford East, on Candlemas day in the morning; at which time the sun (as some write) appeared to the Earle of March like three sunnes and suddenly joyned together in one; upon which sight hee tooke such courage that he fiercely setting one his enemies, put them to flight; and for this cause men imagined he gave ye sun in his full brightnesse for his badge or cognizaunce. Of his enemies were slain to the number of three thousand eight hundred. The Earles of Pembroke and Willshire fled, but Owen Teuther (whom Leland saith should be called Meredicke), father of the said Earle of Pembroke, which Owen Teuther had married (as was said) Katherine mother to King Henry the Sixt, was there taken and beheaded, and afterwards buried in a chappel of the Grey Friars Church in Hereford. There were also taken and beheaded David Floid, Morgan ap Reuther, Sir John Skidmore, John Throckmorton, Thomas Fitzhenry, and others.

The Lancastrians marched towards the Yorkists, meeting about 4 miles south of Wigmore Castle at Mortimer's Cross, where two valleys meet at right angles. Yorkist troops, preparing their camp on the day before the battle, were frightened by the appearance of three suns, the phenomenon known as a parhelion. This can occur when the sun is rising or setting and shines through ice crystals, creating a mirror effect. Edward provided a clever explanation that the three suns represented the blessing of the Holy Trinity upon another trinity, that of himself and his two young brothers, George, later Duke of Clarence, and Richard, later Duke of Gloucester. The 'sun in splendour' became Edward's favourite badge, demonstrating that this unusually tall and muscular eighteen-year-old had been blessed by God. Shakespeare refers to the parhelion in *Henry VI Part 3*:

> Three glorious suns, each one a perfect sun;
> Not separated with the racking clouds,
> But sever'd in a pale clear-shining sky.
> See, see! they join, embrace and seem to kiss,
> As if they vow'd some league inviolable:
> Now are they but one lamp, one light, one sun.
> In this the heaven figures some event.

Edward positioned his three Yorkist battles with the great Wigmore Castle behind them, offering a secure refuge if he had to stage a fighting retreat. The River Lugg was swollen with winter rains, and protected his left flank. Nearby Croft Castle would have supplies and men in reserve. On his right flank, steep wooded slopes offered concealment for Yorkist archers waiting to fire volleys of arrows against the left flank of the Lancastrians advancing from the south. The battle was thought to be fought on 2 February, but was more likely fought on St Blaise's Day, 3 February 1461. The *English Chronicle* reports:

> The iii day of February... Edward the noble earl of Marche fought with the Walsshmen beside Wygmore in Wales, whose captains were the earl of Penbrook and the earl of Wylshyre, that would finally have destroyed the said earl of Marche... And so by His grace, he had the victory of his enemies, and put the ii earl to flight, and slew of the Walsshemen to the number of four thousand.

Giles wrote that around 11,000 Yorkists faced 8,000 Lancastrians. There is no proper contemporary account of the battle, but Hodges has researched the likely positions of the armies. It is believed that the Lancastrians approached from the south via the Hereford Lane. Although they did not wish to seek battle, the Lancastrians advanced as victory was necessary for them to cross the River Lugg. It is suggested that the Yorkists faced south with the River Lugg to their left. There seems no evidence of cannon being used. The Yorkists are believed to have had more archers than the Lancaster army, probably many of them among the Herbert forces from Monmouthshire. The positions of York's three battles and archers were probably recommended by Sir Richard Croft.

The Yorkists would have been drawn up on foot, with their centre probably near the 'Battle Oak'. We do not know whether the Lancastrians entered a trap, as suggested by some, but in advancing across flat, open fields on the flood plain they would have suffered a storm of arrows before reaching the enemy. It seems that the battles were laid out horizontally, to make the Lancastrians suffer maximum damage from the arrow storm. If the enemy was up to 300 yards away then 'flight arrows' would be used to rain down upon the advancing force, but heavier arrows were used under 150 yards, capable of piercing armour at that range. Assuming there were only 1,000 archers – probably an underestimate – and considering that they could each unleash twelve arrows a minute, if the Lancastrians, in armour, came into range and took a minute to cover 300 yards and reach close quarters, this could have meant 12,000 arrows aimed directly into their midst.

The Yorkist right battle was commanded by Sir Walter Devereux, the centre by Edward of York and the left battle by Sir William Herbert. The Lancastrian left battle, under the command of Wiltshire, included the more experienced and professional mercenaries and faced Devereux. The centre, under Jasper Tudor, charged at York's men. The right flank was under the joint command of Owen Tudor and Sir John Throckmorton.

Wiltshire may have started the battle proper by leading the advance on the York right wing, which was pushed back and may have scattered, but Worcester comments that Wiltshire 'fled the field at the start of the battle'. Jasper advanced on Edward's centre, and both sides fought for a short time before the Yorkists began to gain ground. Owen Tudor and Throckmorton may have attempted to encircle the Yorkists, but in doing so they exposed their left flank to Herbert's troops, and the Yorkist commander ordered his men to advance towards Owen's forces, who could offer little resistance and fled the field. Despite possibly losing the early stages of the battle on their right wing, the Yorkists were now assured of victory, and their archers could begin shooting volleys of arrows from both flanks into the Lancastrian centre, causing it to collapse. With the day lost, Jasper fled the field. Wiltshire had already disappeared. Owen may have staged a fighting retreat to Hereford, where he was taken.

In such a murderous struggle, with axes, maces, swords, glaives and bill-hooks smashing, hewing and slashing, the lighly armed Irish would have suffered particularly badly. According to Drayton, they were in the vanguard:

> The Earl of Ormond ....
> Came in the vanguard with his Irishmen,
> With darts and skains; those of the British blood,
> With shafts and gleaves, them seconding again,
> And as they fall still make their places good,
> That it amaz'd the Marchers to behold
> Men so ill-armed, upon their bowes so bold.

A story told by Flavell Edmunds from an anonymous guide to Leominster of 1808 claims that Jasper sent troops on to Leominster to reinforce a Lancastrian garrison already stationed there. The Lancastrians then drove Yorkist detachments away, but were themselves dislodged while battle was raging at Mortimer's Cross, and were driven back to Kingsland to join the routed main army. However, it is doubtful whether Jasper would have divided his army deep inside hostile country. It is also unlikely that there were Lancastrian troops in Leominster, an unwalled monastery town. Blue Mantle Cottage stands near the battlefield and gives weight to the rumours that Edward's herald, Blue Mantle, was slain during attempts to hold peace talks before the battle.

Local folklore says that the River Lugg ran red with the blood of the massacred Welshmen. Tradition suggests that some fled past Covenhope to the Lugg, only to be pursued and massacred when cornered at a river gorge near Kinsham. Here we see the names Slaughterhouse Covert and Bank. Evidence collected by Brooke makes it probable that some sort of last stand was made somewhere near Battle Acre, bearing out accounts of a second battle. The battle monument is a mile from the site of the main battle, and uses the words 'near this spot'. This could have been where Owen Tudor, Throckmorton, a Scudamore and other royalist captains may have been taken prisoner. Jasper, Wiltshire, Perrot, Sir John Scudamore II, Sir William and Sir James Scudamore all escaped, though James was killed later that year 'at a Herefordshire manor house'. Many of the dead soldiers slain on the battlefields now lie buried in a field just south of Mortimer's Cross known as the Clamp.

Perhaps 4,000 men were killed, mostly Lancastrians. If Owen Tudor had attempted the flanking manoeuvre, he would have been in the wrong position to try to escape back to Wales, with the three Yorkist battles in line blocking his route. It may be that he was caught south of the battlefield, trying to get back to Wales. One account is that some Yorkists pursued the remnants of Owen's battle all the way to Hereford, where, after a brief skirmish, Owen Tudor and other Lancastrian captains were captured. Owen, by tradition, was held prisoner overnight in a coaching inn, which is now the Green Dragon Hotel on the remarkably wide Broad Street, leading to the Bishop's Palace and Cathedral Close, in the formerly walled city of Hereford. His captors would have kept him in reasonable comfort as the uncle of the king, hoping for a ransom or prisoner exchange. Other accounts place Owen in captivity at Hereford Castle. However, Edward was in no mood for mercy after the heads of his father and brother had been spiked at York a few weeks previously. Mortimer relates:

> all those who had the misfortune to be taken prisoners were put to death with unrelenting barbarity. Thus, with more than savage rage, did Englishmen bury their daggers in the breasts of their countrymen, contending with each other for the horrid palm [first prize] of brutality; among others who suffered on this occasion, our historians have mentioned Owen Tudor, the husband of Queen Catherine, and father to the earls of Richmond and Pembroke.

Dozens of Lancastrians were captured, taken to Hereford and held there for up to three weeks before they were beheaded, but Owen was executed the day after his capture. It is said that Owen expected to receive amnesty because of his relationship with the royal family. Owen was led to the block in Hereford marketplace by Roger Vaughan of Tretower, and apparently was not convinced of his approaching death until his collar was ripped off his doublet by the executioner. *Gregory's Chronicle* states that he still trusted to the good fortune, 'wenyng and trustvng all eway that he shulde not be hedyd tylle he saw the axe and the block, and when that he was in hys dobelet he trusted on pardon and grace tylle the coler of hys redd vellvet dobbelet was ryppyd of.' Tradition is that his final words were: 'This head which used to lie in Queen Catherine's lap would now lie in the executioner's basket.'

However, according to *Ricart's Kalendar* Owen was executed on 7 February. *The Historical Collections of a citizen of London* states he was buried in a chapel of the now vanished Greyfriars Church in Hereford. Under the title of Hereford, Leland notes, 'Owen Meredek, corruptly cawled Owen Thider, father to Edmund Erie of Richmond and grandfather to King Henry the Seventh, buried in the Greye Freres in the north syde of the body of the churche, in a chapell.' Elsewhere he writes, 'Owen Meredith alias Tuder buried in the Greye Freyers in navi ecclesice in Bacello sine ulla sepulchri memoria.' According to *Gregory's Chronicle*, a 'mad woman' set Owen's head on top of the market cross and combed his hair. She washed away the blood from his face and placed more than hundred burning candles around his head. It may well be that this was the mother of Owen's illegitimate son David, born just a year before at Pembroke.

Evans sums up the life of Owen Tudor well:

Owen Tudor typifies that spirit of adventure and chivalry which in the fifteenth century sent Welshmen abroad to win fame on the battlefields of Europe or in the courts of princes. He carried to the grave that intrepidity and dignified bearing which had characterised him in life. But he mistook the age, not indeed in which he had lived, but in which he was to die. The age of chivalry was passing by and giving way to the ungovernable passions and truculent savagery of meaner days. Owen Tudor bridges the two; he lived in the one, and died in the other.

Robin Ddu of Anglesey noted the passing of a comet in 1477, writing that it signified the expulsion of Englishmen from Wales. His exact contemporary, the wealthy nobleman Ieuan ap Rhydderch, wrote that the juxtaposition of the dates of Lady Day and Easter was a good omen, foretelling the freedom of Wales through the children of Owen Tudor. Roberts translated Ieuan's *cywydd brud* (prophecy), and the relevant passage reads: 'When Lady Day and Good Friday become one, and Easter is early, gentle and mellow, and there is also a long sunlit summer, and the armed host is moving to and fro, through the one true God deliverance will come.' Robin Ddu was constant in his prophesying support for Owen Tudor, being his contemporary and probably knowing him. Bards from across Wales bemoaned the death, with Robin Ddu's elegy being the most famous:

Marwnad Owain Tudur

Brudio y bûm: brud heb wyw
A frudiais, ofer ydyw.
Gwynedd, ei chlod a ganwyd,
Llyma'i rhoi yn y llam rhwyd.

Ni bu er a fu ar Fôn
Dirwy oer hyd yr awron.
Y wlad aeth i wylo dŵr
Drwy gwyno'i daroganwr.

Nid oedd o gŵyn, dydd o gur,
Ond hoedyl Owain Tudur.
Gwennol y daroganoedd,
Ac un o ddawn Gwynedd oedd.

A châr diwarth i Arthur,
A thad ieirll gwnâi waith a dur,
Iesu llas urddas y llwyth
O'r dialedd ar dylwyth.

Diddig y bu yn dioddef,
Aberth Nudd aeth i borth Nef.
Pen Ieuan, hoywlan helynt,
A dorres gŵr di-ras gynt.

Pedr o lid ŵr pwdr ei lu
A las yng nghweryl Iesu.
Owain a las, annwyl iôn,
Yn wrol ac yn wirion.

Er torri pen y wennol,
Mae eryr ynn mawr ar ôl.
Gwinau yw'n daroganwr,
Gwyn ein byd i gyd o'r gŵr.

Y tarw corniog tir Cernyw,
A'r tri chorn o'r teiriach yw.
A'r marchog llidiog yw'r llu,
Dau hanner ydyw hwnnw.

Ni bydd llai i fintai faeth
Ym mrwydr nog ymerodraeth.
Ym mhlaid Brytaniaid y tyn,
I roi olew ar elyn.

Aderyn i wlad arall
I fordwy cyrch, fwriad call.
Rhodied hi, rhaid ydyw hyn,
Heb wledd bûm han ner blwyddyn.

Yr edn a ddaw â'r adar
O bell i ddial y bâr.
A llynges a ollyngir,
Gwynt a'i dwg i Gent i dir.

A brad a ddaw o Brydyn,
Penfro hai pan fo ar hyn.
Manaw yn fflam, cytgam cur,
Dulyn yn yr un dolur.

Ffurf oer ac anffurf a fydd.
A ffawr Môn a ffy i'r mynydd.
Diwedd y gwŷn bonheddig
Drwy'r awel a ddêl yn ddig.

Eryr addfwyn o'r Wyddfa
A ddaw, ac o daw nid â.
Pwy uwch y pridd a ddiddawr?
Pam y plyg y pump i lawr?

Gwyliwn bawb am gael ein bwyd,
Gwleddau y mab a gladdwyd.
Pan ddêl y tân yn felyn,
Drwy'r coed y syrth derw rhag hyn.

Draig wen ddibarch yng ngwarchae,
A draig goch a dyr y cae.
Pedair blynedd heb heddwch,
Y bydd trais a beiddio trwch.

Y gŵr glew â'r gaerog lain
A gawn ni ac enw Owain.
A phen a gorffen y gwaith,
A'n ynys oll yn uniaith.

Dr Heledd Haf Williams has translated Robin Ddu's elegy, in couplet form as follows:

Elegy for Owen Tudor

I prophesied an undying prophecy in vain.
I have sung Gwynedd's praise, and now its fate has been sealed.
A punishment like this has not been seen since that on Anglesey,
The country has been weeping and lamenting the son of prophecy.
Owain Tudur's life - day of pain! - is lamented.
He was the swallow of the prophecies, and a gift from Gwynedd.
A noble kinsman of Arthur, and father of earls. He acted with steel [weapons].
Jesus, the nobility of the family was killed through vengeance on the lineage.
He suffered meekly; Nudd's treasure went to Heaven's gate.
John [the Baptist]'s fine head was [also] cut off by an abominable man.
Peter was killed for Jesus' cause, by the wrath of a man with a corrupt army.
Owain, beloved lord, brave and pure, has been killed.
Although the swallow [Owen] has been beheaded, the great eagle [Jasper]
   remains.
The son of prophecy is of auburn [hair]; we are blessed because of him.
The horned bull of Cornwall; he is the three horns of the three lineages.
The fierce knight is of two halves.
The sustenance of an army in battle is authority.
The enemy is anointed in the Brytainiaid [Brythoniaid, Welsh] cause.
The bird has journeyed overseas to another country for a wise purpose.
It must go. Half a year has been without a feast.
The bird [eagle, Jasper] will bring the other birds [followers] from afar to
   avenge other birds from afar to avenge that brutality.
A fleet will be sent - the wind will bring it to Kent.
A betrayal will come from Prydyn [Pictland]. When this happens, go
   Pembroke!
The Isle of Man and Dublin will burn.
There will be misery. And the grace of Anglesey [Jasper] will flee to the
   mountains.
The pain will come to an end.
The noble eagle [Jasper] will come from Snowdon, and when it comes it will
   not depart.
Who on earth will care? Why does the five yield?
We will feed on the feast of the man that was buried.
When the fire comes, oak trees will fall.
The red dragon will be triumphant against the dishonourable white dragon.
There will be four years without peace – there will be violence and adversity.
The courageous man with the mighty sword and the name 'Owain' will
   come.
The task will be done, and our island will belong to one nation.

Sir John Throckmorton, of Coughton, Warwickshire, was the most notable of between eight and thirteen Lancastrian captains beheaded alongside Owen. David Lloyd and Morgan ap Rhydderch were also executed. Some sources state that Gruffydd ap Nicolas was present with his sons, but he probably died before the event. Two of his sons found safety in flight. There escaped several who are recorded as having been either beheaded or captured. For instance, Phillip Mansel, Hopkyn ap Rhys of Gower, and Lewis ap Rhys of Strata Florida were still fighting a few years later. Sir John Scudamore was said to be killed but later held Pembroke Castle against Sir William Herbert. He surrendered Jasper's castle on being promised a pardon, but his lands were confiscated. Philip Mansel was said to have been killed but survived, though two of his sons were also killed in the wars, John being killed in 1465 and Leonard being killed on 21 May 1471. There were no notable casualties on the Yorkist side.

Born around the same time as Owen, Ieuan Gethin of Baglan, Glamorgan, had sung the praises of Owen Tudor of Penmynydd in a *cywydd* when Owen was imprisoned in Newgate between 1437 and 1439. After the beheading at Hereford, Ieuan bitterly lamented the last *mab darogan* (son of prophecy) to bear the name of Owain, with Tudor's death following the assassination of Owain Lawgoch and the disappearance of Owain Glyndŵr. However, he still raised hopes for a future deliverer from the French conquerors: 'Er clybod darfod â dur / Newid hoedl Owain Tudur, / Gwilio Siasbar a Harri, / Ei ŵyr a'i fab, yr wyf i' (Although it is said that giving up steel / Changed the life of Owen Tudor / To keep watching out for his son and grandson / Jasper and Tudor, I will.)

Apart from Jasper, the major escapee was Wiltshire. As mentioned previously, in 1456 Wiltshire had deserted the field during the First Battle of St Albans – he had hidden his armour in a ditch and donned a monk's habit. *Gregory's Chronicle* noted: 'He fought mainly with his heels for he was called the most handsome knight in the land and was afraid of losing his beauty.' Wiltshire was afterwards known as 'the flying earl'. After fleeing Mortimer's Cross he would take part in the Battle of Towton, which ended with the Yorkists massacring the Lancastrians; he again fled the field, finally being captured at Cockermouth while trying to escape by sea. He was beheaded at Newcastle on 1 May 1461 and his head was displayed on London Bridge.

However, there were others escapees; some would prove invaluable to the Tudor cause in future. Mirehouse recounts the flight of Thomas ap Gruffudd and his son Rhys:

After the battle of Mortimer's Cross in 1461, Thomas ap Gruffudd, the leader of the Welsh, retired with his younger son Rhys to Burgundy, where young Rhys was brought up and educated; when they returned later to Wales, he was in consequence a soldier and a gentleman, very different from his half-savage brothers, who had never stirred from home. Thomas ap Gruffudd was murdered after his return to Wales, and Rhys ap Thomas became the head of the house. Being a man of sound judgment and broad views, he made friends with the English, and took Carew Castle on mortgage from Sir Edmund Carew, who was going abroad. Lord William Herbert had now become Earl of Huntingdon instead of Pembroke, and Edward IV had granted the latter to his young son Prince Edward, so there was no one there on the spot to rival Rhys ap Thomas, Lord of Carew. Rhys married Eva, the heiress of Count Henry.

After the death of Edward V (Earl of Pembroke), 1483, a boy of thirteen, who only reigned two months, Rhys swore fealty to Richard III, the Hunchback, in 1484. Later on Margaret Beaufort, Countess of Richmond, approached Rhys cautiously in 1484 in favour of her son, young Henry, then abroad in Brittany with his uncle, Jasper Tudor. Rhys was very cautious, but at length gave way, being absolved from his oath to Richard by the Bishop of St David's, and 'Henry ap Edmund ap Owen ap Meredydd ap Tudyr' (or Henry Tudor, Earl of Richmond) sailed from Harfleur with his uncle Jasper in 1485, and landed at Dale on August 1, after fourteen years exile. He was there met by Rhys ap Thomas, Lord of Carew, at Dale, riding on his charger 'Grey Fetterlocks'.

Without the assistance of Rhys ap Thomas, Henry could not have passed through Wales to fight at Bosworth.

On 17 February 1461, just two weeks after Mortimer's Cross, Warwick tried to stop Margaret's Lancastrian army from taking London, setting up his position at St Albans. Hearing that the northern army was nearing London, Warwick brought King Henry VI with him. Margaret had begun her southward march before news of Jasper's defeat had reached her. Under cover of darkness, the Lancastrians outflanked Warwick and took him by surprise as his force was facing north. Warwick realised the situation was hopeless and withdrew west to link up with Edward's army. The Yorkists then marched to London, where they received a warm welcome; the city had previously barred its doors to Margaret of Anjou and the rescued Henry VI.

Edward's men then chased the Lancastrians into Wales, probably searching for the fleeing Jasper and Wiltshire. Lewys Glyn Cothi addressed an ode to Maredydd ap Maredydd, who hid the bard and Jasper in Trefeglwys, Montgomeryshire, at this time. Jasper and Lewys Glyn Cothi are described as flying from place to place, hiding in mountains and forests. At Maredydd's mansion they found both a welcome reception and a kind protector. Also escaping with them was Owen ap Gruffudd ap Nicolas, brother of Thomas ap Gruffudd, who had escaped with his son Rhys ap Thomas to Burgundy.

Fresh troops were raised by York, and other preparations made for his return to London. Soon after the battle he was given a commission by the Privy Council to raise fresh levies in Warwick, Bristol and the border counties, having in the meantime moved from Hereford to Gloucester. Jasper Tudor had probably ridden south-west from Trefeglwys to Pembroke Castle and then to Tenby Castle. On 25 February 1461, three weeks after Mortimer's Cross, he wrote to his followers Puleston and Eyton, who were defending Denbigh Castle for him, pleading with them to stay faithful and to prepare to avenge the beheading of Owen Tudor. The letter was written from Tenby (spelling modernised):

> To the right-trusty and well-beloved Roger à Puleston, and to John Eyton, and to either of them. Right-trusty and well-beloved Cousins and friends, we greet you well. And suppose that ye have well in your remembrance the great dishonour and rebuke that we and ye now late have by traitors March, Herbert, and Dunns, with their affinities, as well in letting us of our Journey to the King, as in putting my father your Kinsman to the death, and their traitorously demeaning, we purpose with the might of our Lord, and assistance of you and other our kinsmen & friends, within short time to avenge. Trusting verily that ye will be well-willed and put your hands unto the same, and of your disposition, with your good advice therein we pray you to ascertain us in all hast possible, as our especial trust is in you. Written at our town of Tenbye the xxvth of February. PEMBROKE.

Sir John ap Elis Eyton was later rewarded for fighting at Bosworth with estates around Rhiwabon, and his monumental effigy can be seen in St Mary's Church. His collar is marked SS to signify his bravery, and Henry VII awarded him an annuity of ten marks 'in consideration of the time and faithful service performed for us ... in the course of our triumphal victory'. Jasper's great servant Roger Puleston served him faithfully through the wars, and before had served Edmund Tudor, as on 19 September 1456 Edmund had written to him granting an annuity of 10 marks for his services. Another letter from Jasper Tudor, probably written a few days after Mortimer's Cross, commits Flint Castle to Puleston's custody. The letter, jointly addressed to Puleston and Eyton, tells us that Jasper blamed the Welsh Yorkists for his defeat. The Herberts had Welsh-speaking courts and bards, and their kinsmen like the Vaughans and Dwnns had usually been enemies of the Tudors. Other letters will have been despatched to Jasper's allies across Wales and elsewhere, to inspire men to 'within short time to avenge' his loss. Ten years would pass before Jasper took the life of Roger Vaughan, who had walked Owen to the block; after this he was in exile for a further fourteen years with his nephew Henry Tudor.

Greyfriars, where Owen Tudor was buried, suffered badly in later years. His illegitimate son Sir David Owen had paid for a tomb there, and Jasper would leave the friary his best cloth of gold for vestments, but during Henry VIII's dissolution of the monasteries the building was demolished and the land sold off, so there is no lasting trace of Owen Tudor beyond a simple plaque in the Hereford marketplace where he is thought to have been beheaded. The only record of the site is in the naming of Greyfriars Bridge, which spans the River Wye. When Jasper himself died, around Christmas 1495, he left substantial funds for masses to be sung in the monastery of Keynsham, his own burial place, 'for the soul of his father, and the soul of Katherine late queen of England, his mother'; Keynsham Abbey has all but vanished as well.

10

The Legacy

Loxdale wrote of Owen's death and his enormous influence over future royalty:

So died Owen Tudor, from whom every English sovereign from his grandson, Henry VII, to the present King is descended. In Scotland, also, two Kings, James V and James VI, one Queen Consort, the wife of James IV, and one Queen in her own right, the ill-fated Mary Stuart, all numbered him among their ancestors. Nor is this all: five Kings of France, Louis XV, Louis XVI, Louis XVIII, Charles X and Louis Phillippe, four Queen Consorts, Mary, wife of King Louis VII, Mary Stuart, Marie Antoinette, and Marie Amelia, and one Empress, Marie Louise, consort of the great Napoleon, were all descendants of Owen Tudor. The Austrian Emperors through the union of Prince Charles of Lorraine and the Empress Marie-Theresa had also his blood in their veins. Even so, the tale is not yet completed. In Germany, from 1713, the descendants of the Welshman included Frederick the Great, the Emperor William I, the Emperor and Empress Frederick, and the ex-Kaiser, and in Russia, the Dowager Tsarina and the late Tsar. Further the Kings and Queens of Spain, Norway and Greece, the Queen of Roumania, the Kings of Italy, Denmark, Bulgaria and Belgium are all descended from Owen Tudor. Among those of his royal descendants who met with a similar death to his own, may be mentioned, Lady Jane Grey, Mary Queen of Scots, Charles I of England, and Louis XVI of France, and Marie-Antoinette.

Henry VI had been deeply unpopular. Abbot Wheathampstead of St Albans met Henry VI several times and was laudatory of his monarch until the usurpation of Edward of York in 1461. Wolffe tells us that at this time the abbot described Henry VI as 'his mother's stupid offspring, not his father's, a son greatly degenerated from the father, who did not cultivate the art of war... a mild-spoken, pious king, but half-witted in affairs of state'. Similarly, Warwick's brother the Bishop of Exeter called Henry VI 'this puppet king' in a letter to a papal legate after the Battle of Towton in 1461, referring to how Henry was manipulated by his wife and ministers. Even Pius II, Pope from 1458 to 1464, described the king in his memoirs as 'more timorous than a woman, utterly devoid of wit or spirit, who left everything in his wife's hand'. Pius II also recorded Warwick's conversation at Calais with a papal legate in 1460, calling Henry 'a dolt and a fool who is ruled instead of ruling. The royal power is in the hands of his wife and those who defile the king's chamber.' To Pius, the October 1460 agreement that disinherited Prince Edward in favour of Richard of York was the best solution for England in light of Henry's deficiencies; he wrote that 'by the wisdom of the Legate the dispute was settled'.

With this in mind, it says a great deal for Jasper Tudor that he did not take the side of York and Warwick even though he had several opportunities to do so. To continue to faithfully serve a king who was patently mentally ill when other nobles were changing sides for advantage shows a remarkable strength of character. After Mortimer's Cross there was no longer any thought of him switching to a winning side – the Yorkists had killed his brother and father, and the Lancastrians had done to the same to his enemy Edward of York, who now assumed the throne as Edward IV.

Jasper travelled constantly, fighting and organising support for Henry VI, and in the 'Readeption' of Henry VI in 1470–71 he was briefly given back his earldom of Pembroke, which had been given to William Herbert by Edward IV. His nephew Henry Tudor had been in Yorkist custody from 1461, when Pembroke Castle was taken, until 1470, after which Jasper kept the young man close to him. Jasper was recruiting for Margaret's army when it was annihilated at Tewkesbury in 1471. The Yorkist brothers Edward IV, George of Clarence and Richard of Gloucester killed the Prince of Wales, Edward of Westminster (probably murdered after the battle), and Sir John Courtenay, Earl of Devon. Edmund Beaufort, Duke of Somerset, the Lancastrian commander, seems to have been responsible for the defeat, during which he killed one of his own commanders, Lord Wenlock. Somerset's younger brother John was killed in the battle, and Somerset and other leaders including Devon's younger brother and Sir John Langstrother were dragged out of Tewkesbury Abbey two days after the battle and beheaded on 6 May 1471.

Both Beauforts died unmarried, and Pollard noted that 'the house of Beaufort and all the honours to which they were entitled became extinct'. The murder of Henry VI on 21 May 1471 left Somerset's first cousin Margaret Beaufort and her son Henry Tudor as the senior representatives of the House of Lancaster. Jasper was at Chepstow Castle at this time, and he disbanded his forces rather than lead them to certain defeat and the death of the only Lancastrian claimant. Edward sent a troop under Sir Roger Vaughan, who had personally led Owen Tudor to the block, to ambush and kill Jasper and Henry, the only surviving threat to the House of York. Jasper, with Henry and a small band that probably included Owen's illegitimate son David, escaped to Pembroke Castle, where they broke out of a siege and hid in cellars in the walled town of Tenby. They managed to take a boat at night to France, where the royal family was closely related to Jasper, but were shipwrecked in Brittany, then an independent duchy. Edward IV and Richard III made many attempts to secure their capture to take them to England, but the Tudors escaped to France. Within weeks of Richard III accessing the throne in 1483 there was a rising across the south of England; the followers of his brother Edward IV were outraged following the disappearance of the young Edward V and his brother Prince Richard. Perhaps 400 former Yorkists, including close friends of Edward IV, then joined Henry and Jasper in exile.

Owen did not escape reproach from marrying a queen, nor did Henry, Earl of Richmond, find his way to the throne smoother, or his seat upon it softer, for being the son of a Welsh country gentleman. Richard III., whom the strong hand of the Welshman at last overcame on Bosworth Field, despised, pursued, and maligned him. '[From] oure Castell of Notyngham, in the 2nd yere of our reign,' he issued a proclamation in which he complains that 'the rebeles and traitours' had chosen 'to be their capitayne oon Henry Tidder, son of Edmand Tidder, son of Owen Tidder, whiche of his ambitious and insatiable covetise incroacheth and usurpeth upon hym the name and title of royal estate of this roiaulme [realm] of Englande, whereunto he hath no manner of interest, right, title, or colour, as every man wel knoweth, for he is descended of bastarde blod both of the fader side and moder side; for the said Owen, the grandfader, was a bastard borne, and his moder was doughter unto John Due of Somerset, sone unto John Erie of Somerset, sone unto dame Kateryne Swynford, and of her in double advoutrow goten.

Henry, however, gained the throne, and, with true Tudor spirit, to repel the imputation cast on his descent, issued a commission 'to make inquisition' concerning the pedigree of Owain Tudor, his grandfather.

Dr Powel, referring to the subject in his 'Historie of Cambria,' published in 1584, says, 'I cannot passe, but must – something answere the reproachfull and slanderous assertions of Johannes Bernardus, Pontus, Henterus, and others, who go about to abase the noble parentage of the said Owen, this King's grandfather, following more their owne affectionate humors, than anie good proofe or authoritie, for if they would read that noble worke of Matthew Paris, they shall finde in pag. 843 of the printed booke, that Ednyvet Fachan, one of his ancestors, was the chiefest of Counsell to Llewelyn ap Iorwerth, otherwise called Leolinus Magnus, and to David ap Llewelyn, Princes of Wales...

They may also finde in the records of the Towre in Ann. 29 Edw. I. in the generall homage done to Edward Carnarvon, first Prince of Wales of the English blood, that Tudor ap Grono, another of the ancestors of the said Owain, did his homage awwmong the nobles of Wales, as appeareth in the said records. Further, the said Owain's grandmother, the wife of Tudor ap Grono, was Margaret, the daughter of Thomas, the sonne of Eleanor, which was the daughter of the Countie of Barr by Eleanor his wife, daughter to Edward the first, King of England.'

The Commission, Powel adds, 'comming to Wales, travelled in that matter and used the helps of Sir John Leyaf, Guttyn Owen Bardh, Gruffyth ap Llewelyn ap Evan Vachan, and others in the search of the Brytish or Welsh bookes of petigrees, out of which they drew his perfect genealogie from the ancient Kings of Brytaine and Princes of Wales, and so returned their Commission, which returne is extant at this daie to be scene.'

(Nicholas, *Anglesey Origin of the Royal House of Tudor*)

Hopefully this author's biographies of Richard III, Jasper Tudor and Henry VII will supplement this volume, and make readers wonder at the recent cathedral interment of Richard III. Henry Tudor's success in taking the throne of England was owing to four major factors. One was the incapacity of Henry VI, and another was the early death of Edward IV. The third was the disappearance of the young Edward V and his brother Prince Richard in 1483, and the consequent hatred of Richard shown by formerly faithful Yorkist supporters of his brother Edward IV, demonstrated by the remarkable lack of support the usurper had at Bosworth Field. The fourth element is the unending Welsh belief in a *mab darogan*. Without it, there is no way that Henry would have landed in Pembroke and marched unopposed into the Midlands, with men flocking to his banner from Wales and the Marches.

On the outbreak of the War of the Roses in 1455, the bards had seen the breakdown of civil order in England as an opportunity for the Tudors of

Penmynydd to at last provide the much desired 'son of prophecy'. Owen Tudor had married the widow of Henry V, and the bards now expected Jasper to lead Wales in its struggle for freedom. In 1468 Sir William Herbert led Yorkists throughout north Wales to try to capture Jasper Tudor and break down the power of the Lancastrians, pillaging the country as he went. He failed to find Jasper, but he did take Harlech Castle after it had held out for eight years. Yorke relates that Herbert 'beheaded Thomas ap Robin of Cochwillan, of the tribe of Marchudd, near the castle of Conway, because he was an adherent of the house of Lancaster; his wife, a pattern of conjugal fidelity and affection, witnessed the execution, and carried away her consort's head in an apron.'

Of Herbert's devastations in north Wales, Sir John Wynne of Gwydir says that 'Earl Herbert's desolation consumed the whole borough of Llanrwst, and all the vale of Conway, to cold cinders, whereof the print is yet extant; the very stones of the ruins of many habitations carrying yet the colour of fire'. On the occasion of the raid, Guto'r Glyn, a poet who spent much of his time in Raglan with Sir William, sang an important *cywydd* reproaching Herbert for the evil he had done in the north. A part (translated by Adrian Price) reads:

> Owen Tudor was on Anglesey
> Henry has taken the name by now
> There is hope to get our nation back
> Living became hopeless.
> Despite hearing that there happened with steel
> A change to the life of Owen Tudor,
> Watching Jasper and Henry,
> His grandson and son am I.

Owen Tudor's grandson Henry VII was, to this author, the greatest king of England – he restored unity and the nation's finances and was the most merciful king in Europe, a fact remarked upon across the Continent. His Tudor dynasty gave us our finest king – his reign was not measured by bloodshed but in the prosperity of his people, who saw the beginnings of the Renaissance. Unfortunately, his eldest son Arthur died, and Henry VIII was never the same man after a severe concussion altered his personality and he became the monster remembered today. Edward VI was manipulated throughout his short life, and Queen Mary has been unfairly assessed. However, the last of Owen Tudor's dynasty, Elizabeth, oversaw the greatest flourishing of culture in our history.

Owen Tudor in Literature

There was originally little interest in the Tudor monarchs' Welsh connection. However, in 1600 a play called *Owen Tudor* was commissioned by the London impresario Philip Henslowe, who paid an advance of £4 to the playwright Anthony Munday and three collaborators – sadly, there is no trace of any performance. The Admiral's Men company at the Rose theatre paid £4 for *Owen Tudor* between 10 and 18 January 1600. The website *lostplays. org*, organised by Professor Roslyn Knutson, tells us of this lost play, which was seemingly a collaboration between the well-known playwrights Michael Drayton, Richard Hathway, Robert Wilson and Anthony Munday. Philip Henslowe's Diary notes a payment on 10 January 1599: 'Lent vnto mihell drayton antony monday mr hathwaye & mr willsone at the apoyntment of Thomas downton in earneste of a playe Boocke called owen teder the some of ... iiijli.' There is also a diary fragment in the collection of the Duke of Rutland at Belvoir Castle on the same date: 'ye 10 of Jeneway 1599 Receyved in pt of payment & in er[e]nest of a playe called Owen Tweder the somme of foure poundes wittnes or hands ... iiijli Ri: Hathwaye R Wilson. An: Mundy witnes Robt Shaa.'

In November 1599 the Admiral's Men had bought the play *Henry Richmond, Part 2*, by Robert Wilson, costing £8. Knutson has suggested *Owen Tudor* was the first part to this latter play and she pointed out that 'the fate of his grandfather would ... have provided additional motive for Henry Richmond to lead an army against Richard III'. *Holinshed's Chronicles* would have been a source for historical details of the lives of Owen Tudor and Catherine of Valois, but Michael Drayton's *England's Heroical Epistles* (1597) is probably the main source for the love story of Owen and Catherine, according to Knutson. The *Epistles* are a series of letters to and from heroic lovers. The first 1597 edition sold out, and they were reissued with additions in 1598. The number was again enlarged in 1599 and 1602. Between the first issue and Drayton's death, the *Heroical Epistles* were issued thirteen or fourteen times. Twelve couples exchange letters, in chronological order: Henry II and Fair Rosamond; King John and Matilda Fitzwater; Queen Isabel and Roger Mortimer; the Black Prince and the Countess of Salisbury; Richard II and Isabel; Queen Catherine and Owen Tudor; Eleanor Cobham and Humphrey of Gloucester; William de la Pole and Queen Margaret; Edward IV and Jane Shore; the Queen of France and Charles Brandon; the Earl of Surrey and Geraldine; and Lady Jane Grey and Lord Guilford Dudley.

The first letter in the relevant 'couple' is Catherine's, when she asks Owen not to think less of her for being so forward. Owen has won her affection with his courtier's skills, comparing these with her dead husband's martial skills. She recalls first seeing him at Windsor, and in a couplet compares the respective courtships: 'A march, a measure, battell, or a daunce,/ A courtly rapier, or a conquering launce.' She tells him that the only titles that matter are 'Wife, Daughter, Mother, Sister to a King', and relates her lineage and his, and according to Knutson in so doing she is 'indirectly celebrating Welsh history. She again praises Henry and "England's flower" of knighthood before turning to blazon-like compliments of Owen's physical beauty. She ends by urging him to ignore the impediments to their love.'

Owen's letter opens with his excitement at receiving her letter. Knutson:

He says that destiny drew him to England so that Wales could be united through their marriage with England and France. He too remembers the meeting at Windsor and adds a charming detail about his missing a step in the dance and falling into her lap. In a modesty trope, he catalogues the mythological ancestry he cannot claim, then praises his Welsh descent and the honour of Wales in defending their land and language. He acknowledges that he has competition for her hand and expresses an impatience in having to wait. He ends with a fervent declaration of love.

Owen Tudor was seemingly ignored by Shakespeare in his sequence of English history plays, but any such work may have been lost, along with one on Henry VII. Catherine of Valois appears in two scenes of *Henry V* (1600). First she is seen with her lady, Alice, inquiring on how to say a number of words in English, since England may soon be taking over parts of France. She is then seen again in the play's final scene, where Henry V attempts to woo her, after the two are betrothed as a condition of the Treaty of Troyes. Catherine agrees to do whatever her father feels is best for her, and part of the final scene reads:

KATHARINE
Is it possible dat I sould love de enemy of France?
KING HENRY V
No; it is not possible you should love the enemy of
France, Kate: but, in loving me, you should love
the friend of France; for I love France so well that
I will not part with a village of it; I will have it
all mine: and, Kate, when France is mine and I am
yours, then yours is France and you are mine.
KATHARINE
I cannot tell vat is dat.
KING HENRY V
No, Kate? I will tell thee in French; which I am
sure will hang upon my tongue like a new-married
wife about her husband's neck, hardly to be shook
off. Je quand sur le possession de France, et quand
vous avez le possession de moi,—let me see, what
then? Saint Denis be my speed!—donc votre est
France et vous etes mienne. It is as easy for me,
Kate, to conquer the kingdom as to speak so much
more French: I shall never move thee in French,
unless it be to laugh at me.
KATHARINE
Sauf votre honneur, le Francois que vous parlez, il
est meilleur que l'Anglois lequel je parle.
KING HENRY V
No, faith, is't not, Kate: but thy speaking of my
tongue, and I thine, most truly-falsely, must needs
be granted to be much at one. But, Kate, dost thou
understand thus much English, canst thou love me?
KATHARINE
I cannot tell.
A month and more, to make the Queene his slave,
He fought by all such traines and trickes of his
As knowe ye lovers (God from them me save!)

KING HENRY V

Can any of your neighbours tell, Kate? I'll ask
them. Come, I know thou lovest me: and at night,
when you come into your closet, you'll question this
gentlewoman about me; and I know, Kate, you will to
her dispraise those parts in me that you love with
your heart: but, good Kate, mock me mercifully; the
rather, gentle princess, because I love thee
cruelly. If ever thou beest mine, Kate, as I have a
saving faith within me tells me thou shalt, I get
thee with scambling, and thou must therefore needs
prove a good soldier-breeder: shall not thou and I,
between Saint Denis and Saint George, compound a
boy, half French, half English, that shall go to
Constantinople and take the Turk by the beard?
shall we not? what sayest thou, my fair
flower-de-luce?'

KATHARINE

I do not know dat…

…

KING HENRY V

O Kate, nice customs curtsy to great kings. Dear
Kate, you and I cannot be confined within the weak
list of a country's fashion: we are the makers of
manners, Kate; and the liberty that follows our
places stops the mouth of all find-faults; as I will
do yours, for upholding the nice fashion of your
country in denying me a kiss: therefore, patiently
and yielding.

(Kissing her)

You have witchcraft in your lips, Kate: there is
more eloquence in a sugar touch of them than in the
tongues of the French council; and they should
sooner persuade Harry of England than a general
petition of monarchs. Here comes your father.'

*(Re-enter the FRENCH KING and his QUEEN, BURGUNDY, and other
Lords)*

In 1603, Welsh writer Hugh Holland (1571–1633) published the first (and
only) book of *Pancharis*, a poem which related the love between Owen Tudor

and Catherine of Valois. Holland was a queen's scholar and contemporary of
Ben Jonson at Westminster, attending Trinity College Cambridge from 1590.
He contributed a sonnet to the *First Folio* of Shakespeare. He travelled on
the Continent and in the Middle East, and after converting to Catholicism
was imprisoned in Constantinople for abusing Elizabeth I. He declared in
the preface to *Pancharis* that his work had been 'long since intended to her
Maiden maiestie' (Elizabeth I) but her death had cheated him of the honour as
the book was going through the press. He dedicated it instead to James I and
his son Prince Henry. James I was descended from Henry VII, whose daughter
Margaret Tudor was Queen of Scots to James IV from 1503 to 1513, then
regent for her son James V. James V died after the Battle of Solway Moss,
leaving a single six-day-old daughter, Mary, Queen of Scots. Her son James VI
of Scotland became James I of England. Below is an excerpt of his *Pancharis*:

> For all yet that betide them could, or can,
> Here lives one still, and stil I hope he shall,
> A gallant and resolved gentleman,
> Faire Owen Tudyr: fire thou hir in love
> With him, my boy. Mother (said he) your swanne
> Shall not exceede this eagle, nor your dove:
> Hereafter shall she stoope so to the lure,
> Though now awhile the clowds she toure above;
> For her pure bosome with a brand as pure
> I wil so kindle, yet before the sunne
> Get out of Libra, that none may recuse
> Her heart, but onely Owen. Well saide, sonne!
> (Him answered she) why should I then despaire?
> But (as one Owen hath us all undone)
> Another Owen may those harmes repaire.
> For who doth know, but that in time to come,
> There may spring from this wel conforted paire
> (I will so blesse and fructifie her wombe)
> He that seaven times happy man, who one day may
> Sit on this throne, and thence with mercy doome
> His and my people? O! when will that day
> Shine from the east upon this northerne clime?
> Then, then may well both Welch and English say,
> That they were borne in a most blessed time.
> Mother, quoth he, thereof mine be the care,
> And if I faile therein, mine be the crime;

...

They all together in the wardrobe met,
And them among (though far above them all)
The gentle Owen was: a man well set;
Broad were his shoulders, though his waist but small;
Straight was his back, and even was his breast,
Which no less seemly made him show then tall.
Such as Achilles seemed among the rest
Of all his army clad in mighty brass:
Among them such (though all they of the best)
The man of Mone [Anglesey], magnifique Owen, was.
He seemed another oak among the briars;
And as in stature, so did he surpass
In wit, and active feats, his other peers.
He nimbly could discourse, and nimbly dance,
And aged he was about some thirty years:
But armed had ye seen him go to France,
Ye would have said, that few on foot or horse
Could have so tossed a pike, or couched a lance,
Wherewith to ground he brought full many a corpse;
That oft alone when I recount the fame,
My tender heart cannot but have remorse:
To write it then, alas! I were too blame.

...

It alfo pleafde the Queene to walke a round,
The courtly fportes the more to countenance,
With whom (bicaufe he did the meafures leade)
To couple it was Owens happy chance.

...

Love that did all the while no will forfloe,
That holp to fett afire her fnowy breft,
Refolv'd, at laft, that it muft needs be fo.

...

Wherefore, as Owen did his galliard daunce,
And grac'd it with a turne upon the toe;
(Whether his eyes afide he chaunc'd to glaunce,
And, like the lovely God, became fo blinde,
Or elfe, perhaps, it were his happy chaunce,
I know not, and record none can I finde.)
This is the fhorte: the Queene being very nigh,

He fell, and (as he forwarde downe declinde)
His knee did hit againſt her ſofter thigh.
I hope hee felt no great hurt by the fall,
That happy fall which mounted him ſo high;
For up he quickly ſprang, and therewithall
He fetch'd me ſuch a friſk above the ground
That, O well doone! cried out both great and ſmall.

...

The Queene aroſe then, and dealt thanks around
To all of them, but unto Owen moſt:
The trumpets alſo they began to found,
For on (he paſſt, and after her an hoaſt
Of lovely ladies, while the people praied,
That God would guide her with his holy ghoſt.

...

Thus all the court was very well apaide,
And every dauncer in delight did ſwimme,
But Owen onely, who was ſo diſmaide,
That all the company came to comfort him.
Amongſt all, one wiſht it had beene his happe:
I can not blame him, though he loft a lim,
That long'd to pitch in ſuch a princely lappe.

Roger Boyle (1621–79) was the Earl of Orrery, and his *The History of Henry the Fifth* was performed at His Highness the Duke of York's Theatre in 1664. According to *The Broadview Anthology of Restoration and Early Eighteenth-Century Drama*, Samuel Pepys loved the play, which was on for ten days. His diary for 13 August 1664 records:

And to the new play at the Duke's house, of *Henery the 5*th, - a most noble play, writ by my Lord Orery; wherein Batterton [*sic*], Harris and Ianthes [Mary Betterton] parts are most nobly wrote and done, and the whole play the most full of heighth [*sic*] and raptures of wit and sense that ever I heard; having but one incongruity or what did not please me in it – that is, that King Harry promises to plead for Tudor to their mistress, Princess Katherine of France, more then [*sic*] when it comes to it he seems to do; and Tudor refused by her with some kind of indignity, not with the difficulty and honour that it ought to have been done in to him.

The play was published in 1668, and 'Owen Tudor, the King's Favourite' was a leading role, played by the leading actor of his day, Thomas Betterton (*c.* 1635–1710). A favourite actor of Charles II, he was highly praised by Pepys, Cibber, Pope and Steele, and his career marked the high point of Restoration drama. Betterton was an actor-manager and was extremely influential in the development of the English theatre. In this play, his wife Mary Saunderson played Catherine of Valois. Mary was the first woman to portray several of Shakespeare's female characters on the professional stage, including Juliet and Lady Macbeth. Boyle has Owen serving with Henry V in France and falling in love with Catherine of Valois there. As the best friend of Henry, he is conflicted by his love for the French princess. Meanwhile, Henry makes Owen the head of a special bodyguard arranged for Catherine.

No spelling or punctuation has been altered below – 'Tudor' is italicized throughout the original. Relevant parts are as follows:

THE FIRST ACT.

[*Enter* King Henry *the 5th, the Duke of* Exeter, *the Duke of* Bedford, *and* Owen Tudor, *with their Attendants.*]

King

This is the day in which our Valour must
Prove to the *French,* our claim to *France* is just;
Since 'twill no other way be understood,
It must be writ in Characters of blood.
By injuries they us to Battel call;
Denying us our part, they forfeit all:
'Tis fit in number they should us exceed;
That odds the *French* against the *English* need;
That odds which both obliges them and me,
Brings them to Fight, and us to Victory.

Exeter

Heav'n left us purposely but few for fight,
To shew the world, by your success, your right.

Bedford

They seem t'acknowledge Heav'n is not their Friend,
Since on their boasted numbers they depend;
Which when their cause is reckon'd, we should prize,
As Heav'n accounts them, for a Sacrifice.

[Enter Earl of *Warwick*].

Exeter

The Earl of *Warwick* in his looks does bring

Some News of high importance to the King.
Warw.
Arm! Arm! Great Sir, the Foe is in our view,
And has a Herauld sent to challenge you.
Warw.
How short a time and narrow space of ground
Is't 'twixt your Conquest, and your being Crown'd?
King
To make both shorter, I will straight advance,
And by two Titles wear the Crown of *France*.
Uncle, to your command with speed repair;
The right wing, Brother, does expect your care;
Both to the field of Battel lead the way,
Whilst but a moment I with *Tudor* stay.
Exeunt Exeter, Bedford, Warwick.
Oh my Best Friend! thy sadness I must blame,
[*Tudor* appears.]
Canst thou now think on any thing but Fame?
Tudor.
When I reflect how many dangers still
You must attempt, how many more you will—
King
Reflect on dangers which must glory win.
Tudor.
Excuse me, if my duty makes me sin:
Since I no other way can grateful prove,
I'le rather shew my fear, then hide my love.
King
That I to thee may proofs of mine dispence,
I now stay here, though glory calls me hence:
When Fame, when Life, and Empire are at stake,
All thoughts of those for thee I can forsake;
Banish thy grief by thinking on that praise,
Which shall thy name so high in Battel raise,
That all my future favours men may say,
Are not what I bestow, but what I pay.
Tudor
What you have said and done brings me relief;
This day I will deserve your love or grief.

King

Speak not of grief, but think on that applause

Which Heav'n doth still allow the juster cause.

Tudor

Why should he be by too much courage lost,

Of whom alone this world has cause to boast?

[Exeunt.] ...

[*Enter the* Queen *of* France, Princess Katharine, Princess Anne *of* Burgundy,

Duke *of* Burgundy, *and their Train...*]

Blam. [the Count of Blaumont]

Young *Tudor,* Madam, much renown'd you know,

To whom all *France* her gratitude does owe;

For he, when all did dangers face decline,

Met it to serve the Princess *Katherine;*

He 'gainst my will this hated life did save,

And when he heard those orders *Henry* gave,

Fearing their rigour might extend to me,

Above my hope, or wish, did set me free;

He told me as we parted that he knew,

I had the honour to belong to you.

Bowing to Princess Katherine.

Queen

'Tis Heav'n has strucken us; and when we know

That hand, who dares want patience for the blow?

My Lord, 'tis needful I resolve with speed

Who shall the fatal Constable succeed.

Burg. [Duke of Burgindy]

And counsel needful is how far 'tis fit,

After defeat to struggle or submit.

Queen

Assemble strait. Heav'n does occasion give

Of Mourning, yet allows no time to grieve.

Exeunt Queen, Burgundy, Blamount, Lady.

Prin. An. [Princess Anne of Burgundy]

Madam, methought when *Tudors* name you heard,

A new Vermilion in your face appear'd;

That word did raise a trouble there as great,

As you discover'd hearing our defeat:...

Owen Tudor

Indeed, Owen is said to have saved Catherine from drowning:

Prin. Kath.
Tudor, whom fortune led that way, descry'd
What many more with vain compassion spy'd;
They at the horrour of my danger wept,
He from the bridge into the River leapt,
And stemm'd the raging Current, till he bore
My breathless body to the neighbouring shore;
Him to the Court this timely service brought,
In whom so many Charms concurring wrought,
As I can scarce without some blushes owne,
That I did grieve he sat not on a Throne;
For to a Princess, who like me would do,
He who a Throne does want, wants all things too.

Owen is torn between his duty to the king, and his love for Henry's intended bride:

Prin. Kath.
He who resigns his Love, though for his King,
Does, as he is a Lover, a low thing:
But, as a Subject, a high Crime does do;
Being at once, Subject and Rebel too:
For, whilst to Regal pow'r he does submit,
He casts off Love, a greater pow'r then it.
Tudor
I fear you now are glad of a pretence
To punish what you cannot recompence.
Else could you think Loves pow'r I do not know
Because my Love all others does out-go?
If I by that seem guilty in your Eye,
Oh happy guilt which raises Love so high!
For I but shew in what I now have done,
That I your Int'rest prize above my own.
Prin. Kath.
But justly I admire how you can prove
So true to Friendship, and so false to Love;
Since in effect they both are but the same,
Only the Sex gives them a diff'rent name.

Tudor
You Friendship tax for being too sublime,
And make its duty, ev'n to Love a Crime.

It is notable that Owen is in conference with Henry V, his brother Bedford, the Duke of Exeter and the Earl of Warwick. Anne of Burgundy is the daughter of John the Fearless, and married to Bedford. As a child, she had been with Catherine of Valois at Poissy. The 'Count of Blaumont' may possibly be Henri IV, Comte de Blâmont (1376–1421). One wonders if his spoken part refers to Owen Tudor refusing to allow him to be killed at Agincourt? It is known, at least, that one of Blâmont's brothers fought at the battle. Again, could Owen have been the 'squire' who organised 200 archers to kill the captured French nobles? Nicolas writes, 'In the main body were placed a number of Knights and Esquires, and archers, who were commanded by the Dukes of Bar and Alençon, the Comtes of Nevers and Vendôme, of Vaudemont, Blâmont, Salmes, Grandpret, and Roussy.' Of these, Bar, Alençon, Vendôme, Vaudemont and Blâmont were said by Monstrelet to have died at Agincourt. According to Barker, 'The main reason the lists of French dead are incomplete is that they were simply so numerous. The final toll included three dukes (Alençon, Bar and Brabant), at least eight counts (Blamont, Fauquembergue, Grandpré, Marle, Nevers, Roucy, Vaucourt and Vaudémont) and one viscount (Pulsaye, younger brother of the Duke of Bar), which is suggestive. Even the usually indefatigable Monstrelet, who devoted a whole chapter to recording those killed or taken prisoner, managed to record more than three hundred names of the dead before admitting 'and many others I omit for the sake of brevity and also because one cannot know how to record them all, because there were too many of them."' However, Henri IV de Blâmont is said in genealogical sources not to have died until 1421: 'In 1382, Henri IV of Blâmont (1376–1421) and his wife Valburge Fénétrange founded Notre-Dame de Blâmont which became the burial place of the lineage.'

In 1751, a novel entitled *The Life and Amours of Owen Tideric, Prince of Wales, Otherwise Owen Tudor* was published. Its anonymous author claimed that the book was based on history widely current in France. In this novel Owen Tudor is sent to the court of France as a representative of Wales, where he and Catherine fall in love before Henry V invades France and defeats the French forces. Believing himself unworthy, Owen goes away, leaving Catherine at the disposal of her father, and Henry claims her for his queen. The relatively low-born but morally superior Owen Tudor had fallen in love with an unattainable beauty and chose exile over rejection. According to Knutson, if the story was known in England as early as 1599, it could 'have provided the Admiral's Men with a counter-narrative to that in the Globe play by Shakespeare, *Henry V*'. Shakespeare's play was first performed in 1660, and depicts Catherine of Valois's marriage to Henry V of England after Agincourt.

Emma Robinson (1814–90) wrote *Owen Tudor: An Historical Romance* in three volumes published by Henry Collins in 1849. Catherine of Valois is the subject of Rosemary Hawley Jarman's novel *Crown in Candlelight* (1978) and Jean Plaidy's *The Queen's Secret* (1989). Dedwydd Jones' 2002 novel *The Lily and the Dragon* tells the story of Owen and Catherine. Vanora Bennett's novel *Blood Royal: The Queen's Lover* (2009) tells the story of Catherine's secret marriage. Joanna Hickson's novel *The Agincourt Bride* (2013) and Anne O'Brien's novel *The Forbidden Queen* (2013) detail the life of Catherine of Valois. Mari Griffith's *Root of the Tudor Rose* (2014) relates the love story of Owen and Catherine with some style. Tony Riches published the well-researched novel *Owen: Part One of the Tudor Trilogy* in 2015, followed by *Jasper: Part Two of the Tudor Trilogy* in 2016, and is completing a work on Henry Tudor.

Select Bibliography

(For the invaluable source of monetary comparison over time, used in all this author's publications, see Officer and Williamson, below)

Abbott, Jacob, *Margaret of Anjou, Queen, consort of Henry VI, King of England 1430–1482*, Harper, New York, 1871

Adams, Tracy, *The Life and Afterlife of Isabeau of Bavaria*, Johns Hopkins University Press, 2010

Allmand, C. T., and Styles, Dorothy, *The Coronations of Henry VI*, History Today, 5 May, 1982

Allmand, Christopher, *Henry V*, Methuen, 1992

Ashdown-Hill, John, *Royal Marriage Secrets: Consorts & Concubines, Bigamists & Bastards*, The History Press, 2013

Ayton, Andrew, *Arms, Armour, and Horses* in Maurice Keen, ed., *Medieval Warfare* Oxford University Press, 1999

Ayton, A., *English Armies in the Fourteenth Century*, in Curry and Hughes, *Arms, Armies and Fortifications*, Boydell, 1999

Baker, Sir Richard (1568–1645) *A chronicle of the kings of England from the time of the Romans government unto the death of King James ... 1670, commonly called Baker's Chronicle*, 1670

Barber, Chris, *In Search of Owain Glyndŵr*, Blorenge, 2004

Bark, Nigel, *Did Schizophrenia change the course of English history? The mental illness of Henry VI*, Medical Hypotheses 2002, 59 (4) 416–421 Elsevier Science Ltd, 2002

Barker, Juliet R. V., *Conquest: The English Kingdom of France 1417–1450* Hachette, 2010

Bassett, Margaret, *Newgate Prison in the Middle Ages*, Speculum 18 (1943)

Baumgertner, W. E, *Squires, Knights, Barons, Kings: War and Politics in Fifteenth Century England*, 2010

Bell, Adrian R; Curry, Anne; King, Andy; Simpkin, David; *The Soldier in Later Medieval England*, Oxford UP, 2013

Belleforest, Francois de, *Les Grandes Annales at histoire generale de France* 2 vols., Paris, 1579

Bennett, Michael, *The Son of Scotangle: Sir John Steward*, Journal of the Sydney Society for Scottish History, Volume 15, May 2015

Bentley, Samuel, *Excerpta Historica, or, Illustrations of English History*, London, 1831

Bicheno, Hugh, *Battle Royal: The Wars of Lancaster and York, 1450–1464*, Head of Zeus, 2015

Biondi, Sir Giovanni Francesco, *L'istoria delle guerre civili d'Inghilterra tra le due case di Lancastre e di Iorc*, published in three volumes in Venice between 1637 and 1644, with a dedication to Charles I. It was translated into English while still in manuscript, by Henry Cary, Earl of Monmouth, and published in two volumes in London in 1641, under the title of: *An history of the civill vvares of England betweene the two Houses of Lancaster and Yorke the originall whereof is set downe in the life of Richard the Second, their proceedings, in the lives of Henry the Fourth, the Fifth, and Sixth, Edward the Fourth and Fifth, Richard the Third, and Henry the Seventh, in whose dayes they had a happy period: written in Italian in three volumes.*)

Blakman (Blacman), John, *Henry VI, King of England 1421–1471* (15th century) edited M.R. James, Cambridge UP, 1919

Blaauw, W.H., *On the Effigy of David Owen in Easeborne Church near Midhurst*, Sussex Archaeological Collections, Vol. VII, London, 1854

Boardman, Andrew W., *The Medieval Soldier in the Wars of the Roses*, Stroud 1998 //

Bradley, A.G., *Owen Glyndwr*, Collections, historical & archaeological relating to Montgomeryshire, Vol. 40, 1923

Breverton, Terry, *The Book of Welsh Saints*, Glyndŵr Publishing, 2000

Breverton, Terry, *Owain Glyndŵr: The Last Prince of Wales*, Amberley, 2013

Breverton, Terry, *Richard III: The King in the Car Park*, Amberley, 2013

Breverton, Terry, *Jasper Tudor: Dynasty Maker*, Amberley, 2015

Breverton, Terry, *Henry VII: The Maligned Tudor King*, Amberley, 2016

Brough, Gideon, The Rise and Fall of Owain Glyn Dŵr: England, France and Welsh Rebellion in the Middle Ages (2016)

Brough, Gideon, Owain's Revolt? Glyn Dŵr's role in the outbreak of the rebellion, Studies in Archaeology, History and Conservation, Cardiff University, Vol. 2 Issue 1: see *cardiff.ac.uk/share/resources/5.%20 Brough%202015%20Owains%20revolt.pdf* 15 May 2015

Carr, A. D., *Gwilym ap Gruffydd and the rise of the Penrhyn estate* Welsh History Review 1990–91

Carr, A.D., *A Welsh knight in the Hundred Years War: Sir Gregory Sais*, Transactions of the Honourable Society of Cymmrodorion, 1977

Carter, M.E., *Groundwork of English History*, 1908

Cavanagh, Harrison Dwight, *Colonial Chesapeake Families, British Origins and Descendants*, Vol 2, available on internet

Chapman, Adam, *Welsh Soldiers of the Later Middle Ages 1282–1422*, PhD thesis, Southampton 2009, available on internet

Clarke, M. V., and Galbraith, V. H., eds., *The Deposition of Richard II: Chronicle of Dieulacres Abbey*, 1381–1403, Bulletin of the John Rylands Library, 14, 1930

Christie, Mabel E., *Henry VI*, Houghton Mifflin, New York 1922

Cole, Teresa, *Henry V: The Life of the Warrior King & the Battle of Agincourt 1415*, Amberley, 2015

Collins, Arthur, *The Baronettage of England: Being an Historical and Genealogical...* Vol 1 (revised John Stockdale), 1806

Cothi, Lewis Glyn, *The Poetical Works of Lewis Glyn Cothi: A Celebrated Bard*, The Honourable Society of Cymmrodorion, Oxford, 1837

Curry, Anne, *Agincourt, A New History*, The History Press, 2006

Davey, Richard, *The Sisters of Lady Jane Grey and their Wicked Grandfather*, London, 1911

Davies, Griffith, *Owain Glyndŵr and Gwent*, Monmouthshire Review, Vol. 1, 1933

Davies, J.S. ed., *An English Chronicle of the Reigns of Richard II, Henry IV, Henry V and Henry VI 1377–1461*, Camden Society, 1856

Davies, R.R., *The Revolt of Owain Glyn Dwr*, Oxford, 1997

D'Escouchy, Mathieu, *Chronique de Mathieu d'Escouchy III*, Societé de l'Histoire de France, Paris, 1863–4 Chapman and Hall, 1911, ed. G. du Fresne de Beaucourt

De Juilly, Nicolas Baudet, *Histoire de Caterine de France, reine d'Angleterre*, Lyons, 1696

Dockray, Keith, *Henry VI, Margaret of Anjou and the Wars of the Roses: A Source Book*, Sutton, 2000

Dockray, Keith, *Warrior King: The Life of Henry V*, Tempus, 2007

Domville, Lady Margaret, *The King's Mother: Memoir of Margaret Beaufort, Countess of Richmond and Derby*, London, 1899

Drayton, Michael, *England's Heroicall Epistles (1597–98)* in *The Works of Michael Drayton in 4 Volumes*, W. Reeve, Fleet Street, 1753 ed. Hebel, J.W., Oxford, 1961

Duruy, Victor, *A History of France*, trans. M. Gary, 1919

Edwards, J. Hugh, *The Life of David Lloyd George: with a short history of the Welsh people*, Vol 1, 1918

Ellis, Henry ed., *Polydore Vergil's English History [1525], Comprising the Reigns of Henry VI, Edward IV and Richard III* Camden Society, 1844

Ellis, Thomas Peter, Welsh Tribal Law and Custom in the Middle Ages, Vol. 1, downloaded from *efm.bris.ac.uk/het/ellis/WelshTribalLaw01.pdf*

Evans, H.T., *Wales and the Wars of the Roses*, Alan Sutton Publishing, 1995

Fabyan, Robert, *The Chronicles of England and France* ed. Henry Ellis London, 1811

Fowler, Kenneth, *Medieval Mercenaries vol.1 The Great Companies*, Blackwell, 2001

French, George Russell, *The ancestry of... queen Victoria, and of... prince Albert*, London, 1841

Fynglwyd, Iorwerth, ed. Howell Ll. Jones and E.I. Rowlands, *Gwaith Iorwerth Fynglwyd* University of Wales Press, 1975

Gairdner, James, *Henry the Seventh*, 1889

Gairdner, James ed., *The historical collections of a citizen of London in the fifteenth century (Gregory's Chronicle)*, Camden Society, 1876

Gairdner, James ed., *A Short English Chronicle in Three Fifteenth Century Chronicles* Camden Society, 1809

Gairdner, James ed., *The Paston Letters 1422–1509*, London, 1900

Gasquet, Cardinal Francis, *The Religious Life of King Henry VI*, London, 1923

Gibbons, Rachel, *Isabeau of Bavaria, Queen of France (1385–1422): The Creation of an Historical Villainess*, Transactions of the Royal Historical Society Vol 6, December, 1996

Giles, J.A. ed., *Incerti Scriptoris Chronicon Angliae de regnis trium regum lancastrensium, Henrici IV, Henrici V, et Henrici VI, commonly known as Giles's Chronicle*, Part 4, London, 1848

Giles, J.A., *Roger of Wendover's Flowers of history, Comprising the history of England from the descent of the Saxons to A.D. 1235; formerly ascribed to Matthew Paris*, 1849

Goodman, Anthony, *The Wars of the Roses:Military Activity and English Society, 1452–97* Dorset Press, 1981

Goch, Iolo, ed. Johnston, D.R., *Iolo Goch Poems*, Gomer Press, 1993

Grafton, Richard, *Grafton's Chronicle*, 1569

Griffiths, Ann, *Rhai agweddau at y syniad o genedl yng nghyfnod y cywydwyr 1320–1603* Unpublished PhD Thesis Aberystwyth, 1988

Griffiths, Margaret Enid, *Early Vaticinations in Wales with English Parallels*, 1937

Griffiths, Ralph A., *The Principality of Wales in the Later Middle Ages*, Cardiff, 1972

Griffiths, Ralph A., *King and Country: England and Wales in the Fifteenth Century*, Hambledon Press, 1991

Griffiths, Ralph A., *The Reign of King Henry VI: The Exercise of Royal Authority 1422–1461*, University of California Press, 1981 (available as Griffiths, Ralph A., *The Reign of King Henry VI*, History Press 2004)

Griffiths, Ralph A., *Queen Katherine of Valois and a missing statute of the realm*, Law Quarterly Review, 93, 1977

Griffiths, Ralph A., *Wales and the Marches*, in S.B. Chrimes, C. D. Ross, and Ralph A. Griffiths, eds., *Fifteenth-Century England, 1399-1509*, Alan Sutton, 1995

Griffiths, Ralph A., ed., *Kings and Nobles in the Later Middle Ages*, St Martin's Press, 1986

Griffiths, Ralph A. and Thomas, Roger, *The Making of the Tudor Dynasty*, St Martin's Press, 1985

Griffiths, Ralph A., 'Prince Henry's War: Armies, Garrisons and Supply during the Glyndŵr Rising', *Bulletin of the Board of Celtic Studies*, 34

Gruffudd, Elis, *Cronicl o Wech Oesoedd* (Chronicle of the Six Ages of the World), *c.* 1545

Haigh, Philip A., *The Military Campaigns of the Wars of the Roses*, Sutton Publishing, 1995

Hall, Edward (1497–1547) *The Union of the Two Noble and Illustre Families of Lancastre and Yorke*, commonly called *Hall's Chronicle*, 1548, later published as Hall, Edward, *Chronicle containing the History of England from Henry VI to Henry VIII*, ed. Henry Ellis London, 1809

Halliwell-Phillipps, James Orchard ed., *Warkworth's Chronicle of the first thirteen years of the reign of King Edward IV*, London, 1839

Halsted, Caroline, *Life of Margaret Beaufort, Countess of Richmond and Derby*, London, 1839

Harriss, G.L. and M.A. (eds.), *John Benet's Chronicle for the years 1400 to 1462*, Camden Miscellany vol. 24 Camden Society, 1972

Harriss, G.L., *Cardinal Beaufort: a study of Lancastrian ascendancy and decline*, 1988

Harrison, David, *The Crusades and the Welsh Princes*, Knights Templar Magazine, February 2102

Hodges, Geoffrey, *Ludford Bridge and Mortimer's Cross the Wars of the Roses in Herefordshire and the Welsh Marches*, Logaston Press, 2001

Holinshed, Raphael (plus John Hooker, Francis Thynne, Abraham Fleming, John Stow, Sir Henry Ellis), *Holinshed's Chronicles of England, Scotland, and Ireland*, England, 1577, 1587

Holland, Hugh *Pancharis: the love between Owen Tudyr and the Queen*, 1603

Hookham, Mary Anne, *The life and times of Margaret of Anjou, queen of England and France; and of her father René 'the Good,' king of Sicily, Naples, and Jerusalem*, Volumes 1 and 2, 1872

Howell, R., *A History of Gwent*, (referring to Rees, W., *South Wales and the March 1284–1415*), 1924

Howells, Adrian, *Owain Glyn Dwr and Gwent – A Reappraisal of his Campaigns...*, Gwent Local History 95, Autumn 2003

Humphreys, Emyr, *The Taliesin Tradition,* Seren, 2000

Iolo Goch, Johnston Dafydd, ed., *Poems,* Gomer, 1993

Jones, Dan, *The Hollow Crown: The Wars of the Roses and the Rise of the Tudors,* Faber & Faber, 2014

Jones, Emyr Wyn, *Robin Ddu's prophecy and 'our lady's lap',* Flintshire Historical Society Journal Vol 29, 1979–80

Jones, Michael K., *The King's Mother: Lady Margaret Beaufort, Countess of Richmond and Derby,* Cambridge University Press, 1992

Jones, Michael K., *The Beaufort Family and the War in France, 1421–1450* unpublished Ph.D. Thesis, Bristol, 1982

Jones, W. Garmon, *Welsh Nationalism and Henry Tudor,* Transactions of the Honourable Society of Cymmrodorion, Session 1917–18

Kingsford, Charles Lethbridge, ed., *The First English Life of King Henry the Fifth, written in 1513 by an anonymous Author known commonly as The Translator of Livius,* Clarendon Press, 1911

Kingsford, C. L., *Chronicles of London,* Oxford, 1905

Leland, John, ed. L. Toulmin Smith, *The itinerary of John Leland,* London, 1907

Lewis, P.S., *Two Pieces of Fifteenth–Century Political Iconography, (b) The English Kill Their Kings,* in his *Essays in Later Medieval French History* pp191–192

Lewis, Samuel, *A Topographical Dictionary of Wales,* 1833

Lisle, Leanda de, *Tudor, the Family Story,* Chatto and Windus, 2013

Lloyd, Sir John E., *Owen Glendower,* Clarendon, Oxford, 1931

Lloyd, Jacob Youde William, *History of the Princes, the Lords Marcher and the Ancient Nobility of Powys Fadog,* T. Richards, London, 1882

Lloyd-Williams, Grace, *Owen Tudor, His Life and Times,* Welsh Outlook Vol 17 et al (4 parts), May 1930

Llwyd, Angharad, *A History of the Island of Mona, or Anglesey, Being the Prize Essay at the Royal Beaumaris Eisteddfod,* 1832

Llwyd, Richard, *Beaumaris Bay,* in *The Poetical Works of Richard Llwyd,* 1837

Lowe, Walter Bezant, *The Heart of Northern Wales: As it was and as it is: Being an Account of the Pre-historical and Historical Remains of Aberconway and the Neighbourhood,* Llanfairfechan, 1912

Loxdale, Florence M., *Romance of the House of Tudor,* Welsh Outlook Vol 11, No 7, July 1924

Luce, Siméon, *Chronique du Mont-Saint-Michel (1343–1468),* Societé des Anciennes Textes Française, Vol 2, Paris 1878, 1883

Major, John, *A History of Greater Britain,* (*c.* 1517) ed. A. Constable, Scottish Historical Society, 1892

Marshal, Anne, *The roles of English War Captains in England and Normandy, 1436–61,* University of Wales MA thesis, 1975

Metcalfe, Walter Charles, *A book of Knights banneret, Knights of the bath, and Knights bachelor, made between the fourth year of King Henry VI and the restoration of King Charles II ... and knights made in Ireland, between the years 1566 and 1698*, 1885

Miller, Michael, *warsoftheroses.co.uk*

Mirehouse, Mary Beatrice, *South Pembrokeshire: Some of its History and Records,* David Nutt London, 1910

Monstrelet Enguerrand de, ed. G. du Fresne de Beaucourt, *Chronique d'Enguerrand de Monstrelet,* 1863–64 (see d'Escouchy)

Mortimer, Ian, *Henry V: the cruel king,* BBC History Magazine September 2014

Mortimer, Ian, *1415: Henry V's Year of Glory,* Vintage, 2010

Mortimer, Thomas, *A New History of England from the Earliest Accounts of Britain to the Treaty of Versailles,* 1764

Mowat, R. B., *Henry V,* Boston, 1920

Myers, A. R., *The Captivity of a Royal Witch: The Household Accounts of Queen Joan of Navarre 1419–1421,* Bulletin of the John Rylands Library, 1940

Nicholas, Thomas, *Annals and Antiquities of the counties and county families of Wales...,* Volume 1 Longmans, 1872

Nicolas, N. H., *Testamenta Vetusta,* Vol. I London, 1826

Norton, Elizabeth, *Margaret Beaufort: Mother of the Tudor Dynasty,* Amberley, 2012

Officer, Lawrence H., and Williamson, Samuel H., *Five Ways to Compute the Relative Value of a UK Pound Amount, 1270 to Present, Measuring Worth,* 2016

URL: measuringworth.com/uk/compare/

O'Flanagan, J. Roderick, *Lives of the Lord Chancellors and Keepers of the Great Seal of Ireland,* 1870

Ormerod, George, *Genealogical Essays illustrative of Cheshire and Lancashire Families...* (unpublished but available on the internet)

Owen, Ann Parry, *Gwaith Ieuan Gethin,* Centre for Advanced Welsh and Celtic Studies, 2013

Pennant, Thomas, *A Tour in Wales,* 1810

Pennant, Thomas, *The History and Antiquities of London,* Vol. 1, London, 1813

Prestwich, Michael, *Armies and Warfare in the Middle Ages: The English Experience,* Yale University Press, 1996

Reese, Peter, *Bannockburn,* Canongate, 2003

Richards, W. Leslie, *Gwaith Dafydd Llwyd of Fathafarn,* Gwasg Prifysgol Cymru, 1964

Roberts, Peter, *The Welsh-ness of the Tudors,* History Today January 1986

Roberts, Glyn, '*Wyrion Eden*': *the Anglesey descendants of Ednyfed Fychan in the fourteenth century*', Transactions of the Anglesey Antiquarian Society and Field Club 1951 (reprinted in Aspects of Welsh History: Selected papers of the late Glyn Roberts, Cardiff, 1969

Roberts, Glyn, *Teulu Penmynydd*, Transactions of the Honourable Society of Cymmrodorion, 1959

Roberts, Thomas, *Pedwar Cywydd Brud*, Bulletin of the Board of Celtic Studies, Vol VII Part III

Roberts, Thomas and Williams, Ifor, *The Poetical Works of Dafydd Nanmor*, Cardiff, 1923

Ross, Charles, *Edward IV*, Yale, 1997

Salmon, Mary, *A Source-Book of Welsh History*, OUP, 1927

Daniel, Samuel, *The Poetical Works of Mr. Samuel Daniel*, 1718

Seward, Desmond, *The Hundred Years War – The English in France 1337–1453*, Penguin, 1999

Simons, Eric N., *Henry VII, the First Tudor King*, 1968 (This may be useful for tales such as Owen's father being a former brewer in Beaumaris, and on page one we see Maredudd ap Tudur being referred to as 'Meredydd ap Tudor', with the spelling altered a few lines down referring to his son Owain as 'Owen ab Meredydd ab Tewdr ab Gronw ab Tewdr'.)

Stephens, Meic, *A Most Peculiar People*, UWP, 1992

Stephenson, David *Political Power in Medieval Gwynedd: Governance and the Welsh princes*, Studies in Welsh History, 2014 (first published in 1984 as *The Governance of Gwynedd*: University of Wales Press)

Skidmore, Chris *Bosworth: The Birth of the Tudors*, Weidenfield and Nicholson, 2013

Stow, John, *A survey of the cities of London and Westminster, borough of Southwark, and parts adjacent ...: Being an improvement of Mr. Stow's, (1598) and other surveys, by adding whatever alterations have happened in the said cities, &c. to the present year*, ed. John Mottley, 1735

Spectator, The, *Provincial History of England – the Welsh March I – Monmouthshire and Hereford*, 19 June 1869

Strecche, John, ed. Taylor, F., *Chronicle of John Strecche for the reign of Henry V (1414–1422)*, Bulletin of the John Rylands Library, 16, 1932

Strickland, Agnes, *Katherine of Valois, surnamed the Fair, Wife of Henry V*, in *Queens of England*, 1840

Paul Strohm, *England's Empty Throne: Usurpation and the Language of Legitimation, 1399–1422*, 1999

Sumption, Jonathan, *The Hundred Years War I: Trial by Battle*, University of Pennsylvania Press, 1999

Thierry, Jacques Nicolas Augustin, *Histoire de la conquête de l'Angleterre par les Normands*, 1841

Thomas, Ceinwen H., *Yr ymdeimlad cenedlaethol yn y Canol Oesoedd*, Heddiw, 6 January 1941

Thomas, Roger Stuart, *The Political Career, Estates and 'Connection' of Jasper Tudor, Earl of Pembroke and Duke of Bedford*, unpublished PhD thesis Swansea, 1971

Thomas, Thomas, *Memoirs of Owen Glendower … with a sketch of the history of the ancient Britons*, 1822

Thorstad, Audrey M., *Establishing a Royal Connection: Tudor Iconography and the Creation of a Dynastic Grand Narrative*, Academia download 5 August 2016

Tout, Thomas Frederick, *The Collected Papers of Thomas Frederick Tout with a Memoir and Bibliography*, Manchester University Press, 1934

Tyler, J. Endell, *Henry of Monmouth Or Memoirs of the Life and Character of Henry the Fifth ….*, 1838

Vale, G.A., *Charles VII*, University of California Press, 1974

Vergil, Polydore, *English History*, Camden Society, 1844

Walker, David, *Medieval Wales*, Cambridge UP, 1991

Warkworth, J., *A Chronicle of the First Thirteen Years of the Reign of King Edward the Fourth 1461–1474* ed. J.O. Halliwell. Camden Society, 1839

Watts, John, *Henry VI and the Politics of Kingship*, Cambridge University Press, 1999

Waurin, Jehan de, *Recueil des Chroniques, etc., Vol. V.*, ed. William Hardy. Rolls Series London, 1864–91

Weir, Alison, *Lancaster and York: The Wars of the Roses*, Vintage, 1995

William of Worcester, ed. Joseph Stevenson, *Annales Rerum Anglicarum*, Rolls Series, London, 1864

Worcester, William, ed. Harvey J. H., *Itineraries [of] William Worcestre*, OMT 1969

Williams, Gruffydd Aled, *The Bardic road to Bosworth: a Welsh view of Henry Tudor*, Transactions of the Honourable Society of Cymmrodorion, 1986

Williams, John, *Ancient & Modern Denbigh: A Descriptive History of the Castle, Borough & Liberties*, 1836

Williams, A.H., *The Early History of Denbighshire*, 1950

Williams, Glanmor, *Harri Tudur a Chymru (Henry Tudor and Wales)*, Gwasg Prifysgol Cymru Cardiff, 1985

Williams, Glanmor, *Renewal and Reformation: Wales, c. 1415–1642*, Oxford University Press, 1993

Williams, J., *Penmynydd and the Tudors*, Archæologia Cambrensis, 1869

Williams, Neville, *The Life and Times of Henry VI*, Weidenfeld and Nicolson, 1973.

Williams, Robert of Rhydycroesau, Oswestry *Penmynydd and the Tudor family,* letter to Archæologia Cambrensis 3rd series, Vol. V, No. XVIII, 1859

Williams-Jones, K., *The Taking of Conway Castle,* 1401, Transactions of the Caernarfonshire Historical Society, XXXIX, 1978

Winston, J.E., *English Towns in the Wars of the Roses,* unpublished Ph.D. thesis, Princeton and Oxford, 1921

Winter, Christine, *Prisons and Punishments in Late Medieval London,* PhD thesis Royal Holloway, University of London, 2012

Wolffe, Bertram, *Henry VI,* Methuen, 1983

Woods, Dr Kim, Paper on *the alabaster tomb of Goronwy at Penmynydd,* online

Wright, Thomas, ed., *Political Songs and Poems Relating to English History,* Vols. I and II Rolls Series No. 14 London, 1859–1861

Wynn, Sir John of Gwydir, *The History of the Gwydir Family,* ed. John Ballinger, 1927

Also available from Amberley Publishing

Available from all good bookshops or to order direct
Please call **01453-847-800**
www.amberley-books.com

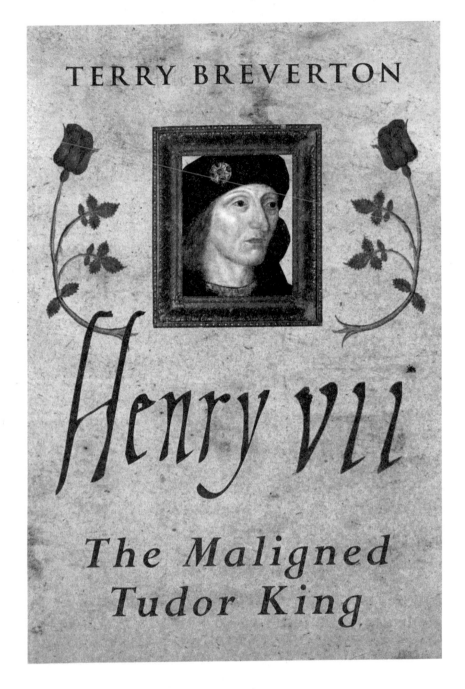

Also available from Amberley Publishing

'A MUCH-NEEDED BIOGRAPHY'
DAN JONES, bestselling author of *THE HOLLOW CROWN*

RICHARD·
·DUKE·OF·YORK
KING BY RIGHT

MATTHEW LEWIS

Available from all good bookshops or to order direct
Please call **01453–847–800**
www.amberley-books.com